Toward an Anthropology of Women

Toward an Anthropology of Women

Edited by

Rayna R. Reiter

AAKAR

TOWARD AN ANTHROPOLOGY OF WOMEN
Edited by Rayna R. Reiter

Published in agreement with Monthly Review Press, New York
for publication and sale only in the Indian Subcontinent
(India, Pakistan, Bangladesh, Nepal, Maldives,
Bhutan & Sri Lanka)

First Published in India 2011

ISBN 978-93-5002-163-7 (Pb)

Published by
AAKAR BOOKS
28 E Pocket IV, Mayur Vihar Phase I, Delhi 110 091
Phone : 011 2279 5505 Telefax : 011 2279 5641
info@aakarbooks.com; www.aakarbooks.com

Printed at
Mudrak, 30 A, Patparganj, Delhi 110 091

Contents

Notes on the Contributors

Judith K. Brown is an Assistant Professor of Anthropology at Oakland University in Rochester, Michigan. Her research interests include the cross-cultural study of the role of women in subsistence, the socialization of children, and the initiation of girls.

Susan Brown received her Ph.D. from the University of Michigan in 1972 and is now doing community advocacy work with Spanish-speaking people in Boston. She also teaches anthropology at Boston University, and is particularly interested in women's perspective and the role of women in prehistory.

Norma Diamond received her degrees from Wisconsin and Cornell and has been teaching anthropology at the University of Michigan since 1963. She has done field research in rural and urban Taiwan, and recently spent two months in the People's Republic of China. She is the author of *K'un Shen: A Taiwan Village,* and several articles on the status of women in Taiwan. Her research interests include social change, problems of the peasantry, and psychological anthropology, as well as an abiding interest in feminist studies.

Patricia Draper received her B.A. from Vassar and her Ph.D. from Harvard. She did her fieldwork in northwestern Botswana in 1968 and 1969, studying child life among the !Kung Bushmen of the Kalahari. She is presently teaching anthropology at the University of New Mexico in Albuquerque.

Elizabeth Faithorn is a doctoral candidate at the University of Pennsylvania and is currently teaching anthropology at the University of California, Los Angeles. Her involvement in the women's movement, as well as her research on female roles and male-female relations in Papua New Guinea, has led to a developing interest in political, ritual, and symbolic anthropology.

Kathleen Gough received her Ph.D. from Cambridge University and has taught in many universities in Britain and North America. She has published widely on Indian social institutions, comparative kinship, and the ethics of social science research. She is a Research Associate in Anthropology at the University of British Columbia.

Susan Harding teaches at the Residential College of the University of Michigan and is writing her doctoral dissertation in anthropology on the recent social history of Oroel, Spain.

Ruby Rohrlich-Leavitt is associate professor in the Social Sciences department at the Borough of Manhattan Community College, City University of New York. She is the author of *The Puerto Ricans: Cultural Change and Language Deviance*, and editor of *Women Cross-Culturally: Change and Challenge*. Her articles, modules, and teaching include the anthropological approach to woman's status and roles.

Lila Leibowitz is Associate Professor of Anthropology at Northeastern University, Boston. Her interest in primate behavior and sex roles is an outgrowth of a concern with the origins of human family arrangements. She is working on a "natural history" of sex and family.

Rayna R. Reiter received her degrees from the University of Michigan, where she was often involved in juggling the relation between anthropology and politics. She now teaches courses on women, peasants, and cities in the Graduate Division of the New School for Social Research in New York City.

Dorothy Remy did her fieldwork with market women in Ibadan, Nigeria, in 1967, and later in Zaria, Nigeria, in 1973, where she came to integrate her work and politics. She received her Ph.D. in 1973 from the University of Michigan. She is now teaching at Federal City College in Washington, D.C.

Anna Rubbo studied architecture in her native Australia before leaving to work in London. She went to Colombia in 1970 and spent two years in rural areas. She is currently a graduate student in architecture at the University of Michigan.

Gayle Rubin is working on her doctorate in anthropology and teaching in the Women's Studies program at the University of Michigan, where she has survived many incarnations of feminist politics.

Karen Sacks has long been active in the women's movement. She received her Ph.D. from the University of Michigan and currently teaches anthropology at Oakland University in Rochester, Michigan. Her current research and writing concerns women and class structure.

Sydel Silverman is a Professor of Anthropology at Queens College, City University of New York. She studied human development at the University of Chicago and received her Ph.D. in anthropology from Columbia. She has done fieldwork in Italy and is currently interested in combining historical and ethnographic approaches to the study of rural-urban relationships in Europe.

Sally Slocum's career has ranged from stripper to anthropologist. She is presently a Ph.D. candidate at the University of Colorado and is teaching anthropology at the University of Montana.

Barbara Sykes was born in Cairo and has spent time in many cultures, including an extended stay among the Lacundones of Mexico. She is currently a graduate student in anthropology at New York University, with research interests in South American women. She has been a long-time activist in the New York women's movement.

Elizabeth Weatherford is currently working on the Ph.D. in cultural anthropology at the New School for Social Research in New York City, and is on the humanities faculty of the School for Visual Arts. She is doing research on women and their participation in the arts.

Paula Webster received her M.A. from the University of Michigan and did her fieldwork in southern Italy. She teaches anthropology in the SEEK program at Queens College, New York City, and plays the cello in her spare time.

Acknowledgments

This book has been nurtured and stimulated by many people who believed it needed to exist. Thanks are due to Lembi Kongas, co-planner and teacher, and the students of the women's anthropology course at the University of Michigan in 1971; also to the Women's Study Program there, which was struggling through its interdisciplinary birth pangs when I worked in it in 1972-73. More recently, students at the New School for Social Research contributed to the effort in their excitement to learn about women. Many friends gave thoughtful criticism and personal support, especially Susan LeVan, Susan Harding, Randy Reiter, Gayle Rubin, and Marilyn Young. Finally, Susan Lowes used her anthropological training and editorial finesse to see this project through. To all, my true gratitude.

This book is dedicated to the women who always want to know why; without their questions, it would never have become necessary. All royalties beyond initial advances will be dedicated to feminist causes selected by the contributors.

Rayna R. Reiter

Introduction

This book has its roots in the women's movement. To explain and describe equality and inequality between the sexes, contemporary feminism has turned to anthropology with many questions in its search for a theory and a body of information. These questions are more than academic: the answers will help feminists in the struggle against sexism in our own society. The subjugation of women is a fact of our daily existence, yet it neither began with modern capitalism nor automatically disappears in socialist societies. In looking at other cultures, we find that sexual inequality appears widespread and that the institutions in which it is embedded have a long and complex history. To truly understand the phenomenon, we must find its roots and trace them in their many permutations and transformations. Our political critique must be based on this understanding of the origins and development of sexism.

Because it incorporates both cross-cultural data and theories about the evolution of society, anthropology at first glance appears to be useful to feminists in this search. It studies the origins and functions of family systems, sex roles and socialization, differences in the division of labor. But underlying all these investigations are certain assumptions about the position of women that make the field suspect. Most anthropologists read rather directly from biology to culture, asserting that woman's role in reproduction is responsible for the earliest forms of the division of labor, and that male supremacy flows from this division.* Feminists, however, have wanted to know *why;* for them, the direct relation of mothering to cultural subordination is anything but obvious, especially in light of the array of cross-cultural data describing the wide range of women's active roles. Mainstream anthropology has been closed to, or has tended to trivialize, the very questions feminist students are asking.

Over several semesters, as I helped to organize and teach a student-initiated course on women from an anthropological perspective, I was forced to reexamine my own training and the theories underlying it. The course was an exciting one, but it was also terribly frustrating. The more we read, the less trusting we became of the authors and their perspectives; anthropology's contribution to a feminist theory is contaminated by the same assumptions that pervade our culture as a whole. A great deal of information on women exists, but it frequently comes from questions asked of men about their wives, daughters, and sisters, rather than from the women themselves. Men's information is too often presented as a group's reality, rather than as only part of a cultural whole. Too often women and their roles are glossed over, underanalyzed, or absent from all but the edges of the description. What women do is perceived as household work and what they talk about is called gossip, while men's work is viewed as the economic base of society and their information is seen as important social communication. Kinship studies are usually centered on males, marriage systems are analyzed in terms of the exchanges men make using women to weave their networks, evolutionary models explain the origin and development of human society by giving enormous weight to the male role of hunting without much consideration of female gathering. These are all instances of a deeply rooted male orientation which makes the anthropological discourse suspect.** All our information must be filtered through a critical

* Marxist anthropologists tend to claim that the earliest human communities were either sexually egalitarian or matriarchal; their claims, however, have been summarily dismissed for reasons having to do with both the data on contemporary societies and the political history of anthropology.

** There have been exceptions to this male bias within anthropology.

lens to examine the biases inherent in it. Theory always underlies the way we collect, analyze, and present data; it is never neutral. Looking for information about ourselves and about women in other societies, feminists have had to join Third World peoples, American Blacks, and Native Americans in expressing their distrust of the body of literature which mainstream anthropology has called objective.*

We need to be aware of the potential for a double male bias in anthropological accounts of other cultures: the bias we bring with us to our research, and the bias we receive if the society we study expresses male dominance. All anthropologists wear the blinders of their own civilization in approaching other cultures; our eyes are as conditioned as those of the people we study.** Our own academic training reflects, supports, and extends the assumptions of male superiority to which our culture subscribes. The vast majority of anthropologists who survive training, fieldwork, degree-getting, and publishing to give us our information are either men, or women trained by men. We might say that the selection for people who agree on what the important questions are and how they are to be answered is strong, and is strongly

---

Classics such as Margaret Mead's *Sex and Temperament* (1935) or Ruth Landes' *Ojibwa Woman* (1938) have found a place in the field. Other researchers and their work have fared less well (see, for example, Salter's book on Daisy Bates [1972]). In the last few years, as women's status within our own culture has again become problematic, there have been articles and books that take the woman's perspective into account. For examples, see Elizabeth Fee's feminist interpretation of nineteenth-century evolutionism (1973); Marilyn Strathern's discussion of the experiences of women in an overtly male-dominant New Guinea group (1972), and Rosaldo and Lamphere's collection of articles providing insights into the role of women in ideological and political systems in a variety of cultures (1974). It must be stressed, however, that there is not a massive amount of such work available, and that what exists is not widely used by most anthropologists in their research or teaching, but is consigned to a feminist ghetto within anthropology.

* See Hymes, 1972; Deloria, 1969; Mafeje, 1971; and Lewis, 1973, for such critiques of anthropological practice and theory, and for responses to them from within the field.

** See Diamond's discussion of the notion of progress as inherent in civilization (1974), or Valentine's work on the relation between anthropological theory and Black Studies (1972) for examples.

male oriented.* Anthropology is no different in this from other disciplines. Male bias is carried into field research. It is often claimed that men in other cultures are more accessible to outsiders (especially male outsiders) for questioning. A more serious and prior problem is that we think that men control the significant information in other cultures, as we are taught to believe they do in ours. We search them out and tend to pay little attention to the women. Believing that men are easier to talk to, more involved in the crucial cultural spheres, we fulfill our own prophecies in finding them to be better informants in the field.

Male bias is surmountable, just as racial bias, or any form of ethnocentrism, is, but only when it is taken seriously as an area for self-critical investigation. Anthropology has developed a theoretical perspective that separates biology from culture in the investigation of race;** it has the potential to make the same discrimination with regard to gender. When investigating other issues, anthropologists rarely make the mistake of reading automatically from a presumed biological base to the superstructure built upon it—yet in analyzing gender, they do exactly this. Recent studies on the biological bases of sex differences and on human gender systems have revealed flexible, culturally influenced structures (for examples, see Money and Ehrhardt, 1972; Maccoby and Jacklin, 1974; Oakley, 1973). Rather than assuming biology-as-destiny (a highly questionable position for a field noted for its studies of cultural plasticity), we need to incorporate subtler information on both biology and culture into new models of how gender operates within all human societies.

The second area of male bias can only be approached once the first is accorded significance. It is the thorny problem of male dominance in the societies we study. In the anthro-

* Popular images of anthropology as a field dominated by Ruth Benedict and Margaret Mead notwithstanding, the facts and figures give us about the same degree of male predominance in the production of academic degrees, publications, and rank within university hierarchies as other social sciences (for recent figures on sexual stratification within anthropology, see Vance, 1975).

** See, for example, Stocking's discussion of Boas' formulation of the distinctions among race, language, and culture (1968).

pological record, cultures seem to display a wide range of variation in the amount of sexual equality or inequality expressed consciously by members of both sexes. Some, such as hunting-gathering groups like the BaMbuti or !Kung, assert minimal or no status differences, while others, such as the Mae Enga horticulturalists or the Fulani pastoralists, show a strong degree of segregation by sex and a hierarchy which accords men more prestige. Groups that have the same mode of production may have radically different sexual status systems depending, for instance, on whether they are matrilineal or patrilineal. Yet we do not even know what we mean when we define a group as having "male dominance." Even among the non-human primates, dominance and aggression are labels that must be used carefully; we should not lump behaviors that have to do with such diverse activities as food-getting, sexual success, leadership in a troop's movement, and so on into one category (see Dolhinow, 1971). When we apply such terms to humans, what are we labeling? Is it a strict division of labor by sex, with more cultural value being awarded to male activities? Or does male dominance refer to situations in which men possess the power to physically control women ("We tame our women with the banana," say Mundurucu men, referring to gang rape). If we only have a vague idea of what constitutes dominance, we cannot know if it reflects the experience of both men and women, or if it is instead something the men assert and the women deny (as in Kaberry's study). In such a case, is dominance a male fantasy? An anthropological fantasy? Or an expression of the internal workings and contradictions of a system for which we have only half the pieces? It is not clear that primitive peoples dichotomize their world into power domains. Coming from an extremely hierarchical cultural milieu, we tend to construct categories to contain social differences, and then rank them in terms of power. We build master-theories out of such notions of difference, but we do not know if the oppositions and hierarchies we construct are universal or simply reflect our own experience in a class-stratified society.*

* For a critical assessment of Lévi-Strauss' structural model of hierarchy built on the principles of binary oppositions, see Diamond, 1974.

If anthropological descriptions of male dominance are ambiguous, interpretations constructed to explain its origins are even more so. Some anthropologists assert that early societies were sexually egalitarian, and that male supremacy arose with the growth of class society and colonial penetration (see, for example, Leacock, 1972). Others assert that the division of labor between male hunting and female mothering has always included some amount of male dominance (notably, Washburn and Lancaster, 1968, and the pop ethology-types, such as Tiger and Fox [1971], Morris [1967], etc.). A third group places the exchange of women by men in marriage alliances at the heart of culture (for instance, see Lévi-Strauss, 1969), and some extend this structuralist perspective to conclude that in the distinction between nature and culture, alleged to be made by all peoples, women fall on the former, devalued side of the "great divide" (see Ortner, 1974). The efficacy of any of these explanations is open for discussion precisely because so many basic questions are barely posed, much less answered.

We need new studies that will focus on women; it cannot be otherwise because of the double bias which has trivialized and misinterpreted female roles for so long. Yet the final outcome of such an approach will be a reorientation of anthropology so that it studies *humankind.* Focusing first on women, we must redefine the important questions, reexamine all previous theories, and be critical in our acceptance of what constitutes factual material. Armed with such a consciousness, we can proceed to new investigations of gender in our own and other cultures.

This collection of essays is presented in support of such radical investigations and redefinitions. The first three papers relate directly to issues of male bias in the interpretation of the biological and cultural evolutionary record. Leibowitz examines the popular belief that physical differences between the sexes (dimorphism) are directly responsible for social-role differentiation, a phenomenon we are alleged to have inherited from our nonhuman primate past. Yet according to her reading of the data, biology is not social destiny, even among monkeys and apes, and she advances another hypothesis to explain sexual dimorphism among these species. Slocum criticizes the widely accepted hypothesis that male hunting was the context in which cultural evolution developed. She combines basic data on the fossil record, our primate ancestors, and contemporary hunting-gathering groups to develop an alternative model of cultural evolution which is more fully human. Gough's article on early forms of the family and contemporary families among hunter-gatherers also reviews a wide range of information and criticizes the bias which has produced a portrait of extensive male dominance among such groups.

The next three essays examine aspects of sexual equality in groups organized primarily along the lines of kinship. Draper compares sexual egalitarianism among the !Kung in their foraging context with the changing sex roles and the beginning of male dominance that accompany sedentarization. Her research may be interpreted as partial support for Engels' hypothesis concerning the development of male predominance as it is linked to acquisition of private property. Leavitt, Sykes, and Weatherford examine the theory, methodology, and data-collection of male and female anthropologists studying the Australian Aborigines. They question both the information and the interpretation that has led to the portrayal of women as subordinate in Aboriginal life, and suggests a reformulation based on the work of women anthropologists with a consciousness that stems from their roles in their own society. Faithorn's fieldwork among the Káfe of Highland New Guinea has led her to reexamine the concepts of pollution and alleged female inferiority that are widespread in the area. Looking at ways in which both sexes can pollute, and heeding the Káfe's own evaluation of sexual relations, she advances a rather different interpretation.

The focus in the next two articles shifts to theories concerning the origin of gender relations. Webster summarizes recent work on the matriarchy debate, including both Marxist and feminist views of the origins of female subordination. She discusses the matriarchy as a vision of female power, assessing its role in our projections for an egalitarian future. Rubin analyzes how the female of the species becomes an oppressed, domesticated woman. Using tools provided by Marx, Engels, Freud, and Lévi-Strauss, she constructs a critical theory of the process of female subordination.

Much of the debate within feminist theory has been centered on acceptance or rejection of Engels' interpretation of the role of women in differing modes of production. The next two papers are informed by this debate. Sacks reworks some of Engels' ideas about the role of socially necessary labor, using as example a comparison of the social adult statuses of women in four African societies. Judith Brown gives us an ethnohistorical analysis of the Iroquois, the group which perhaps comes closest to popular notions of a matriarchy. She claims that it is not only the women's contribution to productive labor, but their control over the distribution of what is produced that forms the basis for female domestic and political power.

The next three papers examine contemporary West European peasant groups. Reiter describes and analyzes the existence of male and female domains, one public, one private, in a southern French village, and uses that example to speculate about the creation of such a division in the evolution of state-organized societies. Harding takes the differences between male and female language in a Spanish village and investigates the ways in which it reflects and reproduces differential access to formal and informal power in peasant life. Silverman uses the anthropological category of life crisis to analyze the tensions in courtship and early marriage for central Italian women, describing differences among women of two economic groups.

The three papers which follow present aspects of the changing role of women in Third World countries. Susan Brown looks at the effects of poverty on women in the Dominican Republic, analyzing the matrifocal household, consensual unions, and extended women's networks as adaptive strategies for survival. Rubbo examines the spread of rural capitalism in Colombia, and shows that it causes an increase in sexual tension and in matrifocality as women become increasingly dependent on both the plantation owners and the men of their households. Remy discusses the differential access to work for men and women in urban Nigeria. Using a range of examples, from totally secluded women to those active in trading and in the petty bourgeois professions, she looks at schooling, religious and community associations, and the availability of investment capital as they affect the wives of men working in the modern capitalist sector. All three papers note that patterns of domination worsen by sex as well as by class with capitalist penetration, especially under conditions of dependency capitalism.

The final essay is an examination of the situation of rural women in the People's Republic of China. Diamond analyzes the changing status of women as the Chinese contend with the patriarchal kinship systems that have endured through the transition to socialism.

Taken together, the papers in this collection provide some guidelines and examples of directions for an anthropology of women. They point to the need for a critical reanalysis of our notions of cultural and biological evolution, and serve as a corrective to the bias of mainstream anthropology. They give us enriched data on the productive roles of women, and on women's own experience of these roles, and sensitize us to the complexities of male supremacy in cultures in which this is expressed. These essays assume that the women's experience may be different from that of the men, and is therefore the legitimate subject for investigation. Above all, they subject our notions of male dominance to specific analysis, and push us to understand that it is anything but natural. As an artifact of culture, such patterns have undergone changes that we can analyze, and are amenable to changes for which we can actively work. This collection aims to provide information and theory on the bases for sexual equality or inequality, and to contribute to the analysis which must always accompany action for fundamental social change.

Lila Leibowitz

Perspectives on the Evolution of Sex Differences

There are very real physical differences between men and women. They differ not only in the appearance of their external genitalia, but in other respects as well. Men are generally bigger, have more facial and body hair, narrower hips, flatter buttocks, and a tendency to greater body mass. Women generally have more fatty tissue on their breasts and buttocks. These anatomical differences were for a long time viewed as intimately related to differences in emotional and intellectual capacities, as well as to differences in physical abilities. The tasks and roles assigned to men and women in our own cultural tradition were assumed to be correlated highly with anatomically based aptitudes. It is still a commonplace belief that anatomy is destiny.

In the era between the late 1930s and the mid-1960s this notion was challenged. Research into the behavior of the sexes in other cultures forced some changes in thinking. Cross-cultural data on the sexual division of labor very quickly dispelled the idea that men (or women) are unable to do some of the tasks assigned women (or men) in our culture. Knitting, weaving, and cooking sometimes fall into the male province, while such things as pearl diving, canoe handling, and housebuilding turn out to be women's work in some settings. Mead's pioneering research on sex roles and personality styles raised some doubts about the biological basis of

---

This is a revised version of a paper presented at the American Anthropological Association Meeting in New Orleans, December 1973.

psychological attributes, for she reported on cultures in which men display such "feminine" emotional qualities as sensitivity, affection, and volatile emotionality, while females are aggressive and calculating. Outside of anthropology, the works of Karen Horney and Viola Klein provided support to the proposition that both men and women are behaviorally flexible, and that the way men and women behave in any particular social setting is a result of circumstances rather than anatomy. Masters and Johnson's startling studies contributed to this view and further undermined many academically propagated assumptions about the workings of the human female's body and psyche. So for a while the main thrust of the respected academic literature on human sexual behavior and social roles challenged the notion that anatomy is destiny, arguing that cultural forces work on the behavioral plasticity of both males and females, shaping their behavior and the roles they assume in society.

Despite the implications of such studies, the issue of men's and women's roles and whether or how to change them was not a significant one at the time these works were appearing. The college women who read Margaret Mead's *Male and Female* in the late 1940s and early 1950s, who admired the highly publicized Yugoslav and Russian army and guerrilla heroines, and who saw Rosie the Riveter in the United States pulling down the same pay as her male co-workers did not agitate for change. They became the ideal *McCalls* magazine mothers of the 1950s. Unaffected by their college readings, they turned to Spock's handbook on child care, gourmet cooking, and interesting arts and crafts hobbies as they pursued the traditional tasks of being wives and mothers. In the early 1960s, an attack on the "feminine mystique" (Friedan, 1963) by a housewife who felt herself cheated attracted a wide audience among them. But the issue of women's roles and whether they are based on genetic capacities or on cultural forces did not emerge onto the political and intellectual scene out of books but out of the Civil Rights struggle. From the precepts of that struggle grew the women's liberation movement and the conviction that anatomy is not destiny.

When women's liberation finally surfaced as an independent entity, it was supported by some academics (like Matina Horner) but opposed by those who felt that physical differences between the sexes are based on and lead to social-role differences. Since the mid-1960s there has been a vigorous revival of the view that social-role and intellectual differences between men and women, and girls and boys, are physiologically based, substantiated by a plethora of books and articles by psychologists and neurophysiologists. Anthropologists and sociologists have picked up on these views and tied them to renewed investigations of biosocial evolution. Interestingly, these academic investigations into sex differences come at a time of a revival of notions of innate differences in intellectual capacities between blacks and whites; both, it would seem, are reactions to efforts at implementing the liberal, nonbiogenetic social-role perspectives that gained respectability during and after World War II.

On the whole, academics no longer hold the position that particular roles or tasks universally belong to either men or women because of simple differences in bones, muscles, and sex organs. The newer arguments for a biogenetic basis in role behavior have acquired a statistical framework, an evolutionary rationale, and sophisticated physiological models of perception and behavior; researchers work with rats, apes, and babies as often as they work with adult human beings. Yet the argument still boils down to the view that because men and women are obviously different physically, they also have different intellectual and emotional capacities. Whether the traits or capacities investigated are shared by a few or many men or women is often considered "statistically insignificant," if not downright irrelevant. In overall characterizations, men, it is argued, are suitable for certain kinds of roles, women for others.

Because men are larger than the females of their species, it is held that they are naturally "dominant" over women. "Dominance," an unclear term at best, may take several forms: having priority of access to food resources, or acting as a provider; fulfilling a leadership position (among nonhuman primates, this means setting the direction and/or pace of group movement); acting as protector of the females and young; taking the initiative in sexual intercourse; or simply getting others to move out of the way. Women—smaller, softer, and fattier tissued—are supposed to be eminently better equipped to be nurturant, affective, docile followers. Dominance and large size (as well as threatening teeth, bony crests, and other male physical characteristics) supposedly go together in nonhuman dimorphised primate species. In fact, it is argued, the reason that men are larger, bonier, and more muscular than women is that these features, and "dominance" in its various expressions, are intrinsically related to one another and gave those males who had them reproductive advantage. By virtue of being leaders, providers, protectors, and sexually aggressive, larger males are more likely to father stronger babies. They are also better able to help their offspring survive than smaller and presumably less dominant males, who are therefore at a reproductive disadvantage. In short, the argument traces physical differences between the sexes (which are supposed to shape contemporary social-role differences) back to social-role differences among our supposed ancestors. Contemporary physical differences are seen as the result of ancient social-role differences, and contemporary social-role differences are treated as the result of physical differences that became established in early human and pre-human populations.

Since we have no way of observing the social arrangements of our ancestors, the social adaptations of living nonhuman primates provide the models from which this theory is drawn because what living primates do as they adapt to the various environments in which they live should, in theory, throw some light on the social behavior of our ancestors. While researchers have tended to pick the one nonhuman primate they consider to be relevant to understanding dimorphism among humans, favoring some species over others, this paper focuses on the behavior and social adaptations of several species in order to examine whether and how their social-role arrangements are related to the presence or absence of sexual dimorphism.

I will first deal briefly with a nondimorphic species, the gibbons, who are found living in the upper reaches of the forest canopies of Southeast Asia, and then touch on the social adaptations of their close neighbors, the extremely dimorphic orangutans. I will look at our closer relations, the African Great Apes: the very dimorphic gorillas and the much less sexually differentiated chimpanzees, who spend much of their time on the ground. Finally, I will examine in somewhat greater detail the adaptations of terrestrial baboons which, despite being rather distantly related to us, have been the most frequent models for speculative reconstructions of early human adaptations.

This brief overview will demonstrate that the sex-role adaptations of the sexually dimorphic nonhuman primate species do not in fact conform to the models used in current explanations of how and why dimorphism developed among humans. In fact, sexual dimorphism cannot easily be equated with sex-role patterns. The data will show, however, that dimorphic primate species do have one thing in common: they all live under environmental conditions that encourage males to range more widely than females. Thus although the data points up the inadequacy of current theory on the sources of physical sex differentiations, it suggests another.

In the closing section, I will examine the possibility that sexual dimorphism is generated not out of selection favoring animals with a predisposition to particular social-role behavior, but is the result of pressures favoring those animals that have growth and maturation rates which give them a reproductive advantage in environments which permit or encourage males to range more widely than females. Thus I am suggesting that while sexual dimorphism is the outcome of sex differences in growth and maturation rates that lead to different body conformations in adults of each sex, sexual dimorphism is at the same time perfectly compatible with a wide variety of sex-role patterns, and even compatible with the ability to adapt to a variety of social-role patterns.

Gibbons, the first of the primates we will consider, are not dimorphic. Males and females look alike; there are no significant characteristics, aside from genitals, that distinguish them. Members of both sexes take the same length of time to achieve full growth and end up in the same size range (13-16 pounds). In the wild, gibbons live in the high trees in pair groups which include an adult male, an adult female, and the immature young of one or both adults. This pair-centered group occupies a relatively fixed range from which adolescent children move off, sometimes with an opposite sexed sibling and at other times with an opposite sexed adolescent from a nearby group. A pair-centered group forages as a unit in its own arboreal niche, and intruders are driven off by either the adult male or the adult female, neither of whom travels far afield from the range the group occupies (Carpenter, 1948). Pairs mate only when females are neither pregnant or nursing, usually at two- or three-year intervals. In some pairs the male tends to give way to the female; in others the reverse is true.

Orangutans are close neighbors of the gibbons, also living in the high trees. Unlike gibbons, orangutans exhibit a marked degree of sexual dimorphism. Males weigh about 160 pounds, females 80 pounds. Males have goiterous-looking throat sacs which lend volume to their voices. They also have much larger canine teeth than do females and heavier bony prominences around their faces. Females reach sexual maturity and full growth at around age nine; males produce viable sperm at that age, but do not stop growing until several years later. An orang female and her young occupy a stable range which may overlap that of another female and her young. Where mothers and daughters with young live in adjacent areas, they sometimes join together temporarily to make a multi-female group.

Adult males travel alone, moving back and forth across a

wide area that cuts across the ranges of several female groups; sometimes they visit, accompany, or follow these groups for awhile. Although these visits do not necessarily involve sexual activity, males mate when they can. Females are rarely receptive, since nursing is quite prolonged. One obvious rape episode was observed by David Horr, but uninterested females usually avoid and rarely excite males, rejecting them without difficulty. Vocalizations appear to help the animals locate one another in dense foliage and males vocalize fairly frequently. They are assiduous in avoiding one another. The large orangutan male is rarely involved in aggressive interactions and has even less opportunity to function as a leader or protector than the male gibbon, but unlike the gibbon he is a traveler and ranges much more widely than the females of his species.*

Gorillas are the largest of the apes: up to 600 pounds for males and 400 or so for females. Adult males differ from females in that they sometimes develop flaring sagital crests, have furry backs that turn silvery at maturity, and usually have larger canine teeth. Gorillas are ground-browsing vegetarians who build tree nests each night, and adult females are always found in groups in which there is at least one, and usually more, silver-backed males, whose presence is a deterrant to predators. Direction-setting leadership is assumed by a silver-back. Males, especially black-backed adolescents, are not infrequently found outside such groups, evidently joining and leaving them with ease. Females never travel alone. They become pregnant almost immediately on reaching sexual maturity and are nursing an infant or pregnant nearly all their adult lives. Among female gorillas sexual receptivity is rare indeed. In a full year's observation of several groups, Schaller saw only two episodes of intercourse, and neither involved a silver-backed leader. In one case a silver-back approached a copulating pair, displacing the younger male, who ran off. The female displayed no interest whatsoever in the silver-

* An informal presentation by David Horr to a class at Northeastern University is the source of this information on orangs.

back, who finally left the scene. The female then turned back to her preferred partner, an "outsider" who had just joined, and soon left, the group (Schaller, 1964).

Chimpanzee males weigh around 150 pounds; females weigh about 130, but there are small males as well as big females (in the 140-pound range). Aside from a tendency to larger canine teeth, males develop no marked secondary sexual characteristics, but adolescent females develop perineal sexual skins which swell and recede periodically in conjunction with the changing hormonal balance of the estrus cycle. Chimpanzees in the wild are found in several habitats: gallery forests, a mosaic of plain and forest, and on cultivated plantations or near stocked feeding stations. Although there are local variations in social organization which include troop-like arrangements, semi-stable nursery groups of mothers and children, mixed adolescent groups, all-male groups, and general assemblages, all these are essentially fluid. Groups dissolve, change personnel, and in so doing change form. The "nursery group" of mothers and their young occurs in a variety of environments, including stocked feeding station situations. Like orangutans, gibbons, and gorillas, chimpanzee females in the wild are infrequently free from pregnancy and nursing. Chimpanzee females are rather more lively than gorillas, however, when they are in estrus. Males mate with interested females wherever and whenever they find them and wait side by side, without friction or competitive scrambling (Goodall, 1965).

Before going on to describe sex differences and social behavior among baboons, let me point out how the social arrangements among gibbons, orangutans, gorillas, and chimpanzees do not confirm current popular and academic theories which associate sex-role behaviors with physical sex differences and then use these associations to account for the evolution of human sex differences. Popular notions about the kinds of sex roles that lead to dimorphism, and about how dimorphism leads to sex roles, are far too simplistic. Sex-related differences among humans, particularly the possession by females of breasts and buttocks, have been tied to pair bonding, a pair bonding in which males are protectors, aggressors, and leaders. Yet pair bonding shows up only among gibbons, who lack any significant sex differentiation either physically or with respect to social roles. Chimp, gorilla, and orangutan populations lack pair bonding but *are* dimorphic.

The sex differences typical of these species—the males are larger, stronger, hairier, and have more formidable dentition—have in turn been tied to a certain kind of social-role pattern: large males are supposed to be the protectors and leaders of the young and female members of the group, and are therefore supposed to have a sexual advantage over smaller males. Females, according to this theory, are more passive, sexually and otherwise. Similarly, the lack of dimorphism among gibbons has been attributed to an adaptation in which males do not play particularly distinctive roles as leaders, protectors, or aggressors. But orangutan males show a similar lack of leadership, and orangutans are dimorphic. And what do we find in the field? Among the dimorphic primate species, the sexes play different roles in different circumstances. Gorillas are the only dimorphic apes to live in groups stable enough to have leaders. Yet while the silver-backed males may set the direction of troop movement, they are mild mannered. Schaller's observations indicate that silver-backed males have no sexual prerogatives, have no pre-emptive rights over food, and can protect others only while they are within the safety of the group.

Further, while many reporters describe chimpanzee dominance hierarchies as being based on who "gives way" to whom, the largest male around is not necessarily dominant. In fluid chimpanzee aggregates, "leadership"—in terms of direction-setting—is temporary and unstable. There is no evidence that some males have sexual prerogatives denied others; nor does a dominant male have special access to vegetable food or in hunting small game. Even when begging meat from animals (male or female) who have taken game, a dominant male does not receive any special or exorbitant quantity of food (Teleki, 1973). Furthermore, chimpanzee and gorilla males do not go in for fights in which big canines are used. Orangutan males are neither group leaders nor protectors, for they do not live with groups. Since orangutan males generally avoid each other, they rarely get into fights. Predators are not significant threats to any of these animals as long as they can escape into trees or remain in large enough groupings to scare them off. Thus the sexual dimorphism in these primate species is not tied to the social-role arrangements that are often cited as the basis of sexual dimorphism among humans.

The physical traits discussed above continue to be attributed to such role patterns largely because of the behavior of certain baboons, who fit our cultural model of our primate past. Baboons live in the kind of terrestrial plains environment early humans apparently became adapted to. They obviously do not and did not compete directly with humans for the same econiche; if they had, they probably would not have survived. Presumably, however, they now face problems similar to those faced by our early ancestors. Baboon males are much bigger than females, and have heavier mantles and bigger canine teeth, which they display quite often. Males and females are both very volatile in temperament.

The plains-living populations of baboons first described in the anthropological literature by DeVore and Washburn (1961) are called cynocephalous baboons (Buettner-Janusch in Rowell, 1972:45). Cynocephalous baboons also live in forest and "farming" settings. The forest and farm adaptations have been described by Rowell and Maples respectively (Rowell, 1972; Maples, 1971). DeVore and Washburn's early study of plains adaptations in "protected" reserves reported that baboons live in large, peaceful, and rather stable groups. Active adolescent males circulate around the periphery of the closed moving troop, while females with infants stick to the central area and cluster around subgroups of "alpha," or dominant, males. Alpha male subgroups involve alliances between several, mostly older, males, who reportedly rush to place themselves between threatening situations and the troop. Alpha males are chosen as sexual consorts by females at the height of estrus, displace other males and compete with or threaten them when they are offered delectable foods in limited quantities, and seem to set the direction of troop movements. In short, early studies of plains-living social adaptations among baboons provide a neat model which nicely correlates sex-role behavior and physical sex differences, corroborating the theory outlined above.

Forest-living cynocephalous baboons behave differently (Rowell, 1972), as do baboons who raid farms and garden plots (Maples, 1971). Groups travel in a linear pattern, with a male in the front and one at the rear. Old females "choose" and set the direction of daily movement. Adult and young males change groups rather frequently. (In at least one instance, some young adult females also changed groups.) When danger threatens males usually issue warning barks and station themselves near the threat and along an escape route; one may stay behind until the others disappear. But if danger is imminent, the first animals into the safety of the trees are those unencumbered by infants—the males. Rowell observed no patterned preferences for particular consorts by females. Females initiate intercourse, even at the height of estrus, with various males.

Hamadryas baboons live in the dry Ethiopian highlands. They congregate in large assemblages at night and disperse during the day in what has been called—erroneously—one-male groups (Kummer, 1968). Characterized by some authors as "harem" groups, one-male groups often include a junior male, as well as an older male who herds or guides one or several females with or without young. As they age, senior males spend less and less time with the group and the younger males take over herding and mating. These quasi-"family" arrangements provide substantial support for the notion that male-female role differences are related to physical sex differences; in addition, they suggest that a propensity to harem and nuclear "family" arrangements is innate.

Yet an interesting change occurred in one generation in an artifically created colony of hamadryas baboons. An elderly female took over herding-type activities when all the older males born in the wild died off and colony-reared males failed to fulfill the herder role. Behavioral plasticity and sex-role adaptability, it seems, are part of baboon behavioral capacities, since not only do we see a change of social patterning in one short generation in a group of hamadryas that was shifted from one ecological setting to another, but we encounter, as already noted, social patterns among cynocephalous baboons that vary from one setting to another.

The hamadryas one-male group pattern may not mean quite what current theorists argue for yet another reason. It is doubtful that hamadryas are a distinct species of baboon since they have mated successfully with cynocephalous types, both in the wild and in captivity (Rowell, 1972). If they are not a separate species, then their particular social adaptations may represent local adaptations, one of several alternatives available to them. In any case, when we consider all the baboon adaptations side by side—plains, forest, farm, and Ethiopian upland—we are once again left with no neat and inevitable tie between sex-role behavior and physical sex differences. The baboons join the orangutans, chimpanzees, and gorillas in what appears to be, at best, a loose correlation between sex-role behavior patterning and physical form.

Given that sex-role specializations are but weakly demonstrated in these higher primates, how can we account for the existence of such physical sex differences? Since sex dimorphism among primates is not clearly associated with or attributable to any particular set of sex-role patterns, we need another hypothesis as to the origins and functions of sexual dimorphism. The crucial physical differences boil down to elaborations of a single difference in dimorphic primate species: males continue to grow for some time past the age when females have ceased to grow and have begun to have offspring; sex differences in size and body form begin to become marked only after the age at which both males and females are reproductively mature. If differences in pubertal growth rates are the key to understanding the physical differentiation of the sexes, it seems sensible to ask what factors give a reproductive advantage to females who stop growing shortly after they achieve sexual maturity and to males who continue to grow after they develop viable sperm. In the social adaptations of orangutans, chimps, baboons, and gorillas there is one sex-differentiated behavioral common denominator: for a while males move around more actively than females. It is not that they are more aggressive—they may or may not be—but that they are more *mobile.* I therefore propose that in ecological settings in which mature males are enabled or forced to forage more widely than females, males who continue to grow after reaching sexual maturity have a reproductive advantage over males who do not.

Primate species, as species, vary in size according to the econiche to which they are adapted. For the female of any species, ceasing to grow after becoming pregnant has obvious survival advantages for the female and for her offspring. Eating for two, whether the infant is *in utero* or at breast, requires less intake and less activity for a female who stops growing than for one who continues to grow. Anything that insures a female's efficient reproductive energy allocation will be selectively favored, whether her social group is large or small, open or closed, whether she has one mate or several, or lives in the trees or on the ground.

The optimal size for females is the same as that of males in the vast majority of *arboreal* primate species, for dimorphism is rare among them. This correlates with the fact that in most arboreal primate species males and females have similar foraging patterns and are equally free from predation. Orangutans, who are unusually large when compared to other arboreal primates, also do not conform to the standard arboreal troop or pair arrangements. They are not only markedly dimorphic, but the forage ranges of males are far larger than those of females. Orangutan food resources are strained by these large animals and dispersal is a necessity. Males forage as individuals, roaming widely. A mother and her young forage together in a small area, occasionally joined by another mother and her young. Though orangutans are pre-eminently arboreal, in some ways this adaptation resembles that of ground-living primate species.

Partially or completely terrestrially adapted primates are

more readily subject to predation than arboreal species, and immature animals and infant-carrying females are safe only when in a good-sized group. Mother-young groups, like those of the orangutans, simply could not survive on the ground. Ground-living species are group foragers and the core of the group is made up of immature animals and females with young. The only isolated males that are large enough to travel safely on the ground for any length of time are gorillas. Food resources at the center of a ground-foraging group are under some pressure, and there is thus an impetus for mature unencumbered animals to move toward the periphery of the group, and even to eventually leave and join another. Those males that continue to grow after reaching sexual maturity are peculiarly well adapted to foraging on the margins of a group. For one thing, they do not experience either the decline in activity level that accompanies the cessation of growth, or the decline in activity level that affects pregnant and nursing females. They tend to remain active and exploratory longer than males who stop growing, so they are ready and able to exploit resources on the margins of the group. (Sometimes they even eat foods that other members of the species don't encounter, which may explain some secondary sexual developments in the chewing equipment and head structures of males.) Furthermore, the bigger they become, the safer they are from predators in their edge locations. But most significant of all, the more mobile they become, the greater are their reproductive advantages over less mobile males.

From what does this reproductive advantage derive? Male reproductive success is linked to the number of mating opportunities a male can take advantage of. Since primate females are infrequently in estrus, males who move around on the edges of groups, and from group to group, are more likely to find fertile females than those who are bound to their own small groups all their lives, or who stay in the center with nursing mothers all the time. This means that a delayed cessation of growth can afford a male reproductive advantages whether or not he engages in active sexual competition with other males, and whether or not he becomes a leader or a protector. If he is living in a setting where predation is significant, the size he achieves may help him survive, and this of course also contributes to his reproductive success. (Since predation hardly affects orangutans at all, however, protection seems to be less a cause than a result of size increments, which are tied to mobility.)

For the mobile male the particular role he plays in the groups he encounters often changes from situation to situation. He may or may not become a dominant male capable of getting others to move out of his way, but even if he does settle down to a life of "dominance" in a particular group, the number of offspring he fathers will not be increased by his ability to displace others, since "dominance" is not particularly correlated with any special sexual prerogatives. Indeed, his reproductive success rate may be reduced as his mobility diminishes, even though he has achieved full size. If he settles down to a life of subdominance, the same holds true. The role he plays in a group seems to be less significant than how much he moves around among groups.

The hypothesis I am proposing therefore argues that in ecological settings which encourage males to forage more widely than females, reproductive advantages have fallen to those males who are active enough to move around, large enough to do so safely, and versatile enough to exploit alternative food resources and social situations. At the same time, reproductive advantage falls to those females who stop growing at pubescence and are efficient in using their limited food intakes for reproduction and nursing. This hypothesis provides a way to account for the evolution of physical differences without viewing sex roles, past or present, rigidly. (I might add, briefly and by way of support for some of the ideas incorporated into this hypothesis, that when a female baboon was prevented from becoming pregnant she continued to grow and remained active longer than her compeers.)

This hypothesis is a response to the recent spate of evolutionary theories which stress that our sex-role destiny along with our sexual anatomy, was settled a long time ago. A number of theorists have revived the view that sexual dimorphism among humans is tied to sex-role patterns that are current or idealized in our own culture. New data on nonhuman primate behavior has provided source materials for such theories: without too much difficulty, theorists have been able to find one or another population of nonhuman primates that conforms to their cultural model of how things were, are, or ought to be. Unfortunately for such theories, humans and nonhuman primates utilize a variety of social forms in which females and males play a variety of roles. Explaining human sexual dimorphism in terms which postulate that the sexes are each suited to only certain kinds of role behavior runs contrary to the accumulated evidence. Until we have an explanation that accounts both for the evolution of physical sex differences and for the existence of role plasticity, the belief that anatomy is destiny will linger on. We must familiarize ourselves with the data and deal with it in a sophisticated framework that accounts for its variability. If we don't, the growing body of evidence that role variability and role plasticity run rather deep in the primate heritage will continue to be ignored or distorted.

Sally Slocum

Woman the Gatherer: Male Bias in Anthropology

Little systematic attention has been given in our discipline to an "anthropology of knowledge." While some anthropologists have concerned themselves with knowledge in general, as seen through the varieties of human cultures, few have examined anthropological knowledge itself. An anthropology of knowledge would have several parts. First is what Peter Berger (1967:1-18) has called "philosophical anthropology": a study of the nature of the human species. This has always been a legitimate concern of anthropology, but too often we become so concerned with minute differences that we forget we are studying a single species. Second is how we "know" anything—what is accepted as "proof," what is reality, what are the grounds for rationality (Garfinkel, 1960), what modes are used in gathering knowledge, what are the effects of differences in culture and world view on what we "know." Third is a close examination of the questions asked in anthropology, for questions always determine and limit answers.

This paper originally appeared, under the name Sally Linton, in the first version of *Women in Perspective: A Guide for Cross-Cultural Studies* (Urbana: University of Illinois Press, 1971), edited by Sue-Ellen Jacobs, to whom thanks are due for facilitating its reprinting here.

Many of the ideas were developed during conversations with Jane Kephart and Joan Roos over a period of several months. Since it was the interaction which produced the ideas, it is difficult to credit any particular idea to any one person. Suffice it to say that without their help and encouragement this paper would not have been written.

It is the third point, the nature of anthropological questions, to which I wish to speak in this paper. We are human beings studying other human beings, and we cannot leave ourselves out of the equation. We choose to ask certain questions, *and not others.* Our choice grows out of the cultural context in which anthropology and anthropologists exist. Anthropology, as an academic discipline, has been developed primarily by white Western males, during a specific period in history. Our questions are shaped by the particulars of our historical situation, and by unconscious cultural assumptions.

Given the cultural and ethnic background of the majority of anthropologists, it is not surprising that the discipline has been biased. There are signs, however, that this selective blindness is beginning to come under scrutiny. For example, in the exchange in the journal *Current Anthropology* (1968), anthropologists like Kathleen Gough and Gerald Berreman point out the unconscious efforts of American political and economic assumptions on our selection of problems and populations to be studied. Restive minority groups in this country are pointing to the bias inherent in anthropological studies of themselves through books such as Vine Deloria's *Custer Died for Your Sins.* We have always encouraged members of American minority groups, and other "foreigners," to take up anthropology because of the perspective on the world that they can supply. The invitation is increasingly being accepted. As we had both hoped and feared, repercussions from this new participation are being felt in theory, method, interpretation, and problem choice, shaking anthropology to the roots.

The perspective of women is, in many ways, equally foreign to an anthropology that has been developed and pursued primarily by males. There is a strong male bias in the questions asked, and the interpretations given. This bias has hindered the full development of our discipline as "the study of the human animal" (I don't want to call it "the study of man" for reasons that will become evident). I am going to demonstrate the Western male bias by reexamining the matter of evolution of Homo sapiens from our nonhuman primate ancestors. In particular, the concept of "Man the Hunter" as developed by Sherwood Washburn and C. Lancaster (1968) and others is my focus. This critique is offered in hopes of transcending the male bias that limits our knowledge by limiting the questions we ask.

Though male bias could be shown in other areas, hominid evolution is particularly convenient for my purpose because it involves speculations and inferences from a rather small amount of data. In such a case, hidden assumptions and premises that lie behind the speculations and inferences are more easily demonstrated. Male bias exists not only in the ways in which the scanty data are interpreted, but in the very language used. All too often the word "man" is used in such an ambiguous fashion that it is impossible to decide whether it refers to males or to the human species in general, including both males and females. In fact, one frequently is led to suspect that in the minds of many anthropologists, "man," supposedly meaning the human species, is actually exactly synonymous with "males."

This ambiguous use of language is particularly evident in the writing that surrounds the concept of Man the Hunter. Washburn and Lancaster make it clear that it is specifically males who hunt, that hunting is much more than simply an economic activity, and that most of the characteristics which we think of as specifically human can be causally related to hunting. They tell us that hunting is a whole pattern of activity and way of life: "The biology, psychology, and customs that separate us from the apes—all these we owe to the hunters of time past" (1968:303). If this line of reasoning is followed to its logical conclusion, one must agree with Jane Kephart when she says:

> Since only males hunt, and the psychology of the species was set by hunting, we are forced to conclude that females are scarcely human, that is, do not have built-in the basic psychology of the species: to kill and hunt and ultimately to kill others of the same species. The argument implies built-in aggression in human males, as well as the assumed passivity of human females and their exclusion from the mainstream of human development. (1970:5)

To support their argument that hunting is important to human males, Washburn and Lancaster point to the fact that many modern males still hunt, though it is no longer economically necessary. I could point out that many modern males play golf, play the violin, or tend gardens: these, as well as hunting, are things their culture teaches them. Using a "survival" as evidence to demonstrate an important fact of cultural evolution can be accorded no more validity when proposed by a modern anthropologist than when proposed by Tylor.

Regardless of its status as a survival, hunting, by implication as well as direct statement, is pictured as a male activity to the exclusion of females. This activity, on which we are told depends the psychology, biology, and customs of our species, is strictly male. A theory that leaves out half the human species is unbalanced. The theory of Man the Hunter is not only unbalanced; it leads to the conclusion that the basic human adaptation was the desire of males to hunt and kill. This not only gives too much importance to aggression, which is after all only one factor of human life, but it derives culture from killing. I am going to suggest a less biased reading of the evidence, which gives a more valid and logical picture of human evolution, and at the same time a more hopeful one. First I will note the evidence, discuss the more traditional reading of it, and then offer an alternative reconstruction.

The data we have to work from are a combination of fossil and archeological materials, knowledge of living nonhuman primates, and knowledge of living humans. Since we assume that the protohominid ancestors of Homo sapiens developed in a continuous fashion from a base of characteristics similar to those of living nonhuman primates, the most important facts seem to be the ways in which humans differ from nonhuman primates, and the ways in which we are similar. The differences are as follows: longer gestation period; more difficult birth; neoteny, in that human infants are less well developed at birth; long period of infant dependency; absence of body hair; year-round sexual receptivity of females, resulting in the possibility of bearing a second infant while the first is still at the breast or still dependent; erect bipedalism; possession of a large and complex brain that makes possible the creation of elaborate symbolic systems, languages, and cultures, and also results in most behavior being under cortical control; food sharing; and finally, living in families. (For the purposes of this paper I define families as follows: a situation where each individual has defined responsibilities and obligations to a specific set of others of both sexes and various ages. I use this definition because, among humans, the family is a *social* unit, regardless of any biological or genetic relationship which may or may not exist among its members.)

In addition to the many well-known close physiological resemblances, we share with nonhuman primates the following characteristics: living in social groups; close mother-infant bonds; affectional relationships; a large capacity for learning and a related paucity of innate behaviors; ability to take part in dominance hierarchies; a rather complex nonsymbolic communication system which can handle with considerable subtlety such information as the mood and emotional state of the individual, and the attitude and status of each individual toward the other members of the social group.

The fossil and archeological evidence consists of various bones labeled Ramapithecus, Australopithecus, Homo habilis, Homo erectus, etc.; and artifacts such as stone tools representing various cultural traditions, evidence of use of fire, etc. From this evidence we can make reasonable inferences about diet, posture and locomotion, and changes in the brain as shown by increased cranial capacity, ability to make tools, and other evidences of cultural creation. Since we assume that complexity of material culture requires language, we infer the beginnings of language somewhere between Australopithecus and Homo erectus.

Given this data, the speculative reconstruction begins. As I was taught anthropology, the story goes something like this. Obscure selection pressures pushed the protohominid in the direction of erect bipedalism—perhaps the advantages of freeing the hands for food carrying or for tool use. Freeing the hands allowed more manipulation of the environment in the direction of tools for gathering and hunting food. Through a hand-eye-brain feedback process, coordination, efficiency, and skill were increased. The new behavior was adaptive, and selection pressure pushed the protohominid further along the same lines of development. Diet changed as the increase in skill allowed the addition of more animal protein. Larger brains were selected for, making possible transmission of information concerned tool making, and organizing cooperative hunting. It is assumed that as increased brain size was selected for, so also was neoteny—immaturity of infants at birth with a corresponding increase in their period of dependency, allowing more time for learning at the same time as this learning became necessary through the further reduction of instinctual behaviors and their replacement by symbolically invented ones.

Here is where one may discover a large logical gap. From the difficult-to-explain beginning trends toward neoteny and increased brain size, the story jumps to Man the Hunter. The statement is made that the females were more burdened with dependent infants and could not follow the rigorous hunt. Therefore they stayed at a "home base," gathering what food they could, while the males developed cooperative hunting techniques, increased their communicative and organizational skills through hunting, and brought the meat back to the dependent females and young. Incest prohibitions, marriage, and the family (so the story goes) grew out of the need to eliminate competition between males for females. A pattern developed of a male hunter becoming the main support of "his" dependent females and young (in other words, the development of the nuclear family for no apparent reason). Thus the peculiarly human social and emotional bonds can be traced to the hunter bringing back the food to share. Hunting, according to Washburn and Lancaster, involved "cooperation among males, planning, knowledge of many species and large areas, and technical skill" (1968:296). They even profess to discover the beginnings of art in the weapons of the hunter. They point out that the symmetrical Acheulian biface tools are the earliest beautiful man-made objects. Though we don't know what these tools were used for, they argue somewhat tautologically that the symmetry indicates they may have been swung, because symmetry only makes a difference when irregularities might lead to deviations in the line of flight. "It may well be that it was the attempt to produce efficient high-speed weapons that first produced beautiful, symmetrical objects" (1968:298).

So, while the males were out hunting, developing all their skills, learning to cooperate, inventing language, inventing art, creating tools and weapons, the poor dependent females were sitting back at the home base having one child after another (many of them dying in the process), and waiting for the males to bring home the bacon. While this reconstruction is certainly ingenious, it gives one the decided impression that only half the species—the male half—did any evolving. In addition to containing a number of logical gaps, the argument becomes somewhat doubtful in the light of modern knowledge of genetics and primate behavior.

The skills usually spoken of as being necessary to, or developed through, hunting are things like coordination, endurance, good vision, and the ability to plan, communicate, and cooperate. I have heard of no evidence to indicate that these skills are either carried on the Y chromosome, or are triggered into existence by the influence of the Y chromosome. In fact, on just about any test we can design (psychological, aptitude, intelligence, etc.) males and females score just about the same. The variation is on an individual, not a sex, basis.

Every human individual gets half its genes from a male and half from a female; genes sort randomly. It is possible for a female to end up with all her genes from male ancestors, and for a male to end up with all his genes from female ancestors. The logic of the hunting argument would have us believe that all the selection pressure was on the males, leaving the females simply as drags on the species. The rapid increase in brain size and complexity was thus due entirely to half the species; the main function of the female half was to suffer and die in the attempt to give birth to their large-brained male infants. An unbiased reading of the evidence indicates there was selection pressure on both sexes, and that hunting was not in fact the basic adaptation of the species from which flowed all the traits we think of as specifically human. Hunting does not deserve the primary place it has been given in the reconstruction of human evolution, as I will demonstrate by offering the following alternate version.

Picture the primate band: each individual gathers its own food, and the major enduring relationship is the mother-infant bond. It is in similar circumstances that we imagine the evolving protohominids. We don't know what started them in the direction of neoteny and increased brain size, but once begun the trends would prove adaptive. To explain the shift from the primate individual gathering to human food sharing, we cannot simply jump to hunting. Hunting cannot explain its own origin. It is much more logical to assume that as the period of infant dependency began to lengthen, *the mothers would begin to increase the scope of their gathering to provide food for their still-dependent infants.* The already strong primate mother-infant bond would begin to extend over a longer time period, increasing the depth and scope of social relationships, and giving rise to the first sharing of food.

It is an example of male bias to picture these females with young as totally or even mainly dependent on males for food. Among modern hunter-gatherers, even in the marginal environments where most live, the females can usually gather enough to support themselves and their families. In these groups gathering provides the major portion of the diet, and there is no reason to assume that this was not also the case in the Pliocene or early Pleistocene. In the modern groups women and children both gather and hunt small animals, though they usually do not go on the longer hunts. So, we can assume a group of evolving protohominids, gathering and perhaps beginning to hunt small animals, with the mothers gathering quite efficiently both for themselves and for their offspring.

It is equally biased, and quite unreasonable, to assume an

early or rapid development of a pattern in which one male was responsible for "his" female(s) and young. In most primate groups when a female comes into estrus she initiates coitus or signals her readiness by presenting. The idea that a male would have much voice in "choosing" a female, or maintain any sort of individual, long-term control over her or her offspring, is surely a modern invention which could have had no place in early hominid life. (Sexual control over females through rape or the threat of rape seems to be a modern human invention. Primate females are not raped because they are willing throughout estrus, and primate males appear not to attempt coitus at other times, regardless of physiological ability.) In fact, there seems to me no reason for suggesting the development of male-female adult pair-bonding until much later. Long-term monogamy is a fairly rare pattern even among modern humans—I think it is a peculiarly Western male bias to suppose its existence in protohuman society. An argument has been made (by Morris, 1967, and others) that traces the development of male-female pair-bonding to the shift of sexual characteristics to the front of the body, the importance of the face in communication, and the development of face-to-face coitus. This argument is insufficient in the first place because of the assumption that face-to-face coitus is the "normal," "natural," or even the most common position among humans (historical evidence casts grave doubt on this assumption). It is much more probable that the coitus position was invented *after* pair-bonding had developed for other reasons.

Rather than adult male-female sexual pairs, a temporary consort-type relationship is much more logical in hominid evolution. It is even a more accurate description of the modern human pattern: the most dominant males (chief, headman, brave warrior, good hunter, etc.), mate with the most dominant females (in estrus, young and beautiful, fertile, rich, etc.), for varying periods of time. Changing sexual partners is frequent and common. We have no way of knowing when females began to be fertile year-round, but this change is not a necessary condition for the development of families.

We need not bring in any notion of paternity, or the development of male-female pairs, or any sort of marriage in order to account for either families or food sharing.

The lengthening period of infant dependency would have strengthened and deepened the mother-infant bond; the earliest families would have consisted of *females and their children.* In such groups, over time, the sibling bond would have increased in importance also. The most universal, and persumably oldest, form of incest prohibition is between mother and son. There are indications of such avoidance even among modern monkeys. It could develop logically from the mother-children family: as the period of infant dependency lengthened, and the age of sexual maturity advanced, a mother might no longer be capable of childbearing when her son reached maturity. Another factor which may have operated is the situation found in many primates today where only the most dominant males have access to fertile females. Thus a young son, even after reaching sexual maturity, would still have to spend time working his way up the male hierarchy before gaining access to females. The length of time it would take him increases the possibility that his mother would no longer be fertile.

Food sharing and the family developed from the mother-infant bond. The techniques of hunting large animals were probably much later developments, after the mother-children family pattern was established. When hunting did begin, and the adult males brought back food to share, the most likely recipients would be first their mothers, and second their siblings. In other words, a hunter would share food *not* with a wife or sexual partner, but with those who had shared food with him: his mother and siblings.

It is frequently suggested or implied that the first tools were, in fact, the weapons of the hunters. Modern humans have become so accustomed to the thought of tools and weapons that it is easy for us to imagine the first manlike creature who picked up a stone or club. However, since we don't really know what the early stone tools such as hand-axes were used for, it is equally probable that they were not weapons at all, but rather *aids in gathering.* We know that gathering was important long before much animal protein was added to the diet, and continued to be important. Bones, sticks, and hand-axes could be used for digging up tubers or roots, or to pulverize tough vegetable matter for easier eating. If, however, instead of thinking in terms of tools and weapons, we think in terms of *cultural inventions*, a new aspect is presented. I suggest that two of the *earliest and most important* cultural inventions were containers to hold the products of gathering, and some sort of sling or net to carry babies. The latter in particular must have been extremely important with the loss of body hair and the increasing immaturity of neonates, who could not cling and had less and less to cling to. Plenty of material was available—vines, hides, human hair. If the infant could be securely fastened to the mother's body, she could go about her tasks much more efficiently. Once a technique for carrying babies was developed, it could be extended to the idea of carrying food, and eventually to other sorts of cultural inventions—choppers and grinders for food preparation, and even weapons. Among modern hunter-gatherers, regardless of the poverty of their material culture, food carriers and baby carriers are always important items in their equipment.

A major point in the Man the Hunter argument is that cooperative hunting among males demanded more skill in social organization and communication, and thus provided selection pressure for increased brain size. I suggest that longer periods of infant dependency, more difficult births, and longer gestation periods also demanded more skills in social organization and communication—creating selective pressure for increased brain size without looking to hunting as an explanation. The need to organize for feeding after weaning, learning to handle the more complex social-emotional bonds that were developing, the new skills and cultural inventions surrounding more extensive gathering—all would demand larger brains. Too much attention has been given to the skills required by hunting, and too little to the skills required for gathering and the raising of dependent young. The techniques required for efficient gathering include location and identification of plant varieties, seasonal and geographical knowledge, containers for carrying the food, and tools for its preparation. Among modern hunting-gathering groups this knowledge is an extremely complex, well-developed, and important part of their cultural equipment. Caring for a curious, energetic, but still dependent human infant is difficult and demanding. Not only must the infant be watched, it must be taught the customs, dangers, and knowledge of its group. For the early hominids, as their cultural equipment and symbolic communication increased, the job of training the young would demand more skill. Selection pressure for better brains came from many directions.

Much has been made of the argument that cooperation among males demanded by hunting acted as a force to reduce competition for females. I suggest that competition for females has been greatly exaggerated. It could easily have been handled in the usual way for primates—according to male status relationships already worked out—and need not be pictured as particularly violent or extreme. The seeds of male cooperation already exist in primates when they act to protect the band from predators. Such dangers may well have increased with a shift to savannah living, and the longer dependency of infants. If biological roots are sought to explain the greater aggressiveness of males, it would be more fruitful to look toward their function as protectors, rather than any supposedly basic hunting adaptation. The only division of labor that regularly exists in primate groups is the females caring for infants and the males protecting the group from predators. The possibilities for both cooperation and aggression in males lies in this protective function.

The emphasis on hunting as a prime moving factor in hominid evolution distorts the data. It is simply too big a jump to go from the primate individual gathering pattern to a hominid cooperative hunting-sharing pattern without some intervening changes. Cooperative hunting of big game animals could only have developed *after* the trends toward neoteny and increased brain size had begun. Big-game hunting becomes a more logical development when it is viewed as growing out of a complex of changes which included sharing the products of gathering among mothers and children, deepening social bonds over time, increase in brain size, and the beginnings of cultural invention for purposes such as baby carrying, food carrying, and food preparation. Such hunting not only needed the prior development of some skills in social organization and communication; it probably also had to await the development of the "home base." It is difficult to imagine that most or all of the adult primate males in a group would go off on a hunting expedition, leaving the females and young exposed to the danger of predators, without some way of communicating to arrange for their defense, or at least a way of saying, "Don't worry, we'll be back in two days." Until that degree of communicative skill developed, we must assume either that the whole band traveled *and hunted* together, or that the males simply did not go off on large cooperative hunts.

The development of cooperative hunting requires, as a prior condition, an increase in brain size. Once such a trend is established, hunting skills would take part in a feedback process of selection for better brains just as would other cultural inventions and developments such as gathering skills. By itself, hunting fails to explain any part of human evolution and fails to explain itself.

Anthropology has always rested on the assumption that the mark of our species is our ability to *symbol*, to bring into existence forms of behavior and interaction, and material tools with which to adjust and control the environment. To explain human nature as evolving from the desire of males to hunt and kill is to negate most of anthropology. Our species survived and adapted through the invention of *culture*, of which hunting is simply a part. It is often stated that hunting *must* be viewed as the "natural" species' adaptation because it lasted as long as it did, nine-tenths of all human history. However:

> Man the Hunter lasted as long as "he" did from no natural propensity toward hunting any more than toward computer programming or violin playing or nuclear warfare, but because that was what the historical circumstances allowed. We ignore the first premise of our science if we fail to admit that "man" is no more natural a hunter than "he" is naturally a golfer, for after symboling became possible our species left forever the ecological niche of the necessity of any one adaptation, and made all adaptations possible for ourselves. (Kephart, 1970:23)

That the concept of Man the Hunter influenced anthropology for as long as it did is a reflection of male bias in the discipline. This bias can be seen in the tendency to equate "man," "human," and "male"; to look at culture almost entirely from a male point of view; to search for examples of the behavior of males and assume that this is sufficient for explanation, ignoring almost totally the female half of the species; and to filter this male bias through the "ideal" modern Western pattern of one male supporting a dependent wife and minor children.

The basis of any discipline is not the answers it gets, but the questions it asks. As an exercise in the anthropology of knowledge, this paper stems from asking a simple question: what were the females doing while the males were out hunting? It was only possible for me to ask this question after I had become politically conscious of myself as a woman. Such is the prestige of males in our society that a woman, in anthropology or any other profession, can only gain respect or be attended to if she deals with questions deemed important by men. Though there have been women anthropologists for years, it is rare to be able to discern any difference between their work and that of male anthropologists. Learning to be an anthropologist has involved learning to think from a male perspective, so it should not be surprising that women have asked the same kinds of questions as men. But political consciousness, whether among women, blacks, American Indians, or any other group, leads to reexamination and reevaluation of taken-for-granted assumptions. It is a difficult process, challenging the conventional wisdom, and this paper is simply a beginning. The male bias in anthropology that I have illustrated here is just as real as the white bias, the middle-class bias, and the academic bias that exist in the discipline. It is our task, as anthropologists, to create a "study of the human species" in spite of, or perhaps because of, or maybe even by means of, our individual biases and unique perspectives.

Kathleen Gough

The Origin of the Family

The trouble with the origin of the family is that no one really knows. Since Frederick Engels wrote *The Origin of the Family, Private Property, and the State* in 1884, a great deal of new evidence has come in. Yet the gaps are still enormous. It is not known *when* the family originated, although it was probably between 2 million and 100,000 years ago. It is not known whether it developed once or in separate times and places. It is not known whether some kind of embryonic family came before, with, or after the origin of language. Since language is the accepted criterion of humanness, this means that we do not even know whether our ancestors acquired the basics of family life before or after they were human. The chances are that language and the family developed together over a long period, but the evidence is sketchy.

Although the origin of the family is speculative, it is better to speculate with than without evidence. The evidence comes from three sources. One is the social and physical lives of nonhuman primates—especially the New and Old World monkeys and, still more, the great apes, humanity's closest relatives. The second source is the tools and home sites of prehistoric humans and protohumans. The third is the family lives of hunters and gatherers of wild provender who have been studied in modern times.

This paper originally appeared in *Journal of Marriage and the Family* 33 (November 1971), and is reprinted with the permission of the publisher and author.

Each of these sources is imperfect: monkeys and apes, because they are *not* pre-human ancestors, although they are our cousins; fossil hominids, because they left so little vestige of their social life; hunters and gatherers, because none of them has, in historic times, possessed a technology and society as primitive as those of early humans. All show the results of long endeavor in specialized, marginal environments. But together, these sources give valuable clues.

Defining the Family

To discuss the origin of something we must first decide what it is. I shall define the family as "a married couple or other group of adult kinfolk who cooperate economically and in the upbringing of children, and all or most of whom share a common dwelling."

This includes all forms of kin-based household. Some are extended families containing three generations of married brothers or sisters. Some are "grandfamilies" descended from a single pair of grandparents. Some are matrilineal households, in which brothers and sisters share a house with the sisters' children, and men merely visit their wives in other homes. Some are compound families, in which one man has several wives, or one woman, several husbands. Others are nuclear families composed of a father, mother, and children.

Some kind of family exists in all known human societies, although it is not found in every segment or class of all stratified, state societies. Greek and American slaves, for example, were prevented from forming legal families, and their social families were often disrupted by sale, forced labor, or sexual exploitation. Even so, the family was an ideal which all classes and most people attained when they could.

The family implies several other universals. (1) Rules forbid sexual relations and marriage between close relatives. Which relatives are forbidden varies, but all societies forbid mother-son mating, and most, father-daughter and brother-sister. Some societies allow sex relations, but forbid marriage, between certain degrees of kin. (2) The men and women of a family cooperate through a division of labor based on gender. Again, the sexual division of labor varies in rigidity and in the tasks performed. But in no human society to date is it wholly absent. Child care, household tasks, and crafts closely connected with the household tend to be done by women; war, hunting, and government, by men. (3) Marriage exists as a socially recognized, durable (although not necessarily lifelong) relationship between individual men and women. From it springs social fatherhood, some kind of special bond between a man and the child of his wife, whether or not they are his own children physiologically. Even in polyandrous societies, where women have several husbands, or in matrilineal societies, where group membership and property pass through women, each child has one or more designated "fathers" with whom he or she has a special social, and often religious, relationship. This bond of *social* fatherhood is recognized among people who do not know about the male role in procreation, or where, for various reasons, it is not clear who the physiological father of a particular infant is. Social fatherhood seems to come from the division and interdependence of male and female tasks, especially in relation to children, rather than directly from physiological fatherhood, although in most societies, the social father of a child is usually presumed to be its physiological father as well. Contrary to the beliefs of some feminists, however, I think that in no human society do men, as a category, have *only* the role of insemination, and *no* other social or economic role, in relation to women and children. (4) Men in general have higher status and authority over the women of their families, although older women may have influence, even some authority, over junior men. The omnipresence of male authority, too, goes contrary to the belief of some feminists that in "matriarchal" societies, women were either completely equal to, or had paramount authority over, men, either in the home or in society at large.

It is true that in some matrilineal societies, such as the Hopi of Arizona or the Ashanti of Ghana, men exert little authority over their wives. In some, such as the Nayars of

South India or the Minangkabau of Sumatra, men may even live separately from their wives and children, that is, in different families. In such societies, however, the fact is that women and children fall under greater or lesser authority from the women's kinsmen—their eldest brothers, mothers' brothers, or even their grown-up sons.

In matrilineal societies, where property, rank, office, and group membership are inherited through the female line, it is true that women tend to have greater independence than in patrilineal societies. This is especially so in matrilineal tribal societies where the state has not yet developed, and especially in those tribal societies where residence is matrilocal—that is, men come to live in the homes or villages of their wives. Even so, in all matrilineal societies for which adequate descriptions are available, the ultimate head of a household, lineage, and local group is usually a man.*

There is in fact no true "matriarchal," as distinct from "matrilineal," society in existence or known from literature, and the chances are that there never has been.** This does not mean that women and men have never had relations that were dignified and creative for both sexes, appropriate to the knowledge, skills, and technology of their times. Nor does it mean that the sexes cannot be equal in the future, or that the sexual division of labor cannot be abolished. I believe that it can and must be. But it is not necessary to believe myths of a feminist Golden Age in order to plan for parity in the future.

* See Schneider and Gough, eds., *Matrilineal Kinship* (1961), for common and variant features of matrilineal systems.

** The Iroquois are often quoted as a "matriarchal" society, but in fact Lewis Henry Morgan refers to "the absence of equality between the sexes" and notes that women were subordinate to men, ate after men, and that women (not men) were publicly whipped as punishment for adultery. Warleaders, tribal chiefs, and *sachems* (heads of matrilineal lineages) were men. Women did, however, have a large say in the government of the longhouse or home of the matrilocal extended family, and women figured as tribal counselors and religious officials, as well as arranging marriages. (See Lewis H. Morgan, *The League of the Ho-De'No-Sau-Nee, Iroquois,* 1954.)

Primate Societies

Within the primate order, humans are most closely related to the anthropoid apes (the African chimpanzee and gorilla and the Southeast Asian orangutan and gibbon), and of these, to the chimpanzee and the gorilla. More distantly related are the Old, and then the New World, monkeys; and finally, the lemurs, tarsiers, and tree shrews.

All primates share characteristics without which the family could not have developed. The young are born relatively helpless. They suckle for several months or years and need prolonged care afterwards. Childhood is longer, the closer the species is to humans. Most monkeys reach puberty at about four to five and mature socially between about five and ten. Chimpanzees, by contrast, suckle for up to three years. Females reach puberty at seven to ten; males enter mature social and sexual relations as late as thirteen. The long childhood and maternal care produce close relations between children of the same mother, who play together and help tend their juniors until they grow up.

Monkeys and apes, like humans, mate in all months of the year instead of in a rutting season. Unlike humans, however, female apes experience unusually strong sexual desire for a few days shortly before and during ovulation (the estrus period), and have intensive sexual relations at that time. The males are attracted to the females by their scent or by brightly colored swellings in the sexual region. Estrus-mating appears to be especially pronounced in primate species more remote from humans. The apes and some monkeys carry on less intensive, month-round sexuality in addition to estrus-mating, approaching human patterns more closely. In humans, sexual desires and relations are regulated less by hormonal changes and more by mental images, emotions, cultural rules, and individual preferences.

Year-round (if not always month-round) sexuality means that males and females socialize more continuously among primates than among most other mammals. All primates form bands or troops composed of both sexes plus children. The numbers and proportions of the sexes vary, and in some species an individual, a mother with her young, or a subsidiary troop of male juveniles may travel temporarily alone. But in general, males and females socialize continually through mutual grooming* and playing as well as through frequent sex relations. Keeping close to the females, primate males play with their children and tend to protect both females and young from predators. A "division of labor" based on gender is thus already found in primate society between a female role of prolonged child care and a male role of defense. Males may also carry or take care of children briefly, and nonnursing females may fight. But a kind of generalized "fatherliness" appears in the protective role of adult males toward young, even in species where the sexes do not form long-term individual attachments.

Sexual Bonds Among Primates

One group of nonhuman primates has enduring sexual bonds and restrictions, superficially similar to those in some human socities. Among gibbons a single male and female live together with their young. The male drives off other males and the female, other females. When a male juvenile reaches puberty it is thought to leave or be expelled by the parent of the same sex, and he eventually finds a mate elsewhere. Similar de facto, rudimentary "incest prohibitions" may have been passed on to humans from their prehuman ancestors and later codified and elaborated through language, moral custom, and law. Whether this is so may become clearer when we know more about the mating patterns of the other great apes, especially of our closest relatives, the chimpanzees. Present evidence suggests that male chimpanzees do not mate with their mothers.

Orangutans live in small, tree-dwelling groups like gibbons, but their groupings are less regular. One or two mothers may wander alone with their young, mating at intervals with a male; or a male-female pair, or several juvenile males, may travel together.

* Combing the hair and removing parasites with hands or teeth.

Among mountain gorillas of Uganda, South Indian langurs, and hamadryas baboons of Ethiopia, a single, fully mature male mates with several females, especially in their estrus periods. If younger adult males are present, the females may have occasional relations with them if the leader is tired or not looking.

Among East and South African baboons, rhesus macaques, and South American woolly monkeys, the troop is bigger, numbering up to two hundred. It contains a number of adult males and a much larger number of females. The males are strictly ranked in terms of dominance based on both physical strength and intelligence. The more dominant males copulate intensively with the females during the latter's estrus periods. Toward the end of each estrus a female may briefly attach herself to a single dominant male. At other times she may have relations with any male of higher or lower rank provided that those of higher rank permit it.

Among some baboons and macaques the young males travel on the outskirts of the group and have little access to females. Some macaques expel from the troop a proportion of the young males, who then form "bachelor troops." Bachelors may later form new troops with young females.

Other primates are more thoroughly promiscuous, or rather indiscriminate, in mating. Chimpanzees, and also South American howler monkeys, live in loosely structured groups, again (as in most monkey and ape societies), with a preponderance of females. The mother-child unit is the only stable group. The sexes copulate almost at random, and most intensively and indiscriminately during estrus.

A number of well-known anthropologists have argued that various attitudes and customs often found in human societies are instinctual rather than culturally learned, and come from our primate heritage. They include hierarchies of ranking among men, male political power over women, and the greater tendency of men to form friendships with one another, as opposed to women's tendencies to cling to a man. (See, for example, Morris, 1967, and Fox, 1967.)

I cannot accept these conclusions and think that they stem

from the male chauvinism of our own society. A "scientific" argument which states that all such features of female inferiority are instinctive is obviously a powerful weapon in maintaining the traditional family with male dominance. But in fact, these features are *not* universal among nonhuman primates, including some of those most closely related to humans. Chimpanzees have a low degree of male dominance and male hierarchy and are sexually virtually indiscriminate. Gibbons have a kind of fidelity for both sexes and almost no male dominance or hierarchy. Howler monkeys are sexually indiscriminate and lack male hierarchies or dominance.

The fact is that among nonhuman primates male dominance and male hierarchies seem to be adaptations to particular environments, some of which did become genetically established through natural selection. Among humans, however, these features are present in variable degrees and are almost certainly learned, not inherited at all. Among nonhuman primates there are fairly general differences between those that live mainly in trees and those that live largely on the ground. The tree dwellers (for example, gibbons, orangutans, South American howler and woolly monkeys) tend to have to defend themselves less against predators than do the ground dwellers (such as baboons, macaques, or gorillas). Where defense is important, males are much larger and stronger than females, exert dominance over females, and are strictly hierarchized and organized in relation to one another. Where defense is less important there is much less sexual dimorphism (difference in size between male and female), less or no male dominance, a less pronounced male hierarchy, and greater sexual indiscriminacy.

Comparatively speaking, humans have a rather small degree of sexual dimorphism, similar to chimpanzees. Chimpanzees live much in trees but also partly on the ground, in forest or semi-forest habitats. They build individual nests to sleep in, sometimes on the ground but usually in trees. They flee into trees from danger. Chimpanzees go mainly on all fours, but sometimes on two feet, and can use and make simple tools. Males are dominant, but not very dominant, over females.

The rank hierarchy among males is unstable, and males often move between groups, which vary in size from two to fifty individuals. Food is vegetarian, supplemented with worms, grubs, or occasional small animals. A mother and her young form the only stable unit. Sexual relations are largely indiscriminate, but nearby males defend young animals from danger. The chances are that our prehuman ancestors had a similar social life. Morgan and Engels were probably right in concluding that we came from a state of "original promiscuity" before we were fully human.

Judging from the fossil record, apes ancestral to humans, gorillas, and chimpanzees roamed widely in Asia, Europe, and Africa some twelve to twenty-eight million years ago. Toward the end of that period (the Miocene), one appears in North India and East Africa, Ramapithecus, who may be ancestral both to later hominids and to modern humans. This species was small like gibbons, walked upright on two feet, had human rather than ape corner-teeth, and therefore probably used hands rather than teeth to tear their food. From that time evolution toward humanness must have proceeded through various phases until the emergence of modern Homo sapiens, about seventy thousand years ago.

In the Miocene period before Ramapithecus appeared, there were several time spans in which, over large areas, the climate became dryer and subtropical forests dwindled or disappeared. A standard reconstruction of events, which I accept, is that groups of apes, probably in Africa, had to come down from the trees and adapt to terrestrial life. Through natural selection, probably over millions of years, they developed specialized feet for walking. Thus freed, the hands came to be used not only (as among apes) for grasping and tearing, but for regular carrying of objects such as weapons (which had hitherto been sporadic), or of infants (which had hitherto clung to their mothers' body hair).

The spread of indigestible grasses on the open savannahs may have encouraged, if it did not compel, the early ground dwellers to become active hunters rather than simply to forage for small, sick, or dead animals that came their way.

Collective hunting and tool use involved group cooperation and helped foster the growth of language out of the call-systems of apes. Language meant the use of symbols to refer to events not present. It allowed greatly increased foresight, memory, planning, and division of tasks—in short, the capacity for human thought.

With the change to hunting, group territories became much larger. Apes range only a few thousand feet daily; hunters, several miles. But because their infants were helpless, nursing women could hunt only small game close to home. This then produced the sexual division of labor on which the human family has since been founded. Women elaborated upon ape methods of child care, and greatly expanded foraging, which in most areas remained the primary and most stable source of food. Men improved upon ape methods of fighting off other animals, and of group protection in general. They adapted these methods to hunting, using weapons which for millennia remained the same for the chase as for human warfare.

Out of the sexual division of labor came, for the first time, home life as well as group cooperation. Female apes nest with and provide foraged food for their infants. But adult apes do not cooperate in food getting or nest building. They build new nests each night wherever they may happen to be. With the development of a hunting-gathering complex, it became necessary to have a G.H.Q., or home. Men could bring several days' supply of meat to this place. Women and children could meet men there after the day's hunting, and could bring their vegetable produce for general consumption. Men, women, and children could build joint shelters, butcher meat, and treat skins for clothing.

Later, fire came into use for protection against wild animals, for lighting, and eventually for cooking. The hearth then provided the focus and symbol of home. With the development of cookery, some humans—chiefly women, and perhaps some children and old men—came to spend more time preparing food so that all people need spend less time in chewing and tearing it. Meals—always less frequent because of the change to a carnivorous diet—now became brief, periodic events instead of the long feeding sessions of apes.

The change to humanness brought two bodily changes that affected birth and child care. These were head size and width of the pelvis. Walking upright produced a narrower pelvis to hold the guts in position. Yet as language developed, brains and hence heads grew much bigger relative to body size. To compensate, humans are born at an earlier stage of growth than apes. They are helpless longer and require longer and more total care. This in turn caused early women to concentrate more on child care and less on defense than do female apes.

Language made possible not only a division and cooperation in labor but also all forms of tradition, rules, morality, and cultural learning. Rules banning sex relations among close kinfolk must have come very early. Precisely how or why they developed is unknown, but they had at least two useful functions. They helped to preserve order in the family as a cooperative unit, by outlawing competition for mates. They also created bonds *between* families, or even between separate bands, and so provided a basis for wider cooperation in the struggle for livelihood and the expansion of knowledge.

It is not clear when all these changes took place. Climatic change with increased drought began regionally up to twenty-eight million years ago. The divergence between prehuman and gorilla-chimpanzee stems had occurred in both Africa and India at least twelve million years ago. The prehuman stem led to the Australopithecines of East and South Africa, about three million years ago. These were pygmylike, two-footed, upright hominids with larger than ape brains, who made tools and probably hunted in savannah regions. It is unlikely that they knew the use of fire.

The first known use of fire is that of cave-dwelling hominids (Sinanthropus, a branch of the Pithecanthropines) at Choukoutien near Peking, some half a million years ago during the second Ice Age. Fire was used regularly in hearths, suggesting cookery, by the time of the Acheulean and Mousterian cultures of Neanderthal man in Europe, Africa, and Asia before, during, and after the third Ice Age, some 150,000 to 100,000 years ago. These people, too, were often cave dwellers, and buried their dead ceremonially in caves. Cave dwelling by night as well as by day was probably, in fact, not safe for humans until fire came into use to drive away predators.

Most anthropologists conclude that home life, the family, and language had developed by the time of Neanderthal man, who was closely similar and may have been ancestral to modern Homo sapiens. At least two anthropologists, however, believe that the Australopithecines already had language nearly two million years ago, while another thinks that language and incest prohibitions did not evolve until the time of Homo sapiens some 70,000 to 50,000 years ago.* I am inclined to think that family life built around tool use, the use of language, cookery, and a sexual division of labor, must have been established sometime between about 500,000 and 200,000 years ago.

Hunters and Gatherers

Most of the hunting and gathering societies studied in the eighteenth to twentieth centuries had technologies similar to those that were widespread in the Mesolithic period, which occurred about 15,000 to 10,000 years ago, after the Ice Ages ended but before cultivation was invented and animals domesticated.

Modern hunters live in marginal forest, mountain, arctic, or desert environments where cultivation is impracticable. Although by no means "primeval," the hunters of recent times do offer clues to the types of family found during that 99 percent of human history before the agricultural revolution. They include the Eskimo, many Canadian and South American Indian groups, the forest BaMbuti (pygmies), and the

* For the former view, see Hockett and Ascher, 1968; for the latter, Livingstone, 1969.

desert Bushmen of southern Africa, the Kadar of South India, the Veddah of Ceylon, and the Andaman Islanders of the Indian Ocean. About 175 hunting and gathering cultures in Oceania, Asia, Africa, and America have been described in fair detail.

In spite of their varied environments, hunters share certain features of social life. They live in bands of about 20 to 200 people, the majority of bands having fewer than 50. Bands are divided into families, which may forage alone in some seasons. Hunters have simple but ingenious technologies. Bows and arrows, spears, needles, skin clothing, and temporary leaf or wood shelters are common. Most hunters do some fishing. The band forages and hunts in a large territory and usually moves camp often.

Social life is egalitarian. There is of course no state, no organized government. Apart from religious shamans or magicians, the division of labor is based only on sex and age. Resources are owned communally; tools and personal possessions are freely exchanged. Everyone works who can. Band leadership goes to whichever man has the intelligence, courage, and foresight to command the respect of his fellows. Intelligent older women are also looked up to.

The household is the main unit of economic cooperation, with the men, women, and children dividing the labor and pooling their produce. In 97 percent of the 175 societies classified by G. P. Murdock, hunting is confined to men; in the other 3 percent it is chiefly a male pursuit. Gathering of wild plants, fruits, and nuts is women's work. In 60 percent of societies, only women gather, while in another 32 percent gathering is mainly feminine. Fishing is solely or mainly men's work in 93 percent of the hunting societies where it occurs.

For the rest, men monopolize fighting, although interband warfare is rare. Women tend children and shelters and usually do most of the cooking, processing, and storage of food. Women tend, also, to be foremost in the early household crafts such as basketry, leather work, the making of skin or bark clothing, and, in the more advanced hunting societies, pottery. (Considering that women probably *invented* all of these crafts, in addition to cookery, food storage and preservation, agriculture, spinning, weaving, and perhaps even house construction, it is clear that women played quite as important roles as men in early cultural development.) Building dwellings and making tools and ornaments are variously divided between the sexes, while boat-building is largely done by men. Girls help the women, and boys play at hunting or hunt small game until they reach puberty, when both take on the roles of adults. When the environment makes it desirable, the men of a whole band or of some smaller cluster of households cooperate in hunting or fishing and divide their spoils. Women of nearby families often go gathering together.

Family composition varies among hunters as it does in other kinds of societies. About half or more of known hunting societies have nuclear families (father, mother, and children), with polygynous households (a man, two or more wives, and children), as occasional variants. Clearly, nuclear families are the most common among hunters, although hunters have a slightly higher proportion of polygynous families than do nonhunting societies.

About a third of hunting societies contain some "stem-family" households—that is, older parents live together with one married child and grandchildren, while the other married children live in independent dwellings. A still smaller proportion live in large extended families containing several married brothers (or several married sisters), their spouses, and children.* Hunters have fewer extended and stem families than do nonhunting societies. These larger households become common with the rise of agriculture. They are especially found in large, preindustrial agrarian states such as ancient Greece, Rome, India, the Islamic empires, China, etc.

Hunting societies also have few households composed of a

* For exact figures, see Murdock, 1957; Coult, 1965; and Murdock, 1967. In the last-named survey, out of 175 hunting societies, 47 percent had nuclear family households, 38 percent had stem families, and 14 percent had extended families.

widow or divorcée and her children. This is understandable, for neither men nor women can survive long without the work and produce of the other sex, and marriage is the way to obtain them. That is why so often young men must show proof of hunting prowess, and girls of cooking, before they are allowed to marry.

The family, together with territorial grouping, provides the framework of society among hunters. Indeed, as Morgan and Engels clearly saw, kinship and territory are the foundations of all societies before the rising of the state. Not only hunting and gathering bands, but the larger and more complex tribes and chiefdoms of primitive cultivators and herders organize people through descent from common ancestors or through marriage ties between groups. Among hunters, things are simple. There is only the family, and beyond it the band. With the domestication of plants and animals, the economy becomes more productive. More people can live together. Tribes form, containing several thousand people loosely organized into large kin groups such as clans and lineages, each composed of a number of related families. With still further development of the productive forces the society throws up a central political leadership, together with craft specialization and trade, and so the chiefdom emerges. But this, too, is structured through ranked allegiances and marriage ties between kin groups.

Only with the rise of the state does class, independently of kinship, provide the basis for relations of production, distribution, and power. Even then, kin groups remain large in the agrarian state, and kinship persists as the prime organizing principle within each class until the rise of capitalism. The reduction in significance of the family that we see today is the outgrowth of a decline in the importance of "familism" relative to other institutions, which began with the rise of the state but became speeded up with the development of capitalism and machine industry. In most modern socialist societies, the family is even less significant as an organizing principle. It is reasonable to suppose that in the future it will become minimal or may disappear, at least as a legally constituted unit for exclusive forms of sexual and economic co-operation and of child care.

Morgan and Engels (1972) thought that from a state of original promiscuity, early humans at first banned sex relations between the generations of parents and children, but continued to allow them indiscriminately among brothers and sisters and all kinds of cousins within the band. They called this the "consanguineal family." They thought that later, all mating within the family or some larger kin group became forbidden, but that there was a stage (the "punaluan") in which a group of sisters or other close kinswomen from one band were married jointly to a group of brothers or other close kinsmen from another. They thought that only later still, and especially with the domestication of plants and animals, did the "pairing family" develop in which each man was married to one or two women individually.

These writers drew their conclusions not from evidence of actual group marriage among primitive peoples but from the kinship terms found today in certain tribal and chiefly societies. Some of these equate all kin of the same sex in the parents' generation, suggesting brother-sister marriage. Others equate the father's brothers with the father, and the mother's sisters with the mother, suggesting the marriage of a group of brothers with a group of sisters.

Modern evidence does not bear out these conclusions about early society. All known hunters and gatherers live in families, not in communal sexual arrangements. Most hunters even live in nuclear families rather than in large extended kin groups. Mating is individualized, although one man may occasionally have two wives, or (very rarely) a woman may have two husbands. Economic life is built primarily around the division of labor and partnership between individual men and women. The hearths, caves, and other remains of Upper Paleolithic hunters suggest that this was probably an early arrangement. We cannot say that Engels' sequences are completely ruled out for very early hominids—the evidence is simply not available. But it is hard to see what economic arrangements among hunters would give rise to group, rather than individual or "pairing," marriage arrangements, and this Engels does not explain.

Soviet anthropologists continued to believe in Morgan and Engels' early "stages" longer than did anthropologists in the West. Today, most Russian anthropologists admit the lack of evidence for "consanguineal" and "punaluan" arrangements, but some still believe that a different kind of group marriage intervened between indiscriminate mating and the pairing family. Y. I. Semyonov (1967), for example, argues that in the stage of group marriage, mating was forbidden within the hunting band, but that the men of two neighboring bands had multiple, visiting sex relations with women of the opposite band.

While such an arrangement cannot be ruled out, it seems unlikely because many of the customs which Semyonov regards as "survivals" of such group marriage (for example, visiting husbands, matrilineal dwelling groups, widespread clans, multiple spouses for both sexes, men's and women's communal houses, and prohibitions of sexual intercourse inside the huts of the village), are actually found not so much among hunters as among horticultural tribes, and even quite complex agricultural states. Whether or not such a stage of group marriage occurred in the earliest societies, there seems little doubt that pairing marriage (involving family households) came about with the development of elaborate methods of hunting, cooking, and the preparation of clothing and shelters—that is, with a full-fledged division of labor.

Even so, there *are* some senses in which mating among hunters has more of a group character than in archaic agrarian states or in capitalist society. Murdock's sample shows that sex relations before marriage are strictly prohibited in only 26 percent of hunting societies. In the rest, marriage is either arranged so early that premarital sex is unlikely, or (more usually) sex relations are permitted more or less freely before marriage.

With marriage, monogamy is the normal *practice* at any

given moment for most hunters, but it is not the normal *rule.* Only 19 percent in Murdock's survey prohibit plural unions. Where polygyny is found (79 percent), the most common type is for a man to marry two sisters or other closely related women of the same kin group—for example, the daughters of two sisters or of two brothers. When a woman dies it is common for a sister to replace her in the marriage, and when a man dies, for a brother to replace him.

Similarly, many hunting societies hold that the wives of brothers or other close kinsmen are in some senses wives of the group. They can be called on in emergencies or if one of them is ill. Again, many hunting societies have special times for sexual license between men and women of a local group who are not married to each other, such as the "lights out" games of Eskimos sharing a communal snowhouse. In other situations, an Eskimo wife will spend the night with a chance guest of her husband's. All parties expect this as normal hospitality. Finally, adultery, although often punished, tends to be common in hunting societies, and few if any of them forbid divorce or the remarriage of divorcées and widows.

The reason for all this seems to be that marriage and sexual restrictions are practical arrangements among hunters designed mainly to serve economic and survival needs. In these societies, some kind of rather stable pairing best accomplishes the division of labor and cooperation of men and women and the care of children. Beyond the immediate family, either a larger family group or the whole band has other, less intensive but important, kinds of cooperative activities. Therefore, the husbands and wives of individuals within that group can be summoned to stand in for each other if need arises. In the case of Eskimo wife-lending, the extreme climate and the need for lone wandering in search of game dictate high standards of hospitality. This evidently becomes extended to sexual sharing.

In the case of sororal polygyny or marriage to the dead wife's sister, it is natural that when two women fill the same role—either together or in sequence—they should be sisters, for sisters are more alike than other women. They are likely to care more for each other's children. The replacement of a dead spouse by a sister or a brother also preserves existing intergroup relations. For the rest, where the economic and survival bonds of marriage are not at stake, people can afford to be freely companionate and tolerant. Hence premarital sexual freedom, seasonal group-license, and a pragmatic approach to adultery.

Marriages among hunters are usually arranged by elders when a young couple is ready for adult responsibilities. But the mates know each other and usually have some choice. If the first marriage does not work, the second mate will almost certainly be self-selected. Both sexual and companionate love between individual men and women are known and are deeply experienced. With comparative freedom of mating, love is less often separated from or opposed to marriage than in archaic states or even in some modern nations.

The Position of Women

Even in hunting societies it seems that women are always in some sense the "second sex," with greater or less subordination to men. This varies. Eskimo and Australian aboriginal women are far more subordinate than women among the Kadar, the Andamanese or the Congo Pygmies—all forest people.

I suggest that women have greater power and independence among hunters when they are important food-providers than when they are mainly processors of meat or other supplies provided by men. The former situation is likelier to exist in societies where hunting is small-scale and intensive than where it is extensive over a large terrain, and in societies where gathering is important by comparison with hunting.

In general in hunting societies, however, women are less subordinated in certain crucial respects than they are in most, if not all, of the archaic states, or even in some capitalist nations. These respects include men's ability to deny women sexuality or to force it upon them; to command or exploit their labor to control their produce; to control or rob them of their children; to confine them physically and prevent their movement; to use them as objects in male transactions; to cramp their creativeness; or to withhold from them large areas of the society's knowledge and cultural attainments.

Especially lacking in hunting societies is the kind of male possessiveness and exclusiveness regarding women that leads to such institutions as savage punishments or death for female adultery, the jealous guarding of female chastity and virginity, the denial of divorce to women, or the ban on a woman's remarriage after her husband's death.

For these reasons, I do not think we can speak, as some writers do, of a class division between men and women in hunting societies. True, men are more mobile than women and they lead in public affairs. But class society requires that one class control the means of production, dictate its use by the other classes, and expropriate the surplus. These conditions do not exist among hunters. Land and other resources are held communally, although women may monopolize certain gathering areas, and men, their hunting grounds. There is rank difference, role difference, and some difference respecting degrees of authority, between the sexes, but there is reciprocity rather than domination or exploitation.

As Engels saw, the power of men to exploit women systematically springs from the existence of surplus wealth, and more directly from the state, social stratification, and the control of property by men. With the rise of the state, because of their monopoly over weapons and because freedom from child care allows them to enter specialized economic and political roles, some men—especially ruling-class men—acquire power over other men and over women. Almost all men acquire it over women of their own or lower classes, especially within their own kinship groups. These kinds of male power are shadowy among hunters.

To the extent that men *have* power over women in hunting societies, this seems to spring from the male monopoly of heavy weapons, from the particular division of labor between the sexes, or from both. Although men seldom use weapons against women, they *possess* them (or possess superior weapons) in addition to their physical strength. This does give men an ultimate control of force. When old people or babies must be killed in order to ensure band or family survival, it is usually men who kill them. Infanticide—rather common among hunters, who must limit the mouths to feed—is more often female infanticide than male.

The hunting of men seems more often to require them to organize in groups than does the work of women. Perhaps because of this, about 60 percent of hunting societies have predominantly virilocal residence—that is, men choose which band to live in (often, their fathers'), and women move with their husbands. This gives a man advantages over his wife in terms of familiarity and loyalties, for the wife is often a stranger. Sixteen to 17 percent of hunting societies are, however, uxorilocal, with men moving to the households of their wives, while 15 to 17 percent are bilocal—that is, either sex may move in with the other on marriage.

Probably because of male cooperation in defense and hunting, men are more prominent in band councils and leadership, in medicine and magic, and in public rituals designed to increase game, to ward off sickness, or to initiate boys into manhood. Women often do, however, take part in band councils; they are not excluded from law and government as in many agrarian states. Some women are respected as wise leaders, storytellers, doctors, or magicians, or are feared as witches. Women have their own ceremonies of fertility, birth, and healing, from which men are often excluded.

In some societies, although men control the most sacred objects, women are believed to have discovered them. Among the Congo Pygmies, religion centers about a beneficent spirit, the Animal of the Forest. It is represented by wooden trumpets that are owned and played by men. Their possession and use are hidden from the women and they are played at night when hunting is bad, someone falls ill, or death occurs. During the playing, men dance in the public campfire, which is sacred and is associated with the forest. Yet the men believe that women originally owned the trumpet and that it was a woman who stole fire from the chimpanzees or from the forest spirit. When a woman has failed to bear children for several years, a special ceremony is held. Women lead in the songs that usually accompany the trumpets, and an old woman kicks apart the campfire. Temporary female dominance seems to be thought necessary to restore fertility.

In some hunting societies women are exchanged between local groups, which are thus knit together through marriages. Sometimes men of different bands directly exchange their sisters. More often there is a generalized exchange of women between two or more groups, or a one-way movement of women within a circle of groups. Sometimes the husband's family pays weapons, tools, or ornaments to the wife's family in return for the wife's services and, later, her children.

In such societies, although they may be well treated and their consent sought, women are clearly the movable partners in an arrangement controlled by men. Male anthropologists have seized on this as evidence of original male dominance and patrilocal residence. Robin Fox (1967) and others, for example, have argued that until recently, *all* hunting societies formed out-marrying patrilocal bands, linked together politically by the exchange of women. The fact that fewer than two-thirds of hunting societies are patrilocal today, and only 41 percent have band exogamy, is explained in terms of modern conquest, economic change, and depopulation.

I cannot accept this formula. It is true that modern hunting societies have been severely changed, deculturated, and often depopulated, by capitalist imperialism. I can see little evidence, however, that the ones that are patrilocal today have undergone less change than those that are not. It is hard to believe that in spite of enormous environmental diversity and the passage of thousands, perhaps millions, of years, hunting societies all had band exogamy with patrilocal residence until they were disturbed by Western imperialism. It is more likely that early band societies, like later agricultural tribes, developed variety in family life and the status of women as they spread over the earth.

There is also some likelihood that the earliest hunters had matrilocal rather than patrilocal families. Among apes and monkeys, it is almost always males who leave the troop or are driven out. Females stay closer to their mothers and their original site; males move about, attaching themselves to females where availability and competition permit. Removal of the wife to the husband's home or band may have been a relatively late development in societies where male cooperation in hunting assumed overwhelming importance.* Conversely, after the development of horticulture (which was probably invented and is mainly carried out by women), those tribes in which horticulture predominated over stock raising were most likely to be or to remain matrilocal and to develop matrilineal descent groups with a relatively high status of women. But where extensive hunting of large animals, or later, the herding of large domesticates, predominated, patrilocal residence flourished and women were used to form alliances between male-centered groups. With the invention of metallurgy and of agriculture as distinct from horticulture after 4000 B.C., men came to control agriculture and many crafts, and most of the great agrarian states had patrilocal residence with patriarchal, male-dominant families.

Conclusions

The family is a human institution, not found in its totality in any prehuman species. It required language, planning, cooperation, self-control, foresight, and cultural learning, and probably developed along with these.

The family was made desirable by the early human combination of prolonged child care with the need for hunting with

* Upper Paleolithic hunters produced female figurines that were obvious emblems of fertility. The cult continued through the Mesolithic and into the Neolithic period. Goddesses and spirits of fertility are found in some patrilineal as well as matrilineal societies, but they tend to be more prominent in the latter. It is thus possible that in many areas even late Stone Age hunters had matrilocal residence and perhaps matrilineal descent, and that in some regions this pattern continued through the age of horticulture and even—as in the case of the Nayars of Kerala and the Minangkabau of Sumatra—into the age of plow agriculture, of writing, and of the small-scale state.

weapons over large terrains. The sexual division of labor on which it was based grew out of a rudimentary prehuman division between male defense and female child care. But among humans this sexual division of functions for the first time became crucial for food production and so laid the basis for future economic specialization and cooperation.

Morgan and Engels were probably right in thinking that the human family was preceded by sexual indiscriminacy. They were also right in seeing an egalitarian group-quality about early economic and marriage arrangements. They were without evidence, however, in believing that the earliest mating and economic patterns were entirely group relations.

Together with tool use and language, the family was no doubt the most significant invention of the human revolution. All three required reflective thought, which above all accounts for the vast superiority in consciousness that separates humans from apes.

The family provided the framework for all pre-state society and the fount for its creativeness. In groping for survival and for knowledge, human beings learned to control their sexual desires and to suppress their individual selfishness, aggression, and competition. The other side of this self-control was an increased capacity for love—not only the love of a mother for her child, which is seen among apes, but of male for female in enduring relationships, and of each sex for ever widening groups of humans. Civilization would have been impossible without this initial self-control, seen in incest prohibitions and in the generosity and moral orderliness of primitive family life.

From the start, women have been subordinate to men in certain key areas of status, mobility, and public leadership. But before the agricultural revolution, and even for several thousands of years thereafter, the inequality was based chiefly on the unalterable fact of long child care combined with the exigencies of primitive technology. The extent of inequality varied according to the ecology and the resulting sexual division of tasks. But in any case it was largely a matter of survival rather than of man-made cultural impositions. Hence the impressions we receive of dignity, freedom, and mutual respect between men and women in primitive hunting and horticultural societies. This is true whether these societies are patrilocal, bilocal, or matrilocal, although matrilocal societies, with matrilineal inheritance, offer greater freedom to women than do patrilocal and patrilineal societies of the same level of productivity and political development.

A distinct change occurred with the growth of individual and family property in herds, in durable craft objects and trade objects, and in stable, irrigated farm sites or other forms of heritable wealth. This crystallized in the rise of the state, about 4000 B.C. With the growth of class society and of male dominance in the ruling class of the state, women's subordination increased, and eventually reached its depths in the patriarchal families of the great agrarian states.

Knowledge of how the family arose is interesting to women because it tells us how we differ from pre-humans, what our past has been, and what have been the biological and cultural limitations from which we are emerging. It shows us how generations of male scholars have distorted or overinterpreted the evidence to bolster beliefs in the inferiority of women's mental processes—for which there is no foundation in fact. Knowing about early families is also important to correct a reverse bias among some feminist writers, who hold that in "matriarchal" societies women were completely equal with or were even dominant over men. For this, too, there seems to be no basis in evidence.

The past of the family does not limit its future. Although the family probably emerged with humanity, neither the family itself nor particular family forms are genetically determined. The sexual division of labor—until recently, universal—need not, and in my opinion should not, survive in industrial society. Prolonged child care ceases to be a basis for female subordination when artificial birth control, spaced births, small families, patent feeding, and communal nurseries allow it to be shared by men. Automation and cybernation remove most of the heavy work for which women are not as well equipped as men. The exploitation of women that came with the rise of the state and of class society will presumably disappear in post-state, classless society—for which the technological and scientific basis already exists.

The family was essential to the dawn of civilization, allowing a vast qualitative leap forward in cooperation, purposive knowledge, love, and creativeness. But today, rather than enhancing them, the confinement of women in homes and small families—like their subordination in work—artificially limits these human capacities. It may be that the human gift for personal love will make some form of voluntary, long-term mating and of individual devotion between parents and children continue indefinitely, side by side with public responsibility for domestic tasks and for the care and upbringing of children. There is no need to legislate personal relations out of existence. But neither need we fear a social life in which the family is no more.

Patricia Draper

!Kung Women: Contrasts in Sexual Egalitarianism in Foraging and Sedentary Contexts

Most members of the Harvard !Kung Bushman Study Project who have thought about the subject of !Kung women's status agree that !Kung society may be the least sexist of any we have experienced. This impression contradicts some popularly held stereotypes about relations between the sexes in hunting and gathering societies. Because sex is one of the few bases for the differentiation of social and economic roles in societies of this type, it has probably been attributed more weight than it deserves. The men are commonly depicted in rather romantic terms, striving with their brothers to bring home the precious meat while their women humbly provide the dull, tasteless vegetable food in the course of routine, tedious foraging. Contrary evidence is now emerging from several researchers that men and women of band-level societies have many overlapping activities and spheres of influence (Gale, 1970). The distinction between male and female roles is substantially less rigid than previously supposed,

---

Fieldwork for this project was supported by National Institute of Mental Health Grant No. MH-136111 to Irven DeVore and Richard B. Lee. This paper has benefited from my discussions with many people. Dr. Nancy Howell (University of Toronto, Scarboro College) and I have discussed these issues for several years, beginning with our common experience in the Kalahari. Drs. Carol Smith and Henry Harpending (University of New Mexico), with whom I taught the undergraduate course, "Bio-Cultural Bases of Sex Roles," have done much to further my thinking in the area of human sex roles.

though there is variation among band-level peoples in the degree of autonomy and influence that women enjoy.

This paper describes relations between the sexes for two groups of !Kung: those living a traditional hunting and gathering life at /Du/da and those who have recently adopted a settled way of life in the !Kangwa Valley and who are now living by agriculture, animal husbandry, and a small amount of gathering.

The point to be developed at some length is that in the hunting and gathering context, women have a great deal of autonomy and influence. Some of the contexts in which this egalitarianism is expressed will be described in detail, and certain features of the foraging life which promote egalitarianism will be isolated. They are: women's subsistence contribution and the control women retain over the food they have gathered; the requisites of foraging in the Kalahari which entail a similar degree of mobility for both sexes; the lack of rigidity in sex-typing of many adult activities, including domestic chores and aspects of child socialization; the cultural sanction against physical expression of aggression; the small group size; and the nature of the settlement pattern.

Features of sedentary life that appear to be related to a decrease in women's autonomy and influence are: increasing rigidity in sex-typing of adult work; more permanent attachment of the individual to a particular place and group of people; dissimilar childhood socialization for boys and girls; decrease in the mobility of women as contrasted with men; changing nature of women's subsistence contribution; richer material inventory with implications for women's work; tendency for men to have greater access to and control over such important resources as domestic animals, knowledge of Bantu language and culture, wage work; male entrance into extra-village politics; settlement pattern; and increasing household privacy.

Background to !Kung Research

The !Kung Bushmen of the Kalahari Desert are one of the better described primitive cultures, with the literature steadily increasing in the last twenty years. The work of Lorna Marshall, John Marshall, and Elizabeth Marshall Thomas gives a background to !Kung social organization and economy. The publications of the Marshall family concern primarily !Kung living in South-West Africa in the Nyae nyae area.

Since the early 1960s other researchers have entered the field of !Kung studies, in particular members of the Harvard !Kung Bushman Study Project. This team worked in western Botswana with populations of !Kung who overlap with the !Kung of South-West Africa first studied by the Marshall expedition. Members of the Harvard research team have focused on more narrow, specialized topics. Some of their publications have already appeared, and many others are currently in preparation (see Biesele, Draper, Howell, Katz, Konner, Lee, Lee and DeVore, Shostak, and Yellen).

Ethnographic Background to the !Kung: Traditional Population

The !Kung are a hunting and gathering people living today mostly on the western edge of the Kalahari sand system in what is now southern Angola, Botswana, and South-West Africa. The great majority of !Kung-speaking people have abandoned their traditional hunting and gathering way of life and are now living in sedentary and semi-squatter status in or near the villages of Bantu pastoralists and European ranchers. A minority of !Kung, amounting to a few thousand, are still living by traditional hunting and gathering techniques. It is to these bush-living peoples and a few groups of very recently settled !Kung, that this paper refers.

The bush-living peoples subsist primarily on wild vegetable foods and game meat. They are semi-nomadic, moving their camps at irregular intervals of from several days to several weeks. The average size of individual groups (also referred to as bands or camps) is about thirty-five people, though the numbers range from seventeen to sixty-five people. Season and the availability of water are the chief factors affecting group size. During the rainy season (October to March), group censuses are lower due to the fact that water and bush foods are widely available in most regions of the !Kung range. Smaller numbers of people in the form of two- and three-family groups spread out over the bush. As the dry season approaches, the small, temporary water pans dry up and the people begin to regroup and fall back on the remaining water sources that continue throughout the dry season. As there are relatively few water sources in the heart of the drought, as many as two or three different camps may be found within one to three miles of the same water hole.

The rules governing the composition of these bands are extremely flexible. It appears there is no such thing as "band membership." Close relatives move together over much of the year, though individuals and segments of large kin groups frequently make temporary and amicable separations to go live some miles distant with other relatives and affines.

Material technology is extremely simple. Men hunt with small bows and arrows (tipped with poison) and metal-pointed spears. Women's tools include a simple digging stick, wooden mortar and pestle, and leather kaross which doubles as clothing and carrying bag. Both sexes use leather carrying bags, hafted adzes, and net slings made from handwoven vegetable fiber. Clothing, particularly among the bush people, consists of leather garments; in addition, various cloth garments are worn, especially by the settled !Kung, but also by the peoples of the bush.

Settled Population

As stated before, the great majority of !Kung-speaking peoples are settled around the villages of technologically more advanced peoples and have been there for as many as three generations. Among other !Kung, sedentarization is much more recent. In the case of the Mahopa people, in the

!Kangwa area of Botswana, !Kung commitment to settled life is perhaps fifteen to twenty years old. I observed these people and the people of /Du/da for two years in 1968 and 1969.

About fifty !Kung lived in three separate villages around the permanent water hole at Mahopa. Bantu-speaking pastoralists also lived at Mahopa and watered their herds of cattle, horses, donkeys, and goats at the Mahopa well. These Bantu were chiefly of the Herero tribe and, like the !Kung, lived in about six villages, whose total population consisted of perhaps fifty people. Some !Kung lived in the Herero villages, but my research and remarks here do not refer to them.

The Mahopa people whom I describe lived in villages composed only of !Kung. The decision of the !Kung to avoid close proximity with the Herero is conscious, for relations between the two groups are not entirely amicable—Bantu of the area have a superior attitude and often (according to the !Kung) do not treat !Kung people fairly. Bantu see the !Kung as irresponsible, poor workers who are prone to killing occasional steers from Bantu herds.

The subsistence practices of the recently settled !Kung are mixed. The women continue to gather bush food, but not with the effort or regularity of the women of the traditional groups. Hunting by Mahopa men has virtually ceased. The people keep small herds of goats and plant small gardens of sorghum, squash, melons, and corn. For the most part, the Mahopa !Kung do not own their own cattle (at least, they did not during my fieldwork). Some !Kung women receive milk in payment for regular chores they do for nearby Herero women.

In the first discussion of !Kung women my remarks will pertain to women of the bush-living groups, unless otherwise specified. Description of the women's life in the settled Mahopa villages of the !Kangwa area will be handled second. The traditional, or bush-living !Kung lived in the /Du/da area, which straddles the border of Botswana and South-West Africa and stretches over a north-south distance of about seventy miles.

Self-Esteem Derived from Subsistence Contribution

Women are the primary providers of vegetable food, and they contribute something on the order of 60 to 80 percent of the daily food intake by weight (Lee, 1965). All !Kung agree that meat is the most desirable, most prestigious food, but the hunters cannot always provide it. Without question, women derive self-esteem from the regular daily contribution they make to the family's food.

A common sight in the late afternoon is clusters of children standing on the edge of camp, scanning the bush with shaded eyes to see if the returning women are visible. When the slow-moving file of women is finally discerned in the distance, the children leap and exclaim. As the women draw closer, the children speculate as to which figure is whose mother and what the women are carrying in their karosses.

Often when women return in the evening they bring information as well as bush food. Women are skilled in reading the signs of the bush, and they take careful note of animal tracks, their age, and the direction of movement. On several occasions I have accompanied gathering expeditions in which, when the group was about thirty to forty minutes out of camp, one of the women discovered the fresh tracks of several large antelope. This find caused a stir of excitement in the group. Quickly the women dispatched one of the older children to deliver the report to the men in camp. In general, the men take advantage of women's reconnaissance and query them routinely on the evidence of game movements, the location of water, and the like.

A stereotype of the female foraging role in hunting and gathering societies (in contrast with men's work, which is social in character) is that the work is individualized, repetitious, and boring (Service, 1966: 12). Descriptions of the work of gathering leave the reader with the impression that the job is uninteresting and unchallenging—that anyone who can walk and bend over can collect wild bush food. This stereotype is distinctly inappropriate to !Kung female work, and it promotes a condescending attitude toward what women's work is all about. Successful gathering over the years requires the ability to discriminate among hundreds of edible and inedible species of plants at various stages in their life cycle. This ability requires more than mere brute strength. The stereotype further ignores the role women play in gathering information about the "state of the bush"—presence of temporary water, evidence of recent game movements, etc. On a given day, !Kung hunters consciously avoid working the same area in which women are foraging, knowing that movements of the women may disturb the game, but also knowing that the women can be questioned at the end of the day (Yellen, personal communication).

!Kung women impress one as self-contained people with a high sense of self-esteem. There are exceptions—women who seem forlorn and weary—but for the most part, !Kung women are vivacious and self-confident. Small groups of women forage in the Kalahari at distances of eight to ten miles from home with no thought that they need the protection of the men or of the men's weapons should they encounter any of the several large predators that also inhabit the Kalahari (for instance, hyena, wild dog, leopard, lion, and cheetah). It is unusual, but not exceptional, for a lone woman to spend the day gathering. In the times I observed at the /Du/da camps, the solitary foragers were either postmenopausal women or young, unmarried women who were still without children. Women with children or adolescent, unmarried girls usually gather bush food in the company of two or more other women. The !Kung themselves claim that lovers (as well as married couples) sometimes arrange to meet privately in the bush. !Kung sleeping arrangements may promote these tactics, for at night whole families sleep outdoors together gathered around individual campfires and within a few feet of other families sleeping at their own fires.

Control by Women Over Gathered Food

Not only do women contribute equally, if not more than men, to the food supply; they also retain control over the food they have gathered after they return to the village. This is even more true of the vegetable food of women than of the meat brought in by the men. Lorna Marshall and Richard B. Lee have described how the distribution of meat is circumscribed by social rules as well as by the spontaneous demands of fellow camp members. With the exception of small game kills, a hunter has little effective control over the meat he brings into the camp. In contrast, the gatherer determines the distribution of vegetable food, at least when it concerns anyone outside her immediate family. An example may help to illustrate this point. One late afternoon I watched N!uhka return from an unusually long gathering trip. Her kaross was bulging with food, and her face showed fatigue from the weight and from dust, heat, and thirst. She walked stolidly through camp to her own hut. When she reached her hearthside, still stooping with the load, she reached to her shoulder, where the kaross was knotted. Wearily she gave the knot one practiced yank. The bush food spilled out of the kaross, clattering and thumping onto the sand behind her. She had not even squatted before releasing the burden. At the sound, several people looked up, but only briefly. No one greeted her or came over to look at the day's collection. N!uhka sat down at her hut, reached inside for an ostrich-egg shell, and slowly drank water from it for several minutes, sitting with her elbows on her knees and staring blankly ahead. Fifteen minutes later her grown daughter and a younger son joined her. The daughter, without talking, blew the coals back to life and started a fire. By then N!uhka had regained her strength, the listlessness had gone, and she picked up a wooden poke and began raking some of the freshly picked ≠nd≠dwa bean pods into the hot ashes for roasting. This done, she began gathering up the bush food she had dropped earlier. Most of it she heaped into the rear of her own hut, but she also made two additional small piles. Calling next door to her twelve-year-old grandnephew, she said, "Take this to your grandmother" (her brother's wife), and she motioned for him to take one of the heaps of bean pods. Later, when her daughter rose to return to her own fire, N!uhka had her take away the second pile for her own use. It is common for women to make these individual gifts, but it is not mandatory. Food that is brought in by women may also be redistributed during a family meal when other people visit at the fire and are served along with family members.

The fact that !Kung women retain control over their own production is, of course, related to the simplicity of !Kung economy, technology, rules of ownership, and social organization. In more complex societies, there are kin groups, lineages, or other corporate units that control essential resources. Even in the relatively rare cases (matrilineages) where women nominally own the land and household property, it is usually men who control the production and distribution of resources. The gathering work of !Kung women can be done by women alone. They do not need to ask permission to use certain lands; they do not need the assistance of men in order to carry out their work, as in the case of many agricultural societies where men must do the initial heavy work of clearing fields, building fences, and the like, before the less strenuous work of women can begin.

Similar Absenteeism for Men and Women

A similarity in the gathering work of women and the hunting work of men is that both activities take adults out of the camp, sometimes all day for several days each week. The pattern of both sexes being about equally absent from the dwelling place is not typical of most middle-range, agriculturally based tribal societies. In these latter groups one finds an arrangement whereby women, much more than men, stay at home during child tending, domestic chores, food preparation and the like, while the men are occupied with activities that take them outside the household and keep them away for many hours during the day. Frequent (daily) male absence may result in viewing men as a scarce commodity with higher value than women, who are constantly present in the household. If men in this sense are a scarce commodity, their homecoming must have greater significance to those who stay at home, and their influence even in routine domestic affairs may be heightened simply because others are less habituated to their presence. Among the !Kung a case could be argued for the equal, or nearly equal, scarcity value of men and women. Both leave the village regularly, and the return of both is eagerly anticipated—as illustrated earlier in this paper with reference to women.

It seems likely that !Kung men and women have similar knowledge of the larger hunting and gathering territory within which their kin and affines range. Both men and women range out from the camp in the course of their subsistence work, and they are equally affected by group moves in search of bush food, game, and water. More recently, however, /Du/da men have gained larger knowledge of the "outside" world, for some young men have spent months, and even years, doing wage work at such towns as Ghanzi, Gobabis, and Windhoek. Women are less likely to have had these experiences. Henry Harpending (1972 and in press) has collected demographic data on the !Kung of the !Kangwa and /Du/da areas which shows that the space occupied over a lifetime does not differ for the two sexes. For example, the distribution of distances between birthplaces of mates and birthplaces of parents and offspring are almost identical for the two sexes, both currently and for marriages that took place prior to substantial Bantu contact in these areas.

The absence of warfare or raiding, either among !Kung themselves or between !Kung and neighboring Bantu, undoubtedly facilitates the freedom of movement of the women. If threat of enemy attack were a recurrent fact of life, many features of !Kung social organization undoubtedly would change, particularly in the area of political leadership, but probably in the area of sex egalitarianism as well. (See Murdock, 1949:205 for a discussion of conditions, including warfare, that increase status discrepancy between the sexes.)

Sexual Division of Labor

When asked, !Kung will state that there is men's work and women's work, and that they conceive of most individual jobs as sex-typed, at least in principle. In practice, adults of both sexes seem surprisingly willing to do the work of the opposite sex. It often appeared to me that men, more than women, were willing to cross sex lines.

One afternoon while visiting in one of the /Du/da camps, I came across Kxau, a rather sober middle-aged man, industriously at work building his own hut. Building huts is predominantly women's work, and I had never seen such a thing. It happened that Kxau's wife was away visiting at another settlement many miles distant, or she would have made the hut. However, Kxau's daughter, an unmarried girl about seventeen years old, was in camp, and even she did not offer to make the hut or help him once he had started. Kxau proceeded to build the structure methodically and without embarrassment. I deliberately stayed in the vicinity to observe the reaction of other people. No one commented or joked with him about how his women were lazy.

Gathering is women's work, but there are times when men also gather (Draper, in preparation). Some married couples collected mongongo nuts together, but in my observation, the couples most likely to do this were elderly couples and a young couple who had been married for several years but had no children. Water collection is normally considered to be women's work, particularly when the water source is close to camp, perhaps fifteen to twenty minutes' walk. However, when the people are camped several miles from water, men participate regularly in carrying water back to camp. In the months of August, September, and October of 1969, I observed two of the /Du/da camps where water was three miles distant. In this situation men and women both worked at bringing in water. Only on the occasions when several of the men were absent from camp for several nights on hunting trips did their wives collect water daily for the remaining members of the family.

I mentioned earlier that men seem more willing (or accustomed) than women to do work normally associated with the opposite sex. Gathering and water-collecting are outstanding examples of female tasks that frequently involve men. While there are undoubtedly sound economic and evolutionary reasons for the male monopoly on hunting (Judith K. Brown, 1970b), there is one aspect of male hunting tasks that could easily absorb female help but typically does not. I refer here to the job of carrying the meat back to camp from the kill site.

A common pattern among the hunters of /Du/da was for a group of three or four hunters to stay out three or more nights in a row. Frequently by the fourth or fifth day one of their number would appear back in camp with the news that an antelope had been killed and that volunteers were needed to carry in the meat. On such occasions the remainder of the original hunting party stayed with the carcass, cutting the meat into biltong and allowing it to dry and lose much of its weight and volume. Always the helpers recruited were men. Often, but not necessarily, they were young males in late adolescence who had not yet begun serious hunting. I personally never knew of a woman (or women) assisting in such a venture, and never heard of any woman having done it.

The !Kung recognize no taboo against women being present at a kill site. On the contrary, when one or two hunters have killed a large animal some distance from camp, one of the hunters will return to camp and bring back his own and the other hunter's family to camp temporarily by the slain animal. Quite possibly the !Kung could verbalize their feelings about why it would be inappropriate to ask women to carry butchered meat. Unfortunately, while I was in the field it never occurred to me to ask; such blind spots are apparently an unavoidable hazard of fieldwork. Professor Cora DuBois warned me of this problem a few months before I began my work in the Kalahari: "Beware that the scale of custom will form over your eyes and you will no longer see."

Child-Rearing Practices and Sexual Equality

As children grow up there are few experiences which set one sex apart from the other. Living in such small groups, !Kung children have relatively few playmates to choose from.* Play groups, when they do form, include children of both sexes and of widely differing ages. This habit of playing in heterogeneous play groups probably minimizes any underlying, biologically based sex differences in style—differences which in other societies may be magnified and intensified by the opportunity of playing in same-sex, same-age play groups.

The child nurse is a regular feature of many African agricultural societies. The custom of assigning child-tending responsibility to an older child (usually a girl) in a family is one example of sex-role typing which can begin at an early age. This responsibility shapes and limits the behavior of girls in ways not true for boys, who are usually passed over for this chore. The training a girl receives as an infant caretaker doubtless has benefits for her eventual role performance and more immediately for the family economy, since she frees the mother from routine child care and allows her to resume subsistence production. However, the typical nine-year-old who is saddled with carrying and supervising a toddler cannot range as widely or explore as freely and independently as her brothers. She must stay closer to home, be more careful, more nurturant, more obedient, and more sensitive to the wishes of others. Habits formed in this way have social value, but my point is that such girls receive more training in these behaviors and that they form part of the complex of passivity and nurturance which characterizes adult female behavior in many cultures.**

* The average size of camps in the /Du/da area was thirty-four persons of whom an average of twelve were children ranging from new-born to fourteen years of age.

** See Barry, Bacon, and Child, 1957, and Whiting and Whiting, 1973 for further discussion of cross-cultural regularity and variability in sex differences in nurturance training.

!Kung do not use child nurses of either sex on a routine basis; this fact follows from the long birth intervals and the pattern of adult subsistence work. The average birth interval is approximately four years (Howell, in press). !Kung mothers can and do give lengthy, intensive care to each child because no new infant arrives to absorb her attention. Such mothers are comparatively unpressured and do not need to delegate the bulk of child-tending responsibility to another caretaker. Naturally, older children interact with younger children and in the process give help, protection, and attention to them. But one or more older children are rarely, if ever, the sole caretakers of younger charges for an appreciable length of time.

The rhythm of adult work also makes the role of child nurse unnecessary. !Kung adults work about three days per week, and they vary their time of being in and out of the camp, with the result that on any given day one-third to one-half of the adults are in camp. They can easily supervise their own children and those whose parents are absent. Older children are helpful in amusing and monitoring younger children, but they do so spontaneously (and erratically), and not because they are indoctrinated with a sense of responsibility for the welfare of a particular child or children.

A reflection of !Kung women's effectiveness in family life is the fact that a mother deals directly with her children when they are in need of correction. A different type of maternal strategy is common in cultures where women's status is clearly subordinate to that of the fathers and husbands. David Landy's study (1959) of rural Puerto Rican socialization techniques, Robert A. and Barbara LeVine's study (1963) of East African Gussi child training practices, and the L. Minturn and John T. Hitchcock study (1963) of child rearing among the Rajputs of Khalapur are particularly good examples of how a mother's ability to control her children is undermined by male superordinance, particularly when accompanied by patrilineal structures and patrilocal residence rules. Such mothers will hold up the father as the ultimate disciplinarian in an attempt to underscore their own power. !Kung women do not resort to the threat, "I'll tell your father . . . !"

Among the !Kung, both parents correct the children, but women tend to do this more often because they are usually physically closer to the children at any given time than the men. When such situations arise, a mother does not seek to intimidate the children with the father's wrath. In this milieu children are not trained to respect and fear male authority. In fact, for reasons which will be elaborated later, authoritarian behavior is avoided by adults of *both* sexes. The typical strategy used by !Kung parents is to interrupt the misbehavior, carry the child away, and try to interest him or her in some inoffensive activity.

This way of disciplining children has important consequences in terms of behaviors that carry over into adulthood. Since parents do not use physical punishment, and aggressive postures are avoided by adults and devalued by the society at large, children have relatively little opportunity to observe or imitate overtly aggressive behavior. This carries over into relations between adult men and women in the society. Evidence from various sources is mounting in support of the notion that human males (and males of nonhuman species) are innately more aggressive than their female counterparts (Bandura *et al.*, 1961; Hamburg and Lunde, 1966; Kagan and Moss, 1962; Sears *et al.*, 1957 and 1965). But among the !Kung there is an extremely low cultural tolerance for aggressive behavior by anyone, male or female. In societies where aggressiveness and dominance are valued, these behaviors accrue disproportionately to males, and the females are common targets, resulting in a lowering of their status. !Kung women are not caught by this dimension of sex-role complementarity. They customarily maintain a mild manner, but so do their men.

Relations of Men with Children

A further example of the equality between the sexes and the amount of overlap in their activities is the relationship between men and their children. In cultures where men have markedly superordinant status, women and children are expected to show deference to the male head of the family by staying away from him, observing routine formalities. !Kung fathers, in contrast, are intimately involved with their children and have a great deal of social interaction with them. The relation between fathers and young children is relaxed and without stylized respect or deference from the children. In fact, the lack of tact with which some children treated their parents was at first quite shocking to me.

As an example, I can relate an incident in which Kxau was trying to get his youngest son, Kashe, to bring him something from the other side of camp. Kxau was sitting at one edge of the village clearing with another man older than himself. Kxau repeatedly shouted to his son to bring him his tobacco from inside the family hut. The boy ignored his father's shouts, though !Kung camps are small, and the boy clearly could hear his father. Finally Kxau bellowed out his command, glaring across at his son and the other youngsters sitting there. Kashe looked up briefly and yelled back, "Do it yourself, old man." A few minutes later Kxau did do it himself, and Kashe received no reprimand.

Most fathers appear ill-at-ease when they hold very young infants, although by the time a child is nine or ten months old it is common to see the father playing with the child and holding it close to his face, blowing on its neck, and laughing. In the late afternoon and evening in a !Kung camp one often sees a father walking among the huts with a two- or three-year-old boy perched on his shoulder. The father ambles along, accepting an offer of a smoke at one hut, then moving on to squat elsewhere while watching a kinsman scraping a hide or mending a tool. At such times the father is mindful of the boy at his shoulder but pays him no special attention, aside from now and then steadying the child's balance.

There are certain aspects of child care that men unanimously eschew. Most prefer not to remove mucous from the runny nose of a child. Most adults of both sexes have a rather high tolerance for this sight, but occasionally a man will see his child with an especially unwholesome-looking smear on his upper lip, and will call out to his wife, "Ugh! Get rid of that snot." Men are also loath to clean up feces left by children. Usually the mother or an older child will scoop up the offending mess with a handful of leaves. If, however, a child's defecation has gone unnoticed by all except the father, he will call out to his wife to remove it.

Effect of Group Size and Settlement Pattern on Relations Between the Sexes

!Kung camps are typically quite small; the average camp size at /Du/da was thirty-four with a range of seventeen to sixty-five. The small group size is related to the low order of specialization of sex roles. Given the rather small numbers of able-bodied adults who manage group life and subsistence in these camps, the lack of opposition (or specialization) of the sexes is highly practical. Especially in the rainy seasons when local group size falls to about fifteen people, it is useful and necessary for adults to be relatively interchangeable in function.

Observing the way people group themselves during leisure hours in a !Kung camp gives one a feeling for the tone of informal heterosexual interaction. Men and women (children, too) sit together in small clusters—talking, joking, cracking and eating nuts, passing around tobacco. Individuals pass among these groups without causing a rift in the ambiance, without attracting attention. In general, the sexes mix freely and unselfconsciously without the diffidence one might expect to see if they thought they were in some way intruding.

If there were a prominent opposition between the sexes, one would expect some expression of this in the organization and use of space within the !Kung camps. However, there are no rules and definitions that limit a person's access to various parts of the village space on the basis of sex. The overall small size of the settled area almost removes this type of symbolism from the realm of possibility.

To an outsider, particularly a Westerner, the small size of

!Kung camps and the intimate, close living characteristic of them can seem stifling.* Essentially, thirty to forty people share what amounts to (by our standards) a large room. The individual grass scherms, one to each married couple, ring an elliptical village space. The huts are often placed only a few feet apart and look a mere forty to fifty feet across the cleared, central space into the hearth and doorway of the hut on the opposite side of the circle. Daily life goes on in this small, open space. Everything is visible with a glance; in many camps conversations can be carried on in normal tones of voice by people sitting at opposite ends of the village. In this setting it is easy to see why the sexes rub elbows without embarrassment. In other societies, where sex roles and the prerogatives which attach to them are more exclusively defined, one generally finds architectural features used to help people manage their interaction and/or avoidance: walls, fences, separate sleeping and/or eating arrangements, designated spaces allocated to only one sex, etc.

In summary, many of the basic organizing features of this hunting and gathering group contribute to a relaxed and egalitarian relationship between men and women. The female subsistence role is essential to group survival and satisfying to the women. The foregoing remarks have illustrated a framework within which egalitarian relations are a natural or logical outcome. There are other issues bearing on the question of women's influence and control which are not answered here. Decision-making is one such issue. Leadership and authority are difficult problems to research in band-level societies generally, and in this one in particular. Still, the question of whether women or men more often influence group or family decisions is an empirical one, albeit one on which I have no data. Other areas that bear on the topic of women's influence and power are marital relations, access to extramarital relations, the influence of young women in determining the selection of their first husbands, changes in

* For further discussion of living density of !Kung camps, see Draper, 1973.

women's influence over their life cycles, etc.* So far as I know, these issues have yet to be researched in a systematic way among the !Kung.

The Sedentary !Kung of Mahopa

As stated earlier, my fieldwork was conducted in two areas of northwestern Botswana: the /Du/da area and the !Kangwa area. The second area was the locus of research similar to that conducted on the social life of the bush-living !Kung at /Du/da. Within the !Kangwa area (about seventy miles from the /Du/da water hole) I worked at Mahopa, one of several permanent water sources in the !Kangwa Valley. Around Mahopa are various settlements, of which three were the focus of my study. The three settlements were composed almost exclusively of !Kung. (Of about fifty persons living there, only one was non-!Kung—a middle-aged Tswana man married to a !Kung woman.)

The Mahopa "well" forms a small pan, or pool of standing water, in the rainy season; but in the dry season it shrinks to a muddy, clay-ringed ditch. This ditch is dug out periodically during the dry season to ensure seepage of an adequate amount of water to supply the approximately one hundred human residents of the Mahopa area and the various domestic animals owned by !Kung and non-!Kung alike. Mahopa is like other settlements of the !Kangwa area such as !Goshi, !Ubi, !Kangwa, and !Xabi in these respects: it has the only permanent water source in its immediate environs, and it hosts a mixed population of !Kung and Bantu-speaking pastoralists of the Tswana and Herero tribes. At all of these water holes a variety of villages are found, some having non-!Kung only, some having !Kung only, some having a mixture of both.

During my fieldwork at Mahopa I deliberately avoided those villages in which both !Kung and Bantu lived. I was concerned with observing the effects of sedentism on a pattern of life which I had observed in the bush. I was not

* Some of these issues are discussed by Shostak, in press.

directly interested in the nature of !Kung-Bantu interaction. It goes without saying that in some respects (especially goat herding and crop planting) the local pastoralists were a model for the subsistence practices of the sedentary !Kung.

The additional question—whether or not Bantu sex-role ideals influence the changes in !Kung sex roles, especially in the direction away from egalitarianism—will not be answered in this discussion. Adequate handling of this topic would require greater knowledge of (particularly) Herero social organization and the dynamics of !Kung-Bantu acculturation than I possess. It remains, however, an important research question, both for the full description of !Kung sedentarization and for understanding general factors that accompany or produce shifts in status relations between the sexes. I will confine myself here to dealing with the sedentary !Kung and some of the changes in the relations between the sexes which appear to follow from the shift from nomadism to sedentism.

The Effect of Sedentism on Sex Egalitarianism

Stated most simply, my strong impression is that the sexual egalitarianism of the bush setting is being undermined in the sedentary !Kung villages. One obvious manifestation of status inequality is that at Mahopa sex roles are more rigidly defined, and at the same time women's work is seen as "unworthy" of men. In the bush setting, although adult roles are sex-typed to some extent—particularly with respect to the exclusive male hunting, and the fact that gathering is primarily done by women—men do not lose face when they do work typically done by women, such as gathering. But in the sedentary villages of Mahopa there is definitely a feeling that it is unmanly for a man to do the jobs that should be done by women. The following example is offered as an illustration of this and of how the community brings social pressure on women (not, in this case, men) to conform.

At the largest of the three Mahopa villages lived a wife, !Uku, about sixteen years of age, and her husband /Gau, about thirty. Like many first marriages of !Kung women, this union was not happy and had not been for some time. The primary source of discontent was the wife's refusal to do the normal domestic chores expected of her. Her husband ranted publicly, claiming that she refused to collect water for their household. !Uku in those days was looking sullen; she avoided her husband and refused to sleep with him. This kind of marital standoff was not unusual among any of the !Kung I knew. !Kung brides are notorious for being labile, uncooperative, and petulant. Young husbands, though usually five to ten years older than their wives, can also be fractious and emotionally ill-equipped to make a first marriage last. !Kung have an expression which invariably crops up when one or both partners to a young marriage sabotage domestic life. They say "*Debi !oa kxwia //wa,*" which translates literally: "Children spoil marriage."

The atypical feature of the Mahopa couple's difficulty was that the husband made a continuing issue of it. He berated his wife's behavior loudly in public and enlisted her relatives to "shame" her into good behavior, etc. Though I never observed a precisely parallel episode in the bush, my prediction is that such a husband would have grumbled quietly, shrugged his shoulders, and either collected the water himself or tried to drink the water of friends and relatives. He also might have waited until his wife complained that he never provided her with meat and then reminded her that he could not spend all day hunting and still have to supply his own water.

By the time I was living at Mahopa and knew of this marital problem, it appeared to me that the elders of the village were working harder at trying to keep the couple together than would be usual in the bush. In the bush concerned relatives will work to keep a young couple together up to a certain point, but if the individuals themselves feel mismatched, there are few, if any, arguments that will persuade them to stay together. When (as often happens) the young couple divorces, no one loses a great deal—no property of any economic weight has changed hands, etc. If both the ex-spouses (together with some of their respective kin) go their separate ways, their departure causes no special disruption in the context of routinely shifting residence patterns.

At Mahopa there were larger political factors at work in the village that may have accounted for the pressure on the couple to get along. Both spouses were related in different ways to the most influential couple of the largest of the three villages. The wife, !Uku, was indirectly related as "niece" to the man who was spoken of as the "owner" of the village. !Uku's husband, /Gau, was the actual brother of the village "owner's" wife. This older, influential couple needed to attract stable, permanent residents to their village. They were extremely "progressive" in comparison with other !Kung of the !Kangwa area. Both had had many years of experience living in various Bantu cattle camps but were now striving to maintain a separate community of sedentary !Kung who could live by agriculture and animal husbandry. Their village needed personnel; /Gau and !Uku were, in theory, ideal recruits to the village on account of their age and kin connections.

What is important for us here is that certain influential persons had vested interests in the success of the marriage, and that the bulk of social criticism was directed at the wife, not the husband. In this sedentary situation, various persons stood to lose a good deal in the event of a divorce. From the point of view of the village "owner" and his wife, a divorce might result in both young people leaving the village. This would be undesirable for reasons already stated. From the point of view of !Uku's parents, who also lived in this village—if their daughter divorced the brother of the "landlady," then their own welcome in the village might become jeopardized.

Although social pressure was being brought to bear on !Uku, it appeared that these pressures were not having the desired effect. !Uku's mother told me privately that she was disgusted with her daughter, that she had tried to get her to change her ways, but that !Uku was obdurate and had even used insulting language to her. !Uku at this time seemed to go out of her way to irritate her husband, had seriously offended her mother, and appeared quite regressive in her behavior. For example, although she was then sixteen years old, she spent hours each day playing dolls with three other girls, ten, nine, and seven years of age. From the bush-living groups I was well acquainted with five adolescent females (both married and unmarried, and approximately the age of !Uku), but I never observed any of them playing so continuously and with such absorption with children five or six years younger.

In the sedentary situation individuals have a different kind of commitment to the place and the persons with whom they are living. People have invested time and energy in building substantial housing, collecting a few goats, clearing and planting fields, and processing and storing the harvested food. It is not easy for an individual to leave these resources behind merely because he or she is at odds with someone else in the village. The couple just described were aware of what they had to lose; the head couple needed neighbors and village mates, not only for the purposes of economic cooperation but because they wanted the human company that would come of a stable settlement around them.

The unhappy marriage remained with no solution or even the hint of one during the time I observed it. Neither party to the marriage appeared ready to leave, so their plight festered and spread into the lives of other people in the village. It was not clear to me why the greatest criticism was leveled at the wife. At sixteen, she was at least fifteen years younger than her husband (a greater age difference than is usual for !Kung couples), and as a juvenile she may have been an easier target than her mature husband. /Gau was known for his hot temper and general unpredictability. The concerned parties may have felt uneasy about urging him to a compromise. Such a marriage in the bush setting would have had a different history. !Uku would have left her husband long before, in all likelihood to spend another year or two in casual flirtations before marrying again.

Childhood Practices and the Greater Separation of Adult Sex Roles

Previously I have stated that in the bush children of both sexes lead very similar lives. Girls and boys do equally little work within the village. For similar reasons both girls and boys are not encouraged to routinely accompany adults of the same sex on their respective food-getting rounds. Children sometimes accompany the women on gathering trips (particularly in the rainy season when the women do not have to carry drinking water for them), but up to about twelve years of age the children make little or no contribution to the collected food which their mothers carry home. Children do, however, pick their own food and eat it during the trek.

In the settled life children continue to have a great deal of leisure, but there is a shift in the adult attitude toward a child as a potential or real worker.* Boys, for example, are expected to help with the animal tending.** They do not herd the animals during the day, but at sundown they are expected to scout the outskirts of the village and to hasten the returning animals into their pens. In each of the three Mahopa villages there was one boy who was primarily responsible for herding chores. In the largest village there were other boys also available, and these youths were frequently asked to help with the herding. Girls were not expected to help in the animal tending, and they in fact made no regular contribution.

An important feature of the herding work of the boys was that it regularly took them out of the village, away from adults and out on their own. There was no comparable experience for girls. They tended to stay in or near the village, unless they were accompanying older women to the water hole to collect water. On such occasions they quickly walked

* The Barry, Child, and Bacon (1957) cross-cultural study reported this as a general attribute of societies with a high degree of accumulation of surplus.

** See Whiting and Whiting (1973) for a discussion of factors that affect the development of responsibility in boys.

the mile or more to the well, where they filled their buckets and then returned more or less promptly to the village. In contrast, the boys drove their animals to the water and then, their work done, they lingered at the water hole. Herero men also came to the well, driving animals to water. Herero and Tswana women frequently came to the well to wash clothing. !Kung boys hung around the fringes of this scene, listening and observing. Experiences like these are no doubt related to the superior knowledge of Bantu languages which !Kung men exhibit in comparison to !Kung women. Such experiences must foster for boys a better and earlier knowledge of the greater !Kangwa area and a more confident spirit when moving within it—or outside of it, for that matter.

Women and girls appear to inhabit more restricted space—that space being largely their own village or neighboring villages. The Mahopa women gather wild plant foods, but they do this infrequently and forage in an area much closer to the village and for shorter intervals as compared with the bush women.

Overall, the Mahopa women seem homebound, their hands are busier, and their time is taken up with domestic chores.* A number of factors enter into this change. Under settled conditions food preparation is more complicated, although the actual diet is probably less varied in comparison with that of the foragers. Grains and squash must be brought in from the fields and set up on racks to dry. Sorghum and corn are pounded into meal; squash and melons are peeled and then boiled before eating. Women do the greatest part of the cooking, and they also do most of the drying and storing.

The material inventory of the settled villagers is richer than that of the bush-living !Kung. People have more possessions and better facilities, and all of these things require more time and energy for maintenance. Housing, for example, is more substantial than in the bush. Round, mud-walled houses with

* Unfortunately, during the period of study I collected systematic information on adult work effort only at /Du/da and not at any of the settled !Kung villages.

thatched roofs are replacing the traditional grass scherms at Mahopa. More durable structures are a response to at least two changes. Once committed to settled life, it makes sense to build better and more permanent shelters. Also, the presence of domestic animals in and near the villages means that grass houses are either protected by barricades or they are literally eaten up. Most people believe it is easier to build the mud-dung earth houses and to close them with inedible doors, rather than being continually on the lookout against stock. These structures provide better shelter, but they also require more upkeep. The women periodically resurface the interior walls and lay new floors. The men do some domestic maintenance work, but it is more likely to be fencing, roof-thatching, and other nonroutine work. It appears that the Mahopa men are becoming peripheral to their households in ways that are completely uncharacteristic of the easy integration of bush-living men into their own households. More will be said about this later.

At Mahopa the work of adult women is becoming more specialized, time-consuming, and homebound, and these women are quite willing to integrate their daughters into this work. Girls have no regular chores to compare with the herding work of some of the boys, but their mothers give them frequent small tasks such as pounding grain, carrying away a troublesome toddler, fetching earth from termite hills to be used in making mud, etc. The little girls are usually on the premises and easy targets for their mothers' commands; little boys seem to be either gone from the village (on errands already described) or else visible but distant enough from the women so that their help cannot be enlisted conveniently.

Earlier in this paper I suggested that bush-living men and women are about equally absent from their respective households, due to the similarities in the location and frequency of their work. This is less true at Mahopa. Women are in the village a great deal. The greatest part of their work takes place there, and foraging occupies only a small part of their weekly work. Mahopa men are increasingly absent from the households as their women become more consistently present. There are tasks and activities for men in the village which have already been described, though they are not routine. What work the men do often takes them away from the village. They water animals, and when the goats are giving birth to kids the men who own pregnant goats check on the grazing herd during the day to make sure the newborn are not lost or rejected by the mothers. During planting season the men clear the fields and erect brush fences around the gardens to keep out the animals. Some men leave home for several days at a time to do wage work for Bantu employers living at other settlements in the !Kangwa Valley.

It is difficult to specify precisely what effect this increasing male absenteeism had on family life or relations between the sexes. The activities of the sedentary men are different not only in form but in content from those of the women. They leave home more frequently, travel more widely, and have more frequent interaction with members of other (dominant) cultural groups. In their own villages the men carry an aura of authority and sophistication that sets them apart from the women and children. For example, occasionally some incident, such as a legal case pending before the Tswana headman at !Xabi, would attract attention in the !Kangwa area. In the afternoons I often saw a group of men composed of several !Kung and one or two Hereros sitting in a shady area of one of the !Kung villages. The men would be discussing the case, carrying on the talks in a Bantu language. Women never joined these groups, and even children seemed to give these sessions a wide berth.

What these episodes conveyed to me is that at Mahopa political affairs are the concern of men, not women. Why or how women have been "eased out" (at least in comparison with the influence they had in the bush) is not clear. The /Du/da people, so long as they remained in the bush, had only rare and fleeting contacts with members of different cultural groups. If one postulates that men are the natural political agents in intergroup contacts, then the /Du/da milieu would not elicit that potential of the male role. At Mahopa three cultural groups mixed. !Kung men, as already described, were more sophisticated than the women, and on those occasions when !Kung became involved in extragroup events, the !Kung men came prominently to the fore.

Organization of Space and Privacy in the Bush Setting

To recapitulate, in the bush, village space is small, circular, open, and highly intimate. Everyone in the camp can see (and often hear) everyone else virtually all of the time, since there are no private places to which people can retire. Even at nightfall people remain in the visually open space, sleeping singly or with other family members around the fires located outside the family huts (Draper, 1973). Elsewhere (Draper, in press), I have suggested that !Kung egalitarianism and commitment to sharing are more than coincidentally associated. The intensity of social pressure, in combination with the absence of privacy, makes hoarding virtually impossible, at least for individuals who wish to remain within the group. I am suggesting that the nature of village space in the bush acts as a "lock" on other aspects of culture that are congruent but capable of sliding apart. While it is true that !Kung values oppose physical fighting and anger, ranking of individuals in terms of status, material wealth, and competition, the context in which social action occurs is such that the earliest and subtlest moves in these directions can be perceived immediately by the group. Various forms of negative reinforcement can be employed by anyone and everyone, and the effect is to discourage anti-social behavior, whatever form it may take.

Obviously a continuous socialization process is not unique to the !Kung. All of us experience our fellows shaping our behavior throughout our lives. What I would like to stress about the !Kung is that in this small, face-to-face society it is much more difficult to compartmentalize one's motives, feeling states, and (most of all) actions. In ways not true of our life, !Kung remain in continuous communication, though they may not be directly conscious of the exchanges of information that are occurring.

This potential for continuous socialization exists among

the !Kung; if it works in the ways I have suggested, it need have no single effect on sexual egalitarianism among hunter-gatherers. There is, for example, abundant literature on other band-level peoples (notably Australian aborigines), where similar technology, economy, and settlement patterns produce at least formally similar settings for social action without attendant equality in male and female statuses (A. Hamilton, 1970; Hiatt, 1970; Peterson, 1970; White, 1970; Hart and Pilling, 1960). In the !Kung case, a number of factors appear to be working directly and indirectly to insure high autonomy of females and immunity of females to subordination by males. Several of these factors have been isolated in the foregoing discussion in an attempt to "explain" sexual egalitarianism from *inside* the system—to show how sexual egalitarianism is a logical outcome given the realities of the !Kung life.

Looked at from the point of view of factors *outside* the normative system, another argument can be made for why an egalitarian, mutual interdependence prevails among these people. The nature and distribution of the resources used by the hunting and gathering !Kung probably have indirect consequences for potential competition between and within !Kung groups. Both vegetable and animal foods are thinly and unevenly distributed over the bush. This is particularly true of the large antelope, which move erratically and seldom in the large herds that are more typical in East Africa and Arctic North America. Under conditions as these, hunting success for a particular individual depends as much on luck as it does on skill. Among the !Kung, even the best hunters readily admit that there are times when game is unavailable or when conditions do not permit the stalk-and-close approach to game required by bow-and-arrow hunting. As a result, any individual man cannot count on success, and in this context sharing of meat is an essential form of social insurance—a way of distributing food to the have-nots against the time when their fortunes change. Not surprisingly, the rules about sharing meat constitute one of the most important values in !Kung culture. My guess is that in such a system where males are continually leveled and divested of their ownership of the single most valued item (meat), the potential for male competition is largely removed. The strict sharing ethic, together with the values against interpersonal aggression described earlier, are checks on male agonistic behavior that leave the field open for female autonomy and influence.*

Organization of Space and Privacy in the Settled Villages

In the settled villages the organization of space and the notion of privacy have undergone some interesting changes. Instead of the circular, closed settlement pattern of the bush, the settled villages typically are arranged in an open crescent; individual households have moved farther apart; and household privacy is substantially increased, particularly for those people who have acquired more material wealth. With individual houses farther apart, the pattern of social usage of the village space is different. The average distance between interactive clusters of people also increases. In the settled village different activities are more typically separated in space, as contrasted with the bush setting where it is typical to find people carrying on a conversation and/or activity while sitting back-to-back with other people who are engaged in a wholly different enterprise.

At the time I was living at Mahopa a few families already lived in permanent mud-walled houses and some other families were in the process of building Bantu-style rondavels to replace their smaller grass scherms. Occupants of the completed rondavels build log fences around their houses; slender logs or poles are placed upright in the ground, reaching to a height of five to six feet, and spaced one to two inches apart. These fences encircle individual households and create an inner courtyard. Obviously, privacy is increased substantially

* Lee (1969) provides a fascinating description of how an anthropologist's pride in making a gift of meat to a !Kung village was deflated by the !Kung expertise in putting down boastfulness.

by the changed house type, settlement pattern, and fencing.

When I asked settled villagers why people erected the fences, the typical response was that it is a means of keeping domestic animals away from people's living quarters. Goats, in particular, can be a nuisance. They steal food, knock over pots, even come into houses in search of food. Their fresh dung attracts flies which are also bothersome. If domestic animals entail a new style of building, the solid, roomy houses, fences, and more linear placement of separate households also change the quality of social interaction in the villages. There are internal boundaries within the village space, which people recognize and manipulate in ways completely foreign to the bush setting. In the bush people can see each other and determine, on a variety of grounds,* whether it is appropriate or timely to initiate social interaction. In the Mahopa villages one heard such exchanges as "So-and-so, are you at home?" and "Shall I enter [your space] ?"

There are differences in material wealth among the people of the settled villages that would not be tolerated in the bush. These differences are manifest in terms of household size and elaborateness of construction, unequal ownership of domestic animals, clothing, jewelry, and food reserves. The differences are not large in an absolute sense, but in comparison with the similar material wealth of individuals in the bush, the differences are impressive. Some !Kung live simply, still using grass scherms and owning few possessions; others are better off, though the men in particular seem to avoid some kinds of ostentation. For example, the two men who were the most influential males in their villages often dressed very simply and did not have the outward appearance of "big men."** Yet, if invited into their houses, one would see a remarkable collection of *things:* clothing, dishes, blankets,

*** My impression while working in the field was that a student of proxemics would find a wealth of material in the area of nonverbal communication among the foraging groups of !Kung.**

**** Yet the middle-aged wives of these men often wore jewelry and clothing beyond the means of other women living in the settled villages.**

bottles, trunks with locks, etc. As a guest in such a house one could sit on the floor, lean back against the cool, sound-deadening wall, and enjoy being *alone* with one's host while he or she made tea and murmured small talk.

Ranking of individuals in terms of prestige and differential wealth has begun in the settled villages. Men, more than women, are defined as the managers or owners of this property. One would hear, for example, such expressions as "Kxau's [a man's name] house" or "Kxau's village." Children are most often identified as being the child of the father rather than the child of the mother. Goats are also referred to as belonging to one or another adult male, though in fact a given man's herd generally includes several animals which in fact belong to his wife or other female relatives. These expressions can be heard in the bush setting, for individual ownership exists among the foragers as well, but the "owners" referred to are as likely to be women as men. At Mahopa this linguistic custom is being replaced by one in which the adult male stands as the symbol of his domestic group. It is a linguistic shorthand, but I believe it signifies changes in the relative importance attached to each sex.

Earlier I referred to the increasing peripheralization of males in the settled villages and the opposite centripetal moving of women to the local domestic sphere. As households and possessions become private, I believe women are becoming private as well. (Perhaps this is one reason the women can afford to be ostentatious of their wealth.) In contrast bush men and women are equally "public," mobile, and visible. I believe this exposure of women is a form of protection in the bush setting. For instance, residence choices of bush-living couples are such that over time the couples live about equally (often simultaneously) with the kin of both husband and wife (Lee, in press). (At present there is not even an ideal of patrilocal residence, so far as my own interviews could establish.) This means that the wife typically has several of her own close kin nearby. These people are already on the premises and can support her interests should they conflict with the interests of her husband or his close kin.

When husbands and wives argue, people are at hand to intervene if either spouse loses self-control. Wife-beating in these settings is extremely difficult to effect.

Once, during my work in Mahopa, I had a conversation with two middle-aged women who lived in the largest of the settled villages where I was camped. I often asked !Kung adults about the Herero, what they thought of them, how they perceived the differences between the groups, mainly because for reasons already stated I seldom visited the Herero settlements and knew little from direct observation about the pattern of life there. In one such conversation I asked Kxarun!a, a woman of about fifty, "Who do you think has the better life—a !Kung woman or a Herero woman?" She answered in a serious, thoughtful way, "The !Kung women are better off. Among the Herero if a man is angry with his wife he can put her in their house, bolt the door and beat her. No one can get in to separate them. They only hear her screams. When we !Kung fight, other people get in between." The other woman sitting with us agreed earnestly.

It would be unwise to attach too much significance to this remark. People are always accusing the people "over there" of various dread offenses ranging from wife-beating to much worse practices. Still, the remark chilled me and I remember deliberately not looking at the Bantu-style rondavels which were going up in the middle of the village where we sat.

In this paper I have pointed out differences in sexual egalitarianism in the hunting and gathering groups versus the settled groups of !Kung. I have discussed factors in the bush setting which favor high autonomy for females and freedom from subordination by males. Once the !Kung shift their subsistence to animal husbandry and crop planting, a number of changes occur in the area of sex roles. A major aspect of this change is the decrease in women's autonomy and influence relative to that of the men.

Ruby Rohrlich-Leavitt, Barbara Sykes, and Elizabeth Weatherford

Aboriginal Woman: Male and Female Anthropological Perspectives

The initial purpose of this paper was to compare the findings of male and female anthropologists about Australian aboriginal women to see if there were sex-based divergences. But even a cursory survey of the studies showed such marked discrepancies in both the range and quality of the data collected in the field that the analysis was extended to include the differences in the theoretical and methodological approaches and in the concomitant ideologies.

It is generally acknowledged that an exclusively male study of a culture is usually incomplete. Male ethnographers use male informants, whether by inclination or because of cultural requirements, and observe the activities of males or those involving both sexes, but rarely those in which women alone participate. A partial ethnography is already a distorted picture, but that it is further distorted by the androcentric theory and methodology of many male ethnographers is only now beginning to be dealt with, chiefly by women anthropologists. Most of the men in the discipline find it difficult to face this reality, for it would bring into question much of the data accumulated for more than a century about non-Western cultures.

In the education of anthropologists, little or no attention has been directed to eliminating androcentrism. The major focus is on expunging that aspect of ethnocentrism that involves unconscious assumptions of superiority over non-Western peoples. Yet, despite deliberate and concerted training to this end, anthropologists find it almost impossible to rid themselves of these assumptions. In his *New York Times* review of Carlos Castaneda's books Paul Riesman notes:

> The belief that all people are human has not saved Western anthropologists from feeling superior to the people they study and write about, and it has not prevented serious distortions in our picture of non-Western peoples (and of ourselves) from arising and influencing our actions.

How much more serious must be the distortions that arise from androcentrism. How is it possible for the male ethnographer, socialized from birth to his superior status in his own culture and in no way held accountable for androcentrism, to report objectively on the relationships between women and men, and on the roles and status of women, in other cultures? Moreover, socialization into the discipline must only fortify androcentrism, since men are so obviously preferred for research grants, fieldwork, and employment.

The prototype for the androcentric approach of the anthropologist is the century-long debate over the existence of matriarchal civilizations, a debate unique for the particular emotionality of its tone. The multitude of contradictions that permeated this controversy are still with us. For example, although it is generally accepted that religious practices reflect the secular life, when the archaeological record reveals the prevalence of goddesses, the corresponding secular dominance of women is denied, despite the acceptance of a masculine secular supremacy when male gods are found to predominate.

At the same time the universality of the patriarchal system is asserted, for most anthropologists insist that even in matrilineal, matrilocal societies it is not the women but their brothers who wield political power. This flies in the face of historical evidence. The political leadership of women is well documented for many states of Southeast Asia and Africa. And in the northern Andean states, "the matrilineal tendencies of the circum-Caribbean area" led "to female as well as male warriors and rulers" (Steward, 1970: 221).

The very selection of the political institution as the defining criterion of social organization is itself a projection of Euro-American society. The high status of women among gathering-hunting and agricultural peoples was based on their crucial economic, religious, and medical roles. But such societies, it seems, may not be termed "matriarchies" because, as defined by most anthropologists, a matriarchy is the mirror image of the patriarchy, particularly of the Euro-American type in which men exercise iron control over all institutions. But the patriarchal concept of power as the means of control over the mass of the people by a ruling elite is in no way applicable to band and tribal cultures. As Eleanor Leacock points out (1972: 34), in such societies "the participation of women in a major share of socially necessary labor did not reduce them to virtual slavery, as is the case in class society, but afforded them decision-making power commensurate with their contribution."

According to David Kaplan and Robert Manners (1972:186), "The purpose for which the research and description are undertaken will determine whether an ethnographic account is couched in 'native categories' (emic terms), in the 'anthropologist's categories' (etic terms), or, as is overwhelmingly the case, in some combination of the two." But in the male ethnographies of the Australian aborigines the "anthropologist's categories" predominate; the societies are represented as male-dominated, with women in a subordinate, degraded status. However, in *Aboriginal Woman* and *Tiwi Wives*, Phyllis Kaberry and Jane Goodale succeed in combining the "anthropologist's categories" with those of the native. Their theory and methodology seem to stem from "double-consciousness," a concept that W. E. B. DuBois evolved to define the special awareness of black people in a racist society. Themselves women in a society that is also sexist, Kaberry and Goodale have the special sensitivity that members of subordinated groups must, if they are to survive, develop to those who control them, at the same time as they are fully aware of the everyday reality of their oppression, a quality the superordinate groups lack. Thus Kaberry and Goodale develop ethnographies from the actual lives and world views of the people they study, and with a thoroughgoing awareness of the "anthropologist's categories," their theory is generated both emically and etically.

In contrast, C. W. M. Hart states (Spindler, 1970:147) that when he studied the Tiwi of North Australia, he focused on the genealogical system and deliberately ignored their mythology and subsistence techniques because they "bored" him. Pointing to the limitations of this approach, Leacock says (1972:7): "Unfortunately, the debate over women's status in primitive society has largely ignored the actual role of women ... in favor of an almost exclusive focus on descent systems." But the emic-etic perspective of Kaberry and Goodale goes beyond the particular system chosen by the male ethnographer. As Kaberry notes (1939:39): "Anthropology as a science must have its laws and abstractions, yet human beings ... are apt to prove intractable to scientific manipulation."

The sensitivity of the women ethnographers to the "scientific manipulation" of people is another facet of "double-consciousness," an accurate term for a truly emic-etic perspective. This kind of manipulation is illustrated by the Aristotelian device of dichotomy, widely used by Western male social scientists to establish and perpetuate, in the case of male and female roles, status, and temperament, the "natural" superiority of men and the "natural" inferiority of women. In the anthropology of the Australian aborigines, functionalists and structuralists like Durkheim, Warner, and Lévi-Strauss have set up fictitious and simplistic dichotomies that arbitrarily designate men as sacred and women as profane, or men as actors and women as acted upon, at the same time as women are devalued, incongruously, precisely on the grounds that they *are* actors, involved with doing. Such polarizations are tellingly challenged by Kaberry and Goodale as they focus on the revealing interactions between the quotidian and ritual activities of these people.

With the exception of Daisy Bates (1938) and a few other women whose works were somehow doomed to obscurity, for more than a century the data on the Australian aborigines came from male fieldworkers. What emerged was a view of these Australian women as pawns in a male exchange system, or as "mere drudges, passing a life of monotony and being shamefully ill-treated by their husbands" (Elkin, 1939:xxii). This perspective was amazingly consistent, and, as late as 1964 *The Tiwi of North Australia* was described as "a case study of a system of influence and power which is based on a strange currency . . . woman . . . Because men compete for prestige and influence through their control over women, women have the value of a scarce commodity" (Spindler, in Hart and Pilling, 1960:v).

But Kaberry and Goodale present a totally different picture of aboriginal women. They describe their crucially important economic roles, and show that these determine the nature of their spiritual roles, refuting the male view that women are excluded from the sacred state. For Australian totemic ceremonies reflect the total social organization that the women and men have evolved in their struggle to adapt to a precarious environment.

Referring to the division of labor by sex, Ashley Montagu (1937:23) reports that the women are nothing but "domesticated cows," while Malinowski states (1913:278) that the women are forced to do the heavier work "by the 'brutal' half of society" and that "the relation of a husband to a wife in its economic aspect [is] that of a master to its slave." Kaberry, however, demonstrates that the women's work is less onerous than the men's. Hunting over rugged hills and under a blazing sun is very exhausting and often disappointing, but the women forage at a leisurely pace, rest and gossip in the shade, swim in pools to cool off, and always manage to bring food back to the camp. Women carry the burdens as the band moves from place to place in search of food, for the men must be free to use their hunting weapons; but nomadic bands travel light and the women are not unduly taxed by their loads.

The women supply most of the food for the family, since hunting is unpredictable and the amount of meat supplied by the men is uncertain. Foraging requires skill, patience, and an exhaustive knowledge of the environment. The women also bring down small game and even kangaroos, with the help of their hunting dogs, which they raise and train with care and love. According to Kaberry:

> If it was compulsory to search for food, at least they did not travel like beasts of burden, with timorous docility and bovine resignation. They were not driven forth by the men; they departed just as leisurely, chose their own routes, and in this department of economic activities, were left in undisputed sway. If it was left to them alone to provide certain goods, at least it was a province in which they were their own mistresses, acquired their skill from the older women, and served no weary apprenticeship to an exacting husband or father. (1939:23)

In fact, the woman's work is no more compulsory than the man's. Meat is regarded as essential to the diet and "it is just as incumbent on the man to contribute this whenever possible, as it is for the woman to go out for roots and tubers" (ibid.:25).

If the husband returns from a tiring day and thinks his wife has not done her share, he quarrels with her and may try to beat her up, "but there is no question of her submissively accepting punishment for unwifely conduct" (ibid.). Every woman has her fighting stick, which she wields with great skill, and when the man is unlucky in the hunt or the wife thinks he is just plain lazy, she may attack him "with both tongue and tomahawk" (ibid.:26). On the whole, however, there is very real economic cooperation between husband and wife, "an expected and recognized feature of marital life" (ibid.:27). Both Kaberry and Goodale show that women and men sometimes go on hunting and fishing excursions together, although generally they go about their activities separately.

Kaberry suggests that the separation of the sexes during the greater part of the day is carried over into the ritual sphere. But A. P. Elkin maintains (1939:xxvi) that "both the dichotomy manifested in economic life and also in ritual life may arise from the physiological differences between men and women." When confronted by the complexities of cultural roles, many Western social scientists take refuge in the reductionist theme, "anatomy is destiny."

Reflecting the primary importance of technology in the West, W. Lloyd Warner asserts (1937:6) that the dominant religious and social roles of the men reflect their technological skills, while the "more simple" techniques used by the women tend to "simplify their personalities" and social roles, and exclude them from the totemic mysteries. Kaberry, however, points out that the men's skills do not increase the importance of their economic activities, while the tools which the women make and use satisfy the bulk of the nutritional needs of the group. It is by virtue of their essential economic contribution that the women are respected and assured of just and good treatment. Women have a right to their own property, and they trade many of the articles they make with both male and female partners in the system of economic exchanges. With their female partners they also exchange secret corroborees and, like the men, the women practice sorcery against undependable partners.

Many male students of the Australian aborigines, from 1840 onward, dwelt on the marital life of the women, hinting darkly at the dire fate of the young girl handed over to an old man. "Polygamy is practiced in an exceedingly barbarous manner unfit for publication," wrote S. Gason (1879:81). "Within these marriage classes things unspeakable may happen," said E. R. Gribble (1940:175-76). And according to Malinowski, (1913:101), "the husband had a definite sexual 'over-right' to his wife, which secured to him the privilege of disposing of her." With little access to the women, how did these scholars arrive at their unmentionable conclusions?

The assumption that the prepubescent girls were sexually violated by dirty old men seems to reflect the widespread father-daughter incest fantasy among Western men. According to Kaberry, young people of both sexes have casual affairs before marriage, a commonplace in pre-class societies. And if a girl becomes pregnant, the man to whom she is betrothed becomes the child's sociological father, a form of insurance for the mother. But full sexual intercourse, with either lover or husband, is not permitted until after puberty.

The girl's future husband begins to stay in her parents' camp before she reaches puberty, and in this transitional premarital period they get to know each other, so that she is accustomed to him by the time she goes to live in his territory. Both parents and young people indignantly rejected the notion that sexual intercourse took place before the first menstruation. In the myths that Kaberry collected from the various tribes, sexual relations always followed menstruation and never preceded it. Child brides are a feature of patriarchal civilizations, not of most "primitive" societies.

The full force of the Judeo-Christian theme of female uncleanliness is projected on the aboriginal woman by male anthropologists. Warner states (1937:394) that "masculinity is inextricably interwoven with ritual cleanliness, and femininity is equally entwined with the concept of uncleanliness, the former being the sacred principle and the latter the profane." The Murngin, according to Warner, connect the superordinate status of the males with their sacred cleanliness, as well as their technological superiority, and connect the woman's subordination with her profane uncleanliness. The ritual cleanliness of the male is made more sacred through continual ceremonial participation, which unifies the male group, while the subordinate female group is unified by exclusion from the ceremonies and by ritual uncleanliness.

Insofar as menstruation is involved with blood and the genitals, it is endowed with powerful magical properties and associated with taboos. Since it is believed that the power of menstrual blood might harm the men, the menstruating women keep unobtrusively out of their way. However, Kaberry reports that the men never expressed disgust for a menstruating woman. They never spoke of her as "dirty" or "unclean," nor was there a term for "dirty" which implied ritual uncleanliness. Particularly significant, says Kaberry (1939:238), is the fact that the women never think of themselves as unclean, or of menstruation as shameful, which they would do, as do women in the West, if the men viewed them that way. The women are unified not by "their ritual uncleanliness" or their exclusion from male ceremonies, but by their economic cooperation and their participation in their own secret ceremonies.

Male anthropologists insist that the men totally dominate all marriage arrangements and that these are entirely in their own interests. According to Hart and Pilling, Tiwi women are investment commodities, pawns in the male struggles for power. The Tiwi male view is represented in the terms of the Wall Street stockbroker:

> As in our culture, where the first million is the hardest to make, so in Tiwi the first bestowed wife was the hardest to get. If some shrewd father with a daughter to invest in a twenty-year-old decided to invest her in you, his judgment was likely to attract other fathers to make a similar investment. (1960:16)

Hart and Pilling completely ignore the benefits and powers accruing to the women in this system. Goodale points out that the tie between the son-in-law and his future mother-in-law is "one of the most important and enduring social relationships that either may have" (1971:52). In return for the promise of her future daughter, the son-in-law becomes responsible for providing for the needs and wants of his mother-in-law until his or her death: "He must supply her with all she demands in services or goods, including today clothes, tobacco, money and the like" (ibid.). Moreover, if the son-in-law "does not serve his mother-in-law to her satisfaction, she may void the contract. A girl's father does not have the right to void such a contract" (ibid.:56). In the Kimberley tribes of northwest Australia, the large number of elopements and irregular marriages also indicates that many young women do not meekly accept the pre-arranged marriages. Moreover, a young woman married to an old man often has a young lover.

Because of the age discrepancy between the Australian woman and her first few husbands, she is often widowed and often remarries. But just as older men marry young women, so the woman as she grows older marries younger and younger men, and exercises increasing choice as to whom she marries. When a widowed woman outlives her brothers, her sons have the nominal right to arrange her next marriage. But even Hart describes Tiwi widows as "highly vocal and pretty tough old ladies who are not easily pushed around by anybody, even by their adult and ambitious sons. Whom they remarried in their old age was a matter upon which they themselves had a good deal to say" (1960:20). What is more, these older women not only arrange their own marriages, but also, according to Goodale, those of their sons: "Since all contracts involve an exchange . . . mothers anxious for their sons' advance might agree to exchange sons!" (1971:57).

Ashley Montagu asserts that throughout Australia the physiological bond between mother and child is even less recognized than that between father and child. The Arunta woman, he says, is merely "the medium through which a spirit-child is transformed into a baby," and much more significance is attached to "the relationship between father and child than that which should exist between a mother and the child to which she has given birth" (1937:74). But this appears to be a projection of the typical patriarchal denial of the female generative power.

"Primitive" peoples everywhere have an enormous respect and awe for the woman's reproductive functions. Specifically among the Kimberley tribes, Kaberry clearly demonstrates that the physiological relationship between mother and child is not only fully recognized, but that the mother is accorded a special respect and affection. The pregnant woman observes food taboos because certain foods are believed to injure the child within the mother's womb. The natives of south and central Australia believe that the individual inherits the body, flesh, and blood from the mother. Children from about the age of six onward distinguish between their own biological mothers and "other mothers," such as mothers' sisters. Men who have the same mother but different fathers call each other "brother," and children have close ties with their mother's group. The mother receives a share of the gifts when her son is initiated, as well as gifts from her daughter's husband, and participates in the negotiations for her daughter's marriage. Mothers and married daughters visit and give each other gifts, and both sons and daughters care for their mother when she is old.

Ashley Montagu also maintains that "the actual experience involved in giving birth to a child is so minimized and the social implications of the result of the birth so magnified that the former wilts away into the obscure background before the all-embracing consequences of the latter" (1937:72). With no access to the rituals surrounding the woman's life crises, he somehow discovered that "childbirth among the Australians . . . is a comparatively light affair for the woman . . . There is no great affect normally associated with childbirth, nor is it in any way climatic" (ibid.:73).

This attitude, says Kaberry, typifies the male ethnographer's casual approach to childbirth and its rites. Although the Australian woman enjoys her children and the advantages that accrue from being a mother, she regards children as the consequence of marriage and not the reason for it: "Where she does bear children, they do not anchor her the more securely in a position of inferiority, nor circumscribe her activities" (1939:156). But women in the gathering and hunting societies deliberately space childbirths. Far from childbirth being lightly treated, many aboriginal women disliked the prospect of the pain and trouble, and the burden of carrying the baby about afterward. A most important secret ritual is performed to lessen the difficulties of childbirth. Goodale notes that young wives "may have several abortions to postpone their motherhood so as not to interfere with their love life" (1971:145). And Kaberry points out that "we cannot assume the existence of a maternal instinct prior to pregnancy or even after conception, since so many aboriginal women resort to abortion" (1939:157-58). It appears that the women in "primitive" cultures have far greater control over their bodies and reproductive functions than their "civilized" sisters.

When it comes to the spiritual life of the aboriginal women, male anthropologists are guilty of the most serious distortions. Durkheim, Warner, and Elkin all assert that only the men are sacred and make sacred progress. But Kaberry points out that if the men really represented the sacred element, the women would surely be cognizant of the fact and accept it (ibid.:230). The women, however, do not regard the men as sacred; they "remained regrettably profane in their attitude toward the men." Elkin insists that the men do become sacred in the course of their secret ritual life, whether or not the women regard them as sacred. But if half the population withholds recognition of the sacredness of the other half, by what magical authority does this other half become sacred?

Many male anthropologists seem to be as bedazzled as any Western tourist by the spectacular rites of the aboriginal men. While the women participate in fewer and less elaborate rituals, the ceremonies of both women and men are closely related to their respective problems. Just as the men are mainly concerned with male rituals, so the women are involved principally with those relating to their own sex, which the male ethnographers are inclined to treat as a minor or exotic feature of native life. Spencer and Gillen, for example, describe women's rites in a chapter they call "Peculiar Native Customs."

The patriarchal identification of women with evil and danger is particularly marked in Géza Róheim's denigration of the women's spiritual life:

> What is her religion? . . . We might just as well put this question in another form and ask what are her fears, anxieties? For it is only this phase of religion that is open to women. All aspects of religion that contain any hint at a supernatural world that protects mankind . . . or any element of identification are limited to the male half of the population. For a woman, religion means a supernatural or semi-supernatural danger, it means demons . . . or demon-like avengers or foreign tribes. (1933:259)

According to Kaberry and Goodale, both women and men have the same deeply rooted beliefs in the totemic ancestors, and the egalitarian relationships between the sexes are reflected in the myths that depict male and female totemic ancestors as existing together from the first. In a Tiwi creation myth a female deity created the earth, trees, and animals, fresh and salt water; and a goddess is both the sun, which gives forth heat at mid-day, and the Milky Way at night. Unlike the patriarchal creation myths that teach men and women that a male god first created a man, the myths related by the Australian women teach them to identify with female totemic ancestors who are responsible for and protect childbirth and menstruation.

As the girl begins to approach puberty the old women chant songs to bring her to sexual maturity, and just before the first menstruation they perform secret rituals to prepare her for marriage. During the first menstruation rituals are performed to bring the secluded girl safely through the period, and the women sing sacred songs, jealously guarded from the men, to stop the flow of menstrual blood, to facilitate childbirth, and to prevent hemorrhaging. After childbirth, rites are performed to strengthen the mother and the baby.

In northwest Australia the men are barred from the women's secret corroborees. Although some of the men oppose these events, they cannot prevent them from taking place, and the women relish the disadvantage to which they put the men. Like the male rituals, the corroborees provide the opportunity for joking and teasing, and for display and recreation. These dramatic and vivid affairs are organized and led by the middle-aged and old women. The painted and costumed dancers use their husbands' boomerangs and their own fighting sticks, which are endowed with magical qualities for the occasion, to simulate sexual intercourse. Many of the songs sung by the women during these corroborees, as well as at other ceremonies, emphasize the clitoris in love-making. It seems that among the Kimberley tribes the myth of the vaginal orgasm is absent.

With increasing age Australian women become more assertive and wield more power and authority, but some male ethnographers project on them the contempt and disrespect experienced by older women in Western society. Hart, for example, usually refers to older Australian women as "ancient hags" or "toothless old hags," in contrast to his respectful references to "powerful old men." Nevertheless, the male ethnographers cannot entirely ignore the influential status of the older woman in band life, as well as in the camp.

The older women teach the younger ones their economic skills, and preside over the women's rites and secret corroborees. According to Kaberry:

> Together with the old men, they are the repositories of myth, responsible for handing on tribal law and custom, and are one of the forces which make possible the stability and continuity of tribal life. (1939: 184)

The older women take the initiative in settling disputes "when anger mounts high and threatens the peace. . . . Amidst the shouting, the barking of dogs, the voice of an old woman will make itself heard above the uproar as she harangues men and women impartially" (ibid.).

Summarizing the major differences between the studies by the male and female ethnographers, it is evident that the androcentrism of male scholars results in an etic perspective which blinds them to the actual realities of aboriginal life. Androcentrism prevents male scholars from recognizing that the natives fully acknowledge the importance of the women's economic contribution so that they participate commensurately in the other institutions. Androcentrism leads male scholars to exaggerate the importance of political power and technology for the natives. Androcentric male scholars project on the aborigines the patriarchal notion that the physiological differences between the sexes determine all sex-role differences, as well as the patriarchal concepts denying the female generative principle, attaching female uncleanliness to menstruation, asserting the subordinate status of the wife and mother, and identifying women with evil and danger. Androcentric male scholars ignore or minimize the importance of the ritual life for the women. In addition, male scholars who are androcentric are also misanthropic, for they misrepresent Australian men as brutal, domineering, and oblivious to the humanity of the women.

The women ethnographers, on the other hand, show us

men and women living together in equal partnership, the rights, self-respect, and dignity of the members of both sexes being guaranteed. Although the men play a more important political role in intergroup relationships, political institutions are not highly developed and are geared to economic survival, in which women play a central role. Australian women are shown to have complete control over the reproductive function, and they are not regarded, either by the men or by themselves, as contaminating, polluting, unclean, evil, or dangerous. The women gain the same benefits as the men from their ritual experiences: emotional security during the life crises, and opportunities for drama, recreation, and display. And the women ethnographers reveal the Australian men to be concerned and caring husbands and fathers.

The basic inference to be drawn from the differences between the male and female ethnographies is that many Western male anthropologists are unwilling or unable to expunge their ethnocentrism, of which the predominant elements are androcentrism and sexism. Androcentrism and sexism lead to the misinterpretation and distortion of the status and roles of women in non-Western cultures. But if the status and roles of women are misinterpreted and distorted, so inevitably must be those of men. Since the relationships of women and men interlock, the distortion of the roles of men and women leads to a distortion of the total social system.

Those women anthropologists, however, who are aware of the oppression of women in an androcentric society, and are sensitive to male misperceptions of women, bring a double consciousness to their research which results in holistic, accurate, and objective studies. It is such women ethnographers as Kaberry and Goodale who achieve a truly emic-etic perspective.

A Note on Daisy Bates

The research of Daisy Bates should be a primary source on the Australian aborigines, for she spent fifty years with them.

But to date no anthropologist appears to have investigated the ninety-four folios of her papers at the National Library in Canberra, Australia. Although she was a member of the same racial and cultural group as the male ethnographers who studied the aborigines, Bates, as a woman, seems to have experienced the misogyny they displayed toward the aboriginal women.

Before his first expedition to Australia in 1910, Radcliffe-Brown wrote Bates that her description of aboriginal social organization represented "a large amount of very valuable information which will be of immense value to us in the work we propose to do" (Salter, 1972:135), and accepted her offer to participate in the expedition. Despite her own poverty, Bates had tapped all possible sources to finance the expedition, and had introduced Radcliffe-Brown to the bands she knew so well. But shortly after the fieldwork began he left her behind. He then delayed editing the manuscript she had entrusted to him, and it was eventually lost. After Radcliffe-Brown's first published reports Bates wrote a friend that "some of my manuscript is being printed as new discoveries by those who had access to it. You will remember that I mentioned the Ngargalulla of the Broome district natives some years ago. I see in a recent paper that those spirit babies are Mr. A. R. Brown's discoveries" (ibid.:152).

In 1923 Elkin contacted Bates before beginning his expedition. But when she asked for help in obtaining a government stipend, as she was financially destitute, all she received was twenty pounds, which she refused indignantly (ibid.:199). Thereafter, according to Salter, Elkins seems to have interfered with Bates' attempts to obtain a decent stipend from the government to support her researches. Although many high officials recommended that she be appointed as the aborigines' representative to the new government, Bates did not get the position on the ground that the risks involved would be too great for a woman. "For one who has lived alone amongst aborigines, wild and civilized, it was a galling decision, made worse" by the title of honorary protector, an unpaid post, "conferred on her as a consolation prize" (ibid.:195).

Daisy Bates continued to function productively, but there is no doubt that the discipline lost in her a most valuable ethnographer, who constantly insisted that "the native questions should be looked at from the native point of view" (Bates, 1938:25).

Elizabeth Faithorn

The Concept of Pollution Among the Káfe of the Papua New Guinea Highlands

Papua New Guinea, formerly the Australian-administered half of the island of New Guinea, has a population of some 2.5 million people. Nearly half this number live in the extensive Highlands region, their existence unknown to Europeans until the early 1930s, when contact was first established by gold prospectors, government patrol officers, and missionaries. Since that time a growing number of anthropologists have conducted intensive field research among Highlands cultural groups, studying such diverse subjects as kinship systems, political structures, land tenure, sorcery and witchcraft, death ritual, male-female relations, and social change. There are some fifty distinct language groups in the Papua New Guinea Highlands, with minimal contact among these groups because of the rugged mountainous terrain; nevertheless, ethnographers have outlined many features of cultural and social life characteristic of Highlands populations in general.

All Highlanders are horticulturalists, subsisting primarily on a diet of sweet potatoes or yams, supplemented by a variety of other foods such as taro, legumes, corn, pumpkins, bananas, sugarcane, greens, and edible palms. Males and females participate in the daily food-producing activities, and husbands and wives in particular frequently perform interdependent but separate gardening tasks. Some minor hunting and gathering occur for small arboreal mammals, rodents,

The research on which this paper is based was supported by the National Science Foundation. Dissertation Grant # GS-28085.

birds, insects, and wild plants, but these activities are irregular and relatively infrequent.

Highlanders are also pig breeders. Pigs are important items of wealth and are a significant feature of the major cultural rituals, such as marriage, funerals, first menstruation, and initiation ceremonies. Pigs are never slaughtered and cooked simply for food; they are always used to fulfill an obligation to another party. Consequently, households rarely eat their own pigs; rather, they eat pork as recipients of presents from others. Most adults own pigs, and pig raising is an activity dependent upon both female and male labor. Women are generally responsible for the daily gathering of food for the pigs owned by the members of their households, whereas men are expected to build and maintain the pig houses. Men or women may periodically perform various kinds of magic to insure their pigs' health and continued growth.

The most significant unit from the point of view of social structure is the localized residence group, regardless of whether Highlanders live in villages, as in the Eastern Highlands, or in scattered households, as is more typical of the Central and Western Highlands. These groupings, alternatively referred to by anthropologists as clans, clan-villages, parishes, or sibs, are generally composed of a cluster of agnatically related males, and their dependents, who espouse an ideology of patrilineal descent and patrilocal residence.* Nevertheless, there is considerable discrepancy between the ideology and the actual composition of local groups. Kinship in the Highlands is not solely a reflection of biological fact, but a system of social relations providing the organizing principles for the residence group. There is considerable flexibility in residence patterns, and people frequently relocate themselves and their dependents in order to maximize their available resources, usually potential gardening land. When residence is changed,

* Anthropological terminology defined: agnatically related means related through males; patrilineal descent refers to the tracing of descent through the male line; patrilocal residence refers to a married couple living with or near the husband's father.

real or fictive kin ties are activated, providing the newcomers with a place in the ongoing social system.

Most adults in the Highlands expect to marry, though the average age at marriage may vary from one cultural group to the next. Polygynous marriage is found throughout the Highlands; however, monogamy, nowadays as well as in the past, is a more frequent occurrence. Missionaries have discouraged the practice of a man taking more than one wife, and the Highlanders themselves discuss the hazards and difficulties of polygyny, particularly the friction that can develop among co-wives, or between a husband and a wife who feels she has been neglected. Women usually reside in their husbands' villages, although they and their children maintain strong ties with, and obligations to, their own kin, and visiting and gift exchange are frequent.

Political power among the Highlanders is acquired, not inherited, and is based on oratorical skill and proficiency in leading discussions, resolving conflicts, influencing decisions, and maximizing resources. Anthropologists have written of politics as a male domain in the Highlands, and have described the "Big Man" complex as characteristic of Melanesian political systems in general (e.g., Sahlins, 1963). However, in some Highlands societies, as among the Káfe with whom I worked, women also participate in the political decision-making processes, and their influence may extend well beyond their own domestic units.

Another feature of Highlands societies, according to several anthropologists, is the basic aggressiveness of the Highlanders themselves, and in particular the hostile and antagonistic relationship that is purported to exist between men and women (cf. Langness, 1967; Meggitt, 1964; Read, 1965). I have argued elsewhere (Faithorn, in press) that this characterization of intersexual relations may not apply to all Highlands groups, and have suggested that it is an oversimplification of a much more complicated process of interaction. Anthropologists have tended to view Highlands women primarily in their role as wives. Marriage is relatively unstable in the Highlands, and the relationship between husband and wife may be tense, given the interdependence of their major daily activities, and their reliance on one another to fulfill their respective duties in order to enhance their own personal reputations. The potential for friction between spouses—or, more broadly, people who may potentially have a sexual relationship, as defined by the rules of society—is expressed in a variety of ways in both ritual and daily life, and has led to what I believe is the mistaken conclusion that men as a group vis-à-vis women as a group are hostile to one another.

In this paper I wish to focus on the concept of pollution as it relates to the general portrayal of Highlands men and women by anthropologists. I shall first briefly discuss the concept of pollution as it has been used by ethnographers working in the Highlands, and then proceed to a consideration of a similar complex of beliefs regulating the behavior of individuals among the Káfe of the Eastern Highlands. Data collected among the Káfe indicate that the capacity to endanger others through improper management of powerful substances is shared by both men and women. The fact that only women have been recognized by anthropologists as potential polluters, and that the dangers of pollution are seen as threatening only to males, is related to the generally perfunctory and negative ways in which Highlands women are depicted in the enthographic literature.

The Concept of Pollution

In anthropological writings on the Papua New Guinea Highlands, pollution is used in the context of sex and gender, and refers to the capacity that women have to endanger men, through their bodily substances and through their overall femaleness. The traditional segregation of the sexes, menstrual and postpartum taboos, male initiation ceremonies, and rules regulating the frequency and appropriateness of sexual intercourse have been related by anthropologists to the concept of female pollution and to the need for men to avoid potentially dangerous contacts with women.

Although the general tenor of male-female relations clearly

varies from one group to the next in the Highlands, male fears of pollution by women, especially through contact with menstrual blood, are widespread. The most extreme views of women as polluters of men appear to be found among the Mae Enga of the Western Highlands.

> They believe that contact with it [menstrual blood] or a menstruating woman will, in the absence of counter-magic, sicken a man and cause persistent vomiting, turn his blood black, corrupt his vital juices so that his skin darkens, and wrinkles as his flesh wastes, permanently dull his wits, and eventually lead to a slow decline and death. (Meggitt, 1964:207)

In the Central and Eastern Highlands, fears of female pollution are less extreme, and the relations between men and women are described as more complementary than in the Western Highlands. Nevertheless, menstrual and postpartum taboos, as well as social pressure on men to avoid frequent contact with sexually fertile women, prevail everywhere.

Lindenbaum has argued that ideas of female pollution are correlated with population pressure on scarce resources, and that the greater the need for population control the greater the fear of female pollution. Thus "fear of pollution is a form of ideological birth control" (Lindenbaum, 1972:248) limiting male access to women in societies that need to curtail population growth.

I agree with Lindenbaum that

> People are also telling us something of their problems by the way they mix or separate sex and the staple crop. Enga men, with magic to protect them from female pollution, copulate with their wives in the bush . . . Fore males in contrast, purchase love magic to enchant the women they desire, and they copulate in the gardens. (Ibid.:249)

Ecology, social structure and social values are related domains. Nevertheless, I think Lindenbaum's analysis leaves three relevant issues unresolved: (1) the capacity men have to endanger others through improper control of their own powerful substances, particularly semen; (2) the seeming paradox that taboos surrounding sexual intercourse and fears of menstrual blood are most effective in limiting intercourse during periods when a woman is least fertile (during menstruation and nursing), thus promoting a greater frequency of intercourse during the time she may well be ovulating; and (3) the fact that not only may men and women endanger one another, they may also threaten or contaminate others of the same sex, or even themselves.

I have suggested that both men and women are potentially polluting and that the concept of pollution may be relevant in analyzing behavior patterns other than the relations between the sexes. I would like now to illustrate these points by considering data collected among the Káfe, an Eastern Highlands group with whom I lived and worked for nineteen months, from June 1971 through January 1973.

Pollution and Káfe Culture

The Káfe live in villages and homesteads at altitudes of 4,600 to 6,800 feet, scattered mainly throughout the Kamanontina and Dunantina river valleys of the Henganofi Sub-District. These valleys are narrow and steep, and residential and agricultural land has literally been burned out of the bush or dense forest that covers much of the region.

The two villages in which I worked, Hómaya and Báfo, are located at the headwaters of the Dunantina River, and have a total population of nearly four hundred people living in some seventy-five to eighty households. In the past, the Káfe, like most other Highlands groups, maintained separate living quarters for husbands and wives. The adult males of the local residence group lived together in a men's house, often accompanied by their older sons. Their wives each had a separate dwelling in which they lived with their daughters, younger sons, and perhaps a mother-in-law or other female kin. After contact husbands and wives began to reside together in the same house, which is the typical pattern nowadays. However, Káfe houses are internally divided so that husband and wife still maintain separate sleeping quarters.

The most important daily activities are related to food

production and pig raising. Women spend at least part of their time tending their gardens, which may be quite a distance from the village, harvesting sweet potatoes and other foods for the members of their households and their pigs, collecting firewood, and at the end of the day carrying food to the pigs that are housed outside the main village areas. Men may also work in the gardens (particularly if a new one is being prepared), build and maintain the surrounding fences, garden huts, and pig houses, gather firewood, and help their wives herd up and feed the pigs.

Coffee production is another important agricultural activity, and it requires intensive periods of labor by both men and women at various times throughout the growing cycle, particularly when the berries are ripe and must be harvested, fermented, washed, and dried in order to sell to buyers.

Child-rearing is generally an activity that occupies both men and women, though small children remain closely tied to their mothers, or the women who are nursing them, until they are weaned at about three years of age. Different patterns of work and activity according to sex class are learned starting at an early age, young girls accompanying their mothers to the garden and carrying home one small sweet potato in the tiny net bags they hang from their heads when they can barely walk alone. Young boys frequently accompany their fathers to the bush to fell trees for fence building, collect vines for rope, or hunt the small creatures of the forest. Nevertheless, there is really no significant difference in the daily lives of boys and girls—what they are permitted to do or where they are permitted to go—until puberty.

Sexual pollution: female. First menstruation is a very important event for a young women, as it marks the beginning of that period in her life as a sexually potent and fertile female. Accompanying the changes in status and role are specific rules of behavior she must follow in her interactions with others. When a girl first menstruates she is secluded inside her parents' house for a period of about a week, and is allowed to eat only sweet potatoes roasted in the fire. She must abstain from eating sugarcane or from drinking water, apparently to prevent her from menstruating too much in the future. Other young girls of her age group sit with her inside the dark hut and listen to the adult women as they instruct her in her new responsibilities as a maturing female. She is told to work hard, help her parents and "adoptive" parents,* obey her elders, go directly to and from the gardens, not straying off where she might encounter strange young men, and begin preparing for her future adult roles.

She is also instructed about her own sexuality, and cautioned that she must seclude herself each month while she is menstruating, refrain from cooking food, and carefully and properly dispose of the leaves and rags used to absorb her menstrual blood. She is told that during this time she may be extremely dangerous to herself and others if she does not abide by these rules, and that it is her responsibility to see that she does.

After the period of seclusion, the young woman is dressed in new skirts made for her by her mother and adoptive mother, washed, rubbed with pig grease and brought outside to a feast traditionally of pork, but nowadays perhaps of tinned fish and rice, provided by her adoptive parents. She remains for a few days resting within the village before she returns to her arduous daily routine.

As long as she is unmarried, a woman will seclude herself in her parents' house during her menses. After marriage her husband or his kin are expected to build her a special menstrual hut, outside the confines of the village, where she retires for menstruation and also for childbirth. During this time her female friends and relatives bring food they have cooked for her, and she may be expected to return the favor when they are in their menstrual huts. A woman is not permitted to have intercourse with her husband during her menses, for

* In Káfe society, all young girls have, in addition to their own biological parents, a set of "adoptive" parents, who are responsible for helping to raise them to maturity and negotiate their marriages.

fear of endangering him through contact with her menstrual blood. After her menses, she washes herself thoroughly and returns to her own house, though she generally refrains from cooking for another couple of days, relying on others in her household to provide her with food.

When a young woman is to be married, she again is counseled by her elders, particularly her older female relatives, about her duties and responsibilities to others, and cautioned that she must be sure to follow the taboos surrounding menstruation. She is warned particularly not to go into her gardens during her menses, for she may accidentally contaminate the crops and endanger those who eat them. The illness that results should a man, woman, or even a pig ingest or become contaminated by menstrual blood is the same—the skin wrinkles, there is a significant weight loss, general weakness, and if the illness is untreated, perhaps death.

Similar taboos surround childbirth. When a woman is ready to give birth, she retires to her menstrual hut, usually accompanied by another woman to help her during labor, particularly if this is her first child. The blood lost during childbirth is regarded as potent and dangerous in the same ways as menstrual blood, and must be collected and disposed of so that others will not come into contact with it. After birth, the mother washes herself and her child and remains in her menstrual hut for about a week, following the same taboos concerning cooking and handling food that are associated with menstruation. After a week has passed she generally moves into her own house, where she stays for about a month, until the baby's eyes are "clear" and the child is considered strong enough to withstand exposure to the outside world. During the day the woman and her infant may be visited by males and females, friends and relatives, but she is prohibited from cooking food, and her husband may not sleep in the same house with her and the baby.

The placenta is also regarded in the same class of dangerous substances as menstrual blood and blood lost during childbirth. When the umbilical cord is cut after birth, the placenta is generally buried to prevent others from accidentally coming into contact with it. When I was in the field I was asked by the Káfe if it was true that Europeans preserved the placenta after birth, keeping it in a special box in their homes. It had been rumored that this was a common practice, the object being to receive information from the placenta in some mystical way about how to be successful in various life ventures, particularly economic ones. Apparently several sets of parents in Hómaya and Báfo had kept the placentas after the birth of their children but had not received any instructions from them. Nevertheless, the Káfe regard the placenta as potent, and dangerous if improperly handled.

These substances—menstrual blood, blood lost in childbirth, and the placenta—all emanate from the bodies of sexually fertile females, and it is considered every woman's responsibility to see that she does not endanger herself or others through her own carelessness in controlling them.

Sexual pollution: male. Semen is also regarded as dangerous and potent by the Káfe. This seems to be true in other parts of the Highlands as well. Marilyn Strathern, in her discussion of pollution and poison among the Hageners of the Western Highlands, mentions in passing that there is "... danger attributed to menstrual blood or semen out of place" (1972:163), and also claims that one of the rationales for long postpartum taboos in Hagen is the fact that "... semen can pollute the young child" (ibid.:168). Langness (personal communication) has said that among the Bena Bena of the Eastern Highlands semen is regarded as a dangerous and powerful substance and figures as an important element in male initiation ceremonies. Nevertheless, no systematic attention has been paid to semen and the taboos surrounding male sexuality by anthropologists working in the Highlands.

The Káfe regard semen and menstrual blood as the essential elements in the conception of a child. They believe that repeated intercourse is necessary in order to accumulate enough of these substances in the woman's body for conception to occur. Furthermore, in the early stages of pregnancy, intercourse is desirable so that additional semen can help the fetus to grow. Thus semen is an extremely potent substance, and men must control it carefully in order not to endanger themselves or others.

After sexual intercourse, both men and women are required to wash themselves thoroughly to avoid contaminating others with semen and other substances produced by their bodies during copulation. If a couple has had intercourse during the night, the next morning they must both refrain from cooking food for themselves or others as semen might be transmitted to the food and ingested. The illness that results, should this occur, is the same as that caused by the ingestion of menstrual blood.

Care is also taken to avoid the ill effects of male pollution in other contexts as well. Káfe women may refuse to wash their husbands' clothing, particularly their shorts or skirts, for fear of accidentally touching semen that may have gotten on the clothing during or after intercourse. Men as well as women are prohibited from stepping over food, or over people, as they could endanger them in this way.

Such restrictions on the behavior of males, and taboos surrounding male sexuality are clearly related to the fact that men as well as women are regarded by the Káfe as potentially dangerous through mismanagement of the substances produced by their bodies.

Pollution in other contexts. The discussion above has examined the concept of pollution in the context of Káfe beliefs about male and female sexuality and rules regulating sexual behavior. Ideas about pollution are also relevant to the analysis of other kinds of behavioral taboos. A few examples will be briefly discussed to illustrate this point.

There are some behavioral taboos related to pollution that are dependent upon the person's kin relationship to others involved. One such restriction has to do with the cooking of food. If a person sits near the firepit so that his or her "shadow"* falls on the roasting sweet potatoes, for example, his or her spouse, or affinal kin of either sex, may not eat the food. However, consanguineal kin may eat it with no fear of ill effects. The same rules apply to the handling of net bags used to carry food and other goods and valuables. If men or women should sit on their bags, they can no longer use them to carry food for their spouses or affines. They must either destroy the bags or pass them on to their consanguines. A third example has to do with the wearing of one another's clothing. Nowadays, many adults, males and females, wear laplaps, pieces of cloth wrapped around the body and tied at the waist. Consanguines of either sex may each wear others' laplaps, but spouses may not share these items of clothing, nor may other affinal kin. These rules are related to the belief that in general consanguineal kin are inherently less dangerous to one another—inherently less polluting—than individuals who are not related by blood.

Conclusion

The Káfe data indicate that among this Highlands group at any rate, women are not the only polluters, nor are men the only victims of pollution. Furthermore, pollution does not only relate to sexual taboos. Given the cultural similarities between the Káfe and other Highlands groups, it seems reasonable to postulate that this may be true in other Highlands societies as well.

One problem has been that anthropologists working in the Highlands have focused their attention on women as polluting agents, rather than on the substances that, out of proper context, can be polluting. Thus they have not systematically identified what these substances are, or where they come from. The point is that menstrual blood, blood lost in child-

* "Shadow" is not really the correct translation of the Káfe word, but there is no better way to refer to this concept in English. What is meant in this context is a symbolic extension of the body, an intangible substance surrounding the physical body.

birth, the placenta, semen, and perhaps other substances that I have not mentioned, are not inherently polluting, rather they are extremely powerful substances that may be dangerous if not carefully controlled.

Menstrual blood and semen in particular, when properly channeled, are regarded as life-producing forces in society. However, if they are improperly channeled they can cause death. Because these substances emanate from the bodies of women and men, individuals are charged with the responsibility of managing their bodies in such a way as to protect society, including themselves as well as others. Because of their biology, women are potentially more dangerous more of the time than men during the sexually fertile period of the life cycle. However, this does not diminish the very real danger posed by men as well.

The concept of pollution has been very narrowly used by anthropologists working in the Highlands. As Strathern comments:

> "Pollution" should perhaps refer strictly to the transference of ritual uncleanliness, as when persons of lower status contaminate those of higher . . . but its use has become accepted in the Highlands ethnographies to describe the harmful consequences of contact between males and females under certain conditions. (1972:163, n.1)

Furthermore, women as polluters are depicted as weak, disgusting, and inferior to men, who as potential victims of pollution are portrayed as naturally pure and strong. This does not accurately represent the way the Káfe themselves regard women. They say that women are also strong and important in the functioning of society. As one Káfe man put it, women work so hard and so constantly that they are like machines. Another man explained that if it weren't for women, nothing would get done, and society would fall apart. Women themselves regard their strengths and weaknesses as different from those of men, but they do not view themselves as inherently inferior or less important.

If the concept of pollution were used in the analysis of

Highlands societies in the broader sense suggested by Mary Douglas (1966) as related to fundamental disorder, things out of context and hence dangerous and threatening to society, it would then be possible to raise questions concerning the relationship of one set of behavioral taboos to another, and the fundamental nature of society as a symbolic system. For example, taboos relating to the practice of sorcery, and to death and death ritual, also have to do with controlling danger and keeping things in proper context, drawing the boundaries between life and death.

As it stands now, the concept of pollution is only used in reference to sex in the Highlands. In the ethnographic literature women, when discussed in any detail at all, are generally portrayed in rather negative ways. The multiplicity of female roles, the importance of women in daily and ritual life, and their participation in political and economic affairs have, on the whole, been neglected. More attention must be focused on Highlands women in order to correct this negative bias and move on to an analysis of taboos related to pollution in its broadest sense.

Paula Webster

Matriarchy: A Vision of Power

When Esther Newton and I decided to explore the issue of matriarchy, our colleagues were skeptical. They reminded us that the acceptance of the notion of an age of female power had had a short life and an undoubtedly well-deserved death in the nineteenth century. The Victorian school of anthropology, with all of its cultural biases, had no evidence for a matriarchal stage of culture, and contemporary ethnographic data cannot support those early claims. Our own anthropological training had led us to accept, though not without disappointment and some anger, that males had *always* been dominant in society, that even in matrilineal societies this was so. But as feminists we found ourselves in an awkward position. Women in the movement were asking us why women had never been politically powerful, why men had always had higher status, and why a matriarchy was impossible. They insinuated that we had rejected the idea of a matriarchy because we had been brainwashed by the male academic establishment, and the more we thought about it, the more we began to wonder if they were not right. The

This is a revision of a paper written by myself and Esther Newton and called "Matriarchy: Puzzle and Paradigm," presented at the 71st Annual Meeting of the American Anthropological Association, Toronto, 1972. It was later published in APHRA—A Feminist Literary Magazine (Spring/Summer 1973) as "Matriarchy: As Women See It." Since this version is no longer the work of both authors, I accept full responsibility for all changes made. It would have been nicer to have revised it together, but I can only hope that it retains some of its original spirit and energy, which flowed from our passionate collective effort.

least we could do was to discuss with other feminist anthropologists the question of female power and powerlessness and pool whatever information we had about the status of women in other cultures.

In a feminist anthropology collective we struggled with the question of women's universal subordination. Perhaps, as some of our sisters argued, women's high status and contributions to culture have not been recorded because of the male bias of the ethnographers. One of the first papers to start us questioning the universality of women's inferior status was Sally (Slocum) Linton's "Woman the Gatherer" (which appears in this volume). The evidence she presented for a male bias in the reconstruction of early hominid evolution was a little unnerving, for many of us had accepted without question the greater importance of hunting, and, by implication, of the hunter, in Paleolithic society. Linton's paper encouraged us to reexamine our anthropological assumptions about women and to reevaluate the ethnographic data for possible male bias. Once we had become aware of these limitations, we felt we could begin to answer some of our questions. If women's position in different cultures was "better" than the male ethnographers had reported, then maybe a matriarchy *had* once existed. Excited by the prospect, we decided to settle the controversy once and for all.

We began by examining the claims and evidence for the existence of a matriarchy. We assumed that since patriarchy meant the dominance of men as a class over women as a class, then matriarchy would be defined as the mirror opposite: a society in which women as a class had power and authority over men.* We did not expect that hierarchy itself would have been eliminated, but that if someone had to be "on the top" it would be women. This was the social organization we expected to find described by J. J. Bachofen in his *Das Mutterrecht* (1861) and by Frederick Engels in *The Origin of the Family, Private Property, and the State* (1884). Since both authors used the term and asserted it was a universal stage in

* The use of the word *class* is not used in the Marxian sense but as simply a grouping based upon gender.

culture, we thought that we might find in their work sufficient evidence to support the claim of women's past dominance.

Bachofen, using ancient myths as his evidence, writes that after an initial stage of promiscuity, women brought about a matriarchy through the military defeat of lustful males. The social order they created was based on the primacy of the mother—the feminine principle—and was reflected in mother goddess religions emphasizing fertility. Ultimately (and logically, to the male Victorian mind) men rebelled and developed patriarchy, with its emphasis on the "divine father principle." If women had symbolized material nature, then men brought with their dominance "spirituality" (Fee, 1973:27).

Bachofen's work has been appropriately criticized for its lack of empirical data and its substitution of mythology for history. Even the existence of mother goddesses, no matter how well documented in the archeological record, does not automatically prove the existence of an entire social organization based on women's power or fertility, or even higher social status for women (Hultkrantz, 1961:85). It is highly problematic to argue directly from a belief system, or the artistic representations of one, to social organization on the ground when the evidence is so scanty and so open to alternate interpretations. Motherhood has often placed abstract *woman* on a pedestal, but it has at the same time left concrete *women* in the home and powerless. Reverence, a highly ambivalent expression of awe and fear, but most clearly of distance, does not necessarily result from or lead to the high status or power of the revered object that is symbolically presented.

In addition to the problems of methodology, Bachofen's schema reflects the widespread Victorian effort to demonstrate that patriarchy was the logical culmination of civilization, the inevitable result of man's long and difficult struggle with nature and its unbridled passions. Therefore, even if women in their role of mothers had power for a time, the *proper* order of things was achieved when men in the role of fathers took the reins (Fee, 1973:28). Paradoxically, a past age of female power was used to support patriarchal ideology.

Engels, while criticizing Bachofen's mystical causality for its lack of a material basis, applauded his predecessor's pioneering effort to understand the evolution of social forms. For Engels, the matriarchal stage also followed an initial period of promiscuity and was characterized by group marriage. Since the only known parent was the mother, descent was traced through women and men lived with their wives' families. Women, according to this reconstruction, had supremacy in the household, which was the productive unit (though Engels never states explicitly that they had political power as a group).* It was not fertility or religious organization but the social relations of production that gave women high status. The change in property relations from communal to private, with inheritance then traced in the male line, plus the institution of monogamous marriage and the beginning of classes, led to what Engels calls the "world historic defeat of the female sex" (Engels, 1972:120).

From the many useful revisions and critiques of Engels' work, one significant issue emerges which threatens the foundation of his evolutionary structure. Engels points to property relations, with their associated kinship organization, as determining social structure, specifically in relation to male and female power. This explanation seems insufficient since it does not account for the organization of work, the social networks that link people to power, or the differing kinds of subsistence bases that influence the precise division of labor (Schein and Lopate, 1972). What we know about the position of women in societies where property is held and passed on through matrilineages does not conform to Engels' notion of "supremacy" in the household (Schneider and Gough, 1961). In these societies a woman's brother exercises the

* Engels does say that the term "mother-right" is "ill-chosen since at this stage of society there cannot yet be any talk of right in the 'legal' sense" (Engels, 1972:106). I take this to mean that the rule of women *or* men was inconceivable at this time (savagery of lower stage of barbarism), since, according to Engels, power is not a political variable in early communal societies.

power and authority usually reserved for fathers and husbands in patrilineal societies. Since Engels based much of his work on Morgan's study of the matrilineal Iroquois, it is safe to assume that this was the matriarchy that he was describing. Women's social position may have been "better" in matrilineal societies, but we have no evidence to support the claim that women had power.

Although we continued to search for evidence that would prove conclusively that there had been societies in which women had power equal to or greater than the power of men, there did not appear to be sufficient data to prove that such a society existed.* We were therefore left with the question: Why continue to discuss matriarchy if there is no evidence for its past existence?

We do not agree with some of our sisters within anthropology that any attention paid to the matriarchy question is a waste of time at best, or a destructive diversion at worst. The more we read, the clearer it became that matriarchy is the only *vision* we have of a society in which women have power, or at least one in which men do not. As such it forced us to imagine a form of social organization that we had never experienced, and to pose critical questions about the relationship between power, gender, and social structure. We will here review the work of five feminist authors, all of whom discuss the matriarchy issue in their attempts to delineate the status of women in early, pre-class societies.** We will see how

* I think that *any* suggestive leads should be followed in the search for women's history. There is a matriarchal tradition among such classicists as Jane Ellen Harrison, Robert Graves, Erich Neumann, and Mary Renault that should be re-examined. Also the Amazons, a tradition that stresses the daughters rather than the mothers, should not be ruled out as pure fantasy until more archeological and ethnographic work is done in the regions where they are supposed to have existed (see Helen Diner's *Mothers and Amazons*).

** In the original version of this paper we reviewed the work of eight authors, but this has been reduced to five, since they sufficiently represent the different points of view. Our original choice was based on what women in the movement were reading and what anthropologists were writing. We also included Evelyn Reed, Minda Borun et al. (The Philadelphia Collective), and Helen Diner.

their positions as to the existence of matriarchy relate to their explanations of women's present-day oppression; and, given their views of the past, we will see what each author envisions for the future liberation of women. We will focus on the ways in which these authors answer the following questions: (1) Was there ever a matriarchy, defined as class power of women over men? (2) What was the actual position of women in pre-class societies? (3) What are the sources of women's present-day oppression? (4) What is liberation and how will it come about?

Review of the Literature

Eleanor Leacock, an anthropologist and a Marxist, has written an excellent introduction to Engels' *Origin of the Family, Private Property, and the State.* Setting out to evaluate what is still valid in Engels' historical reconstruction of women's past, she states that although Engels used the term "matriarchy," he was actually referring to the matrilineal organization of society before the advent of private property and class relations. Therefore a matriarchy, defined as the class power of women, never existed because power as such was not a component of egalitarian society (Leacock in Engels, 1972:35). Although she questions the universal priority of matrilineal over patrilineal descent systems, Leacock also suggests that in these early societies descent traced through the female line probably conferred more status to women—certainly more than they have in class societies today. Women in pre-class societies were neither oppressed nor exploited. The expression of authority and power did not reflect gender differences. Under the prehistoric conditions of hunting-gathering and horticulture, there existed egalitarian social relations:

> . . . since in primitive communal society decisions were made by those who would be carrying them out, the participation of women in a major share of socially necessary labor did not reduce them to virtual slavery, as is the case in class society, but accorded them decision-making powers commensurate with their contribution. (Ibid.:34)

and

> The significant point for women's status is that the household was communal, and the division of labor between the sexes reciprocal; the economy did not involve the dependence of the wife and children on the husband. . . . (Ibid.:33)

What, then, was the source of women's oppression? Was it childbearing or child-rearing? Leacock claims neither:

> In some ways it is the ultimate alienation in our society that the ability to give birth has been transformed into a liability . . . [the fact that women bear children] was not a handicap even under the limited technology of hunting and gathering life: *it certainly has no relevance today*. (Ibid.:40; my italics)

For Leacock the oppression of women rests upon the "transformation of their socially necessary labor into private service through the separation of the family from the clan" (ibid.:41). It is with the development of private property, and of monogamous marriage within a class society, that women lose their egalitarian position. Liberation will be brought about by the destruction of class society. The specific role that women as a class, or women within their class, are to play in the coming revolution is not developed, but it is suggested that middle-class women make alliances with their working-class sisters around such women's issues as child care, housing, and health. Women's consciousness will promote class consciousness and this will facilitate the attack on the monogamous nuclear family, which is the basic economic unit of class society and the "central buttress of class exploitation" (ibid.:45).

In her article "The Origin of the Family" (1971 and reprinted in this volume), Kathleen Gough, an anthropologist and a Marxist, also concludes that there is no evidence to prove that there ever was a matriarchy, but she argues that it seems that even in hunting societies women are in some ways "the second sex, with greater or lesser subordination to men" (K. Gough, 1971:767), and that "from the start women have been subordinate to men in certain key areas of status, mobility and public leadership" (ibid.:770). Although women were never equal to, much less dominant over men,

> the extent of inequality varied according to ecology and the resulting sexual division of tasks. But in any case it was largely a matter of *survival* rather than man-made cultural imposition. Hence the impressions we receive of dignity, freedom and mutual respect between men and women in primitive hunting and horticultural societies. (Ibid.:770)

How did women lose this "better" position? While not pointing to women's child-bearing role as an agent of her oppression, Gough does indicate that perhaps this and the *cultural elaboration* of the physical differences in strength between men and women might have led to women's subordination. Agreeing with Engels, she says that the shift in property relations, the emergence of the state and of classes gave men power over women "because of their monopoly over weapons, and because freedom from child care allows them to enter specialized economic and political roles, some men—especially ruling class men—acquire power over other men and over women . . ." (ibid.:768). The most interesting part of her explanation of male power in hunting societies ("*shadowy*" as she thinks it is) is its basis on the sexual division of labor and/or the monopoly over heavy weapons that gives men, with their greater strength, the *ultimate control of force.* This is an area that should be further investigated. Do men turn their weapons or their strength against women in primitive societies? Is this strength used as a means of social control? If so, then it seems that anthropologists will have to redefine the term "egalitarian."

For Gough, the exploitation of women will "presumably disappear in post-state, classless society" (ibid.:770). Since we now have the technology to alter the division of labor, to relieve women of the prolonged and exclusive responsibility for child care, and to minimize physical differentials in terms of work, the adaptational imperatives that were operating in pre-class societies will no longer have an effect in subordinating women. The contemporary nuclear family must be altered, although the role women are to play is not worked out.

Both Leacock and Gough use extensive data from both historical and contemporary primitive societies to support their belief that the status of women deteriorates with the rise of class society. While the general assertion is undoubtedly correct, there remain both methodological and empirical questions about this data, and consequently about the status of women in primitive society.

Gough states that in hunting societies women are "less subordinate" in crucial areas of their lives than women in our own society. Men cannot "deny women their sexuality or force it upon them; . . . command or exploit their produce; control or rob them of their children; confine them physically or prevent their movement; or withhold from them large segments of the society's knowledge and cultural attainments" (ibid.:768). Yet there are many ethnographic examples which contradict this view: cases of extreme sexual hostility (most of the New Guinea data); forced sexuality in the form of gang rape (the Cheyenne of the Plains and the Hazda in South-West Africa); general brutality toward women (the Yanamamo of Brazil). Add to this the general cultural devaluation of women in symbolic systems (Ortner:1974) and another picture emerges. To what can we attribute this discrepancy? Contact with Western imperialism? Poor ethnographic reporting? Male bias in reading social relations? Even those anthropologists who have spoken of egalitarian societies define them in terms of equal access to resources, bounded by age and *sex*. What does it mean to women today if there were *no* egalitarian societies in terms of the distribution of power and sex roles?

Feminist anthropologists will have to reevaluate the ethnographic data in order to resolve these empirical dilemmas. However, there is always the possibility that one's ideological stance will influence one's interpretation. As Slocum (in this volume) and others who have turned their attention to the sociology of knowledge point out, one can take the same assortment of ethnographic "facts" and have them support two quite divergent theories. Thus, the "fact" that women are excluded from much of Australian aboriginal ritual life can be seen as either insignificant in light of their role in subsistence activities, or as yet another example of subordination and of the exclusion from the culturally valued activities of the group. There are some feminists who will use their data to demonstrate women's universal subordination and powerlessness because this adds weight to their belief in the inadequacies of the Marxist model of pre-class egalitarianism, their distrust of what they see as economic determinism, and their criticism of sexual "equality" in contemporary socialist countries. Feminists who accept the Marxist model, on the other hand, may seek to expand it to take account of the apparent contradiction between the symbolic devaluation of women in cultures where women's contribution to production is substantial and even critical for survival. Feminists must thus approach ethnographic materials very critically; there are no simple solutions, and reductionist models—whether economic, idealist, or psychobiological—that attempt to account for women's position in *all* societies only limit our analysis.

Furthermore, if a reexamination of the data finds women everywhere are subordinated to men and are without political power, and if these conditions seem *not* to be related to such outside factors as contact with Western civilization, then we must expand our theoretical constructs and reformulate our political strategies.

Some authors *do* believe that women have been universally oppressed. Simone de Beauvoir in *The Second Sex* (1953) and Shulamith Firestone in *The Dialectic of Sex* (1970) both see the original and root cause of women's oppression in the biologically given unequal distribution of reproductive labor. Because of reproduction and associated child-care burdens, woman has always been restricted to a maintaining, nurturing role, while man has appropriated the creative, and for de Beauvoir transcendent, role:

> The Golden Age of woman is only a myth. To say that woman was the other is to say that there did not exist between the sexes a reciprocal relation: Earth, Mother, Goddess—she was no fellow creature in man's eyes; it was beyond the human realm that her power was confirmed and she was therefore outside that realm. Society has always been male; political power has always been in the hands of men. (de Beauvoir, 1952:64-65)

However, de Beauvoir believes that woman's status declined even further in class society and, leaving the problem of biology unsolved, she calls for a socialist revolution as a necessary step toward liberation. Writing much later, Firestone goes beyond the "necessary revolution" to advocate the elimination of inequality through test-tube babies and the complete redistribution of child-care functions. For Firestone *all* forms of hierarchy are ultimately based on the sex distinction and should be done away with, including culture itself. The end goal is "cosmic consciousness." How are women to make sure that revolutionary changes are made in their best interests? Firestone assumes that those in power will have "good intentions" (Firestone, 1970:206).

De Beauvoir and Firestone agree that women have always been the "Other," that their female role, conditioned by childbearing and child-rearing, has always been evaluated as less important, and thus that women have remained socially powerless. The only author who does not accept the universal powerlessness of women is Elizabeth Gould Davis. In her very controversial book, *The First Sex* (1971), Davis claims that women once held power over men in both the public and private spheres. Her bold argument for women's past supremacy is based on very questionable interpretations of history, archaeology, anthropology, biology, and mythology. Davis, like Bachofen, uses myth as history and believes that the religious organization of society determined the form of its social organization. Her reconstruction of history is unique, fantastic, and provocative. Its importance to feminists lies not in its historical veracity, which is doubtful, but in its vision of the domain of women's power.*

According to Davis, the great civilizations of Sumer, Crete, and Egypt grew out of the city-states that women established after they invented the incest taboo and exogamy to control the lust of their sons (an interesting reversal of Freud). The excluded males, uncivilized and violent, existed on the periphery of the "gynocracies" but finally overthrew them in a state of fury:

> Suddenly all is ended. Paradise is lost. A dark age overtakes the world—a dark age brought on by the cataclysm accompanied by a patriarchal revolution. Nomads, barbaric and uncivilized, roving bands of ejected, womanless men, destroy civilized city-states, depose queens, and attempt to rule in their stead. The result is chaos. War and violence make their appearance, justice and law fly out the window, might replaces right, and the Great Goddess is replaced by a stern and vengeful God, man becomes carnivorous, property rights become paramount over human rights, woman is degraded and exploited and civilization starts on the downward path that it still pursues. (Davis, 1971:68-69)

The matriarchy, according to this reconstruction, was not a mirror image of the patriarchy that followed it, for the society that Davis describes was harmonious and spiritual. How does she explain the difference? She does not point to the class system, though she mentions property rights, but instead refers to the "innate moral superiority of women." The cause of oppression, then, is the male principle which brought about the military defeat of women and continued to enslave them in a male, materialist society. Child bearing and rearing have an important place in this schema, but not as a cause of oppression: a woman's higher prestige and status rests specifically on her ability to be a mother. Their reproductive abilities and consequent attachment to life over

* The recent focus on women's power has not been confined to the matriarchy debate. A number of feminists are looking at women's power within male-dominated societies (Friedl, 1967; Singer, 1972; Denitch, 1971; Shapiro, 1971; Lewin et al., 1971). But this work is *re*visionary rather than visionary. For a critical review of Davis's visionary work, see Hackett and Pomeroy, 1973.

death, creation over destruction, and harmony over conflict make women innately different from, and superior to, men. These psychological and/or temperamental differences transcend time, place, and material conditions. In this view, how will women attain their liberation? Since women were originally overthrown by force, one would expect Davis to call for a new Amazon army to redress the situation, but she avoids this by claiming that patriarchy is bringing about its own destruction. When this has been accomplished, "woman will once again be the pivot—not as sex but divine woman—about whom the next civilization will, as of old, revolve" (ibid.:339).

Davis's vision, apocalyptic and utopian, has numerous methodological problems, but its internal contradictions are far more interesting. The fundamental problem has to do with the use of power. If women are to be supreme, won't men be necessarily subordinate? *Can* power in the hands of women be wholly different from what it has been in the hands of men?* Is gender more important than social structure in determining the way in which power is used? Is it impossible to have a balance of power? For Davis, no reforms of the "sick" civilization based on "masculist" principles are possible. The spiritual force of women is the only cure for the social body: "Only the overthrow of the three-thousand-year-old beast of masculist materialism will save the race" (ibid.:339). The contradictions are resolved by the assurance that women will be benevolent rulers.

In spite of the many differences between the authors (including political ideology and academic training), there are two areas of agreement. Each wants to see an end to the oppression of women, and each wants a radically new society in which technology will be used for human ends. Yet when the issue is one of power and how it will be distributed in the

* As far as we know, the only feminist to work out power in the hands of women to a logical, if unlikely, conclusion is Valerie Solanis (1967), who advocated the overthrow of patriarchy by the simple means of physically eliminating men, except for reproductive or exhibition purposes. If men are eliminated, so is sex oppression.

"new" society, a fundamental vagueness emerges. There is a tendency to *hope* that with a socialist revolution and the destruction of class society the structural basis for equality will be established. But what does this mean? Does it mean that sex distinctions, including roles, will be eliminated, so that women and men will in some sense be the "same"? Or does it mean a "balance" of power? What kind of social organization will insure such a balance? What role will women play in bringing it about? Can women's oppression as a group be ended *without* women holding power as a group? These are the questions that remain to be explored if we are to proceed to a future that will alter significantly the power distribution of the present.

The first thing that becomes apparent after reading the literature on the position of women in society (past and present) is the need for sharper, explicit, and cross-culturally applicable definitions of power, authority, influence, and status. Our own male-biased socialization as women and as anthropologists has allowed us to accept and use conceptually limited descriptions of social reality. We need to develop new concepts to identify clearly the areas of women's power and the factors that facilitate or obstruct its exercise.

Second, we have to evaluate the relative importance of revisionary work that seeks to locate women's power within male-dominated societies, and of visionary work that seeks to create new models of society. The recent research of feminist historians and anthropologists helps us identify the variables that relate to women's power in particular cultures and at specific times in history. It reveals that in some cultural contexts and under some conditions women have more power, more prestige, or more influence than originally assumed. From this we *may* conclude that women are not necessarily universally, or at least not equally, oppressed. But the data, and the theories that are constructed around them, do not provide guides for action or visions of the future in which our liberation is posited as a given.

For this reason many have turned to examine the socialist countries' efforts to create "equality." Although radical social changes have been effected in China and Cuba, we will have to see if men under socialism will give up their power, and if women will share it. We will have to investigate how a balance of power functions, if women in power are treated like men, if women's participation in government is restricted to women's caucuses. Until we can answer these questions we will not be able to predict how sex roles and the distribution of power will change in the future.

If it is the future that interests us, what is the value of a vision of the past? Whatever past history women think they had (primitive matriarchy, communal egalitarianism, or ubiquitous and unrelenting inequality), none produces a blueprint for the future. Even utopian literature (written for the most part by men) in no way satisfactorily resolves the issues of power for women.*

Though the matriarchy debate revolves around the past, its real value lies in the future: not as a model for a future society, for ultimately it doesn't resolve the problems of hierarchy, sex oppression, or class relations, and not in its mythic evocation of past glories, but in its rejection of power in the hands of men, regardless of the form of social organization. It pushes women (and men) to imagine a society that is not patriarchal, one in which women might for the first time have power over their lives. Women have been powerless, and have had their reality defined for them, for so long that imagining such a society is politically important. Because the matriarchy discussion uncovers the inadequacies of old paradigms, it encourages women to create new ones.

In the process of building these new paradigms, we will have to reexamine old theories, weigh old and new evidence, initiate new research. Our history has been denied us; it is yet to be written. Whatever we can learn from this work must be shared with all women, inside and outside the academic com-

* For an interesting discussion of the male vision of Utopia see Daphne Patai (1974). A brilliant exception to these male visions is *Les Guérillères* by Monique Wittig (1973).

munity. I would not encourage women to confuse myth with history or exchange vision for science, for the creative energy that each affords the other should not be lost. Thus, even if feminists reject the existence of matriarchy on empirical and/or theoretical grounds, we should acknowledge the importance of the vision of matriarchy and use the debate for furthering the creation of feminist theory and action.

Gayle Rubin

The Traffic in Women: Notes on the "Political Economy" of Sex

The literature on women—both feminist and anti-feminist—is a long rumination on the question of the nature and genesis of women's oppression and social subordination. The question is not a trivial one, since the answers given it determine our visions of the future, and our evaluation of whether or not it is realistic to hope for a sexually egalitarian society. More importantly, the analysis of the causes of women's oppression forms the basis for any assessment of just what would have to be changed in order to achieve a society without gender hierarchy. Thus, if innate male aggression and dominance are at the root of female oppression, then the feminist program would logically require either the extermination of the offending sex, or else a eugenics project to modify its character. If sexism is a by-product of capitalism's relentless appetite for profit, then sexism would wither away in the advent of a successful socialist revolution. If the world histor-

Acknowledgments are an inadequate expression of how much this paper, like most, is the product of many minds. They are also necessary to free others of the responsibility for what is ultimately a personal vision of a collective conversation. I want to free and thank the following persons: Tom Anderson and Arlene Gorelick, with whom I co-authored the paper from which this one evolved; Rayna Reiter, Larry Shields, Ray Kelly, Peggy White, Norma Diamond, Randy Reiter, Frederick Wyatt, Anne Locksley, Juliet Mitchell, and Susan Harding, for countless conversations and ideas; Marshall Sahlins, for the revelation of anthropology; Lynn Eden, for sardonic editing; the members of Women's Studies 340/004, for my initiation into teaching; Sally Brenner, for heroic typing; Susan Lowes, for incredible patience; and Emma Goldman, for the title.

ical defeat of women occurred at the hands of an armed patriarchal revolt, then it is time for Amazon guerrillas to start training in the Adirondacks.

It lies outside the scope of this paper to conduct a sustained critique of some of the currently popular explanations of the genesis of sexual inequality—theories such as the popular evolution exemplified by *The Imperial Animal*, the alleged overthrow of prehistoric matriarchies, or the attempt to extract all of the phenomena of social subordination from the first volume of *Capital*. Instead, I want to sketch some elements of an alternate explanation of the problem.

Marx once asked: "What is a Negro slave? A man of the black race. The one explanation is as good as the other. A Negro is a Negro. He only becomes a slave in certain relations. A cotton spinning jenny is a machine for spinning cotton. It becomes *capital* only in certain relations. Torn from these relationships it is no more capital than gold in itself is money or sugar is the price of sugar" (Marx, 1971b:28). One might paraphrase: What is a domesticated woman? A female of the species. The one explanation is as good as the other. A woman is a woman. She only becomes a domestic, a wife, a chattel, a playboy bunny, a prostitute, or a human dictaphone in certain relations. Torn from these relationships, she is no more the helpmate of man than gold in itself is money . . . etc. What then are these relationships by which a female becomes an oppressed woman? The place to begin to unravel the system of relationships by which women become the prey of men is in the overlapping works of Claude Lévi-Strauss and Sigmund Freud. The domestication of women, under other names, is discussed at length in both of their *oeuvres*. In reading through these works, one begins to have a sense of a systematic social apparatus which takes up females as raw materials and fashions domesticated women as products. Neither Freud nor Lévi-Strauss sees his work in this light, and certainly neither turns a critical glance upon the processes he describes. Their analyses and descriptions must be read, therefore, in something like the way in which Marx read the classical political economists who preceded him (on this, see Althusser and Balibar, 1970:11-69). Freud and Lévi-Strauss are in some sense analogous to Ricardo and Smith: They see neither the implications of what they are saying, nor the implicit critique which their work can generate when subjected to a feminist eye. Nevertheless, they provide conceptual tools with which one can build descriptions of the part of social life which is the locus of the oppression of women, of sexual minorities, and of certain aspects of human personality within individuals. I call that part of social life the "sex/gender system," for lack of a more elegant term. As a preliminary definition, a "sex/gender system" is the set of arrangements by which a society transforms biological sexuality into products of human activity, and in which these transformed sexual needs are satisfied.

The purpose of this essay is to arrive at a more fully developed definition of the sex/gender system, by way of a somewhat idiosyncratic and exegetical reading of Lévi-Strauss and Freud. I use the word "exegetical" deliberately. The dictionary defines "exegesis" as a "critical explanation or analysis; especially, interpretation of the Scriptures." At times, my reading of Lévi-Strauss and Freud is freely interpretive, moving from the explicit content of a text to its presuppositions and implications. My reading of certain psychoanalytic texts is filtered through a lens provided by Jacques Lacan, whose own interpretation of the Freudian scripture has been heavily influenced by Lévi-Strauss.*

I will return later to a refinement of the definition of a sex/gender system. First, however, I will try to demonstrate

* Moving between Marxism, structuralism, and psychoanalysis produces a certain clash of epistemologies. In particular, structuralism is a can from which worms crawl out all over the epistemological map. Rather than trying to cope with this problem, I have more or less ignored the fact that Lacan and Lévi-Strauss are among the foremost living ancestors of the contemporary French intellectual revolution (see Foucault, 1970). It would be fun, interesting, and, if this were France, essential, to start my argument from the center of the structuralist maze and work my way out from there, along the lines of a "dialectical theory of signifying practices" (see Hefner, 1974).

the need for such a concept by discussing the failure of classical Marxism to fully express or conceptualize sex oppression. This failure results from the fact that Marxism, as a theory of social life, is relatively unconcerned with sex. In Marx's map of the social world, human beings are workers, peasants, or capitalists; that they are also men and women is not seen as very significant. By contrast, in the maps of social reality drawn by Freud and Lévi-Strauss, there is a deep recognition of the place of sexuality in society, and of the profound differences between the social experience of men and women.

Marx

There is no theory which accounts for the oppression of women—in its endless variety and monotonous similarity, cross-culturally and throughout history—with anything like the explanatory power of the Marxist theory of class oppression. Therefore, it is not surprising that there have been numerous attempts to apply Marxist analysis to the question of women. There are many ways of doing this. It has been argued that women are a reserve labor force for capitalism, that women's generally lower wages provide extra surplus to a capitalist employer, that women serve the ends of capitalist consumerism in their roles as administrators of family consumption, and so forth.

However, a number of articles have tried to do something much more ambitious—to locate the oppression of women in the heart of the capitalist dynamic by pointing to the relationship between housework and the reproduction of labor (see Benston, 1969; Dalla Costa, 1972; Larguia and Dumoulin, 1972; Gerstein, 1973; Vogel, 1973; Secombe, 1974; Gardiner, 1974; Rowntree, M. & J., 1970). To do this is to place women squarely in the definition of capitalism, the process in which capital is produced by the extraction of surplus value from labor by capital.

Briefly, Marx argued that capitalism is distinguished from all other modes of production by its unique aim: the creation and expansion of capital. Whereas other modes of production might find their purpose in making useful things to satisfy human needs, or in producing a surplus for a ruling nobility, or in producing to insure sufficient sacrifice for the edification of the gods, capitalism produces capital. Capitalism is a set of social relations—forms of property, and so forth—in which production takes the form of turning money, things, and people into capital. And capital is a quantity of goods or money which, when exchanged for labor, reproduces and augments itself by extracting unpaid labor, or surplus value, from labor and into itself.

> The result of the capitalist production process is neither a mere product (use-value) nor a *commodity*, that is, a use-value which has exchange value. Its result, its product, is the creation of *surplus-value* for capital, and consequently the actual *transformation* of money or commodity into capital. . . ." (Marx, 1969:399; italics in the original)

The exchange between capital and labor which produces surplus value, and hence capital, is highly specific. The worker gets a wage; the capitalist gets the things the worker has made during his or her time of employment. If the total value of the things the worker has made exceeds the value of his or her wage, the aim of capitalism has been achieved. The capitalist gets back the cost of the wage, plus an increment—surplus value. This can occur because the wage is determined not by the value of what the laborer makes, but by the value of what it takes to keep him or her going—to reproduce him or her from day to day, and to reproduce the entire work force from one generation to the next. Thus, surplus value is the difference between what the laboring class produces as a whole, and the amount of that total which is recycled into maintaining the laboring class.

> The capital given in exchange for labour power is converted into necessaries, by the consumption of which the muscles, nerves, bones, and brains of existing labourers are reproduced, and new labourers are begotten . . . the individual consumption of the labourer, whether it proceed within the workshop or outside it,

> whether it be part of the process of production or not, forms therefore a factor of the production and reproduction of capital; just as cleaning machinery does. . . . (Marx, 1972:572)

> Given the individual, the production of labour-power consists in his reproduction of himself or his maintenance. For his maintenance he requires a given quantity of the means of subsistence. . . . Labour-power sets itself in action only by working. But thereby a definite quantity of human muscle, brain, nerve, etc., is wasted, and these require to be restored. . . . (Ibid.:171)

The amount of the difference between the reproduction of labor power and its products depends, therefore, on the determination of what it takes to reproduce that labor power. Marx tends to make that determination on the basis of the quantity of commodities—food, clothing, housing, fuel—which would be necessary to maintain the health, life, and strength of a worker. But these commodities must be consumed before they can be sustenance, and they are not immediately in consumable form when they are purchased by the wage. Additional labor must be performed upon these things before they can be turned into people. Food must be cooked, clothes cleaned, beds made, wood chopped, etc. Housework is therefore a key element in the process of the reproduction of the laborer from whom surplus value is taken. Since it is usually women who do housework, it has been observed that it is through the reproduction of labor power that women are articulated into the surplus value nexus which is the *sine qua non* of capitalism.* It can be further argued that since no wage is paid for housework, the labor of women in the home contributes to the ultimate quantity of surplus value realized

* A lot of the debate on women and housework has centered around the question of whether or not housework is "productive" labor. Strictly speaking, housework is not ordinarily "productive" in the technical sense of the term (I. Gough, 1972; Marx, 1969:387-413). But this distinction is irrelevant to the main line of the argument. Housework may not be "productive," in the sense of directly producing surplus value and capital, and yet be a crucial element in the production of surplus value and capital.

by the capitalist. But to explain women's usefulness to capitalism is one thing. To argue that this usefulness explains the genesis of the oppression of women is quite another. It is precisely at this point that the analysis of capitalism ceases to explain very much about women and the oppression of women.

Women are oppressed in societies which can by no stretch of the imagination be described as capitalist. In the Amazon valley and the New Guinea highlands, women are frequently kept in their place by gang rape when the ordinary mechanisms of masculine intimidation prove insufficient. "We tame our women with the banana," said one Mundurucu man (Murphy, 1959:195). The ethnographic record is littered with practices whose effect is to keep women "in their place" —men's cults, secret initiations, arcane male knowledge, etc. And pre-capitalist, feudal Europe was hardly a society in which there was no sexism. Capitalism has taken over, and rewired, notions of male and female which predate it by centuries. No analysis of the reproduction of labor power under capitalism can explain foot-binding, chastity belts, or any of the incredible array of Byzantine, fetishized indignities, let alone the more ordinary ones, which have been inflicted upon women in various times and places. The analysis of the reproduction of labor power does not even explain why it is usually women who do domestic work in the home, rather than men.

In this light it is interesting to return to Marx's discussion of the reproduction of labor. What is necessary to reproduce the worker is determined in part by the biological needs of the human organism, in part by the physical conditions of the place in which it lives, and in part by cultural tradition. Marx observed that beer is necessary for the reproduction of the English working class, and wine necessary for the French.

> ... *the number and extent of his [the worker's] so-called necessary wants, as also the modes of satisfying them, are themselves the product of historical development,* and depend therefore to a great extent on the degree of civilization of a country, more

> particularly on the conditions under which, and consequently on the habits and degree of comfort in which, the class of free labourers has been formed. *In contradistinction therefore to the case of other commodities, there enters into the determination of the value of labour-power a historical and moral element....* (Marx, 1972:171, my italics)

It is precisely this "historical and moral element" which determines that a "wife" is among the necessities of a worker, that women rather than men do housework, and that capitalism is heir to a long tradition in which women do not inherit, in which women do not lead, and in which women do not talk to god. It is this "historical and moral element" which presented capitalism with a cultural heritage of forms of masculinity and femininity. It is within this "historical and moral element" that the entire domain of sex, sexuality, and sex oppression is subsumed. And the briefness of Marx's comment only serves to emphasize the vast area of social life which it covers and leaves unexamined. Only by subjecting this "historical and moral element" to analysis can the structure of sex oppression be delineated.

Engels

In *The Origin of the Family, Private Property, and the State*, Engels sees sex oppression as part of capitalism's heritage from prior social forms. Moreover, Engels integrates sex and sexuality into his theory of society. *Origin* is a frustrating book. Like the nineteenth-century tomes on the history of marriage and the family which it echoes, the state of the evidence in *Origin* renders it quaint to a reader familiar with more recent developments in anthropology. Nevertheless, it is a book whose considerable insight should not be overshadowed by its limitations. The idea that the "relations of sexuality" can and should be distinguished from the "relations of production" is not the least of Engels' intuitions:

> According to the materialistic conception, the determining factor in history is, in the final instance, the production and repro-

> duction of immediate life. *This again, is of a twofold character: on the one hand, the production of the means of existence, of food, clothing, and shelter and the tools necessary for that production; on the other side, the production of human beings themselves,* the propagation of the species. The social organization under which the people of a particular historical epoch and a particular country live is determined by both kinds of production: by the stage of development of labor on the one hand, and of the family on the other ... (Engels, 1972:71-72; my italics)

This passage indicates an important recognition—that a human group must do more than apply its activity to reshaping the natural world in order to clothe, feed, and warm itself. We usually call the system by which elements of the natural world are transformed into objects of human consumption the "economy." But the needs which are satisfied by economic activity even in the richest, Marxian sense, do not exhaust fundamental human requirements. A human group must also reproduce itself from generation to generation. The needs of sexuality and procreation must be satisfied as much as the need to eat, and one of the most obvious deductions which can be made from the data of anthropology is that these needs are hardly ever satisfied in any "natural" form, any more than are the needs for food. Hunger is hunger, but what counts as food is culturally determined and obtained. Every society has some form of organized economic activity. Sex is sex, but what counts as sex is equally culturally determined and obtained. Every society also has a sex/gender system—a set of arrangements by which the biological raw material of human sex and procreation is shaped by human, social intervention and satisfied in a conventional manner, no matter how bizarre some of the conventions may be.*

* That some of them are pretty bizarre, from our point of view, only demonstrates the point that sexuality is expressed through the intervention of culture (see Ford and Beach, 1972). Some examples may be chosen from among the exotica in which anthropologists delight.

The realm of human sex, gender, and procreation has been subjected to, and changed by, relentless social activity for millennia. Sex as we know it—gender identity, sexual desire and fantasy, concepts of childhood—is itself a social product. We need to understand the relations of its production, and forget, for awhile, about food, clothing, automobiles, and transistor radios. In most Marxist tradition, and even in Engels' book, the concept of the "second aspect of material life" has tended to fade into the background, or to be incorporated into the usual notions of "material life." Engels' suggestion has never been followed up and subjected to the refinement which it needs. But he does indicate the existence and importance of the domain of social life which I want to call the sex/gender system.

Among the Banaro, marriage involves several socially sanctioned sexual partnerships. When a woman is married, she is initiated into intercourse by the sib-friend of her groom's father. After bearing a child by this man, she begins to have intercourse with her husband. She also has an institutionalized partnership with the sib-friend of her husband. A man's partners include his wife, the wife of his sib-friend, and the wife of his sib-friend's son (Thurnwald, 1916). Multiple intercourse is a more pronounced custom among the Marind Anim. At the time of marriage, the bride has intercourse with all of the members of the groom's clan, the groom coming last. Every major festival is accompanied by a practice known as *otiv-bombari,* in which semen is collected for ritual purposes. A few women have intercourse with many men, and the resulting semen is collected in coconut-shell buckets. A Marind male is subjected to multiple homosexual intercourse during initiation (Van Baal, 1966). Among the Etoro, heterosexual intercourse is taboo for between 205 and 260 days a year (Kelly, 1974). In much of New Guinea, men fear copulation and think that it will kill them if they engage in it without magical precautions (Glasse, 1971; Meggitt, 1970). Usually, such ideas of feminine pollution express the subordination of women. But symbolic systems contain internal contradictions, whose logical extensions sometimes lead to inversions of the propositions on which a system is based. In New Britain, men's fear of sex is so extreme that rape appears to be feared by men rather than women. Women run after the men, who flee from them, women are the sexual aggressors, and it is bridegrooms who are reluctant (Goodale and Chowning, 1971). Other interesting sexual variations can be found in Yalmon (1963) and K. Gough (1959).

Other names have been proposed for the sex/gender system. The most common alternatives are "mode of reproduction" and "patriarchy." It may be foolish to quibble about terms, but both of these can lead to confusion. All three proposals have been made in order to introduce a distinction between "economic" systems and "sexual" systems, and to indicate that sexual systems have a certain autonomy and cannot always be explained in terms of economic forces. "Mode of reproduction," for instance, has been proposed in opposition to the more familiar "mode of production." But this terminology links the "economy" to production, and the sexual system to "reproduction." It reduces the richness of either system, since "productions" and "reproductions" take place in both. Every mode of production involves reproduction—of tools, labor, and social relations. We cannot relegate all of the multi-faceted aspects of social reproduction to the sex system. Replacement of machinery is an example of reproduction in the economy. On the other hand, we cannot limit the sex system to "reproduction" in either the social or biological sense of the term. A sex/gender system is not simply the reproductive moment of a "mode of production." The formation of gender identity is an example of production in the realm of the sexual system. And a sex/gender system involves more than the "relations of procreation," reproduction in the biological sense.

The term "patriarchy" was introduced to distinguish the forces maintaining sexism from other social forces, such as capitalism. But the use of "patriarchy" obscures other distinctions. Its use is analagous to using capitalism to refer to all modes of production, whereas the usefulness of the term "capitalism" lies precisely in that it distinguishes between the different systems by which societies are provisioned and organized. Any society will have some system of "political economy." Such a system may be egalitarian or socialist. It may be class stratified, in which case the oppressed class may consist of serfs, peasants, or slaves. The oppressed class may consist of wage laborers, in which case the system is properly labeled "capitalist." The power of the term lies in its implication that, in fact, there are alternatives to capitalism.

Similarly, any society will have some systematic ways to deal with sex, gender, and babies. Such a system may be sexually egalitarian, at least in theory, or it may be "gender stratified," as seems to be the case for most or all of the known examples. But it is important—even in the face of a depressing history—to maintain a distinction between the human capacity and necessity to create a sexual world, and the empirically oppressive ways in which sexual worlds have been organized. Patriarchy subsumes both meanings into the same term. Sex/gender system, on the other hand, is a neutral term which refers to the domain and indicates that oppression is not inevitable in that domain, but is the product of the specific social relations which organize it.

Finally, there are gender-stratified systems which are not adequately described as patriarchal. Many New Guinea societies (Enga, Maring, Bena Bena, Huli, Melpa, Kuma, Gahuku-Gama, Fore, Marind Anim, ad nauseum; see Berndt, 1962; Langness, 1967; Rappaport, 1975; Read, 1952; Meggitt, 1970; Glasse, 1971; Strathern, 1972; Reay, 1959; Van Baal, 1966; Lindenbaum, 1973) are viciously oppressive to women. But the power of males in these groups is not founded on their roles as fathers or patriarchs, but on their collective adult maleness, embodied in secret cults, men's houses, warfare, exchange networks, ritual knowledge, and various initiation procedures. Patriarchy is a specific form of male dominance, and the use of the term ought to be confined to the Old Testament-type pastoral nomads from whom the term comes, or groups like them. Abraham was a Patriarch—one old man whose absolute power over wives, children, herds, and dependents was an aspect of the institution of fatherhood, as defined in the social group in which he lived.

Whichever term we use, what is important is to develop concepts to adequately describe the social organization of sexuality and the reproduction of the conventions of sex and gender. We need to pursue the project Engels abandoned when he located the subordination of women in a development within the mode of production.* To do this, we can imitate Engels in his method rather than in his results. Engels approached the task of analyzing the "second aspect of material life" by way of an examination of a theory of kinship systems. Kinship systems are and do many things. But they are made up of, and reproduce, concrete forms of socially organized sexuality. Kinship systems are observable and empirical forms of sex/gender systems.

Kinship
(On the part played by sexuality in the transition from ape to "man")

To an anthropologist, a kinship system is not a list of biological relatives. It is a system of categories and statuses which often contradict actual genetic relationships. There are dozens of examples in which socially defined kinship statuses take precedence over biology. The Nuer custom of "woman marriage" is a case in point. The Nuer define the status of fatherhood as belonging to the person in whose name cattle bridewealth is given for the mother. Thus, a woman can be married to another woman, and be husband to the wife and father of her children, despite the fact that she is not the inseminator (Evans-Pritchard, 1951:107-09).

In pre-state societies, kinship is the idiom of social interaction, organizing economic, political, and ceremonial, as well as sexual, activity. One's duties, responsibilities, and

* Engels thought that men acquired wealth in the form of herds and, wanting to pass this wealth to their own children, overthrew "mother right" in favor of patrilineal inheritance. "The overthrow of mother right was the *world historical defeat of the female sex.* The man took command in the home also; the woman was degraded and reduced to servitude; she became the slave of his lust and a mere instrument for the production of children" (Engels, 1972:120-21; italics in original). As has been often pointed out, women do not necessarily have significant social authority in societies practicing matrilineal inheritance (Schneider and Gough, 1962).

privileges vis-à-vis others are defined in terms of mutual kinship or lack thereof. The exchange of goods and services, production and distribution, hostility and solidarity, ritual and ceremony, all take place within the organizational structure of kinship. The ubiquity and adaptive effectiveness of kinship has led many anthropologists to consider its invention, along with the invention of language, to have been the developments which decisively marked the discontinuity between semi-human hominids and human beings (Sahlins, 1960; Livingstone, 1969; Lévi-Strauss, 1969).

While the idea of the importance of kinship enjoys the status of a first principle in anthropology, the internal workings of kinship systems have long been a focus for intense controversy. Kinship systems vary wildly from one culture to the next. They contain all sorts of bewildering rules which govern whom one may or may not marry. Their internal complexity is dazzling. Kinship systems have for decades provoked the anthropological imagination into trying to explain incest taboos, cross-cousin marriage, terms of descent, relationships of avoidance or forced intimacy, clans and sections, taboos on names—the diverse array of items found in descriptions of actual kinship systems. In the nineteenth century, several thinkers attempted to write comprehensive accounts of the nature and history of human sexual systems (see Fee, 1973). One of these was *Ancient Society*, by Lewis Henry Morgan. It was this book which inspired Engels to write *The Origin of the Family, Private Property, and the State.* Engels' theory is based upon Morgan's account of kinship and marriage.

In taking up Engels' project of extracting a theory of sex oppression from the study of kinship, we have the advantage of the maturation of ethnology since the nineteenth century. We also have the advantage of a peculiar and particularly appropriate book, Lévi-Strauss' *The Elementary Structures of Kinship.* This is the boldest twentieth-century version of the nineteenth-century project to understand human marriage. It is a book in which kinship is explicitly conceived of as an imposition of cultural organization upon the facts of biological procreation. It is permeated with an awareness of the importance of sexuality in human society. It is a description of society which does not assume an abstract, genderless human subject. On the contrary, the human subject in Lévi-Strauss's work is always either male or female, and the divergent social destinies of the two sexes can therefore be traced. Since Lévi-Strauss sees the essence of kinship systems to lie in an exchange of women between men, he constructs an implicit theory of sex oppression. Aptly, the book is dedicated to the memory of Lewis Henry Morgan.

"*Vile and precious merchandise*"
—*Monique Wittig*

The Elementary Structures of Kinship is a grand statement on the origin and nature of human society. It is a treatise on the kinship systems of approximately one-third of the ethnographic globe. Most fundamentally, it is an attempt to discern the structural principles of kinship. Lévi-Strauss argues that the application of these principles (summarized in the last chapter of *Elementary Structures*) to kinship data reveals an intelligible logic to the taboos and marriage rules which have perplexed and mystified Western anthropologists. He constructs a chess game of such complexity that it cannot be recapitulated here. But two of his chess pieces are particularly relevant to women—the "gift" and the incest taboo, whose dual articulation adds up to his concept of the exchange of women.

The Elementary Structures is in part a radical gloss on another famous theory of primitive social organization, Mauss' *Essay on the Gift* (See also Sahlins, 1972:Chap. 4). It was Mauss who first theorized as to the significance of one of the most striking features of primitive societies: the extent to which giving, receiving, and reciprocating gifts dominates social intercourse. In such societies, all sorts of things circulate in exchange—food, spells, rituals, words, names, ornaments, tools, and powers.

> Your own mother, your own sister, your own pigs, your own yams that you have piled up, you may not eat. Other people's mothers, other people's sisters, other people's pigs, other people's yams that they have piled up, you may eat. (Arapesh, cited in Lévi-Strauss, 1969:27)

In a typical gift transaction, neither party gains anything. In the Trobriand Islands, each household maintains a garden of yams and each household eats yams. But the yams a household grows and the yams it eats are not the same. At harvest time, a man sends the yams he has cultivated to the household of his sister; the household in which he lives is provisioned by his wife's brother (Malinowski, 1929). Since such a procedure appears to be a useless one from the point of view of accumulation or trade, its logic has been sought elsewhere. Mauss proposed that the significance of gift giving is that it expresses, affirms, or creates a social link between the partners of an exchange. Gift giving confers upon its participants a special relationship of trust, solidarity, and mutual aid. One can solicit a friendly relationship in the offer of a gift; acceptance implies a willingness to return a gift and a confirmation of the relationship. Gift exchange may also be the idiom of competition and rivalry. There are many examples in which one person humiliates another by giving more than can be reciprocated. Some political systems, such as the Big Man systems of highland New Guinea, are based on exchange which is unequal on the material plane. An aspiring Big Man wants to give away more goods than can be reciprocated. He gets his return in political prestige.

Although both Mauss and Lévi-Strauss emphasize the solidary aspects of gift exchange, the other purposes served by gift giving only strengthen the point that it is an ubiquitous means of social commerce. Mauss proposed that gifts were the threads of social discourse, the means by which such societies were held together in the absence of specialized governmental institutions. "The gift is the primitive way of achieving the peace that in civil society is secured by the state. . . . Composing society, the gift was the liberation of culture" (Sahlins, 1972:169, 175).

Lévi-Strauss adds to the theory of primitive reciprocity the idea that marriages are a most basic form of gift exchange, in which it is women who are the most precious of gifts. He argues that the incest taboo should best be understood as a mechanism to insure that such exchanges take place between families and between groups. Since the existence of incest taboos is universal, but the content of their prohibitions variable, they cannot be explained as having the aim of preventing the occurrence of genetically close matings. Rather, the incest taboo imposes the social aim of exogamy and alliance upon the biological events of sex and procreation. The incest taboo divides the universe of sexual choice into categories of permitted and prohibited sexual partners. Specifically, by forbidding unions within a group it enjoins marital exchange between groups.

> The prohibition on the sexual use of a daughter or a sister compels them to be given in marriage to another man, and at the same time it establishes a right to the daughter or sister of this other man. . . . The woman whom one does not take is, for that very reason, offered up. (Lévi-Strauss, 1969:51)

> The prohibition of incest is less a rule prohibiting marriage with the mother, sister, or daughter, than a rule obliging the mother, sister, or daughter to be given to others. It is the supreme rule of the gift. . . . (Ibid.:481)

The result of a gift of women is more profound than the result of other gift transactions, because the relationship thus established is not just one of reciprocity, but one of kinship. The exchange partners have become affines, and their descendents will be related by blood: "Two people may meet in friendship and exchange gifts and yet quarrel and fight in later times, but intermarriage connects them in a permanent manner" (Best, cited in Lévi-Strauss, 1969:481). As is the case with other gift giving, marriages are not always so simply activities to make peace. Marriages may be highly competitive, and there are plenty of affines who fight each other. Nevertheless, in a general sense the argument is that the taboo on incest results in a wide network of relations, a set of people whose connections with one another are a kinship structure. All other levels, amounts, and directions of exchange—including hostile ones—are ordered by this structure. The marriage ceremonies recorded in the ethnographic literature are moments in a ceaseless and ordered procession in which women, children, shells, words, cattle names, fish, ancestors, whale's teeth, pigs, yams, spells, dances, mats, etc., pass from hand to hand, leaving as their tracks the ties that bind. Kinship is organization, and organization gives power. But who is organized?

If it is women who are being transacted, then it is the men who give and take them who are linked, the woman being a conduit of a relationship rather than a partner to it.* The exchange of women does not necessarily imply that women are objectified, in the modern sense, since objects in the primitive world are imbued with highly personal qualities. But it does imply a distinction between gift and giver. If women are the gifts, then it is men who are the exchange partners. And it is the partners, not the presents, upon whom reciprocal exchange confers its quasi-mystical power of social linkage. The relations of such a system are such that women are in no position to realize the benefits of their own circulation. As long as the relations specify that men exchange women, it is men who are the beneficiaries of the product of such exchanges—social organization.

> The total relationship of exchange which constitutes marriage is not established between a man and a woman, but between two groups of men, and the woman figures only as one of the objects in the exchange, not as one of the partners. . . . This remains true even when the girl's feelings are taken into consideration, as, moreover, is usually the case. In acquiescing to the proposed

* "What, would you like to marry your sister? What is the matter with you? Don't you want a brother-in-law? Don't you realize that if you marry another man's sister and another man marries your sister, you will have at least two brothers-in-law, while if you marry your own sister you will have none? With whom will you hunt, with whom will you garden, whom will you go visit?" (Arapesh, cited in Lévi-Strauss, 1969:485).

> union, she precipitates or allows the exchange to take place, she cannot alter its nature. . . . (Lévi-Strauss in ibid.:115)*

To enter into a gift exchange as a partner, one must have something to give. If women are for men to dispose of, they are in no position to give themselves away.

> "What woman," mused a young Northern Melpa man, "is ever strong enough to get up and say, 'Let us make *moka*, let us find wives and pigs, let us give our daughters to men, let us wage war, let us kill our enemies!' No indeed not! . . . they are little rubbish things who stay at home simply, don't you see?" (Strathern, 1972:161)

What women indeed! The Melpa women of whom the young man spoke can't get wives, they *are* wives, and what they get are husbands, an entirely different matter. The Melpa women can't give their daughters to men, because they do not have the same rights in their daughters that their male kin have, rights of bestowal (although *not* of ownership).

The "exchange of women" is a seductive and powerful concept. It is attractive in that it places the oppression of women within social systems, rather than in biology. Moreover, it suggests that we look for the ultimate locus of women's oppression within the traffic in women, rather than within the traffic in merchandise. It is certainly not difficult to find ethnographic and historical examples of trafficking in women. Women are given in marriage, taken in battle, exchanged for favors, sent as tribute, traded, bought, and sold. Far from being confined to the "primitive" world, these practices seem only to become more pronounced and commercialized in more "civilized" societies. Men are of course also trafficked—but as slaves, hustlers, athletic stars, serfs, or as

* This analysis of society as based on bonds between men by means of women makes the separatist responses of the women's movement thoroughly intelligible. Separatism can be seen as a mutation in social structure, as an attempt to form social groups based on unmediated bonds between women. It can also be seen as a radical denial of men's "rights" in women, and as a claim by women of rights in themselves.

some other catastrophic social status, rather than as men. Women are transacted as slaves, serfs, and prostitutes, but also simply as women. And if men have been sexual subjects —exchangers—and women sexual semi-objects—gifts—for much of human history, then many customs, clichés, and personality traits seem to make a great deal of sense (among others, the curious custom by which a father gives away the bride).

The "exchange of women" is also a problematic concept. Since Lévi-Strauss argues that the incest taboo and the results of its application constitute the origin of culture, it can be deduced that the world historical defeat of women occurred with the origin of culture, and is a prerequisite of culture. If his analysis is adopted in its pure form, the feminist program must include a task even more onerous than the extermination of men; it must attempt to get rid of culture and substitute some entirely new phenomena on the face of the earth. However, it would be a dubious proposition at best to argue that if there were no exchange of women there would be no culture, if for no other reason than that culture is, by definition, inventive. It is even debatable that "exchange of women" adequately describes all of the empirical evidence of kinship systems. Some cultures, such as the Lele and the Luma, exchange women explicitly and overtly. In other cultures, the exchange of women can be inferred. In some—particularly those hunters and gatherers excluded from Lévi-Strauss's sample—the efficacy of the concept becomes altogether questionable. What are we to make of a concept which seems so useful and yet so difficult?

The "exchange of women" is neither a definition of culture nor a system in and of itself. The concept is an acute, but condensed, apprehension of certain aspects of the social relations of sex and gender. A kinship system is an imposition of social ends upon a part of the natural world. It is therefore "production" in the most general sense of the term: a molding, a transformation of objects (in this case, people) to and by a subjective purpose (for this sense of production, see

Marx, 1971a:80-99). It has its own relations of production, distribution, and exchange, which include certain "property" forms in people. These forms are not exclusive, private property rights, but rather different sorts of rights that various people have in other people. Marriage transactions—the gifts and material which circulate in the ceremonies marking a marriage—are a rich source of data for determining exactly who has which rights in whom. It is not difficult to deduce from such transactions that in most cases women's rights are considerably more residual than those of men.

Kinship systems do not merely exchange women. They exchange sexual access, genealogical statuses, lineage names and ancestors, rights and *people*—men, women, and children—in concrete systems of social relationships. These relationships always include certain rights for men, others for women. "Exchange of women" is a shorthand for expressing that the social relations of a kinship system specify that men have certain rights in their female kin, and that women do not have the same rights either to themselves or to their male kin. In this sense, the exchange of women is a profound perception of a system in which women do not have full rights to themselves. The exchange of women becomes an obfuscation if it is seen as a cultural necessity, and when it is used as the single tool with which an analysis of a particular kinship system is approached.

If Lévi-Strauss is correct in seeing the exchange of women as a fundamental principle of kinship, the subordination of women can be seen as a product of the relationships by which sex and gender are organized and produced. The economic oppression of women is derivative and secondary. But there is an "economics" of sex and gender, and what we need is a political economy of sexual systems. We need to study each society to determine the exact mechanisms by which particular conventions of sexuality are produced and maintained. The "exchange of women" is an initial step toward building an arsenal of concepts with which sexual systems can be described.

Deeper into the Labyrinth

More concepts can be derived from an essay by Lévi-Strauss, "The Family," in which he introduces other considerations into his analysis of kinship. In *The Elementary Structures of Kinship*, he describes rules and systems of sexual combination. In "The Family," he raises the issue of the preconditions necessary for marriage systems to operate. He asks what sort of "people" are required by kinship systems, by way of an analysis of the sexual division of labor.

Although every society has some sort of division of tasks by sex, the assignment of any particular task to one sex or the other varies enormously. In some groups, agriculture is the work of women, in others, the work of men. Women carry the heavy burdens in some societies, men in others. There are even examples of female hunters and warriors, and of men performing child-care tasks. Lévi-Strauss concludes from a survey of the division of labor by sex that it is not a biological specialization, but must have some other purpose. This purpose, he argues, is to insure the union of men and women by making the smallest viable economic unit contain at least one man and one woman.

> The very fact that it [the sexual division of labor] varies endlessly according to the society selected for consideration shows that . . . it is the mere fact of its existence which is mysteriously required, the form under which it comes to exist being utterly irrelevant, at least from the point of view of any natural necessity . . . the sexual division of labor is nothing else than a device to institute a reciprocal state of dependency between the sexes. (Lévi-Strauss, 1971:347-48)

The division of labor by sex can therefore be seen as a "taboo": a taboo against the sameness of men and women, a taboo dividing the sexes into two mutually exclusive categories, a taboo which exacerbates the biological differences between the sexes and thereby *creates* gender. The division of labor can also be seen as a taboo against sexual arrangements other than those containing at least one man and one woman, thereby enjoining heterosexual marriage.

The argument in "The Family" displays a radical questioning of all human sexual arrangements, in which no aspect of sexuality is taken for granted as "natural" (Hertz, 1960, constructs a similar argument for a thoroughly cultural explanation of the denigration of left-handedness). Rather, all manifest forms of sex and gender are seen as being constituted by the imperatives of social systems. From such a perspective, even *The Elementary Structures of Kinship* can be seen to assume certain preconditions. In purely logical terms, a rule forbidding some marriages and commanding others presupposes a rule enjoining marriage. And marriage presupposes individuals who are disposed to marry.

It is of interest to carry this kind of deductive enterprise even further than Lévi-Strauss does, and to explicate the logical structure which underlies his entire analysis of kinship. At the most general level, the social organization of sex rests upon gender, obligatory heterosexuality, and the constraint of female sexuality.

Gender is a socially imposed division of the sexes. It is a product of the social relations of sexuality. Kinship systems rest upon marriage. They therefore transform males and females into "men" and "women," each an incomplete half which can only find wholeness when united with the other. Men and women are, of course, different. But they are not as different as day and night, earth and sky, yin and yang, life and death. In fact, from the standpoint of nature, men and women are closer to each other than either is to anything else—for instance, mountains, kangaroos, or coconut palms. The idea that men and women are more different from one another than either is from anything else must come from somewhere other than nature. Furthermore, although there is an average difference between males and females on a variety of traits, the range of variation of those traits shows considerable overlap. There will always be some women who are taller than some men, for instance, even though men are on the average taller than women. But the idea that men and women are two mutually exclusive categories must arise out of something other than a nonexistent "natural" opposition.* Far from being an expression of natural differences, exclusive gender identity is the suppression of natural similarities. It requires repression: in men, of whatever is the local version of "feminine" traits; in women, of the local definition of "masculine" traits. The division of the sexes has the effect of repressing some of the personality characteristics of virtually everyone, men and women. The same social system which oppresses women in its relations of exchange, oppresses everyone in its insistence upon a rigid division of personality.

Furthermore, individuals are engendered in order that marriage be guaranteed. Lévi-Strauss comes dangerously close to saying that heterosexuality is an instituted process. If biological and hormonal imperatives were as overwhelming as popular mythology would have them, it would hardly be necessary to insure heterosexual unions by means of economic interdependency. Moreover, the incest taboo presupposes a prior, less articulate taboo on homosexuality. A prohibition against *some* heterosexual unions assumes a taboo against *non*-heterosexual unions. Gender is not only an identification with one sex; it also entails that sexual desire be directed toward the other sex. The sexual division of labor is implicated in both aspects of gender—male and female it creates them, and it creates them heterosexual. The suppression of the homosexual component of human sexuality, and by corollary, the oppression of homosexuals, is therefore a product of the same system whose rules and relations oppress women.

In fact, the situation is not so simple, as is obvious when we move from the level of generalities to the analysis of specific sexual systems. Kinship systems do not merely encourage heterosexuality to the detriment of homosexuality.

* "The woman shall not wear that which pertaineth unto a man, neither shall a man put on a woman's garment: for all that do so *are* abomination unto the LORD thy God" (Deuteronomy, 22:5; emphasis not mine).

In the first place, specific forms of heterosexuality may be required. For instance, some marriage systems have a rule of obligatory cross-cousin marriage. A person in such a system is not only heterosexual, but "cross-cousin-sexual." If the rule of marriage further specifies matrilateral cross-cousin marriage, then a man will be "mother's-brother's-daughter-sexual" and a woman will be "father's-sister's-son-sexual."

On the other hand, the very complexities of a kinship system may result in particular forms of institutionalized homosexuality. In many New Guinea groups, men and women are considered to be so inimical to one another that the period spent by a male child *in utero* negates his maleness. Since male life force is thought to reside in semen, the boy can overcome the malevolent effects of his fetal history by obtaining and consuming semen. He does so through a homosexual partnership with an older male kinsman (Kelly, 1974; see also Van Baal, 1966; Williams, 1936).

In kinship systems where bridewealth determines the statuses of husband and wife, the simple prerequisites of marriage and gender may be overridden. Among the Azande, women are monopolized by older men. A young man of means may, however, take a boy as wife while he waits to come of age. He simply pays a bridewealth (in spears) for the boy, who is thereby turned into a wife (Evans-Pritchard, 1970). In Dahomey, a woman could turn herself into a husband if she possessed the necessary bridewealth (Herskovitz, 1937).

The institutionalized "transvesticism" of the Mohave permitted a person to change from one sex to the other. An anatomical man could become a woman by means of a special ceremony, and an anatomical woman could in the same way become a man. The transvestite then took a wife or husband of her/his own anatomical sex and opposite social sex. These marriages, which we would label homosexual, were heterosexual ones by Mohave standards, unions of opposite socially defined sexes. By comparison with our society, this whole arrangement permitted a great deal of freedom. However, a person was not permitted to be some of both genders—he/she could be either male or female, but not a little of each (Devereaux, 1937; see also McMurtrie, 1914; Sonenschein, 1966).

In all of the above examples, the rules of gender division and obligatory heterosexuality are present even in their transformations. These two rules apply equally to the constraint of both male and female behavior and personality. Kinship systems dictate some sculpting of the sexuality of both sexes. But it can be deduced from *The Elementary Structures of Kinship* that more constraint is applied to females when they are pressed into the service of kinship than to males. If women are exchanged, in whatever sense we take the term, marital debts are reckoned in female flesh. A woman must become the sexual partner of some man to whom she is owed as return on a previous marriage. If a girl is promised in infancy, her refusal to participate as an adult would disrupt the flow of debts and promises. It would be in the interests of the smooth and continuous operation of such a system if the woman in question did not have too many ideas of her own about whom she might want to sleep with. From the standpoint of the system, the preferred female sexuality would be one which responded to the desire of others, rather than one which actively desired and sought a response.

This generality, like the ones about gender and heterosexuality, is also subject to considerable variation and free play in actual systems. The Lele and the Kuma provide two of the clearest ethnographic examples of the exchange of women. Men in both cultures are perpetually engaged in schemes which necessitate that they have full control over the sexual destinies of their female kinswomen. Much of the drama in both societies consists in female attempts to evade the sexual control of their kinsmen. Nevertheless, female resistance in both cases is severely circumscribed (Douglas, 1963; Reay, 1959).

One last generality could be predicted as a consequence of

the exchange of women under a system in which rights to women are held by men. What would happen if our hypothetical woman not only refused the man to whom she was promised, but asked for a woman instead? If a single refusal were disruptive, a double refusal would be insurrectionary. If each woman is promised to some man, neither has a right to dispose of herself. If two women managed to extricate themselves from the debt nexus, two other women would have to be found to replace them. As long as men have rights in women which women do not have in themselves, it would be sensible to expect that homosexuality in women would be subject to more suppression than in men.

In summary, some basic generalities about the organization of human sexuality can be derived from an exegesis of Lévi-Strauss's theories of kinship. These are the incest taboo, obligatory heterosexuality, and an asymmetric division of the sexes. The asymmetry of gender—the difference between exchanger and exchanged—entails the constraint of female sexuality. Concrete kinship systems will have more specific conventions, and these conventions vary a great deal. While particular socio-sexual systems vary, each one is specific, and individuals within it will have to conform to a finite set of possibilities. Each new generation must learn and become its sexual destiny, each person must be encoded with its appropriate status within the system. It would be extraordinary for one of us to calmly assume that we would conventionally marry a mother's brother's daughter, or a father's sister's son. Yet there are groups in which such a marital future is taken for granted.

Anthropology, and descriptions of kinship systems, do not explain the mechanisms by which children are engraved with the conventions of sex and gender. Psychoanalysis, on the other hand, is a theory about the reproduction of kinship. Psychoanalysis describes the residue left within individuals by their confrontation with the rules and regulations of sexuality of the societies to which they are born.

Psychoanalysis and Its Discontents

The battle between psychoanalysis and the women's and gay movements has become legendary. In part, this confrontation between sexual revolutionaries and the clinical establishment has been due to the evolution of psychoanalysis in the United States, where clinical tradition has fetishized anatomy. The child is thought to travel through its organismic stages until it reaches its anatomical destiny and the missionary position. Clinical practice has often seen its mission as the repair of individuals who somehow have become derailed en route to their "biological" aim. Transforming moral law into scientific law, clinical practice has acted to enforce sexual convention upon unruly participants. In this sense, psychoanalysis has often become more than a theory of the mechanisms of the reproduction of sexual arrangements; it has been one of those mechanisms. Since the aim of the feminist and gay revolts is to dismantle the apparatus of sexual enforcement, a critique of psychoanalysis has been in order.

But the rejection of Freud by the women's and gay movements has deeper roots in the rejection by psychoanalysis of its own insights. Nowhere are the effects on women of male-dominated social systems better documented than within the clinical literature. According to the Freudian orthodoxy, the attainment of "normal" femininity extracts severe costs from women. The theory of gender acquisition could have been the basis of a critique of sex roles. Instead, the radical implications of Freud's theory have been radically repressed. This tendency is evident even in the original formulations of the theory, but it has been exacerbated over time until the potential for a critical psychoanalytic theory of gender is visible only in the symptomatology of its denial—an intricate rationalization of sex roles as they are. It is not the purpose of this paper to conduct a psychoanalysis of the psychoanalytic unconscious; but I do hope to demonstrate that it exists. Moreover, the salvage of psychoanalysis from its own motivated repression is not for the sake of Freud's good name. Psychoanalysis contains a unique set of concepts for understanding men, women, and sexuality. It is a theory of sexuality in human society. Most importantly, psychoanalysis provides a description of the mechanisms by which the sexes are divided and deformed, of how bisexual, androgynous infants are transformed into boys and girls.* Psychoanalysis is a feminist theory *manqué*.

The Oedipus Hex

Until the late 1920s, the psychoanalytic movement did not have a distinctive theory of feminine development. Instead, variants of an "Electra" complex in women had been proposed, in which female experience was thought to be a mirror image of the Oedipal complex described for males. The boy loved his mother, but gave her up out of fear of the father's threat of castration. The girl, it was thought, loved her father, and gave him up out of fear of maternal vengeance. This formulation assumed that both children were subject to a biological imperative toward heterosexuality. It also assumed that the children were already, before the Oedipal phase, "little" men and women.

Freud had voiced reservations about jumping to conclusions about women on the basis of data gathered from men. But his objections remained general until the discovery of the pre-Oedipal phase in women. The concept of the pre-Oedipal

* "In studying women we cannot neglect the methods of a science of the mind, a theory that attempts to explain how women become women and men, men. The borderline between the biological and the social which finds expression in the family is the land psychoanalysis sets out to chart, the land where sexual distinction originates." (Mitchell, 1971:167)

"What is the *object* of psychoanalysis? . . . but the *'effects,'* prolonged into the surviving adult, of the extraordinary adventure which from birth the liquidation of the Oedipal phase transforms a small animal conceived by a man and a woman into a small human child . . . the 'effects' still present in the survivors of the forced 'humanization' of the small human animal into a *man* or a *woman*. . . ." (Althusser, 1969:57, 59; italics in original) phase enabled both Freud and Jeanne Lampl de Groot to articulate the classic psychoanalytic theory of femininity.* The idea of the pre-Oedipal phase in women produced a dislocation of the biologically derived presuppositions which underlay notions of an "Electra" complex. In the pre-Oedipal phase, children of both sexes were psychically indistinguishable, which meant that their differentiation into masculine and feminine children had to be explained, rather than assumed. Pre-Oedipal children were described as bisexual. Both sexes exhibited the full range of libidinal attitudes, active and passive. And for children of both sexes, the mother was the object of desire.

In particular, the characteristics of the pre-Oedipal female challenged the ideas of a primordial heterosexuality and gender identity. Since the girl's libidinal activity was directed toward the mother, her adult heterosexuality had to be explained:

> It would be a solution of ideal simplicity if we could suppose that from a particular age onwards the elementary influence of the mutual attraction between the sexes makes itself felt and impels the small woman towards men. . . . But we are not going to find

* The psychoanalytic theories of femininity were articulated in the context of a debate which took place largely in the *International Journal of Psychoanalysis* and *The Psychoanalytic Quarterly* in the late 1920s and early 1930s. Articles representing the range of discussion include: Freud, 1961a, 1961b, 1965; Lampl de Groot, 1933, 1948; Deutsch, 1948a, 1948b; Horney, 1973; Jones, 1933. Some of my dates are of reprints; for the original chronology, see Chasseguet-Smirgel (1970: introduction). The debate was complex, and I have simplified it. Freud, Lampl de Groot, and Deutsch argued that femininity developed out of a bisexual, "phallic" girl-child; Horney and Jones argued for an innate femininity. The debate was not without its ironies. Horney defended women against penis envy by postulating that women are born and not made; Deutsch, who considered women to be made and not born, developed a theory of feminine masochism whose best rival is *Story of O.* I have attributed the core of the "Freudian" version of female development equally to Freud and to Lampl de Groot. In reading through the articles, it has seemed to me that the theory is as much (or more) hers as it is his.

> things so easy; we scarcely know whether we are to believe seriously in the power of which poets talk so much and with such enthusiasm but which cannot be further dissected analytically. (Freud, 1965:119)

Moreover, the girl did not manifest a "feminine" libidinal attitude. Since her desire for the mother was active and aggressive, her ultimate accession to "femininity" had also to be explained:

> In conformity with its peculiar nature, psychoanalysis does not try to describe what a woman is . . . but sets about enquiring how she comes into being, how a woman develops out of a child with a bisexual disposition. (Ibid.:116)

In short, feminine development could no longer be taken for granted as a reflex of biology. Rather, it had become immensely problematic. It is in explaining the acquisition of "femininity" that Freud employs the concepts of penis envy and castration which have infuriated feminists since he first introduced them. The girl turns from the mother and represses the "masculine" elements of her libido as a result of her recognition that she is castrated. She compares her tiny clitoris to the larger penis, and in the face of its evident superior ability to satisfy the mother, falls prey to penis envy and a sense of inferiority. She gives up her struggle for the mother and assumes a passive feminine position vis-à-vis the father. Freud's account can be read as claiming that femininity is a consequence of the anatomical differences between the sexes. He has therefore been accused of biological determinism. Nevertheless, even in his most anatomically stated versions of the female castration complex, the "inferiority" of the woman's genitals is a product of the situational context: the girl feels less "equipped" to possess and satisfy the mother. If the pre-Oedipal lesbian were not confronted by the heterosexuality of the mother, she might draw different conclusions about the relative status of her genitals.

Freud was never as much of a biological determinist as some would have him. He repeatedly stressed that all adult sexuality resulted from psychic, not biologic, development.

But his writing is often ambiguous, and his wording leaves plenty of room for the biological interpretations which have been so popular in American psychoanalysis. In France, on the other hand, the trend in psychoanalytic theory has been to de-biologize Freud, and to conceive of psychoanalysis as a theory of information rather than organs. Jacques Lacan, the instigator of this line of thinking, insists that Freud never meant to say anything about anatomy, and that Freud's theory was instead about language and the cultural meanings imposed upon anatomy. The debate over the "real" Freud is extremely interesting, but it is not my purpose here to contribute to it. Rather, I want to rephrase the classic theory of femininity in Lacan's terminology, after introducing some of the pieces on Lacan's conceptual chessboard.

Kinship, Lacan, and the Phallus

Lacan suggests that psychoanalysis is the study of the traces left in the psyches of individuals as a result of their conscription into systems of kinship.

> Isn't it striking that Lévi-Strauss, in suggesting that implication of the structures of language with that part of the social laws which regulate marriage ties and kinship, is already conquering the very terrain in which Freud situates the unconscious? (Lacan, 1968:48)

> For where on earth would one situate the determinations of the unconsciousness if it is not in those nominal cadres in which marriage ties and kinship are always grounded. . . . And how would one apprehend the analytical conflicts and their Oedipean prototype outside the engagements which have fixed, long before the subject came into the world, not only his destiny, but his identity itself? (Ibid.:126)

> This is precisely where the Oedipus complex . . . may be said, in this connection, to mark the limits which our discipline assigns to subjectivity: that is to say, what the subject can know of his unconscious participation in the movement of the complex structures of marriage ties, by verifying the symbolic effects in his individual existence of the tangential movement towards incest. . . . (Ibid.:40)

Kinship is the culturalization of biological sexuality on the societal level; psychoanalysis describes the transformation of the biological sexuality of individuals as they are enculturated.

Kinship terminology contains information about the system. Kin terms demarcate statuses, and indicate some of the attributes of those statuses. For instance, in the Trobriand Islands a man calls the women of his clan by the term for "sister." He calls the women of clans into which he can marry by a term indicating their marriageability. When the young Trobriand male learns these terms, he learns which women he can safely desire. In Lacan's scheme, the Oedipal crisis occurs when a child learns of the sexual rules embedded in the terms for family and relatives. The crisis begins when the child comprehends the system and his or her place in it; the crisis is resolved when the child accepts that place and accedes to it. Even if the child refuses its place, he or she cannot escape knowledge of it. Before the Oedipal phase, the sexuality of the child is labile and relatively unstructured. Each child contains all of the sexual possibilities available to human expression. But in any given society, only some of these possibilities will be expressed, while others will be constrained. When the child leaves the Oedipal phase, its libido and gender identity have been organized in conformity with the rules of the culture which is domesticating it.

The Oedipal complex is an apparatus for the production of sexual personality. It is a truism to say that societies will inculcate in their young the character traits appropriate to carrying on the business of society. For instance, E. P. Thompson (1963) speaks of the transformation of the personality structure of the English working class, as artisans were changed into good industrial workers. Just as the social forms of labor demand certain kinds of personality, the social forms of sex and gender demand certain kinds of people. In the most general terms, the Oedipal complex is a machine which fashions the appropriate forms of sexual individuals (see also the discussion of different forms of "historical individuality" in Althusser and Balibar, 1970:112, 251-53).

In the Lacanian theory of psychoanalysis, it is the kin terms that indicate a structure of relationships which will determine the role of any individual or object within the Oedipal drama. For instance, Lacan makes a distinction between the "function of the father" and a particular father who embodies this function. In the same way, he makes a radical distinction between the penis and the "phallus," between organ and information. The phallus is a set of meanings conferred upon the penis. The differentiation between phallus and penis in contemporary French psychoanalytic terminology emphasizes the idea that the penis could not and does not play the role attributed to it in the classical terminology of the castration complex.*

In Freud's terminology, the Oedipal complex presents two alternatives to a child: to have a penis or to be castrated. In contrast, the Lacanian theory of the castration complex leaves behind all reference to anatomical reality:

> The theory of the castration complex amounts to having the male organ play a dominant role—this time as a symbol—*to the extent that its absence or presence transforms an anatomical difference into a major classification of humans, and to the extent that, for each subject, this presence or absence is not taken for granted, is not reduced purely and simply to a given, but is the problematical result of an intra- and intersubjective process* (the subject's as-

* I have taken my position on Freud somewhere between the French structuralist interpretations and American biologistic ones, because I think that Freud's wording is similarly somewhere in the middle. He does talk about penises, about the "inferiority" of the clitoris, about the psychic consequences of anatomy. The Lacanians, on the other hand, argue from Freud's text that he is unintelligible if his words are taken literally, and that a thoroughly nonanatomical theory can be deduced as Freud's intention (see Althusser, 1969). I think that they are right; the penis is walking around too much for its role to be taken literally. The detachability of the penis, and its transformation in fantasy (e.g., penis = feces = child = gift), argue strongly for a symbolic interpretation. Nevertheless, I don't think that Freud was as consistent as either I or Lacan would like him to have been, and some gesture must be made to what he said, even as we play with what he must have meant.

> sumption of his own sex). (Laplanche and Pontalis, in Mehlman, 1972:198-99; my italics)

The alternative presented to the child may be rephrased as an alternative between having, or not having, the phallus. Castration is not having the (symbolic) phallus. Castration is not a real "lack," but a meaning conferred upon the genitals of a woman:

> Castration may derive support from . . . the apprehension in the Real of the absence of the penis in women—but even this supposes a symbolization of the object, since the Real is full, and "lacks" nothing. Insofar as one finds castration in the genesis of neurosis, it is never real but symbolic. . . . (Lacan, 1968:271)

The phallus is, as it were, a distinctive feature differentiating "castrated" and "noncastrated." The presence or absence of the phallus carries the differences between two sexual statuses, "man" and "woman" (see Jakobson and Halle, 1971, on distinctive features). Since these are not equal, the phallus also carries a meaning of the dominance of men over women, and it may be inferred that "penis envy" is a recognition thereof. Moreover, as long as men have rights in women which women do not have in themselves, the phallus also carries the meaning of the difference between "exchanger" and "exchanged," gift and giver. Ultimately, neither the classical Freudian nor the rephrased Lacanian theories of the Oedipal process make sense unless at least this much of the paleolithic relations of sexuality are still with us. We still live in a "phallic" culture.

Lacan also speaks of the phallus as a symbolic object which is exchanged within and between families (see also Wilden, 1968:303-305). It is interesting to think about this observation in terms of primitive marriage transactions and exchange networks. In those transactions, the exchange of women is usually one of many cycles of exchange. Usually, there are other objects circulating as well as women. Women move in one direction, cattle, shells, or mats in the other. In one sense, the Oedipal complex is an expression of the circulation of the phallus in intrafamily exchange, an inversion of the circulation of women in interfamily exchange. In the cycle of exchange manifested by the Oedipal complex, the phallus passes through the medium of women from one man to another—from father to son, from mother's brother to sister's son, and so forth. In this family *Kula* ring, women go one way, the phallus the other. It is where we aren't. In this sense, the phallus is more than a feature which distinguishes the sexes: it is the embodiment of the male status, to which men accede, and in which certain rights inhere—among them, the right to a woman. It is an expression of the transmission of male dominance. It passes through women and settles upon men.* The tracks which it leaves include gender identity, the division of the sexes. But it leaves more than this. It leaves "penis envy," which acquires a rich meaning of the disquietude of women in a phallic culture.

Oedipus Revisited

We return now to the two pre-Oedipal androgynes, sitting on the border between biology and culture. Lévi-Strauss places the incest taboo on that border, arguing that its initiation of the exchange of women constitutes the origin of society. In this sense, the incest taboo and the exchange of women are the content of the original social contract (see

* The pre-Oedipal mother is the "phallic mother," e.g., she is believed to possess the phallus. The Oedipal-inducing information is that the mother does not possess the phallus. In other words, the crisis is precipitated by the "castration" of the mother, by the recognition that the phallus only passes through her, but does not settle on her. The "phallus" must pass through her, since the relationship of a male to every other male is defined through a woman. A man is linked to a son by a mother, to his nephew by virtue of a sister, etc. Every relationship between male kin is defined by the woman between them. If power is a male prerogative, and must be passed on, it must go through the woman-in-between. Marshall Sahlins (personal communication) once suggested that the reason women are so often defined as stupid, polluting, disorderly, silly, profane, or whatever, is that such categorizations define women as "incapable" of possessing the power which must be transferred through them.

Sahlins, 1972: Chap. 4). For individuals, the Oedipal crisis occurs at the same divide, when the incest taboo initiates the exchange of the phallus.

The Oedipal crisis is precipitated by certain items of information. The children discover the differences between the sexes, and that each child must become one or the other gender. They also discover the incest taboo, and that some sexuality is prohibited—in this case, the mother is unavailable to either child because she "belongs" to the father. Lastly, they discover that the two genders do not have the same sexual "rights" or futures.

In the normal course of events, the boy renounces his mother for fear that otherwise his father would castrate him (refuse to give him the phallus and make him a girl). But by this act of renunciation, the boy affirms the relationships which have given mother to father and which will give him, if he becomes a man, a woman of his own. In exchange for the boy's affirmation of his father's right to his mother, the father affirms the phallus in his son (does not castrate him). The boy exchanges his mother for the phallus, the symbolic token which can later be exchanged for a woman. The only thing required of him is a little patience. He retains his initial libidinal organization and the sex of his original love object. The social contract to which he has agreed will eventually recognize his own rights and provide him with a woman of his own.

What happens to the girl is more complex. She, like the boy, discovers the taboo against incest and the division of the sexes. She also discovers some unpleasant information about the gender to which she is being assigned. For the boy, the taboo on incest is a taboo on certain women. For the girl, it is a taboo on all women. Since she is in a homosexual position vis-à-vis the mother, the rule of heterosexuality which dominates the scenario makes her position excruciatingly untenable. The mother, and all women by extension, can only be properly beloved by someone "with a penis" (phallus). Since the girl has no "phallus," she has no "right" to love her mother or another woman, since she is herself destined to some man. She does not have the symbolic token which can be exchanged for a woman.

If Freud's wording of this moment of the female Oedipal crisis is ambiguous, Lampl de Groot's formulation makes the context which confers meaning upon the genitals explicit:

> . . . *if the little girl comes to the conclusion that such an organ is really indispensable to the possession of the mother, she experiences* in addition to the narcissistic insults common to both sexes still another blow, namely *a feeling of inferiority about her genitals.* (Lampl de Groot, 1933:497; my italics)

The girl concludes that the "penis" is indispensable for the possession of the mother because only those who possess the phallus have a "right" to a woman, and the token of exchange. She does not come to her conclusion because of the natural superiority of the penis either in and of itself, or as an instrument for making love. The hierarchical arrangement of the male and female genitals is a result of the definitions of the situation—the rule of obligatory heterosexuality and the relegation of women (those without the phallus, castrated) to men (those with the phallus).

The girl then begins to turn away from the mother, and to the father.

> To the girl, it [castration] is an accomplished fact, which is irrevocable, but the recognition of which compels her finally to renounce her first love object and to taste to the full the bitterness of its loss . . . the father is chosen as a love-object, the enemy becomes the beloved. . . . (Lampl de Groot, 1948:213)

This recognition of "castration" forces the girl to redefine her relationship to herself, her mother, and her father.

She turns from the mother because she does not have the phallus to give her. She turns from the mother also in anger and disappointment, because the mother did not give her a "penis" (phallus). But the mother, a woman in a phallic culture, does not have the phallus to give away (having gone through the Oedipal crisis herself a generation earlier). The girl then turns to the father because only he can "give her the phallus," and it is only through him that she can enter into the symbolic exchange system in which the phallus circulates. But the father does not give her the phallus in the same way that he gives it to the boy. The phallus is affirmed in the boy, who then has it to give away. The girl never gets the phallus. It passes through her, and in its passage is transformed into a child. When she "recognizes her castration," she accedes to the place of a woman in a phallic exchange network. She can "get" the phallus—in intercourse, or as a child—but only as a gift from a man. She never gets to give it away.

When she turns to the father, she also represses the "active" portions of her libido:

> The turning away from her mother is an extremely important step in the course of a little girl's development. It is more than a mere change of object . . . hand in hand with it there is to be observed a marked lowering of the active sexual impulses and a rise of the passive ones. . . . The transition to the father object is accomplished with the help of the passive trends in so far as they have escaped the catastrophe. The path to the development of femininity now lies open to the girl. (Freud, 1961b:239)

The ascendance of passivity in the girl is due to her recognition of the futility of realizing her active desire, and of the unequal terms of the struggle. Freud locates active desire in the clitoris and passive desire in the vagina, and thus describes the repression of active desire as the repression of clitoral eroticism in favor of passive vaginal eroticism. In this scheme, cultural stereotypes have been mapped onto the genitals. Since the work of Masters and Johnson, it is evident that this genital division is a false one. Any organ—penis, clitoris, vagina—can be the locus of either active or passive eroticism. What is important in Freud's scheme, however, is not the geography of desire, but its self-confidence. It is not an organ which is repressed, but a segment of erotic possibility. Freud notes that "more constraint has been applied to the libido when it is pressed into the service of the feminine function . . ." (Freud, 1965:131). The girl has been robbed.

If the Oedipal phase proceeds normally and the girl "accepts her castration," her libidinal structure and object choice are now congruent with the female gender role. She has become a little woman—feminine, passive, heterosexual. Actually, Freud suggests that there are three alternate routes out of the Oedipal catastrophe. The girl may simply freak out, repress sexuality altogether, and become asexual. She may protest, cling to her narcissism and desire, and become either "masculine" or homosexual. Or she may accept the situation, sign the social contract, and attain "normality."

Karen Horney is critical of the entire Freud/Lampl de Groot scheme. But in the course of her critique she articulates its implications:

> . . . when she [the girl] first turns to a man (the father), it is in the main only by way of the narrow bridge of resentment . . . we should feel it a contradiction if the relation of woman to man did not retain throughout life some tinge of this enforced substitute for that which was really desired. . . . The same character of something remote from instinct, secondary and substitutive, would, even in normal women, adhere to the wish for motherhood. . . . The special point about Freud's viewpoint is rather that it sees the wish for motherhood not as an innate formation, but as something that can be reduced psychologically to its ontogenetic elements and draws its energy originally from homosexual or phallic instinctual elements. . . . It would follow, finally, that women's whole reaction to life would be based on a strong subterranean resentment. (Horney, 1973:148-49)

Horney considers these implications to be so far-fetched that they challenge the validity of Freud's entire scheme. But it is certainly plausible to argue instead that the creation of "femininity" in women in the course of socialization is an act of psychic brutality, and that it leaves in women an immense resentment of the suppression to which they were subjected. It is also possible to argue that women have few means for realizing and expressing their residual anger. One can read Freud's essays on femininity as descriptions of how a group is prepared psychologically, at a tender age, to live with its oppression.

There is an additional element in the classic discussions of the attainment of womanhood. The girl first turns to the father because she must, because she is "castrated" (a woman, helpless, etc.). She then discovers that "castration" is a prerequisite to the father's love, that she must be a woman for him to love her. She therefore begins to desire "castration," and what had previously been a disaster becomes a wish.

> Analytic experience leaves no room for doubt that the little girl's first libidinal relation to her father is masochistic, and the masochistic wish in its earliest distinctively feminine phase is: "I want to be castrated by my father." (Deutsch, 1948a:228)

Deutsch argues that such masochism may conflict with the ego, causing some women to flee the entire situation in defense of their self-regard. Those women to whom the choice is "between finding bliss in suffering or peace in renunciation" (ibid.:231) will have difficulty in attaining a healthy attitude to intercourse and motherhood. Why Deutsch appears to consider such women to be special cases, rather than the norm, is not clear from her discussion.

The psychoanalytic theory of femininity is one that sees female development based largely on pain and humiliation, and it takes some fancy footwork to explain why anyone ought to enjoy being a woman. At this point in the classic discussions biology makes a triumphant return. The fancy footwork consists in arguing that finding joy in pain is adaptive to the role of women in reproduction, since childbirth and defloration are "painful." Would it not make more sense to question the entire procedure? If women, in finding their place in a sexual system, are robbed of libido and forced into a masochistic eroticism, why did the analysts not argue for novel arrangements, instead of rationalizing the old ones?

Freud's theory of femininity has been subjected to feminist critique since it was first published. To the extent that it is a rationalization of female subordination, this critique has been justified. To the extent that it is a description of a process which subordinates women, this critique is a mistake. As a description of how phallic culture domesticates women, and the effects in women of their domestication, psychoanalytic theory has no parallel (see also Mitchell, 1971 and 1974; Lasch, 1974). And since psychoanalysis is a theory of gender, dismissing it would be suicidal for a political movement dedicated to eradicating gender hierarchy (or gender itself). We cannot dismantle something that we underestimate or do not understand. The oppression of women is deep; equal pay, equal work, and all of the female politicians in the world will not extirpate the roots of sexism. Lévi-Strauss and Freud elucidate what would otherwise be poorly perceived parts of the deep structures of sex oppression. They serve as reminders of the intractability and magnitude of what we fight, and their analyses provide preliminary charts of the social machinery we must rearrange.

Women Unite to Off the Oedipal Residue of Culture

The precision of the fit between Freud and Lévi-Strauss is striking. Kinship systems require a division of the sexes. The Oedipal phase divides the sexes. Kinship systems include sets of rules governing sexuality. The Oedipal crisis is the assimilation of these rules and taboos. Compulsory heterosexuality is the product of kinship. The Oedipal phase constitutes heterosexual desire. Kinship rests on a radical difference between the rights of men and women. The Oedipal complex confers male rights upon the boy, and forces the girl to accommodate herself to her lesser rights.

This fit between Lévi-Strauss and Freud is by implication an argument that our sex/gender system is still organized by the principles outlined by Lévi-Strauss, despite the entirely nonmodern character of his data base. The more recent data on which Freud bases his theories testifies to the endurance of these sexual structures. If my reading of Freud and Lévi-Strauss is accurate, it suggests that the feminist movement must attempt to resolve the Oedipal crisis of culture by reorganizing the domain of sex and gender in such a way that each individual's Oedipal experience would be less destructive. The dimensions of such a task are difficult to imagine, but at least certain conditions would have to be met.

Several elements of the Oedipal crisis would have to be altered in order that the phase not have such disastrous effects on the young female ego. The Oedipal phase institutes a contradiction in the girl by placing irreconcilable demands upon her. On the one hand, the girl's love for the mother is induced by the mother's job of child care. The girl is then forced to abandon this love because of the female sex role—to belong to a man. If the sexual division of labor were such that adults of both sexes cared for children equally, primary object choice would be bisexual. If heterosexuality were not obligatory, this early love would not have to be suppressed, and the penis would not be overvalued. If the sexual property system were reorganized in such a way that men did not have overriding rights in women (if there was no exchange of women) and if there were no gender, the entire Oedipal drama would be a relic. In short, feminism must call for a revolution in kinship.

The organization of sex and gender once had functions other than itself—it organized society. Now, it only organizes and reproduces itself. The kinds of relationships of sexuality established in the dim human past still dominate our sexual lives, our ideas about men and women, and the ways we raise our children. But they lack the functional load they once carried. One of the most conspicuous features of kinship is that it has been systematically stripped of its functions—political, economic, educational, and organizational. It has been reduced to its barest bones—*sex and gender.*

Human sexual life will always be subject to convention and human intervention. It will never be completely "natural," if only because our species is social, cultural, and articulate. The wild profusion of infantile sexuality will always be tamed. The confrontation between immature and helpless infants and the developed social life of their elders will probably always leave some residue of disturbance. But the mechanisms and aims of this process need not be largely independent of conscious choice. Cultural evolution provides us with the opportunity to seize control of the means of sexuality, reproduction, and socialization, and to make conscious decisions to liberate human sexual life from the archaic relationships which deform it. Ultimately, a thoroughgoing feminist revolution would liberate more than women. It would liberate forms of sexual expression, and it would liberate human personality from the straightjacket of gender.

"Daddy, daddy, you bastard, I'm through."
—Sylvia Plath

In the course of this essay I have tried to construct a theory of women's oppression by borrowing concepts from anthropology and psychoanalysis. But Lévi-Strauss and Freud write within an intellectual tradition produced by a culture in which women are oppressed. The danger in my enterprise is that the sexism in the tradition of which they are a part tends to be dragged in with each borrowing. "We cannot utter a single destructive proposition which has not already slipped into the form, the logic, and the implicit postulations of precisely what it seeks to contest" (Derrida, 1972:250). And what slips in is formidable. Both psychoanalysis and structural anthropology are, in one sense, the most sophisticated ideologies of sexism around.*

* Parts of Wittig's *Les Guérillères* (1973) appear to be tirades against Lévi-Strauss and Lacan. For instance:

> Has he not indeed written, power and the possession of women, leisure and the enjoyment of women? He writes that you are currency, an item of exchange. He writes, barter, barter, possession and acquisition of women and merchandise. Better for you to see your guts in the sun and utter the death rattle than to live a life that anyone can appropriate. What belongs to you on this earth? Only death. No power on earth can take that away from you. And—consider explain tell yourself—if happiness consists in the possession of something, then hold fast to this sovereign happiness—to die. (Wittig, 1973:115-16; see also 106-107; 113-14; 134)

The awareness of French feminists of Lévi-Strauss and Lacan is most clearly evident in a group called "Psychoanalyse et Politique" which defined its task as a feminist use and critique of Lacanian psychoanalysis.

For instance, Lévi-Strauss sees women as being like words, which are misused when they are not "communicated" and exchanged. On the last page of a very long book, he observes that this creates something of a contradiction in women, since women are at the same time "speakers" and "spoken." His only comment on this contradiction is this:

> But woman could never become just a sign and nothing more, since even in a man's world she is still a person, and since insofar as she is defined as a sign she must be recognized as a generator of signs. In the matrimonial dialogue of men, woman is never purely what is spoken about; for if women in general represent a certain category of signs, destined to a certain kind of communication, each woman preserves a particular value arising from her talent, before and after marriage, for taking her part in a duet. In contrast to words, which have wholly become signs, woman has remained at once a sign and a value. *This explains why the relations between the sexes have preserved that affective richness, ardour and mystery which doubtless originally permeated the entire universe of human communications.* (Lévi-Strauss, 1969:496; my italics)

This is an extraordinary statement. Why is he not, at this point, denouncing what kinship systems do to women, instead of presenting one of the greatest rip-offs of all time as the root of romance?

A similar insensitivity is revealed within psychoanalysis by the inconsistency with which it assimilates the critical implications of its own theory. For instance, Freud did not hesitate to recognize that his findings posed a challenge to conventional morality:

> We cannot avoid observing with critical eyes, and we have found that it is impossible to give our support to conventional sexual morality or to approve highly of the means by which society attempts to arrange the practical problems of sexuality in life. *We can demonstrate with ease that what the world calls its code of morals demands more sacrifices than it is worth*, and that its behavior is neither dictated by honesty nor instituted with wisdom. (Freud, 1943:376-77; my emphasis)

Nevertheless, when psychoanalysis demonstrates with equal

facility that the ordinary components of feminine personality are masochism, self-hatred, and passivity,* a similar judgment is *not* made. Instead, a double standard of interpretation is employed. Masochism is bad for men, essential to women. Adequate narcissism is necessary for men, impossible for women. Passivity is tragic in man, while lack of passivity is tragic in a woman.

It is this double standard which enables clinicians to try to accommodate women to a role whose destructiveness is so lucidly detailed in their own theories. It is the same inconsistent attitude which permits therapists to consider lesbianism as a problem to be cured, rather than as the resistance to a bad situation that their own theory suggests.**

There are points within the analytic discussions of femininity where one might say, "This is oppression of women," or "We can demonstrate with ease that what the world calls femininity demands more sacrifices than it is worth." It is precisely at such points that the implications of the theory are ignored, and are replaced with formulations whose purpose is to keep those implications firmly lodged in the theo-

* Every woman adores a fascist."—Sylvia Plath

** One clinician, Charlotte Wolff (1971) has taken the psychoanalytic theory of womanhood to its logical extreme and proposed that lesbianism is a healthy response to female socialization.

> Women who do not rebel against the status of object have declared themselves defeated as persons in their own right. (Wolff, 1971:65)
>
> The lesbian girl is the one who, by all means at her disposal, will try to find a place of safety inside and outside the family, through her fight for equality with the male. She will not, like other women, play up to him: indeed, she despises the very idea of it. (Ibid.:59)
>
> The lesbian was and is unquestionably in the avant-garde of the fight for equality of the sexes, and for the psychical liberation of women. (Ibid.:66)

It is revealing to compare Wolff's discussion with the articles on lesbianism in Marmor, 1965.

retical unconscious. It is at these points that all sorts of mysterious chemical substances, joys in pain, and biological aims are substituted for a critical assessment of the costs of femininity. These substitutions are the symptoms of theoretical repression, in that they are not consistent with the usual canons of psychoanalytic argument. The extent to which these rationalizations of femininity go against the grain of psychoanalytic logic is strong evidence for the extent of the need to suppress the radical and feminist implications of the theory of femininity (Deutsch's discussions are excellent examples of this process of substitution and repression).

The argument which must be woven in order to assimilate Lévi-Strauss and Freud into feminist theory is somewhat tortuous. I have engaged it for several reasons. First, while neither Lévi-Strauss nor Freud questions the undoubted sexism endemic to the systems they describe, the questions which ought to be posed are blindingly obvious. Secondly, their work enables us to isolate sex and gender from "mode of production," and to counter a certain tendency to explain sex oppression as a reflex of economic forces. Their work provides a framework in which the full weight of sexuality and marriage can be incorporated into an analysis of sex oppression. It suggests a conception of the women's movement as analogous to, rather than isomorphic with, the working-class movement, each addressing a different source of human discontent. In Marx's vision, the working-class movement would do more than throw off the burden of its own exploitation. It also had the potential to change society, to liberate humanity, to create a classless society. Perhaps the women's movement has the task of effecting the same kind of social change for a system of which Marx had only an imperfect apperception. Something of this sort is implicit in Wittig (1973)—the dictatorship of the Amazon *guérillères* is a temporary means for achieving a genderless society.

The sex/gender system is not immutably oppressive and has lost much of its traditional function. Nevertheless, it will not wither away in the absence of opposition. It still carries the social burden of sex and gender, of socializing the young, and of providing ultimate propositions about the nature of human beings themselves. And it serves economic and political ends other than those it was originally designed to further (cf. Scott, 1965). The sex/gender system must be reorganized through political action.

Finally, the exegesis of Lévi-Strauss and Freud suggests a certain vision of feminist politics and the feminist utopia. It suggests that we should not aim for the elimination of men, but for the elimination of the social system which creates sexism and gender. I personally find a vision of an Amazon matriarchate, in which men are reduced to servitude or oblivion (depending on the possibilities for parthenogenetic reproduction), distasteful and inadequate. Such a vision maintains gender and the division of the sexes. It is a vision which simply inverts the arguments of those who base their case for inevitable male dominance on ineradicable and *significant* biological differences between the sexes. But we are not only oppressed *as* women, we are oppressed by having to *be* women, or men as the case may be. I personally feel that the feminist movement must dream of even more than the elimination of the oppression of women. It must dream of the elimination of obligatory sexualities and sex roles. The dream I find most compelling is one of an androgynous and genderless (though not sexless) society, in which one's sexual anatomy is irrelevant to who one is, what one does, and with whom one makes love.

The Political Economy of Sex

It would be nice to be able to conclude here with the implications for feminism and gay liberation of the overlap between Freud and Lévi-Strauss. But I must suggest, tentatively, a next step on the agenda: a Marxian analysis of sex/gender systems. Sex/gender systems are not ahistorical emanations of the human mind; they are products of historical human activity.

We need, for instance, an analysis of the evolution of sexual exchange along the lines of Marx's discussion in *Capi-*

tal of the evolution of money and commodities. There is an economics and a politics to sex/gender systems which is obscured by the concept of "exchange of women." For instance, a system in which women are exchangeable only for one another has different effects on women than one in which there is a commodity equivalent for women.

> That marriage in simple societies involves an "exchange" is a somewhat vague notion that has often confused the analysis of social systems. The extreme case is the exchange of "sisters," formerly practiced in parts of Australia and Africa. Here the term has the precise dictionary meaning of "to be received as an equivalent for," "to give and receive reciprocally." From quite a different standpoint the virtually universal incest prohibition means that marriage systems necessarily involve "exchanging" siblings for spouses, giving rise to a reciprocity that is purely notational. But in most societies marriage is mediated by a set of intermediary transactions. If we see these transactions as simply implying immediate or long-term reciprocity, then the analysis is likely to be blurred.... The analysis is further limited if one regards the passage of property simply as a symbol of the transfer of rights, for then the nature of the objects handed over . . . is of little importance.... Neither of these approaches is wrong; both are inadequate. (Goody, 1973:2)

There are systems in which there is no equivalent for a woman. To get a wife, a man must have a daughter, a sister, or other female kinswoman in whom he has a right of bestowal. He must have control over some female flesh. The Lele and Kuma are cases in point. Lele men scheme constantly in order to stake claims in some as yet unborn girl, and scheme further to make good their claims (Douglas, 1963). A Kuma girl's marriage is determined by an intricate web of debts, and she has little say in choosing her husband. A girl is usually married against her will, and her groom shoots an arrow into her thigh to symbolically prevent her from running away. The young wives almost always do run away, only to be returned to their new husbands by an elaborate conspiracy enacted by their kin and affines (Reay, 1959).

In other societies, there is an equivalent for women. A woman can be converted into bridewealth, and bridewealth can be in turn converted into a woman. The dynamics of such systems vary accordingly, as does the specific kind of pressure exerted upon women. The marriage of a Melpa woman is not a return for a previous debt. Each transaction is self-contained, in that the payment of a bridewealth in pigs and shells will cancel the debt. The Melpa woman therefore has more latitude in choosing her husband than does her Kuma counterpart. On the other hand, her destiny is linked to bridewealth. If her husband's kin are slow to pay, her kin may encourage her to leave him. On the other hand, if her consanguineal kin are satisfied with the balance of payments, they may refuse to back her in the event that she wants to leave her husband. Moreover, her male kinsmen use the bridewealth for their own purposes, in *moka* exchange and for their own marriages. If a woman leaves her husband, some or all of the bridewealth will have to be returned. If, as is usually the case, the pigs and shells have been distributed or promised, her kin will be reluctant to back her in the event of marital discord. And each time a woman divorces and remarries, her value in bridewealth tends to depreciate. On the whole, her male consanguines will lose in the event of a divorce, unless the groom has been delinquent in his payments. While the Melpa woman is freer as a new bride than a Kuma woman, the bridewealth system makes divorce difficult or impossible (Strathern, 1972).

In some societies, like the Nuer, bridewealth can only be converted into brides. In others, bridewealth can be converted into something else, like political prestige. In this case, a woman's marriage is implicated in a political system. In the Big Man systems of Highland New Guinea, the material which circulates for women also circulates in the exchanges on which political power is based. Within the political system, men are in constant need of valuables to disburse, and they are dependent upon input. They depend not only upon their immediate partners, but upon the partners of their partners, to several degrees of remove. If a man has to return some bridewealth he may not be able to give it to someone who planned to give it to someone else who intended to use it to give a feast upon which his status depends. Big Men are therefore concerned with the domestic affairs of others, whose relationship with them may be extremely indirect. There are cases in which headmen intervene in marital disputes involving indirect trading partners in order that *moka* exchanges not be disrupted (Bulmer, 1969:11). The weight of this entire system may come to rest upon one woman kept in a miserable marriage.

In short, there are other questions to ask of a marriage system than whether or not it exchanges women. Is the woman traded for a woman, or is there an equivalent? Is this equivalent only for women, or can it be turned into something else? If it can be turned into something else, is it turned into political power or wealth? On the other hand, can bridewealth be obtained only in marital exchange, or can it be obtained from elsewhere? Can women be accumulated through amassing wealth? Can wealth be accumulated by disposing of women? Is a marriage system part of a system of stratification?*

These last questions point to another task for a political economy of sex. Kinship and marriage are always parts of total social systems, and are always tied into economic and political arrangements.

> Lévi-Strauss . . . rightly argues that the structural implications of a marriage can only be understood if we think of it as one item in a whole series of transactions between kin groups. So far, so good. But in none of the examples which he provides in his book does he carry this principle far enough. The reciprocities of kinship obligation are not merely symbols of alliance, they are also economic transactions, political transactions, charters to rights of domicile and land use. No useful picture of "how a kinship sys-

* Another line of inquiry would compare bridewealth systems to dowry systems. Many of these questions are treated in Goody and Tambiah, 1973.

> tem works" can be provided unless these several aspects or implications of the kinship organization are considered simultaneously. (Leach, 1971:90)

Among the Kachin, the relationship of a tenant to a landlord is also a relationship between a son-in-law and a father-in-law. "The procedure for acquiring land rights of any kind is in almost all cases tantamount to marrying a woman from the lineage of the lord" (ibid.:88). In the Kachin system, bridewealth moves from commoners to aristocrats, women moving in the opposite direction.

> From an economic aspect the effect of matrilateral cross-cousin marriage is that, on balance, the headman's lineage constantly pays wealth to the chief's lineage in the form of bridewealth. The payment can also, from an analytical point of view, be regarded as a rent paid to the senior landlord by the tenant. The most important part of this payment is in the form of consumer goods —namely cattle. The chief converts this perishable wealth into imperishable prestige through the medium of spectacular feasting. The ultimate consumers of the goods are in this way the original producers, namely, the commoners who attend the feast. (Ibid.:89)

In another example, it is traditional in the Trobriands for a man to send a harvest gift—*urigubu*— of yams to his sister's household. For the commoners, this amounts to a simple circulation of yams. But the chief is polygamous, and marries a woman from each subdistrict within his domain. Each of these subdistricts therefore sends *urigubu* to the chief, providing him with a bulging storehouse out of which he finances feasts, craft production, and *kula* expeditions. This "fund of power" underwrites the political system and forms the basis for chiefly power (Malinowski, 1970).

In some systems, position in a political hierarchy and position in a marriage system are intimately linked. In traditional Tonga, women married up in rank. Thus, low-ranking lineages would send women to higher ranking lineages. Women of the highest lineage were married into the "house of Fiji," a lineage defined as outside the political system. If the highest ranking chief gave his sister to a lineage other than one which had no part in the ranking system, he would no longer be the highest ranking chief. Rather, the lineage of his sister's son would outrank his own. In times of political rearrangement, the demotion of the previous high-ranking lineage was formalized when it gave a wife to a lineage which it had formerly outranked. In traditional Hawaii, the situation was the reverse. Women married down, and the dominant lineage gave wives to junior lines. A paramount would either marry a sister or obtain a wife from Tonga. When a junior lineage usurped rank, it formalized its position by giving a wife to its former senior line.

There is even some tantalizing data suggesting that marriage systems may be implicated in the evolution of social strata, and perhaps in the development of early states. The first round of the political consolidation which resulted in the formation of a state in Madagascar occurred when one chief obtained title to several autonomous districts through the vagaries of marriage and inheritance (Henry Wright, personal communication). In Samoa, legends place the origin of the paramount title—the *Tafa'ifa*—as a result of intermarriage between ranking members of four major lineages. My thoughts are too speculative, my data too sketchy, to say much on this subject. But a search ought to be undertaken for data which might demonstrate how marriage systems intersect with large-scale political processes like state-making. Marriage systems might be implicated in a number of ways: in the accumulation of wealth and the maintenance of differential access to political and economic resources; in the building of alliances; in the consolidation of high-ranking persons into a single closed strata of endogamous kin.

These examples—like the Kachin and the Trobriand ones—indicate that sexual systems cannot, in the final analysis, be understood in complete isolation. A full-bodied analysis of women in a single society, or throughout history, must take *everything* into account: the evolution of commodity forms in women, systems of land tenure, political arrangements, subsistence technology, etc. Equally important, economic and political analyses are incomplete if they do not consider women, marriage, and sexuality. Traditional concerns of anthropology and social science—such as the evolution of social stratification and the origin of the state—must be reworked to include the implications of matrilateral cross-cousin marriage, surplus extracted in the form of daughters, the conversion of female labor into male wealth, the conversion of female lives into marriage alliances, the contribution of marriage to political power, and the transformations which all of these varied aspects of society have undergone in the course of time.

This sort of endeavor is, in the final analysis, exactly what Engels tried to do in his effort to weave a coherent analysis of so many of the diverse aspects of social life. He tried to relate men and women, town and country, kinship and state, forms of property, systems of land tenure, convertibility of wealth, forms of exchange, the technology of food production, and forms of trade, to name a few, into a systematic historical account. Eventually, someone will have to write a new version of *The Origin of the Family, Private Property, and the State*, recognizing the mutual interdependence of sexuality, economics, and politics without underestimating the full significance of each in human society.

Karen Sacks

Engels Revisited: Women, the Organization of Production, and Private Property

This paper reexamines Engels' ideas on the bases of women's social position relative to that of men. Engels is almost alone in providing a materialist theory—one that sees women's position as varying from society to society, or epoch to epoch, according to the prevailing economic and political relationships of the society. Though he made a number of specific ethnographic errors,* I think his main ideas are correct—and remain the best way of explaining data gathered since he wrote—namely ethnographic and historical data which show that women's social position has *not* always been, everywhere or in most respects, subordinate to that of men.

This is a somewhat revised version of a paper of the same title that appeared in *Woman, Culture, and Society*, edited by Michelle Zimbalist Rosaldo and Louise Lamphere, and is reprinted with the permission of the publishers, Stanford University Press. Special personal thanks to Shelley Rosaldo and Louise Lamphere for facilitating this reprinting. Judith K. Brown, Kathleen Gough, Bridget O'Laughlin, Dorothy Remy, Jean Williams, and Soon Young Yoon all contributed a great deal to this paper through their valuable suggestions and criticisms.

* I have excluded enumeration of these partly for lack of space, but also because they are substantively secondary and are more than amply dealt with by others. Two such errors, however, are germane to the discussion in this paper. Engels believed that men were always the collectors or producers of subsistence. It has since become clear that for gathering-hunting societies the reverse is closer to the norm (Lee and DeVore, 1968); and for horticultural societies, it is often the women's

Since capitalism has dominated and transformed the social orders of most of the world's peoples, it is useful to look to the past, as Engels did, through ethnographic and historical reconstruction, both to understand the present state of affairs and to help shape the future. Looking at noncapitalist ways of organizing economic and political relations and how these affected the relative positions of men and women provided Engels with an answer as to why women were subordinate to men in capitalist society, and what political and economic changes were needed to end sexual inequality.

The Origin of the Family, Private Property, and the State (1891) is more than an analysis of women's status. It is a contrast between nonclass and class societies. Set in an evolutionary framework, it shows how private property originated; and how, once on the scene, it undermined an egalitarian tribal order, creating families as economic units, inequality of property ownership, and, finally, exploitative class societies. It includes a description of how women's social position declined as private property gained strength as an organizing principle of society, and weaves in an analysis of why property had the effect it did; specifically, how it transformed women's work organization and, more generally, the relationship of property to class and sex.

The first part of this paper pulls together some of Engels' key points on how the sexual egalitarianism of preclass societies was undermined by changes in women's work, and by the growth of the family as an important economic unit. It is a selective and somewhat interpretive summary: selective in that it focuses on Engels' ideas about public labor, the family, and private property as they relate to women's status, and excludes his discussion of incest, exogamy, and the early

---

horticultural activities which are the basis of subsistence (see Judith Brown, this volume). Engels also believed that the domestication of animals preceded cultivation of the soil. Today, as a result of more recent research, a more commonly accepted theory is that cultivation and pastoralism developed at the same time in the same milieu, as progressively divergent and somewhat interdependent adaptations (Lattimore, 1957).

stages of human social evolution in general*; interpretive in that I have used some of what has been learned since Engels wrote as the lens through which to view his ideas. A second section redefines some of Engels' terminology and framework in the context of nonclass societies. The third section examines, using ethnographic data, Engels' ideas about the importance of public labor, private property, and the family for determining women's status. While these indeed appear to be factors determining women's position, this examination suggests some modification of Engels' idea that women are *either* social adults *or* wifely dependents. Based on this modification, namely that the existence of private property does not directly lead to a lower social status for women, the fourth section suggests an alternate explanation for Engels' observation that class societies have used the family to circumscribe and subordinate women.

Women in Engels' Theory: A Reconstruction

Engels presents a historical process by which women are transformed from free and equal productive *members of society* to subordinate and dependent *wives* and wards. The growth of male-owned private property, with the family as the institution that appropriates and perpetuates it, is the cause of this transformation.

According to Engels, in the early stages of society productive resources were owned communally by the tribe or the clan. Food had to be collected and cooked daily. Production was for use only, that is, to meet people's subsistence needs. There was no surplus produced for exchange.** The group,

* For a full discussion of Engels' entire work in the light of current knowledge, Eleanor Leacock's Introduction to the 1972 edition is of key importance. Kathleen Gough, in "The Origin of the Family" (1971 and this volume), and in "An Anthropologist Looks at Engels" (1972), provides important reexaminations of Engels' theory of women.

** Though Engels does not deal with this situation, people in many nonclass and noncapitalist societies do in fact produce for exchange. The question of how production for exchange in these societies differs consisting of husband, wife, and dependent children, was neither a productive unit nor one for performing housework —nor did it own property. Since Engels saw economic functions (production, consumption, and property ownership), as defining the family, and since this group was in no way an economic unit, the family did not exist at this stage; it had not precipitated out of the larger household. The household, which was the basic social and economic unit, was communistic in that all food stores were held in common, and all work was done for the household rather than for individual members or couples. Women did the housework and ran these households.

> In the old communistic household, which embraced numerous couples and their children, the administration of the household, entrusted to the women, was just as much a public, a socially necessary industry as the providing of food by the men. (Engels, 1891:120)

Instead of the family, the context of men's and women's life and labor was a larger group based on kinship or residence in a common territory. This was a communal property-owning group, called the *gens* by Engels. Although individuals of both sexes owned tools and personal effects, on their death these passed to other members of the same sex in their *gens*, not necessarily to their own children. Decision-making, both economic and political, involved the equal participation of all members, both men and women. Both sexes were equal members of the group because both made crucial contributions to its economic life.

Engels concluded that the absence of private property made men's productive work and women's household work of equal social significance. Men and women were simply involved in different stages of the production of the same

---

from that of capitalist societies is a complex one. A good discussion of the fundamental differences involved can be found in Marshall Sahlins, *Stone Age Economics* (1971).

kinds of goods—the production of subsistence. All production was of the same kind: production for use.

Engels focused on the public rights of women in the early stages of society: their participation in political decision-making and (for the Iroquois) their collective right to depose a chief. These rights came from membership in the *gens*, which in turn was based on the performance of public or social labor. He was also impressed with the high status of a wife relative to that of her husband, which he attributed to the solidarity and kinship among the women, who were the core of the household.

The material base for women's transformation from equal members of society to subordinate wives lay in the development of valuable productive resources, initially the domestication of large animals, as private property. For Engels, the words "private" and "property" had a specific meaning. Only goods or resources with productive potential could be considered *property*. He was aware that people held personal goods individually. Though these were private, they were not property in the sense Engels meant the word. Only things with productive potential can be considered property. Tools (productive means) are unimportant because the skills and materials for their manufacture are equally available to all. In non-industrial societies, the most important types of private property are domesticated animals and cultivated land. These are productive *resources*.

Engles' use of the word "private" is broader than its use under capitalism—where there are almost no restrictions on what the owner can do with property. For Engels, private seems to mean property owned by an individual or by a family where rights to manage it are vested in one of the owners. It also means that these goods can be disposed of with *some* leeway—that is, to acquire wives, clients, or service from others. Engels saw "gaining a livelihood" as always men's work, and the means of production as always having been owned by the user (with the stipulation that inheritance remained in the *gens*). From this he reasoned that the earliest private property, which seemed to be domestic animals, must have been owned by men.* For Engels, private property became possible in human history only when technological development and natural resources allowed a society to develop the skills needed to domesticate animals or to invest labor in land so that its productivity lasted for some appreciable length of time. He believed that enduring productivity led to enduring private ownership.

Domesticated animals were assimilated into the older patterns of tool ownership—that is, they were privately owned. Yet animals were a qualitatively new kind of item: they met subsistence needs, and they reproduced themselves. The growth of private property shattered the communal political economy of the *gens*. The foundation for its egalitarianism had been the collective ownership of productive property. Now that property was privately owned (by men), the family grew in importance and soon overshadowed the *gens* as the key economic and decision-making group. Unlike the *gens*, though, internal family structure was not egalitarian. Families contained propertyless dependents (all women and children, and some propertyless men).

Private property transformed the relations between men and women within the *household* only because it also radically changed the political and economic relations in the larger *society*. For Engels the new wealth in domesticated animals meant that there was a surplus of goods available for exchange between productive units. With time, production by men specifically for exchange purposes developed, expanded, and came to overshadow the household's production for use. Industrial capitalism had now reached the stage where pro-

* It is worth noting that Engels saw these new items (domesticated animals, cultivated land) as being assimilated into an already existing social context: the pattern of owning personal effects. The qualitatively different nature of these new "effects"—that they could reproduce themselves and their fruits—led to the destruction of the communal political and economic order that had created them. Engels does not attribute the development of private property to a greedy male nature.

duction was almost exclusively social, outside the household, and for exchange, leaving women's work as private maintenance for *family* use.

As production for exchange eclipsed production for use, it changed the nature of the household, the significance of women's work within it, and consequently women's position in society. Women worked for their husbands and families instead of for society as a whole. Private property made its owner the ruler of the household. Women and other propertyless dependents worked to maintain and augment the household head's property, for he was now engaged in competitive production and exchange with other heads of households. Women's labor was a necessary but socially subordinate part of producing an exchangeable surplus. Women became wards, wives, and daughters instead of adult members of the society.

Families perpetuated themselves through time by the inheritance of property. Thus changes took place in the definition of children. From new members of a societal group, they became either private heirs or subordinate, dependent workers. This meant that women's reproductive labor, like their productive work, also underwent a transformation from social to private. That is, women bore *men's* heirs—to both property and social position—whereas before they had borne new members of a social group that included men and women. People and property became intertwined, and each became part of the definition of the other.

With the further development of technology and accumulation of wealth, the property owners separated themselves from their subordinate kinsmen and allied with other property owners to preserve and defend their holdings against the claims of the nonpropertied. This marked the end of kinship-based productive groups, and the beginning of class society and the state.

Engels' Theory and Nonclass Societies

To use Engels' concepts of social labor and production for exchange and apply them to nonclass societies, I will have to redefine them so that they are more in line with the ways these societies are organized. Engels' use of social or public labor in nonclass societies emphasizes work for and in the context of one's own corporate property-owning group. But marriage often joins two such groups; this generally means that at least one partner is not working for and in the context of his or her natal group. At the same time, he or she is not necessarily doing what Engels would call domestic work—work for one's own household. Therefore I will stretch his concept of social labor to include any work done (singly or in a group) for use or appropriation by someone of another household. Some examples of social labor, illustrated in the next section, indicate the wide range of organizations it covers: participation in a cooperative work group, tributary labor for a chief, corvée, collective livestock raiding, etc.

Engels' discussion of production for exchange in the context of nonclass societies has to be amplified somewhat. People do not spontaneously work to produce a surplus as Engels implies (1891:264). There has to be some power forcing them to produce more than they use. People in all societies give hospitality and gifts, and these always put the recipient under an obligation to make a return. In a general way, as long as everyone has equal access to the means of subsistence, production is planned to include hospitality and gifts, and these are things which everyone has or can expect to have by his or her own effort—and can thus make an equivalent return in goods. But when the means of subsistence are privately and unequally held, a recipient is often unable to make an equivalent return in goods. He or she may then be expected to return the favor with service and become a loyal dependent or client-follower, perhaps part of a retinue helping enforce unequal exchange.

Both situations, the return of equivalent goods and the return of service for goods, are instances of exchange. But only the second gives one of the parties the ability to harness the labor power of others for his or her own ends. Thus the production of goods to gain control over the services of others must also be included in production for exchange. Indeed, Engels argues that the domestic and private ownership of cattle brought with it increased productivity of labor and the use of cattle to conquer or purchase labor to serve the wealthy (ibid.:265).

While production of goods for trade or barter between groups exists in societies without private property, it exists in the fabric of a political economy geared principally toward production for use. Perhaps this fabric was first rent when private property allowed the use of wealth to gain followers,* and then the need to use the productive and military labor of one's followers to create still more wealth to keep their loyalty. In any case, this particular kind of production for exchange in nonclass societies goes hand in hand with private property, and with economic and political inequality.

For example, there is wealth inequality and clientage in nonclass societies with large domesticated animals. These animals not only contribute to subsistence, but they are also necessary in order for a man to marry and to have some political standing. Thus, in much of East Africa prior to imperialist rule, men obtained cattle from kinsmen or from service to a chief or other wealthy man, to whom they then owed loyalty in exchange for the cattle. The production of cattle was a kind of production for exchange, in that loyalty and service were given for livestock and were used to augment the wealth and power of the benefactor, whether kinsman or not. Regardless of overlapping rights and obligations of various people to the livestock, the cattle were private property because there was some choice in how they would be allocated, and because an individual was empowered to make that choice.

* A discussion of the variety of conditions under which loyal followers would be desirable belongs in a consideration of the origin of stratification and the state, which is beyond the scope of this paper.

Women as Social Adults and Wives: Four African Societies

Though Engels has an integrated theory, at the risk of some distortion I would like to separate out two sets of ideas: (1) Those about the immediate determinants or material bases of women's status—that social or public labor makes men or women adult citizens in the eyes of society and that men's ownership of private property establishes their dominance over women in the family and society. (2) Those about the evolutionary aspect—that women's status became solely subordinate and domestic with the development of male private property, production for exchange, and class society.

In this section I will discuss the immediate determinants of women's status by using ethnographic illustrations. This has the advantage of focusing first on the material bases of women's position. Even if Engels is right in a general way, that women are worse off in class than in nonclass societies, we still need to know what gives rise to this state. Using ethnographic reconstruction allows us to look at some of the variety in women's status in noncapitalist societies—nonclass as well as class—and to use the comparisons to illuminate Engels' ideas.

I do not believe that Engels' evolutionary explanation is correct as it stands: there is too much data showing that women are not the complete equals of men in most nonclass societies lacking private property. There are also many societies, with and without classes, where women do own and inherit property. The final section will use some illustrations from class societies to suggest a different route to Engels' conclusions.

The following illustration is a reconstruction, mainly from ethnographic sources, of women's position in four African societies prior to the imposition of effective imperialist domination.*

* This section summarizes a portion of my dissertation (Sacks, 1971). These societies were selected from the writings on East and Southern Africa because the data on women are adequate and comparable. Thus

The Mbuti of Zaïre can be characterized as a band society with subsistence based on communal net hunting and the gathering of vegetable food. In South Africa, the Lovedu were principally hoe agriculturalists, while the Pondo combined agriculture with livestock. The Ganda, a class society in Uganda, were also hoe agriculturalists.

If we place these societies on a continuum from egalitarian to class society, our rankings can be seen to hold in three principal respects. First, Mbuti and Lovedu have economies of production for use; the Pondo have the beginnings of production for exchange centered around cattle; and in Ganda production for exchange is quite important. Second, in Mbuti and Lovedu both sexes perform social labor in a use economy; among the Pondo, this remains the organization of women's labor, but the men perform social labor at least in part in an exchange economy; and in Ganda women's work is individual domestic production for household use, while men work in groups, almost totally in production for exchange. Third, the Mbuti band owns the productive resources; these are largely patrilineal family estates in Lovedu and Pondo; and in Ganda they become less enmeshed in family obligations and are in male hands.

Among the Mbuti, Lovedu, and Pondo, women's productive activities are social and women have an adult social status. In Ganda, where women's productive activities are domestic, the status of woman is that of wife and ward only—despite the fact that women produce the bulk of the food. This suggests that Engels is right in seeing public or social labor as the basis for social adulthood. A more detailed look, however, shows that women do not have to be characterized as *either* social adults *or* wifely wards. Rather, the data suggest that women can be both simultaneously, and that women's status in a marital relationship seems to vary independently of their status in the larger society. Engels does seem correct in seeing the status of wife relative to husband

---

many aspects—for example, concerning women in trade and marketing roles—though they are important, simply cannot be dealt with here.

as dependent on their relationships to the property of the household; that is, the spouse who owns the property rules the household.

Table 1 summarizes some indices of women's status in society and in the family, and their relationship to women's organization of productive activities and to property ownership.* Essentially, Mbuti and Lovedu women are the equals of men, whereas Ganda women are subordinate, and Pondo women fall somewhere in between. The first nine variables I see as representing social adulthood, and the first five of these involve egalitarian relationships with people outside the household.

A look at the first variable, mutual-aid relationships, suggests that social adulthood is based on performing collective social labor. Though the Mbuti have no categories of relationship that are specifically identifiable as mutual aid, Lovedu men and women both have some sort of age groupings that are mobilized to do some work for the district head and queen.** For women, at least, those of a neighborhood age group may take collective action against the group of a person who has offended one of its members. Pondo women of a neighborhood work together and cooperate in the performance of girls' initiation ceremonies, and women of the same household cooperate in arranging extramarital sexual affairs. Women's collective action is recognized by men when they collectively punish women and girls for what they deem to be sex offenses. Ganda men enter a number of mutual-aid relationships with nonkin, or even non-Ganda; women have no such relationships.

Self-representation in legal proceedings indicates that a woman is regarded as able to be wronged or to do wrong in the eyes of society, as is the case among Mbuti, Lovedu, and

* The variables and their categorization, rather than being determined in advance by a logical scheme, emerged as a result of comparing the position of women in each of these four societies.

** "Queen," the title used in the ethnographies, is a misnomer. The office is actually that of a tribal chief, carrying moral authority but little if any coercive power.

Table 1
Women's Social and Domestic Status Compared with Men's in Four African Societies

Indexes of women's status	*Discrimination against women's participation*			
	Mbuti	*Lovedu*	*Pondo*	*Ganda*
Social				
Mutual aid	n.a.	none	none	active
Self-representation	none	none	none	active
Socializing opportunity	none	none	none	active
Extramarital sex	none	none	none	active
Divorce	none	none	none	active
Social disposal of wealth	none	none	active	active
Political office	none	none	active	active
Extradomestic dispute settlement	none	none	active	active
Extradomestic mediation with supernatural	none	none	active	active
Domestic				
Wife's inheritance of marital estate	none	active	active	active
Wife's authority over domestic affairs	none	active	active	active
Wife as private reproducer (adultery compensation)	none	active	active	active
Menstrual and pregnancy restrictions	none	weak	weak	active

Note: Ownership of major productive resources: the band in Mbuti, the family in Lovedu and Pondo, and the individual in Ganda. Collective social production by women, as against that by men: equal in Mbuti and Lovedu, unequal in Pondo, and absent in Ganda.

Pondo. A Ganda woman, by contrast, needs a male guardian (generally a husband or father) to bring her case to court. The guardian is held responsible for her acts and receives compensation for wrongs done to her.

Though Mbuti, Lovedu, and Pondo men and women participate in most of the same social activities, in the latter two societies young wives are kept busy at domestic work, which significantly restricts their ability to enjoy these events. But as older wives, as sisters visiting their own kinsmen, and as diviners, women attend social events as freely as do men. In Ganda, a large portion of the social activities are patron- or state-oriented; from these, women are excluded.

Mbuti and Lovedu have a single standard regarding extramarital sexual affairs. Pondo women view their extramarital affairs as right and proper, but the men see women's affairs as immoral. A Ganda husband may kill his wife for real or suspected adultery, but a wife has little recourse against her husband. Men may use the courts to deal out severe punishment to their wives' lovers. In general, Ganda restricts extramarital sexual activity much more than do the other societies. Exceptions are made for high-ranking men who have affairs with peasant women, but men and women in the reverse situation are punished severely. Yehudi Cohen's (1969) point that restricted sexual activity serves to strengthen the marital bond at the expense of bonds which could serve as a basis for rebellion in class societies seems borne out here.

While marital and social status are very closely related, the ease of divorce for men versus women indicates the relative importance of marital and social status for each. In Ganda a husband can effectively end a marriage by simply ignoring his wife, but a woman who wishes a divorce must contend not only with her husband but with her brother, who is partial guardian and generally acts to preserve the marriage.

Being able to give and receive food and items of social exchange is the material basis for exercising political power. Engels suggests that real power develops only with production for exchange and private property. In societies without these—that is, in societies based on production for use—the performance of social labor gives a person the right to join with other adults in making political decisions and settling disputes. This is because political decision-making and dispute settlement are responsibilities of adult members of an egalitarian society. Among Mbuti and Lovedu both sexes give and receive food. Lovedu women give and receive cattle and may marry a wife with them; they become husbands in social status. Pondo women, though they are social producers, cannot dispose of the most important exchange item: livestock. Perhaps the explanation lies in the nature of Pondo production for exchange. Women's agricultural work is for use; work is geared over the long and short run to the needs of the households. But men's organization for livestock raiding involves them in production for exchange. Over the short run, warfare is geared more to the power need of a chief, who keeps a following by having cattle to distribute, than to household needs. Over the long run a chief keeps power by actually distributing cattle more or less widely. He owns the cattle captured in warfare, but sooner or later he distributes them among the warriors by virtue of their role in raiding. These livestock are the chief's to allocate. They are the most important item of exchange (in bridewealth, loans, and feasts), and of establishing long-term relationships (marriage and service). Because Pondo women do not participate in production for exchange (raiding), they cannot dispose of the property which establishes these power relationships. Thus, they do not hold overt political power.

Lovedu women hold political office, enter the decision-making arenas of the society, and predominate in officiating in religious rituals on behalf of their lineages. Ganda peasant women are barred from even the minimal access to political positions available to peasant men. Yet the mother and one sister of the king do hold important offices and exercise some power predicated on their relationship to the king.

A wife's position vis-à-vis her husband is based on her ownership, or lack of it, of the marital estate. In Lovedu, Pondo, and Ganda, productive resources are inherited patrilineally. Here there is a contradiction, or opposition, between the fact that production is organized in a social or public way, but that families or individuals appropriate and inherit the productive resources. A wife does not participate in the ownership of resources of her marital household. On the other hand, the Mbuti's appropriation for *use* by families seems to me qualitatively different from the appropriation for inheritance and exchange of the other societies. Mbuti resources are owned by the territorial band as a whole. Residence entitles a person to use these, and there is no inheritance. Thus, Mbuti husbands and wives have the same relationship to the band resources.

Lovedu, Pondo, and Ganda wives labor for their husbands and their husbands' patrikin, but do not belong to the group that appropriates the product of their labor. Wives provide heirs, raise children, and do the bulk of the domestic work under the authority of the husband and his kin. They do not represent the household to outsiders. By contrast, Mbuti marriage carries no restrictions on a woman's authority over her work, children, or socializing. Her fertility cannot be said to be private since her husband receives no compensation for her extramarital sexual relationships.

Menstrual and pregnancy restrictions on women's activities among Lovedu, Pondo, and Ganda seem to operate to separate women's reproductive functions from contact with the social production of exchange goods; that is, from contact with warriors, cattle, craft, and some medical practices. In these three societies children inherit property and continue the family line. Regardless of how women's productive activities are organized, their reproductive potential is private. But among the Mbuti, where children are social members rather than private heirs, menstruation and pregnancy are not surrounded by any such restrictions. This contrast suggests that menstrual and pregnancy restrictions are based on private property, and that they serve to symbolize a contradiction between social production of exchange goods and private or familial appropriation. Since men are also involved in the reproductive process, and contain the same contradiction, logically they should—and actually they do—face analagous restrictions. Lovedu, Pondo, and Ganda men must separate sexual relations from their participation in social production for exchange. By contrast Mbuti regard the collective hunt as an ideal time for sexual liaisons.

A final point remains. Though Ganda is a class society, I have not dealt with the differences between women of ruling and peasant families. There are several privileges accorded to wives, sisters, and daughters of the king. Each category of ruling-class women shares some privilege with ruling-class men which distinguishes them from peasant women: freedom from productive labor for some wives; sexual freedom for sisters and daughters; political and economic power for the queen mother and sister. But none of these women has all the privileges of the men of their class, which seems to reflect the contradictory position of ruling-class women: they are of a privileged class, but of a subordinate sex. I have not dealt with them in depth because their existence does not really change the generalizations made on the basis of peasant women. This should not be surprising if we recall Queen Victoria and her times in England, but it should make one wary of generalizations based on a few women holding prominent positions.

Though I have separated women's position as wives from their position as social beings, in reality the two are interrelated. Wifely subservience reduces the ability of Lovedu and Pondo women to exercise their social prerogatives. They are held back from social activities to the extent that they work under the authority of husband and his kin. Similarly, while Pondo women may become diviners, and while most diviners are women—allowing the women opportunities for travel, socializing, and financial reward—they may not be initiated to practice without their husband's consent.

Things can work the other way also. If a woman is socially regarded as an adult, this can limit the extent to which she can be subordinated as a wife. Thus, while a Pondo woman's fertility may be said to belong to her husband, and while he may claim compensation for her extramarital sexual affairs, this is a matter between men. Women regard these affairs as proper, and are assisted in arranging them by their husband's own kinswomen. Moreover, should a woman choose to end a marriage or visit her own kin, there is little her husband can do to prevent it.

I have suggested that there are two aspects to women's position—women as social adults, and women as wives—and that these can vary somewhat independently. What determines how, or whether, women are regarded as adults is not the same as what determines their positions vis-à-vis their husbands. Basically, women are social adults where they work collectively as part of a productive group larger than or separate from their domestic establishment. The meaning and status of "wife," though, depend on the nature of the family in much the way Engels suggests. Where the estate is familial, and the wife works for it but does not share in its ownership, she is in much the same relationship to her husband and his kin as is a worker to his boss. Where there are no private estates, or perhaps where the family estate is jointly owned, the *domestic* relationship is a more egalitarian one (Friedl, 1967). This last point is overstated, since the domestic and social spheres of life are not really independent. On the basis of the American experience, it is difficult to conceive of a completely egalitarian domestic relationship when only the male partner is regarded as fully adult beyond the bounds of the household.

Women in Class Societies: A Reinterpretation

If we agree that the position of women declined from Mbuti and Lovedu to Ganda, as illustrated above, in direct correlation to the domestication of women's work and the development of production for exchange and private property, it is tempting to conclude that Engels was right after all—that private property and production for exchange lead to women's domestication and subordination. Many anthropologists accept something like Engels' view of the relationship between private property and the growth of social inequality and classes. While I suspect that women in general stand in more equal relationship to men in nonclass societies than in class societies, I do not think that male property ownership is the basis for the male's supremacy. First, not all males own productive property. Second, in many class societies—even in those with a strong pattern of male dominance—women as well as men own productive property, and a wife's ownership of property gives her a substantial amount of domestic power vis-à-vis her husband (ibid.). But class societies make a sharp dichotomy between the domestic and public spheres of life, and this domestic power is not translatable into social power or position in the public sphere. Moreover, in class societies the economic and political autonomy of a household is quite restricted. Thus, in necessary dealings in the public sector women are at an overt or covert disadvantage. This probably militates against even domestic equality.

It seems likely, then, that in class societies the subordinate position of women derives not from domestic property relations but from something outside the household which denies women adult social status. The question is then why do male public power and ideals of male social dominance predominate in class societies? For an explanation, the focus has to shift from the domestic to the societal level.

We have seen that public or social labor is the material basis for adult social status. It follows that a society would have to exclude women from public labor or in some way denigrate women's performance of such labor in order to deny them social adulthood for any length of time.* The former seems to have been the case, at least for many precapitalist agrarian states of Eurasia (Boserup, 1970). Leaving aside for the moment the apparent exception of industrial capitalism, what were the circumstances that may have led class societies to exclude women from social production?

*** An earlier version of this paper argued that all precapitalist class societies excluded women from public labor. Kathleen Gough has pointed out (personal communication) that this was not the case in precapitalist Indian states. I have thus modified this section.**

Class societies are exploitative, which means that many people must work for the benefit of a few. While tithes and taxes on domestically produced goods can serve this end, even agrarian societies do not rely exclusively, or even mainly, on this form of production. Corvée for public works, both sumptuary and productive, conscription and predatory war, and collective agricultural or wage work for the rulers—all collective forms of social or public labor—are important productive activities in class societies. While these may not necessarily seem large from the local viewpoint, they are crucial nationally—for creating the "surpluses" by which rulers and their states are maintained.

Though women may or may not engage in domestic agriculture, they seem rarely to participate in these large-scale forms of social production. It seems that class societies tend to socialize the work of men and domesticate that of women. This creates the material and organizational foundations for denying that women are adults and allows ruling classes to define them as wards of men.

But why would this happen in a class society? With the development of socialized production for a ruling class, domestic production for subsistence becomes more precarious, forcing people into greater reliance on production for exchange—laboring for the rulers in exchange for their subsistence (alternatively, rulers can force people to work for them as a condition of access to subsistence resources). Ruling classes tend to select men as social laborers partly because they are more mobile, but probably more significantly because they can be more intensively exploited than women, not having to nurse and rear children.

Alice Clark (1968) provides rather gruesome data from seventeenth-century England, a period *preceding* and setting the social conditions for later industrialization. Peasants were being forced off the land and swelling a class of rural, landless laborers. The idea of wages as something paid for a task was not yet fully institutionalized; and it conflicted with the earlier notion that an employer was in some way obligated to meet the subsistence needs of the worker. Yet payments were so low that a landless family had difficulty surviving. A man or woman without children could survive, but prevailing remuneration did not allow for reproduction and rearing of the next generation of laborers. Indeed, they did not reproduce themselves. Clark shows that the laboring class grew in size only from constant new recruits from the peasantry. Women and children were deliberately excluded from wage work by employers, who felt an obligation to, but could not or would not, bear the burden of supporting nonproductive dependents. In human terms the results were the abandonment of women and their early death, and in organizational terms a largely male public labor force.

Once such a dichotomy is made—women in domestic work for family use, men in social production for exchange—there is an organizational basis for a sexual divide-and-rule policy. Whether such policy is conscious or not is irrelevant. The *effect* of state legal systems and other aspects of ideology developed mainly by ruling classes has been to convert differences between men and women in terms of their roles in production into differential worth. Through their labor men are social adults; women are domestic wards.

Men are more directly exploited and more often collectively so—a situation which gives them the possibility of doing something about it. Women's field of activity and major responsibility is restricted to the household, which neither produces nor owns the means of production for more than domestic subsistence, a level of organization at which little can be done to institute social change in a class society. This situation has several consequences. First, women are relegated to the bottom of a social pecking order (a *man's* home is his castle). Second, because of their isolation and exclusion from the public sector, women can be used as a conservative force, unconsciously upholding the status quo in their commitment to the values surrounding maintenance of home, family, and children. Finally, the family is the sole institution with responsibility for consumption and for the maintenance of its members and rearing of its children, the future generation of exchange workers. It is necessary labor for the rulers, but women are forced to perform it without compensation.

Modern capitalism has maintained this pattern of exploiting the private *domestic* labor of women, but since industrialization women have also been involved heavily in public or wage labor. Meeting the labor burden that capitalism places on the family remains socially women's responsibility. Responsibility for domestic work is one of the material bases for present barriers to women working for money and for placing them in a more exploitable position than men in the public labor force. As Margaret Benston (1969) shows, this domestic work is not considered "real" work because it has only private use value and no exchange value—it is not public labor. Women's greater exploitability in the modern wage labor force may derive from a preindustrial adaptation to being excluded from public labor (ironically, because women were *less* exploitable in a pre-wage milieu). Only after they had been defined as inadequate for public labor were the conditions right for industrial capitalism to discover women as a source of cheap labor.

However, there have been precapitalist societies where women have participated in social production. On the one hand, this means that the exclusion of women is not a necessary condition for their exploitation, or for sexual divide-and-rule. On the other hand, the position of women involved in such labor seems to reinforce the thesis that social labor is the material basis of social adulthood. It suggests, too, that social adulthood is not synonymous with sexual equality in class societies.

At least some of the precapitalist states of India contained a large class of state slaves—for example, the Chola and Vijayanagar empires.* Both men and women of this class, which was recruited from the "exterior" or Untouchable castes, served as agricultural laborers for religious, military, and government officials, as well as being corvéed for public

* All the information on India has been most generously supplied by Kathleen Gough.

works. However, women were paid considerably less for their labor than men. At the same time, Gough points out that in Untouchable tenant-farming and village-service castes or classes, where women work today for village communities in similar relationships of production, they "have greater sexual freedom, power of divorce, authority to speak and witness in caste assemblies, authority over children, ability to dispose of their own belongings, rights to indemnity for wrongs done to them, rights to have disputes settled outside the domestic sphere, and representation in public rituals." In short, women who perform social labor have a higher status vis-à-vis men of their own class than do women who labor only in the domestic sphere or do no labor.

In sum, I am suggesting two patterns: (1) Intensive exploitation in social production by and for ruling classes favored making this men's work. In turn, ruling classes capitalized on the situation, legitimizing the division of labor by a thoroughgoing system of differential worth. In return for the loss of economic autonomy, they conferred upon men exclusive social adulthood and guardianship of women. Under these circumstances, even if women own property the state intervenes to limit what they can do with it publicly, and to subordinate the household to the larger society. (2) States incorporate women of the poorer or propertyless classes into social production. Here there is a "second line of defense" against equality institutionalized through pay differentials. While these women are social adults with respect to men of their class, economic policies prevent actual equality. The key aspect of women's position, especially in class societies, is social adulthood, and this comes from participation in social production.

This brief examination of the bases of women's domestic and social status suggests some tentative conclusions about the kinds of economic and social changes necessary for full sexual equality. While property ownership seems important for women's domestic position vis-à-vis a husband, the exercise of domestic power, particularly in class societies, is limited by whether or not women have adult status in the social sphere. This in turn is determined by their participation in social production. But the dichotomization of family and society, which is especially strong in class societies, makes women responsible for the production of private use value and makes men responsible for the production of exchange values. The distinction between production for use and production for exchange places a heavy responsibility on women to maintain themselves as well as exchange workers and to rear future exchange and maintenance workers. In this context, wage work (or social labor) becomes an additional burden and in no way changes women's responsibility for domestic work. For full social equality, men's and women's work must be of the same kind: the production of social use values. For this to happen, family and society cannot remain separate *economic* spheres of life. Production, consumption, child-rearing, and economic decision-making all need to take place in a single social sphere—something analogous to the Iroquois *gens* as described by Engels, or to the production brigades of China during the Great Leap Forward. What is now private family work must become public work for women to become fully social adults.

Judith K. Brown

Iroquois Women: An Ethnohistoric Note

My purpose is to investigate the relationship between the position of women and their economic role. At least three possibilities are suggested in the literature. Robert H. Lowie (1961:201) felt that the two were unrelated, that in determining women's status, economic considerations could be "offset and even negatived" by historical factors. On the other hand, Bronislaw Malinowski (1913) maintained that the considerable economic contribution of Australian aborigine women confirmed their subservient position, since their labors were extorted from them through male "brutalization." The opposite point of view is expressed by Jenness:

> If women among the Iroquois enjoyed more privileges and possessed greater freedom than the women of other tribes, this was due . . . to the important place that agriculture held in their economic life, and the distribution of labor . . . [which left] the entire cultivation of the fields and the acquisition of the greater part of the food supply to the women. (1932:137)

His explanation for the high status of women among the Iroquois stresses the extensiveness of their economic contribution. A similar position is taken by B. H. Quain (1961),

---

This is a revised and shortened version of Brown, 1970. Thanks are due to the editors of *Ethnohistory* for permission to use portions of that paper. The research was made possible by the generous support of the Radcliffe Institute. Hilda Kahne, Ying Ying Yuan, and Peter Bertocci have made numerous helpful comments on previous versions of the manuscript.

who also states that matrilineality and matrilocality contributed to the position of Iroquois women. (Stites, 1905; Murdock, 1949; Gough, 1961; Aberle, 1961; D'Andrade, 1966; and Ingliss, 1970, among others, have suggested that matrilineality and matrilocality are related to the subsistence role of women.*)

Thus the high status enjoyed by Iroquois women has been attributed to their considerable contribution to the subsistence of the tribe, or to this in addition to the practice of matrilineality and matrilocality. Closer examination reveals that neither was the case. As will be shown, it was the control of the economic organization of the tribe by Iroquois women that accounted for their high status.

The Position of Women Among the Iroquois

Most authors have described the Iroquois as if they had been a homogeneous group (see, for example, the ratings in the *Ethnographic Atlas*). They will be considered as such here, since the six member nations of the Iroquois Confederacy do not appear to have differed on the variables under consideration.

A further caution must be added. The accounts giving the fullest information describe the Iroquois during the eighteenth and nineteenth centuries. Although the data will be interpreted synchronically, certain historical factors should be kept in mind. The tribe was undergoing rapid change, and its economic organization and the status of its women did not remain constant. Cara Richards (1957) has pointed out the increase in the decision-making power of Iroquois women, and John Noon (1949) has noted the increase in their economic responsibilities in the early part of the period under consideration.

* For the sake of brevity, I have oversimplified the relationship these authors suggest. Thus for example, Gough (1961) does not imply that matrilocality and matrilineality are necessarily based on *current* division of labor. She notes that descent and residence may remain unaltered under certain conditions, in spite of changes in the division of labor.

In dealing with the position of women, two aspects of status must be clearly differentiated. High status may be inferred from deferential treatment. However, as defined here, high status consists of an actual position of power over basic resources and important decisions. The two need not coincide and should be considered separately (D'Andrade, 1966).* Among the Iroquois, women were not accorded deferential treatment. Morgan (1962:324) noted with Victorian bias that such amenities signal the advance of civilization. He observed, "The Indian regarded women as inferior, the dependent, and the servant of man, and from nurture and habit, she actually considered herself to be so." However, the position of power that Iroquois women held has been pointed out by numerous authors, such as Beauchamp (1900), Carr (1887), Goldenweiser (1912), Hewitt (1933), and Randle (1951).** Murdock's statement (1934:302) can be taken as a summary: "Indeed of all the people of the earth, the Iroquois approach most closely to that hypothetical form of society known as the matriarchate."

An early, detailed, and much-cited appraisal was made by Father Joseph Lafitau of the Society of Jesus.† Unlike other early sources, the account is not anecdotal but descriptive. The tone of the book is scholarly, and the information it contains is based on Lafitau's five-year stay in Canada, material supplied by another missionary who worked in Canada for sixty years, and material in the *Jesuit Relations*. According to Lafitau:

* There is at present no consensus on an operational definition of women's status in society. For alternative definitions, the reader is referred to Oliver, 1972; Sanday, 1973; and Sacks, this volume.

** Beauchamp, Carr, and Hewitt published their articles over a span of nearly fifty years, yet all describe Iroquois "matriarchy." Carr's article contains the most documentation. Hewitt's information is somewhat idiosyncratic and contains no documentation. He ends his article with a paraphrase of Lafitau's (1724) famous passage, but does not attribute it to its original source.

† Lafitau's charmingly illustrated four-volume work carries the inscription "avec approbation et privilege du Roy," but no doubt helped to promote the revolutionary idea of the noble savage (Fenton, 1969).

> Nothing, however, is more real than this superiority of the women. It is of them that the nation really consists; and it is through them that the nobility of the blood, the genealogical tree and the families are perpetuated. All real authority is vested in them. The land, the fields and their harvest all belong to them. They are the souls of the Councils, the arbiters of peace and of war. They have charge of the public treasury. To them are given the slaves. They arrange marriages. The children are their domain, and it is through their blood that the order of succession is transmitted. The men, on the other hand, are entirely isolated. . . . Their children are strangers to them. (1724:I:66-67; my translation)

This passage must be interpreted with caution. Lafitau does not specify in these often-quoted lines exactly which "Ameriquains" he is describing. It may be the Iroquois, the Huron, or both. The particular section from which this quotation is taken attempts to establish similarities between tribal customs and those of antiquity (foreshadowing much of late-nineteenth-century anthropology). Moreover, a number of the unusual powers enumerated were not vested in all Iroquois women, but only in the matrons, the elderly heads of households and work groups. However, such a position was achieved and could be aspired to by all women, as Martha Randle has noted. Unfortunately, there is no detailed description of how matrons were chosen. William Fenton's statement (1957:31), "the mild person who speaks easily and kindly succeeds to public roles which the women withhold from the over-anxious person," suggests that women made the selection on the basis of personality traits. However, the author does not specify the sex of the would-be office holder. (Also see Quain, 1961:257.)

The evidence for statements such as those of Murdock and Lafitau must be evaluated by examining the role of Iroquois women in the political, the religious, and the domestic life of the tribe. In the political sphere, Iroquois matrons had the power to raise and depose the ruling elders, the ability to influence the decisions of the Council, and occasional power over the conduct of war and the establishment of treaties.

Although women could not serve on the Council of Elders, the highest ruling body of the League, the hereditary eligibility for office passed through them, and the elective eligibility for office was also largely controlled by them. Alexander Goldenweiser (1912:468) gives a retrospective account of the power of the matrons to raise and depose the ruling elders (whom he called chiefs):

> When a chief died, the women of his tribe and clan held a meeting at which a candidate for the vacant place was decided upon. A woman delegate carried the news to the chiefs of the clans which belonged to the "side" of the deceased chief's clan. They had the power to veto the selection, in which case another women's meeting was called and another candidate selected. . . .

The actions of the new elder were closely watched, and if his behavior deviated from the accepted norms, he was warned by the woman delegate. If after several warnings he still did not conform, she would initiate impeachment proceedings.

It is surprising that Lewis Morgan, whose *League of the Ho-De'-No-Sau-Nee, Iroquois* stands as a classic to this day, should have taken no particular note of the political power of the Iroquois matrons. His account of the raising of the elders in *Ancient Society* (1963) differs in some details from the account given by Goldenweiser. Speaking of the election, he states, "Each person of adult age was called upon to express his *or her* preference" (ibid:72; italics mine). The right to depose "was reserved by members of the gens" (ibid.:73). Thus Morgan's observations do not contradict the fact that the matrons had a voice in these important matters. But for some reason, he did not find this remarkable or did not choose to comment upon it. However, in a later work, Morgan (1965:66) quotes from a letter written by the Reverend Ashur Wright (who had been a missionary among the Iroquois for forty years) as follows:

> The women were the great power among the clans, as everywhere else. They did not hesitate, when occasion required, to "knock off the horns," as it was technically called, from the head of a

> chief and send him back to the ranks of the warriors. The original nomination of the chiefs also always rested with them.*

Morgan's next paragraph begins, "The mother-right and gyneocracy among the Iroquois here plainly indicated is not overdrawn." He ends his paragraph with a footnote to Bachofen. It is therefore surprising when sixty-odd pages later he states:

> But this influence of the woman did not reach outward to the affairs of the gens, phratry, or tribe, but seems to have commenced and ended with the household. This view is quite consistent with the life of patient drudgery and of general subordination to the husband which the Iroquois wife cheerfully accepted as the portion of her sex. (Ibid.:128)

In his earlier work, however, Morgan (1962) noted that women had the power of life or death over prisoners of war, which must certainly be regarded as an influence reaching beyond the household. Furthermore, the women could participate in the deliberations of the Council through their male speakers, such as the Council of 1791 (Snyderman, 1951), the Council of 1804 (Beauchamp, 1900), and the Council of 1839 (Parker, 1916), and had a voice concerning warfare and treaties. Schoolcraft (1860:III:195-96) sums up these powers as follows:

> They are the only tribes in America, north and south, so far as we have any accounts, who gave to woman a conservative power in their political deliberations. The Iroquois matrons had their representative in the public councils; and they exercised a negative, or what we call a veto power, in the important question of the declaration of war. They had the right also to interpose in bringing about a peace.

It appears from the evidence (some of it Morgan's) that the political influence of the Iroquois matron was considerable. The nation was not a matriarchy, as claimed by some, but the

* The letter was written in May 1879 and appears in its entirety in Stern, 1933. Another interpretation by Wright of the "knocking off of horns" appears in Fenton, ed., 1957.

matrons were an *éminence grise*. In this respect the Iroquois were probably not unique. What is unusual is the fact that this power was socially recognized and institutionalized.

In addition, Iroquois matrons helped to select the religious practitioners of the tribe. Half of these "keepers of the faith" were women and, according to Morgan (1962:186), "They had an equal voice in the general management of the festivals and of all their religious concernments." As Randle and Quain have pointed out, women's activities were celebrated in the ceremonial cycle, and female virtues of food-providing, cooperativeness, and natural fertility were respected and revered. Women might become clairvoyants or could join medicine societies; for several of the latter, women were managing officers (Quain, 1961).

Kin-group membership was transmitted through the mother, and since there were rules of exogamy, the father belonged to a kinship group other than that of his wife and children. Morgan (1962:84; 326-27) describes the rules of inheritance and succession as follows:

> Not least remarkable among their institutions, was that which confined transmission of all titles, rights and property in the female line to the exclusion of the male. . . .
>
> If the wife, either before or after marriage, inherited orchards, or planting lots, or reduced land to cultivation, she could dispose of them at her pleasure, and in case of her death, they were inherited, together with her other effects, by her children.

Marriages were arranged by the mothers of the prospective couple, and they also took responsibility for the success of the union thus created. Both marriage and divorce involved little ceremony. The latter could be instigated by either the wife or the husband. In the case of a separation, the children usually remained with the mother (ibid.). Arthur Parker (1926) mentions that spacing the births of children was in the hands of the mother and there was greater delight at the birth of a daughter than at that of a son (Stites, 1905). The mother often had the power to confer a name on her child (Goldenweiser, 1912; 1914). Furthermore, Quain (1961:258) notes that "the women of the maternal line chose the child successors to a series of names which might culminate in high administrative titles of community or nation."

Crucial in consolidating the power of the women was the family longhouse. Traditionally this was a large structure of bark and wood containing many compartments and several fires, all connected by a central aisle. Each family occupied a compartment and shared a fire with several other families (Bartram, 1895:40-41). Rev. Wright is quoted by Morgan (1965:65-66) concerning the domestic arrangements of the tribe:

> As to their family system, when occupying the old long-houses, it is probable that some one clan predominated, the women taking husbands, however, from the other clans; and sometimes, for a novelty, some of their sons bringing in their young wives until they felt brave enough to leave their mothers. Usually, the female portion ruled the house, and were doubtless clannish enough about it. The stores were in common; but woe to the luckless husband or lover who was too shiftless to do his share of the providing. No matter how many children, or whatever goods he might have in the house, he might at any time be ordered to pick up his blanket and budge; and after such an order it would not be healthful for him to disobey; the house would be too hot for him; and unless saved by the intercession of some aunt or grandmother, he must retreat to his own clan, or as was often done, go and start a new matrimonial alliance.

Two features of Iroquois domestic life deserve special mention. First, as noted by Murdock (1934), the authority over the household resided in the matron and not in one of her male relatives. Audrey Richards (1950) has identified as the "matrilineal puzzle" the reconciliation of matrilineal descent with the rule of exogamy, the reconciliation of descent traced through women with authority vested in men. The Iroquois suggest yet another solution to the domestic aspect of this dilemma. Authority over the household was not given to the matron's husband nor to her brother, but was exercised by the woman herself.

Second, as Randle has pointed out, the longhouse was the

analogy on which the League was built. The Iroquois referred to themselves as the people of the longhouse. The figurative longhouse of the League was divided into geographical compartments, each occupied by a tribe. It is probable that this analogy helped to consolidate the considerable political power of the Iroquois matrons.

In sum, Iroquois matrons enjoyed unusual authority in their society, perhaps more than women have ever enjoyed anywhere at any time. The position of matron was open to all women who qualified. The matrons were socially recognized and institutionalized powers behind the throne (though one can hardly term the supremely democratic Council of Elders as a "throne"). Women were able to serve as religious practitioners, and the matrons helped to select all "keepers of the faith." Finally, the matron ruled supreme within the longhouse, and domestic arrangements were such that all women had dominant power within the household.

The Economic Organization of Subsistence Activities

Agricultural activities. The Iroquois supplemented cultivated foods with food gathered by the women, with meat hunted by the men (although women occasionally joined hunting expeditions), and with fish obtained by both men and women. However, the tribe depended upon shifting cultivation for the major portion of its food supply. Agricultural activity consisted of four stages: clearing the ground, planting, cultivating, and harvesting.

Men were in charge of preparing the fields, although Waugh and Quain claim that the women helped. Trees were girdled and allowed to die. The following spring, the underbrush was burned off (Parker, 1910). Planting and cultivating were conducted by the women in organized work groups. Elderly men occasionally helped, but for other men to do this work was considered demeaning. As Sara Stites has pointed out, the warrior in the field was always an assistant, never an owner or director. Men did join in the harvest, although this was occasionally done by women alone. Husking of the corn was a festive occasion, usually joined by the men. The work would be followed by a special meal and by singing and dancing.

Mary Jemison,* a white woman adopted into the Seneca tribe, offers a full description of the activities of the women's work group:

> Our labor was not severe; and that of one year was exactly similar in almost every respect to that of the others. . . . Notwithstanding the Indian women have all the fuel and bread to procure, and the cooking to perform, their task is probably not harder than that of white women, who have those articles provided for them; and their cares certainly are not half as numerous, nor as great. In the summer season, we planted, tended, and harvested our corn, and generally had all of our children with us; but had no master to oversee or drive us, so that we could work as leisurely as we pleased. . . .
>
> We pursued our farming business according to the general custom of Indian women, which is as follows: In order to expedite their business, and at the same time enjoy each other's company, they all work together in one field, or at whatever job they may have on hand. In the spring, they choose an old active squaw to be their driver and overseer, when at labor, for the ensuing year. She accepts the honor, and they consider themselves bound to obey her.
>
> When the time for planting arrives, and the soil is prepared, the squaws are assembled in the morning, and conducted into a field,

* *Life of Mary Jemison: Deh-he-wä-mis* was originally published in 1824 when Mary Jemison was about eighty. The book, written by James Seaver, is supposed to present her narrative, but it is written in a style that can hardly have been the idiom of a woman who spent most of her life as a Seneca. As it is the only source of its kind, it is quoted here. The edition used is that published in 1880 and contains chapters by a number of later authors. By 1924 the book had gone through twenty-two editions at the hands of four revisers, one of whom was Lewis Morgan. Any edition of the book is difficult to obtain today, even the 1961 paperback edition. Milliken (1924:87) writes of the first edition: "Published before the day of the dime novel, at a time when tales of adventure and romance were much less common than now and the thrillers of the silver screen were entirely unknown, it was circulated and read almost to complete destruction."

where each plants one row. [Note: The seeds were first soaked, and then planted in prepared hills.]

They then go into the next field and plant once across, and so on till they have gone through the tribe. If any remains to be planted, they again commence where they did at first, (in the same field,) and so keep on till the whole is finished. By this rule, they perform their labor of every kind, and every jealousy of one having done more or less than another is effectually avoided. (Seaver, 1880:69-71; see also Parker, 1910, and the footnote by Cornplanter in Quain, 1961:250)

Loskiel (1794:part 1:16) emphasizes the toil of the women, adding, "Nothing but hunger and want can rouse the men from their drowsiness, and give them activity." Parker (1910) tends to agree with Mary Jemison that the work of the women was not hard.

The economic organization of the Iroquois was remarkable (and far from unique), for the great separateness of the sexes which it fostered.* Men were often away on war parties for years at a time. Although wives or temporary wives, appointed especially for the purpose, occasionally accompanied men on the hunt, it was more usual for this to be a male pursuit. Even at the daily meal the sexes ate separately. It is no wonder that Morgan wrote:

Indian habits and modes of life divided the people socially into two great classes, male and female. The male sought the conversation and society of the male, and they went forth together for amusement, or for the severer duties of life. In the same manner the female sought the companionship of her own sex. Between the sexes there was but little sociality, as this term is understood in polished society. (1962:323)

Factors of production. In agricultural production, land constitutes the natural resource, seeds constitute the raw

* This separateness of the sexes applied also to the child-rearing methods of the tribe. In the words of Morgan (ibid.:325), "The care of their infancy and childhood was entrusted to the watchful affection of the mothers alone." This must have afforded the growing girl a reassuring continuity, but it contained inherent problems for the young boy.

materials, and agricultural implements constitute the tools. The ownership of these factors of production—the land, the seeds, and the implements—among the Iroquois is difficult to establish from existing evidence. Goldenweiser (1912:469) offers the following information: "The husband, in ancient times, could regard as his own only his weapons, tools, and wearing apparel, his wife owned the objects of the household, the house itself, and the land."

It is also not entirely clear who owned the land. The importance of the fields can be deduced from the fact that village sites were chosen largely for the fertility of the surrounding land. As Randle has pointed out, these sites were changed as land became depleted, and not when an area had been hunted out. The extent of the cornfields can be estimated from the various accounts of their destruction at the hands of white war parties. In one such foray mentioned by Stites, it took the French forces about a week to destroy the fields of four Iroquois villages.

Morgan (1965) stressed that land was communally owned and that its individual ownership was unknown. Snyderman (1951) mentions the belief that land belonged to future generations as well as to the present generation. However, according to Randle, land was often registered in female names. Hewitt states that women owned the lands, the village sites, and the burial grounds. Nominal female ownership is indicated in the following statement by Red Jacket, speaker for the women at the Council of 1791: "You ought to hear and listen to what we women shall speak . . . for we are the owners of the land and it is ours" (Snyderman, 1951:20). In short, the lands of the Iroquois appear to have been communally owned, but held by the women.

The food produced. A great variety of corn was raised. Frank Speck (1945) estimates from fifteen to seventeen varieties, and it was prepared in numerous ways. Murdock (1934) suggests as many as fifty. Even the husks, silk, cobs, and leaves were used to make a number of useful articles (Parker,

1910). Beans were also a popular food—Speck estimates that there were sixty varieties—as were squashes, of which there were eight varieties, according to Speck. All three of these foods were provided by the women and held in high esteem by the Iroquois. The foods were represented in their pantheon as "The Three Sisters," "Our Life," and "Our Supporters" (Morgan, 1962).

These staples were supplemented by foods gathered by the women—maple sugar, berries, wild fruit, nuts, roots, mushrooms, leaf foods—and by other cultivated foods, such as melons. Schoolcraft (1847) referred to the apple as "the Iroquois banana." The fruit was one of several introduced by the Dutch and the French. According to Parker (1910:94), during the Revolutionary War "General Sullivan in his famous raid against the hostile Iroquois cut down a single orchard of 1500 trees." Thus an impressive commissariat was supplied by the women of the tribe. The diet of the Iroquois was ample, varied, and nutritious. One is forced to agree with Morgan (1962), who considered the indigenous diet of the Iroquois far superior to that typical of the Europeans of pre-contact times.

Distributing and dispensing food. The generous hospitality that was customary among the Iroquois was probably the most salient feature of their food distribution. The rule of hospitality was perpetuated and its protocol codified by Handsome Lake, the early nineteenth-century prophet (Parker, 1913). Hospitality was extended to all strangers, and the stranger was to be fed before he was questioned about his mission (Lafitau, 1724). Hospitality was also extended to other members of the village, to the extent that no one went hungry (Parker, 1910). It is of interest to note Morgan's (1962:329) comment: "It [hospitality] rested chiefly upon the industry, and therefore upon the natural kindness of the Indian women." This statement demonstrates that the hospitality of the household reflected favorably on its women, not on its men. Furthermore, hospitality was motivated by generosity, which was valued in and of itself (Fenton, 1957).

There is conflicting evidence concerning the distribution of the fruit of the chase. Beauchamp says that the meat was given to the hunter's wife. Carr claims it was given to the hunter's mother-in-law. Lafitau mentions that the legitimate wife had a prior claim to that of the temporary hunting wife. (The Iroquois were not rigidly monogamous.) Hunting expeditions often lasted as long as a year, and if the hunter's wife refused to go, a special temporary wife might accompany him instead.

Stites cites one *Jesuit Relation* to the effect that one of the women's chief winter tasks was to go into the forest to bring home the deer their husbands had slain. Citing a different *Jesuit Relation*, however, she states that women were sometimes not given a share of the meat at all.* Wright, quoted by Morgan (1965), seems to suggest that the meat was contributed by the hunter to his wife's household. Morgan (ibid.:127) makes a similar statement himself, and this is probably the most correct description.

Thus the distribution of the food of the tribe, even the food procured by the men, appears to have been at the discretion of the matrons. By observing the rules of hospitality, the matrons made it possible for every member of the tribe and for visitors to obtain a share of the food supply.

The dispensing of food within the household also rested with the matrons. As Morgan (1962:327) observed, "The care of the appetite was left entirely with the women, as the Indian never asked for food." No author mentions any specified obligations which the matrons had to meet in performing this task.

* This discrepancy demonstates one of the difficulties in using the *Jesuit Relations*. The *Relations* cover an extended period of time and are anecdotal rather than descriptive. They are the work of many authors, whose prime purpose was to describe not the customs they found but their own missionary activities.

The Iroquois had one meal a day, which was served in the morning. Lafitau (1724:III:79-80) offers a description of this meal. Morgan's (1965:65) later description is as follows:

> Every household was organized under a matron who supervised the domestic economy. After a single daily meal was cooked at the several fires the matron was summoned, and it was her duty to divide the food, from the kettle, to the several families according to their respective needs. What remained was placed in the custody of another person until it was required by the matron. . . . It shows that their domestic economy was not without method, and it displays the care and management of woman.

It was not only in the domestic realm that the matrons controlled the dispensing of food. By supplying the essential provisions for male activities—the hunt, the warpath, and the Council—they were able to control these to some degree. Thus Randle (1951:172) writes, "Indirectly, too, it is stated that the women could hinder or actually prevent a war party which lacked their approval by not giving the supplies of dried corn and the moccasins which the warriors required." Stites (1905:78) makes a similar assertion: "They also had control of the cultivated land and its produce, and gave support to the warriors only in return for their military services." This control was effected by the monopoly that the matrons exercised on the staple food used on both the hunt and the warpath. According to Morgan (1962), this food was prepared while the warriors performed their dance. He gives the recipe for the dried corn–maple syrup provision (see also Bartram, 1895:71), and concludes, "The warrior could carry without inconvenience in his bear-skin pocket a sufficient supply for a long and perilous expedition" (Morgan, 1962:340). Further on he states, "This [the same recipe] was carried in the bear-skin pocket of the hunter, and upon it alone he subsisted for days together" (ibid.:373).

The importance of these provisions was also mentioned by Loskiel, who observed that hunting was not possible on the warpath for fear of giving warning to the enemy. He also describes the importance of the food provided by the matrons for the Council: "Provisions must always be in plenty in the council-house; for eating and deliberating take their turns" (1794:part 1:134; also see Bartram, 1895:58-63).

Iroquois women were in charge of the ingenious methods of preserving and storing the abundant food supplies. Corn, meat, fish, berries, squashes, and even fats were preserved. Some of these foods were buried in specially constructed pits, and some were kept in the longhouse. Stored food constituted one of the major forms of wealth of the tribe. Stites (1905:72) claims, "It was the women's organization which controlled the surplus and represented the owning class." Hewitt describes a tribal public treasury which contained wampum belts, quill and feather work, furs, and assorted stored foods. Its contents were scrupulously guarded by the matrons.

In sum, among the Iroquois, the distribution of food within the tribe was the responsibility of the matrons. They also controlled the provisions within the household, as well as those that made the major male activities possible. Some authors claim that the matrons also controlled the wealth of the tribe (much of it in stored food).

Summary

Iroquois women controlled the factors of agricultural production, for they had a right in the land which they cultivated, and in the implements and the seeds. Iroquois agricultural activities, which yielded bountiful harvests, were highly organized under elected female leadership. Most important, Iroquois women maintained the right to distribute and dispense all food, even that procured by men. This was especially significant, as stored food constituted one of the major forms of wealth for the tribe. Through their control of the economic organization of the tribe, Iroquois matrons were able to make available or withhold food for meetings of the Council and for war parties, for the observance of religious festivals and for the daily meals of the household. These economic realities were institutionalized in the matrons' power to nominate Council Elders and to influence Council decisions. They had a voice in the conduct of war and the establishment of treaties. They elected "keepers of the faith" and served in that capacity. They controlled life in the longhouse.

The unusual role of Iroquois women in politics, religion, and domestic life cannot be dismissed simply as a historical curiosity. It cannot be explained by Iroquois kinship structure, nor can it be attributed to the size of the women's contribution to Iroquois subsistence. The powerful position of Iroquois women was the result of their control of the economic organization of their tribe.

Rayna R. Reiter

Men and Women in the South of France: Public and Private Domains

The village of Colpied is located in Haute Provence in the foothills of the Southern French Alps. Although it is only a two-hour drive north and east from Marseilles, it seems much further removed. In this Mediterranean hinterland, people live in small villages; Colpied's population is 185, a size that is typical for the area. Moreover, they live in agglomerated villages surrounded by their fields. Each village appears distinct and isolated. But this isolation is illusory; although the rugged hills and ravines mask neighboring villages, they are never far away. On twisting roads, there is always a neighboring community to be found five to ten kilometers away, and on foot, walking straight through the fields, the distances are shorter.

When I first began doing field work in Colpied, I was struck by how easy it was to contact village men. They were often in the cafes, or on the square playing boules,* or standing around the mayor's office at regular times during the day.

The fieldwork on which this paper is based was done with Randy Reiter and supported by an NIMH predoctoral training grant and the University of Michigan's Project for the Study of Social Networks in the Mediterranean. Both sources are gratefully acknowledged. Many friends aided me in writing the paper. I am especially grateful to Anton Blok, Susan Harding, Roger McConochie, Randy Reiter, and Gayle Rubin for the insights and support they gave to my work. Helpful criticism was also given by Kathleen Gough and Susan Lowes.

* Boules is a favorite pastime of Provençal men. It is a game like bocci, its Italian counterpart, and is similar to lawn bowling.

I found it much harder in the beginning to meet the women. They were rarely seen in public places, and stayed inside their houses. Throughout the time I lived in the village, I was constantly aware of how distinct the lives of the two sexes were. They inhabited different domains, one public, one private.* While men fraternized with whomever they found to talk to in public places, women were much more enmeshed in their families and their kinship networks. They exchanged visits and errands with female relatives, but didn't do much socializing beyond the kinship sphere. To work among the women, I learned how to live in their private realm.

Private and public forms of sociability were clues to the very different lives of women and men. Women spend their time working and living within a realm that is defined as their own, which has many informal prerogatives attached to it, the realm of their households. It is a domain quite distinct from the more public, highly differentiated spheres where men predominate in activities within the economy, politics, or the church. Although "official" power is vested in the more formal, public arenas occupied by men, women consider their own domestic realm as more important and more formative. Men deny the importance of women's activities and see themselves as predominant in village life. On a day-to-day basis, there is a standoff about which domain is more worthwhile. Are the public and the private spheres separate but equal? Or is there a power differential between them? This was the question I constantly asked myself while living in Colpied.

As an anthropologist, I was struck by the importance of the kinship realm to women's lives. How kinship functions in complex (state-organized) societies became a central concern of my fieldwork. In the anthropological literature, we learn about the role of kinship in pre-state societies. People who live in bands and tribes conduct all of their social relations—

*** Throughout this paper, "distinct" and "separate" refer to the subjective perception of the situation by village women, and by me. The lives of men and women are of course integrated in a holistic view of the way society actually operates.**

politics, economics, rituals—in terms of their kinship alliances. In contrast, state-organized societies have many other forms of social relations based on more highly differentiated spheres of economy and polity. Formally, French society is not structured around family and kinship. There are complex institutions—the government and church, for instance—which have vested and codified powers in society. Kinship takes its place among the other institutions that make up the structure of French society.

Yet for village women, these other, more public institutions seemed tangential; kinship was their way of life. An investigation of the origins and consequences of women's roles within the kinship domain in a complex society was in order. Is the existence of distinct sexual spheres, one private and kinship-oriented, one oriented to public activity, a product of state society? If so, are there differences in status and power assigned to the two realms? There are important questions to explore.

This paper traces that investigation. In the first section sexual segregation and some of its implications in Colpied are described. The second section presents some hypotheses about such distinct domains in state societies in general. While the leap from daily life in a small French village to a theory about sexual roles in state societies is a long one, I think it is one worth making. For it is only on this second level that the more general questions about the role of women in societies such as our own can be asked.

1

One of the earliest patterns of sexual division of domains that I encountered in Colpied was geographic. I began to ask questions about the ties that connected people living in rural villages with other villages, towns, and cities. I tried to trace out the regions in which people traveled and had social ties. Although it was easy enough to discover regional networks for men, I was confronted with a very different pattern when speaking with women. Women do not travel or "fraternize" as men do. For them, life is more contained within the village itself.

Men often spend Saturdays, the traditional market day, in the cantonal capital, a small town ten kilometers away. They travel occasionally to Manosque or Digne, the largest urban centers in the department, and may even go as far as Marseilles for the annual agricultural fair. They own equipment that comes from towns within an hour's drive, and they sometimes visit these agricultural towns because they are members of co-ops centered there. In all such places, they know other men. Some are acquaintances made in the course of doing business—employees of co-ops, agents who sell tractors, bankers and notaries with whom contacts have built up over the course of years. Others fall into the general category of colleague. These are men known by sight, people with whom they shake hands and have a drink on market days, even though they may not know each other's names. Colleagueship is based on a general sense of syndicalism. Although the men of the area rarely belong to agricultural leagues or unions and scarcely participate in social and political clubs, they share a general sense of identification with other agriculturalists, whom they always refer to as colleagues. The same holds true for other men with different jobs. Men tend to claim colleagueship with people of their own professions—bakers with other bakers, merchants with other merchants, masons with other masons.

When asked about their travels, however, women insist they have no such contacts. With the exception of the very young women, it is only men who drive cars and therefore travel with any frequency. Women's shopping is either done in the village, or they give errands to a husband, a neighbor, or the local bus driver. When women do go to the cantonal capital for a market day, they tend to stick together. Village women walk arm in arm with one another. They talk only with each other, unlike their husbands and sons, who fraternize with their colleagues from elsewhere. Women's self-perception does not lead them into colleague relations. While women from other villages live very much as they do, they do not form bonds through contacts. Unlike men, women do not see themselves as social and economic agents linked to one another by the work that they do. They perceive their links through their families. Unless she has a relational tie with another woman via kinship or marriage, a woman from Colpied has a minimal basis for social interaction.

When asked about their visits to large cities, women respond quite differently than men do. Some women visit cities only when in need of medical attention. One can see a midwife, a dentist, an optician in the cantonal capital, but anything more serious prompts travel to cities. Women may also travel to such places because they have kin there. They go to visit their families rather than to use the public resources of the cities. Women have another way to use urban resources without necessarily leaving the village: they can manipulate kin ties. Many women have children who go to secretarial school in Manosque, are studying to be electricians in Marseilles, or work in Digne. They claim they don't need to go to cities because their children, or sisters or nieces, bring whatever goods and information they want. Regions, as defined by how people use them, break sharply along lines of sex: men have cars and colleagues, women have families.

There is a sexual geography to the way people use space within the village as well as outside of it. Throughout the Mediterranean area, a distinction is often made between private and public spheres.* Public places like the village square, the cafes and the mayor's office are the domain of men, while private places such as houses and the back streets that connect them into residential neighborhoods belong to women. Two categories of public space fall into women's domain. One is the church, where no self-respecting man is likely to be seen ("The church is for the women, but we have our own chapel on Sunday mornings—the cafe," men say). It is women who use the church—although the persons who preside over it, from the local priest to the pope, are all men.

* For a further discussion of private and public spheres in the Mediterranean, see Sweet, 1967, and Wolf, 1969.

The three village shops (a grocery, bakery, and butcher shop) also fall into women's domain. Visits to these may be seen as an extension of women's roles within their households, the care and feeding of families. Two of these shops are located in the residential back streets (women's domain), while the bakery is built in the former presbytery of the church (women's territory, once again), which stands on the central square (men's domain). In general, women tend to cross the square to get bread only at times when there are no men congregating. Even then they skirt the edges of the square, walking with their heads down. Men tend to stroll across the square, stopping to form social groups, lounging in front of the cafe or the mayor's office. Similarly, men tend to avoid women's places, sending children to do errands if they need something in a shop, and walking as quickly as possible past the front stoops or benches where women sit to talk in the back streets. Men who are obliged to buy their own bread will often stand around outside the bakery until they are joined by others in a similar situation. They will then all enter the shop together. Their arrival is greeted with jokes: "Let's attack now," they say. "Come on in, now that you're so strong," the women tease. Avoidance of one another's space is general between the sexes. Whenever possible, children will be sent to replace adults if the boundaries must be breached. Thus a son will be sent into the cafe to fetch his father when his mother is ready to serve dinner.

Watching the village day after day, a coordinated choreography can be observed: not only do men and women use different space in different ways, but they use it at different times as well. The men go early to the fields, and congregate on the square or in the cafes for a social hour after work. Sometimes they also fraternize in the evenings. These are the times when women are home cooking and invisible to public view. But when the men have abandoned the village for the fields, the women come out to do their marketing in a leisurely fashion. The village is then in female hands. In the afternoon, when the men return to work, the women form gossip groups on stoops and benches or inside houses, depending on the weather.

Joking is often used to maintain sexual preserves. A woman who enters a cafe will receive stares and be the butt of some jokes for her transgression. Watching a boules game or entering the mayor's office except on well-defined business are other ways to provoke teasing. Men who walk past women's gossip groups will hear the laughter that follows them. Territoriality is strong, and is based on the division of public from private spheres. It is important to realize that the men have a wider domain than the women. Despite the joking from the gossip groups, men have access to the residential areas where they live. Women rarely have access to the public areas within the village or in the larger world.

Women's reaction to such domain-ance is to invert it. They perceive the public areas as the sites of great play-acting. They see men as overgrown children strutting around and holding onto places and roles that are really quite silly; these have less value than their own homes and roles as family-cores. They even consider men's space to be inferior to their own. "Up there on the square it's more windy and chilly, not as comfortable as my own front stoop" (fifty feet away), said an elderly woman, to which her neighbors heartily agreed. As an outsider I was aware that social power and prestige were defined by men, and vested in themselves, their roles, and functions. Beyond the village, the hierarchies that control powerful institutions such as markets and co-ops, schools and churches, are male dominated; in the village, the local representatives of such larger institutions are all men. Men would mock the idea of a woman mayor or municipal counselor, or the suggestion that women participate in the social life of the cafe. But from the women's perspective such a definition of power is not accepted. The arenas and roles forbidden them are discounted as unimportant. They do not see the public sphere as more powerful or imposing than the private one.

Both the male and the female sphere have distinct forms of social organization. In both, people divide themselves into groups that are age-graded and hierarchical for each sex. There is a strong notion of *classe*—literally, those of the same birth-year who make their first communions together and, for men, do military service at the same time. There are three age groups: the elders, the adults in their middle years, and the youth. For women, the age groups are less visible than they are for men; they are cut by ties of kinship and neighborhood which link women across generations.

The men who frequent the boules court, the cafes, and the card games every day identify themselves by *classe*. They generally include the village elders, peasants who represent traditional values vested in the ownership and working of land; they are the patois-speakers, the storytellers, the ones who identify themselves as truly Provençal. Among them are the mayor and the retired or semi-retired wealthier peasants as well as some poorer elderly men. Their solidarity as an age-grade derives from occupying a position that tops what was, in the recent past, a gerontocracy.*

In the social hierarchy younger men between the ages of thirty and fifty (depending on the age at which an individual gets married and has a family to support) come next. They tend to participate in cafe life and games less frequently, spending most of their time in the fields, men's working domain. Such men form a cohesive social unit to themselves, exchanging tools, labor, and information. They tend to fraternize, to go hunting, and to drink in one another's homes. They are the economic backbone (or at least the male vertebrae) of the villages. They are also the ones who drive and own cars, traveling in the widest and most regional pattern.

A third group is formed of the unmarried boys—teenagers, young men in their early twenties, and sometimes older

* The word "gerontocracy" must be used cautiously: in a society where land is a measure of wealth and success, and where inheritance is partible and may take place at any point late in a father's life or be withheld until after his death, elder men retain power over their sons. But in the last two generations so many young men have been leaving the land that it is an exaggeration to claim that their elders continue to form a gerontocracy.

bachelors, socially defined as boys. This group goes to the cafe, where it may set up its own games or join those of the elders as needed to fill in on a hand at cards or listen to a story. They are in training for a role they would traditionally have come to occupy later in life with gradual retirement from agriculture. But it is a role which will remain vacant, since most of these younger men will not pass their adult years in Colpied. They are all being educated for jobs that require their migration. It takes very few electricians, mechanics, and plumbers to service villages of fewer than two hundred inhabitants. After military service, these young men move out to look for jobs elsewhere.

Among all three groups there is a strong sense of diffused sociability. People are publicly friendly, exchanging drinks and stories. The youngest group has ties through school and weekend dances. The middle group has ongoing work ties. The elders are linked by a shared set of memories, and even by the patois language they use. Men in each of the groups behave as colleagues.

Women's social organization is rarely visible in public places. They may stop to chat with one another while doing errands, but their main social contacts are private ones that are strong and enduring. They visit in one another's homes. Like men, they have a strong sense of an age-grade. Elderly widows enjoy each other's company, women with growing families are often most friendly with neighbors of a similar age and status, and young girls parade arm in arm when home from school. Like the men, women identify with members of their own *classe*. But such age-grading seems less important than the ties that flow along kinship lines. Kinship is truly the domain of women. Just as their contacts outside the village extend along family lines, so do their links inside it. Indeed, the strongest tie between women (and perhaps the overall strongest dyadic tie) is the mother-daughter bond.* Any adult woman with a living mother will be found sharing a household or, at most distant, a neighborhood with her. If

* Other emotional, dyadic ties are discussed later.

they do not live together, they will visit frequently, and the younger woman will often shop for the older one. Sometimes the older woman will raise one or more of her daughter's children, if the younger woman must work or doesn't have the house-space or income to care for her whole family. Other affective ties are found between sisters, who visit often. They may replace one another at part-time jobs, or do cooking and cleaning in times of illness. Historically, there are many examples of two sisters marrying two brothers, and of sororate (a woman becomes the second wife of her dead sister's widower). There is the expectation among women that sisters are close and may be taken as equivalent when necessary. Other strong ties are the bonds between female first cousins, and between aunts and nieces. Much of the visiting that goes on daily in the village is between such kinswomen.

Visits are not exclusively kin-oriented. Neighbors will visit, and *quartiers* (neighborhoods) are strong units of identification for women. Outside of kin links, women rarely visit beyond their neighborhoods; that is, within a radius of five or six households, often a few hundred square meters of space. As was explained to me by the women of my *quartier* who adopted me, "We know everyone in this village, but we are intimate only with our *quartier* neighbors." Sexual geography not only limits women in terms of how far they go outside the village, but it defines a very small space for them within the village as well. Inside such a space, it is often widows (at the top of the age hierarchy, a position that holds some prestige but not material power) whose houses become the centers for gatherings. The pattern of centering visits around a widow seems to begin in the early days of widowhood, when other women drop by to console the mourner. It is a pattern easily continued, as there is no man in the house to dictate hours of work or break up the visiting circle. Socializing during widowhood can be seen as the functional equivalent of the male village elders retiring to the cafe; it is the time when women retire from their defined jobs—ministering to husbands and children. Like the cafes, the widows' houses are sexually segregated arenas used regularly by established cliques of people.

How is such a small and tight focus of sociability maintained within a single tiny *quartier* over the years? When asking about neighborhood ties, I was often told by older women that neighborhoods were the locus of marriages: "We married in the *quartier,*" the women claimed. What an astounding thought. Surely in such a small place—even in the last century, when village endogamy accounted for more than 75 percent of all marriages—one did not simply marry the boy next door. Attempting to find out what marriage in the *quartier* might mean, I came up with two possible answers. One is that people *did* marry the boy next door. People claim that until the end of the nineteenth century, marriages were often arranged. Cousins or neighbors would promise one another their children. This is not an easy explanation to prove, since there are no admitted examples of couples with arranged marriages living today.

The second explanation is denied by the villagers themselves but seems quite accurate according to historic records. It has to do with inheritance patterns. Officially, inheritance is partible: all villagers insist that property, both land and houses, must be split among all heirs, and that there is no sexual bias or preference in the division. However, when the history of individual houses is traced, the buildings tend to be inherited through the female line. Whenever feasible, daughters inherit houses and some fields, while sons inherit larger amounts of agricultural land. This pattern of transmission of land to men, and houses to women, has historical precedents in the region. In medieval times, in feudal domains of Provence, partible and productive buildings (especially castles and church-related properties) often passed to females rather than to males (A. Lewis, 1965). To this day, there seems to be a regional inheritance pattern that tends to pass houses and buildings through women, while fields go through men. This pattern is neither recognized nor acknowledged by the villagers themselves.

This pattern of female transmission of houses may get submerged in the life cycle of a family. A young couple may not come into their inheritance immediately, and may have to rent or buy a house outside of their families' property. In recent times, changing marriage patterns have also affected inheritance. In all current marriages in which both partners were born in Colpied, the man has moved into the house his wife inherited. But many marriages include a partner who comes from outside the village. In virtually all such cases, the outsider is the male.* In former times there were some in-marrying women, but currently it is only men without adequate land in their own villages who marry into Colpied. These men all have wives who have inherited adequate farms. The recent influx of outside men marrying into Colpied and moving into their wives' houses strengthens the pattern of female house ownership. While the timing of a move into the wife's house depends on the wealth and life cycle of her family, women sooner or later inherit their childhood houses, in their childhood *quartiers.* When women then say, "We married in the *quartier*," I might translate the statement to "We married and (eventually) moved with our husbands back to our childhood houses in the *quartier*."

In former times, families would sometimes subdivide houses into apartments or buy and build structures next to their own in order to provide equal portions for married children.** This, too, reinforces kinship ties in the *quartier*, as mothers and daughters, sisters and cousins, aunts and nieces often find themselves to be neighbors. Such links in-

* Currently women rarely marry farmers in other villages; they usually migrate and marry in towns and cities. This is a problem throughout rural France, as few women want to be farmers' wives, and many farmers remain bachelors. Several generations ago, women married into Colpied as wives of artisans or shopkeepers—higher-status occupations. In addition to the economics of leaving the land, we may hypothesize that women who remain as farmers' wives prefer to do so in their own villages where they can keep their neighborhood and kin ties intact.

** Both rapid depopulation and a low birth rate currently mean that there are rarely two or more daughters needing houses in the village. In former times when population was greater, this sort of subdivision happened.

crease a sense of neighborhood solidarity, and may serve to protect the reputation of women, since their behavior is constantly being observed by their kinfolk.*

The social organization of men and women varies not only in its structure but in its content. The sexes have a distinctly different relation to information and to behavior. Hidden behind curtains and closed doors, women speak only of their own realm. The topic of their conversation is almost always kinship. Kinship information is their specialty. Ties of family bind them tightly within a narrow space and determine their principal role in life, a role that is much more confined than a man's. They do not have the potential for participation in outside social, economic, and political networks, all of which are thoroughly male-dominated.** Kinship ties define their spheres of interest, influence, and expertise. In visiting groups, between generations as well as within them, stories of peoples' lives are polished through constant retelling. It is here that younger women learn about their ancestors, about the births, marriages, and deaths of people they may never have known, as well as about the lives of the current villagers. Through such telling and retelling a tremendous sense of female solidarity is established. Despite a male-centered naming system (in France, as in the United States, women take the names of their husbands at marriage, of their fathers at birth), women trace kinship stories through other women and not through men. Women born in the village, even if married for fifty years, are identified by their maiden names, while children are identified with their mothers (and thus by maiden names) and rarely through their fathers. Marriages are traced through newspaper announcements to the mothers of the bride and groom, often with some mistakes, as it takes a bit of juggling to drop out the paternal name of each person

* For an Italian case in which female-centered neighborhoods explicitly serve this function, see J. Davis, 1969.

** The young women are now receiving an education and working outside of the home. But, as in other Western capitalist countries, it is debatable whether such experiences will give them equal access to areas of life dominated by men.

in the announcement and recall the maternal maiden name. Houses as well as families are identified with women. It is women who keep and cherish houses, who link houses, and who inherit houses. In the women's discussions, it is as if men are simply stand-ins in the world of the family, semi-autonomous additions whose presence allows for the establishment of a household and the birth of children, and whose death reaffirms the ties of the wife to her neighbors and kinswomen.

Such female-centered preoccupation with kinship information reflects the division of the social universe between women and men. Women do not have the social, professional, suprafamilial ties that govern men's public existence. They cannot create such ties. What they do have is a set of life expectations and a body of knowledge that is centered around the family. They know that they are defined as daughters and wives; they respond by learning and controlling the links that revolve around those roles, and reversing the orientation so as to center themselves not on their links to fathers and husbands but to other women. Examples of such a reversal of links are numerous. In addition to tracing general family ties strongly through women, they will often drop the men out of their own social genealogies. A woman will speak of a visit to her sister-in-law, the children of her daughter-in-law, rather than tracing such ties through a brother or a son. The wife of a brother or a brother-in-law may be spoken of as a sister-in-law, dropping out the alliances through men that bring her into the kinship network. In a sense, kinship information assumes the existence of men but also ignores them.

In addition to a division of kinship information into male and female realms, there is a division of kinship behavior. Women meet in the privacy of their own homes and perceive their links in terms of families. They have no obvious idioms in which to express relationships that are not familial. Even the concept of *classe* is quite limited for women. They say they have to have grown up together, gone to school, and actually made their first communion together to feel that they are of the same *classe.* Having few public roles or relationships with people who are not kin, women tend to familize the exceptional case as it occurs. A woman who maintains a close friendship with someone who has married out of the village (a rare case) will speak of the friend as a sister. Elderly women with whom I visited would say they'd come to feel as if I were a daughter in their house. But younger French women moving into Colpied, like the wife of the postman, or the schoolteacher, have a hard time getting to know the village women. They did not grow up with them, have no kinship ties to them, and are perceived as outsiders. This is less true for men, who can adopt roles that are public rather than familial. Newcomers to the village may participate in the cafe life or at boules and find a role for themselves among the other men, although they are still known as outsiders. Their wives cannot get even this close to the village women.

The information men control is also distinctly different. Their topics of conversation at the cafe or when visiting other villages are usually impersonal. Men will discuss agriculture, politics, the weather or hunting, and will sometimes tell stories about one another. But they do not talk about families, discuss life crises, or retell stories that solidify information about dead or living relatives. Indeed, they are quite bad at remembering names or tracing family links. But ask a man about a plot of land and he can tell you not only the owner, but the lines along which the plot was inherited. He, too, controls some kinship information, but it is filed within knowledge about land, a realm that belongs to men rather than to women.

The division of information about property is reinforced by women, who often claim to know nothing about the land they inherited: "Ask my husband" is a common response to queries about land when made to women. Several women claimed not to know how much land they'd inherited from their own parents, as their husbands took care of the formalities. While I am skeptical about women's ignorance, it certainly works well as a social fiction. The spheres of information and behavior about land, as about families, are conceptually distinct: women have families, men have fields. This distinction of information may also serve to uphold male status and privilege. In an agrarian community where position is based on amount of land and on success as a farmer, but where inheritance is partible, women who bring land to their marriages may potentially have a lot of power.* Yet if they disclaim all concern with and information about land, they yield that power, at least publicly, to the men. This division is reinforced by the system of land records. Property information is kept in the mayor's office, one of the public arenas, and discussed frequently by the men who fraternize there. While occasionally a woman will enter the office to look up a deed, her presence is uncommon; although women inherit land, the records of their inheritances are kept on male turf.

Men also behave quite differently from women around their families. They often subordinate kinship ties to public roles. A woman will keep a daughter-in-law with her in the kitchen or spend time in the house gossiping about the family with a niece, but a man will take a son-in-law to the cafe for a drink and general socializing with other men. Such a pattern diffuses the personal relationship and makes kinsmen into colleagues. The turning of kinship into colleagueship can be seen to result from the female specialization in kinship. In principle, kinship is traced through men. That is, there is an ideological centering of the kinship system on men through patrilineal naming at marriage and at the birth of children. But such male-centering is a formal fiction, undercut by female domestic behavior and knowledge. Since it is women who keep up family ties and initiate visiting, men's kin relations are usually mediated through women. A man is likely to live with or spend weekends in the company of people who are related to him through his mother, sister, wife, or daughter. Relations including two or more men are between or among fathers and sons-in-law; brothers-in-law; brothers-in-law by alliance (that is, the husband of the sister of a sibling's spouse or the brother of a sibling's spouse), as well as fathers and sons and brothers. The men find themselves sharing

* For a case study in which this is true, see Friedl, 1967.

meals and resources, though rarely on their own initiative. They turn relationships which grow out of the female style of family visiting into male-sanctioned patterns. Two brothers will take the husband of their sister to hunt with them, a father-in-law will sign his son-in-law up for a boules tournament, assorted men related by marriage will leave the house to drink together in the cafe. Privately related via women as kin, they publicly relate to one another as colleagues.

The segregation of domains between the sexes along public and private lines is a striking characteristic of village life. At times it felt as if the population were divided into two well-bounded and somewhat hostile moieties.* Activities and places claimed by one group were disclaimed by the other. Women not only avoid the boules courts and cafes, they also state that the activities that go on there are boring and incomprehensible. Men say the same of the gossip groups, adding that they are malicious. Television programs watched by one sex are different from those watched by the other, and quite a bit of impatience with the choices of the opposite sex is expressed. It even seems as if men prefer dogs as pets (for hunting), while women prefer cats (as house pets). Each group accuses the other of wasting time in its leisure activities, and women state that men only go to the cafe because they are such conformists.

But as villagers would point out, such a picture is exaggerated. Men and women are not, after all, two hostile clans. They do spend time together, they do share certain activities. The public school in the village is no longer sexually segregated, and neither is the intermediate school in the cantonal capital, so classes are mixed up to the age of fourteen. Adolescents pass their weekends going to local dances in mixed groups, and it is from these bands that serious relationships leading to marriage filter out. There is marriage itself, a tie between the sexes. But the quality of relations across sex

*** A moiety is one of two basic complementary tribal subdivisions; the term implies that members cannot marry within their own groups and must select partners from other moieties.**

lines (at least where women are concerned) does not seem as strong as the mother-daughter ties described earlier. While young women will speak of romantic love, most women do not express such feelings. Having a husband is one's *destin* (literally, "destiny"); being a wife is a full-time job. Women speak of men with affection, but also as helpless creatures in need of their services. They express concern lest a husband be cruel to a wife, and relief when he is proven reliable and gentle. I do not mean to imply that real concern and caring is lacking; rather, there does not seem to be the emotional involvement with and dependence upon a husband that there is between mothers and daughters. Women, of course, love their sons as well as their daughters. But boys are expected to spend time among men. Even quite small toddlers will be paraded around the cafe by proud fathers or grandfathers. A woman's love for her son is not a dependent sort of love; she is prepared for the day when he will marry and leave her, and she hopes to gain a loving daughter-in-law in return. As a woman, it was harder for me to ask questions about the emotions of the men, and harder for them (given their public, nonintimate orientation) to answer me. From observations rather than discussion, I learned that men tend to turn kinship into colleagueship. Their relation to female kin is less clear; fathers joked about their teen-aged daughters in sexual terms, but they never expressed any feelings about other female kin to me. The feelings of intimacy that people express toward members of their own sex, and distance toward members of the opposite sex, seem to be very much embedded in expectations concerning life cycle. From early childhood through old age, the life cycle of the individual is subordinated to the family's cycle, and to a rather strict division of labor by sex. It is within these contexts that the extreme sex segregation in Colpied must be viewed.

From childhood on, youngsters tend to play in sexually segregated groups, and a child is teased for acting like a member of the opposite sex. Reinforcement for behavior appropriate to girlhood and boyhood is strong. Despite coeducational schooling, children follow their parents' patterns from an early age, little boys accompanying fathers into cafes, girls staying in the home until they approach courting age. Adolescent technical education is de facto segregated by sex. The boys study to be mechanics, electricians, masons, the girls to be secretaries and hairdressers.

Households are often merged so that the nuclear family appears and disappears several times in an individual's life. While ideally a newly married couple lives alone, it may take several years for such a household to get set up, depending on the resources of the couple's families. During this time a young woman and her husband will live with her mother or her mother-in-law. When parents and their children live separately, the women will visit frequently. In widowhood, women move into the homes of their daughters whenever possible. Depending on the life cycle, family resources, and the household cycle, a woman expects to live with her mother or her mother-in-law (if the woman has no married daughters to depend on) for part of her adult life, and to be closely involved with her during the years when they don't share a house. The extensions and contractions of the nuclear family reinforce female ties, especially in terms of socially acceptable work roles.

Many of the expectations about ties within one's own sex originate in the division of labor. Unlike many agricultural communities where women and men work the land together, in Colpied it is claimed that women do not work. The statement is of course false. Women work every day within the household. Though their tasks are considerably lightened by such modern improvements as running water, electricity, and semi-automatic washing machines, they still spend many hours caring for house and family. They also raise the chickens and rabbits. Within the agricultural work force, they form a critical reserve pool of labor. All women claim to hate agricultural work and to know nothing about it (which, once again, keeps them separate from the men, who are the agricultural specialists). But most cut lavender every summer, and in the fall they harvest grapes, as needed. Neither of these tasks is considered "work" by either sex. There is little value attached to the discontinuous but crucial labor women contribute to basic agricultural production, men's sphere. Women's work is also less visible in comparison to former times, when there was more for them to do. They used to harvest almonds and olives, but both crops have disappeared from the village economy, and there were female work groups for cleaning truffles which, until recently, was the major source of cash for village families. Household and local industry, always scarce, is now nonexistent. Compared to women of other generations, or to contemporary women who earn salaries in cities, these women do not consider that they work. Yet it is they who provide the part-time labor at the grocery, the cafes, and for cleaning the homes of elderly and wealthier women. Here, as in agriculture, women remain a part-time, underemployed group. Their self-definition, as well as the role bestowed on them by men, is that of non-worker. In a society increasingly based on a cash economy, such a definition lowers status. It also serves to keep the domains of public and private life distinct, for women who "do not work" are seen by both sexes as having a life that centers uniquely around the household. Women are pre-defined as structurally absent from the work process, even though they actually work. The definition of women as non-workers encourages their exclusion and withdrawal from public life in general. They are not seen, nor do they see themselves, as having anything to do with running the economy or managing village or supravillage affairs through politics or organizational participation. "I don't know anything about land," and "I don't know anything about politics" are both statements frequently made by women.

The legal status in each of these realms is that women and men are equal. Partible inheritance and universal adult suffrage are tenets of French law. In principle, then, women participate in control of land (the village economy) and in electoral politics exactly as men do, but they cede these areas of concern to men: national legal structure is modified by village social structure. The de facto perception of a strict division of labor and domain by sex relegates women to the home and the family.

In Colpied, women are defined by men, and define themselves, as guardians of the private sphere. They have many mechanisms for protecting their roles, and for gaining status from them. They are quick to demean the public sphere in which men operate as having less value than their own. Within the village, women maintain a positive self-image in a small world where the division of sexual realms feels functional. They are secure within their realm and do not experience their position as inferior to men. From inside the village, it is possible to see the two domains as separate but equal, but it is precisely the confinement of village women to the village itself that makes this notion of distinction and equality possible. When the arena is enlarged that notion of equality is challenged, for all the institutions which influence or control regional and national social structure are male-dominated. Rapid social change is going on in the larger society within which the village is integrated. It is the migrating daughters and granddaughters of village women who feel the impact of male domination of the public sector in the nonagricultural communities of the south of France. They experience discrimination in pay rates, a relative lack of educational advancement, and the double duties of housework and paid jobs, much as women in other Western industrial nations do.

Village men have very little power in the world beyond the village. They speak with great fatalism about their inability to influence national economic policies or even regional politicians. Yet they move in a realm that is male-dominated, sharing the public realm with those who control markets, banks, and administrative, educational, and ecclesiastical bureaucracies. This does not give individual men much real power—it is the rare peasant who breaks class barriers to receive an elite education, serve in the senate, or preside over the national office of an agricultural co-op—but the cultural expressions of male dominance permeate the public arena and are translated for all men into an illusion of pre-eminence. Male dominance is an unconscious but cultural fact that village men internalize in the larger arena as well as at home.

2

Colpied displays an extreme division of sexual spheres into public and private. This pattern is found throughout the Mediterranean area and it may be associated with Roman influences and the long history of urbanization of the region. In some other regions of France, and in other peasant cultures, the division of labor between the sexes is less distinct, as are the corresponding social realms. Other factors influence the particular constellation of relations between the sexes, for instance, demographic patterns, the impact of markets and taxation of families, and the history of warfare and peace in the region.

Nonetheless, there is a historical and conceptual case to be made for the hypothesis that all state societies organize a sexual division between private and public spheres. That is, within the variation of male-female relations, there is a strong tendency for state societies to consider public functions as male and private ones as female. Serving and reproducing the kinship network is always the woman's role; participation in the public realm beyond the household is predominantly the man's role. In many contemporary cultures women are increasingly found in the public sphere, but still less so than men. They are usually statistical exceptions, and certain roles are still off limits to them. To see how this private/public sexual distinction has come about, we need to examine some of the foundations of state organization by looking at the pre-state societies from which state societies emerged.

In pre-state societies, social relations are organized by two primary sets of ties: kinship and location. Economy, polity, and ritual are localized processes which are usually organized along genealogical lines. One's obligations and expectations are circumscribed by the local group, and by kinship relations within it. Thus, nomadic gatherers and hunters will share food within their bands according to genealogy; African tribal peoples will allow access to land to, and expect support in warfare from, those whose membership in a group is based on proximity and kinship ties. In such situations, social participation and power are defined within the local group, with kinship as an organizing principle.

Yet based on a universal division of labor by sex, men and women have a different relation to location and to kinship ties. While the variation in the exact content of the division of labor by sex is enormous, the general pattern cross-culturally is that women tend to do the majority of child care, cooking, provisioning of clothing, gathering, and horticulture. These activities serve to reproduce the household in a continuous, daily fashion. They also tend to keep women close to home. Men, too, reproduce the household through their economic contributions (hunting, agriculture). But they also participate in more discontinuous long-distance activities, such as hunting, group politics, feuds, and warfare.* All members of the group are bound by kinship ties; yet there seem to be narrower and wider kin groups, which correspond to geographically narrower and wider activities. Women seem to be involved in the spatially narrower activities that correspond to conceptually narrower kinship space. Thus women are most active in local kinship arenas, while men participate in longer-distance alliances.

Such a sexual division in kinship functions based on geographical activities is not overtly discussed in much of the anthropological literature. We do not, for example, know much about differential access to information and roles in terms of kinship in pre-state societies. But in asking other anthropologists about their own fieldwork, I have found this tentative difference: in addition to assuming virtually all leadership positions, men seem to control the information, the rituals, and the personal ties that are concerned with group structure and alliances between groups. They share with women, or women hold exclusively, information and rituals

* The range of the division of labor by sex is discussed in D'Andrade, 1966. Hypotheses concerning its origins and functions are found in Gough in this volume and Judith Brown, 1970b, as well as many other works.

relating to household and domestic functions. For example, in Fiji, where political position is traced through ranked lineages, it is men who concern themselves with genealogical knowledge. They are "ancestor-obsessed" because alliances among lineages are made and justified by assertions of kinship. It is the women in Fiji who conduct the rituals associated with birth and marriage, subjects which are of less concern to men than are alliances and ancestors (Sahlins, personal communication). In such segregation of access to information and roles, economic and ritual, within kinship-organized societies, there is an incipient sexual division of sphere: kinship-as-politics belongs to men, kinship-as-household-organization belongs to women. It is here that I see the basis for an elaborate distinction between private and public domains in state-organized societies.

As states grow out of pre-state societies, their bases of social organization are transformed. While kinship organization continues to play an important role (especially in archaic states, such as those localized in Mesopotamia, Mesoamerica, and Egypt), it ceases to be the sole mechanism for the control of resources within a territory, and a stratified class system gradually emerges. Under a class system, access to resources and social surpluses is limited to certain groups, rather than being available through kinship redistribution to all persons belonging to a kin group. The power of kin groups to control labor and resources becomes subsumed in the power of emerging classes. Kinship organization is in competition with class organization for the control of resources. Certain classes consolidate their power as state control; in the process, kinship as a form of social organization is curtailed, transformed, and used by them to new ends.

I do not mean to imply that the evolution of a state society is a uniform or unilinear process in which kinship is simply replaced by class as a form of social organization. Surely, the two coexist and there is a flux and flow between their powers. This process is well-illustrated in the development of the French state. In discussing medieval France, Georges Duby claims that "the family is the first refuge in which the threatened individual takes shelter when the authority of the state weakens. But as soon as political institutions afford him adequate guarantees, he shakes off the constraint of the family and the ties of blood are loosened. The history of lineage is a succession of contractions and relaxations whose rhythm follows the modification of the political order" (quoted in Aries, 1962:355). As the state grows stronger, increasing central authority of the upper classes saps the functions of the kin groups. As political ruling segments are differentiated from the general population in kin groups, there is a reduced dependence of individuals on these groups, which undermines their importance. The growth of political centralization corresponded to a weakening of kin-group authority in feudal Europe.

Marc Bloch records the limitations of kinship vendettas by a growing and powerful feudal nobility to illustrate this process. In the tenth century, loyalty to a blood group was a paramount obligation. The murder of a member could be avenged by any member of the kin unit. Over the next few centuries, the nobility limited the scope of avenging members; only those relatives within a certain degree of kinship were reckoned close enough to participate in vendettas. By the thirteenth century, relations could not officially avenge murdered kinsmen, but had to take their demands for retribution to the local nobility: ". . . violence became a class privilege, at least in theory" (Bloch, 1961:130). A more modern example of the replacement of kinship ties by state authority is found in Stanley Diamond's study of the imposition of state legal systems over African kinship groups (1971).

For a state to exist—in the form of specific lineages and specific individuals—it must control resources that were formerly vested in the kin group. In France, social historians have documented the growth of the concept of private property, in distinction to corporate kin-held property. From the thirteenth century onward, there is evidence for an increasingly monetized economy while greater public safety encouraged trading and commerce. At the same time, a battle raged over the definition of the rights of kin groups versus the rights of individuals over property in the form of land. A distinction was drawn between properties owned by joint family estates and those acquired by individuals; properties were also separated into male and female lines. The concept of the sale of property was legitimized, but kinsmen had to be given top priority on bidding for any lands that their group members wish to sell as individuals. By codifying property relations, the centralizing authority limited corporate kin group control over resources in favor of the acquisitions made by individuals and wealthier lineages (Bloch, 1961).

The creation of private property is one example of the separation of a resource base from kinship control. In general, a state must also have access to the labor power of people previously organized to produce for kinship redistribution. Kin groups must continue to exist, for it is within them that the most important resource—people, who are the source of all labor power—is produced. Yet those people must be accessible to the productive demands of the emergent upper classes, which is why the hegemony of the kin group must be supplanted. Elites must be able to conscript persons to build roads and palaces, to fight wars, to produce surpluses to pay taxes. These obligations were extracted in all archaic states. They were characteristic, too, of elite impositions on vassals and serfs in medieval Europe.

A state must hold the monopoly on force (as seen, for example, in the limitation of kinship vendettas) in order to control, administer, and defend its territory, and to tax its inhabitants. Its power must be more, however, than just the power of coercion. A state system must be structured to insure that the acquisition of resources by an elite is institutionalized, and is, to a large extent, accepted by the population. In other words, the state needs to control the minds as well as the bodies of its people. It must be an apparatus for ideological as well as material control. The ideological power of the state is that which political theorists have called the power of legitimacy, the authority to act on the "perceived common will." On a deeper level, it may be characterized as control over the means of orientation. That is, the evolution of the state requires the regulation of knowledge, values, education, religion: the processes by which world views and allegiances are formed. Such ideological components make up the cultural expression of the real relations in people's lives. Orientation is the apparatus through which world views are formed and filtered. It includes the legitimacy of authority. A study of the history of education and of the church would contribute to the understanding of how such orientational controls develop and influence acceptance of state authority. In France, an example of the importance of orientation is found in the Albigensian Crusade. The rationale for the war was stated in religious (orientational) terms; people fought and died for values which can be characterized as ideological dogmas. Beyond religious issues, the Northern bureaucratic kingdom was asserting its hegemony as economic and military ruler over the South, where social organization was much less centralized. Mobilization for the Crusade was called forth through ideological control.

One of the mechanisms that underwrites the control of a central power over the minds of its population is the separation of society into public and private spheres. State structure and its functions are defined as public ("for everyone"; in reality, for the participation of the many in labor, and for the benefit of a select few). Reproducing and sustaining those people whose labor power and goods are essential to that structure is defined as a private function. In pre-state societies, economy, polity, and religion are all familized; in state society, these spheres emerge as separate and public while the family becomes privatized. Kinship, which organizes these private functions, becomes structurally less and less visible. Publicly, legitimately, officially, it is the state which holds power rather than the kinship group. As the state gains hegemony over kinship-based organizations, its political, religious, and military elites increasingly define service to the public realm as having legitimacy and high status. Within this ideological orientation, the incipient distinctions between local, household-oriented roles and extralocal, more political roles get transformed. In the process of elite classes legitimizing service to their ends, it is the sphere that is extralocal, and male, to which prestige is attached. A distinction that was functionally based on the division of labor by sex and its geographical expression becomes transformed into more distinct public and private arenas. The state then uses the distinction to assert its own legitimacy and to devaluate the authority of kinship groups. While I would assert that early and archaic states all needed to transform kin-based organization to serve legitimized, public ends, it is clearly in the development of industrial capitalism in modern states that the division into public and private domains is most radical. And in the process, the separation of the sexes—one defined as serving the private domain, the other, the public—is carried to its greatest degree of segregation.

This development of public and private spheres is a gradual and uneven process. In France, we have evidence of its evolution from later medieval times through the nineteenth century. Aries, in tracing the development of the concept of the family, presents the increasing division between public and private spheres as well.* Using materials from the history of art, he asserts that the concept of private, familial space occurs after the fifteenth century. In sixteenth- and seventeenth-century painting, there is a merger of domestic and social activities; men and women are pictured together with children, in undifferentiated interior scenes. The same room is used for cooking and sleeping, business and crafts. By the later seventeenth century, there are paintings that glorify the realm of the family, and especially of women, as an interior scene with segregated rooms for various activities. Men are often pictured outside the home, conducting business and participating in craft production. He is describing a differentiation of space by function—public versus private activity—

* There is an obvious class bias inherent in using art history and even written records; paintings and contracts are seldom produced by the peasantry. Nonetheless, fascinating analyses such as Aries' have implications for other groups in the society.

and by sex, which is linked to the flowering of European capitalism (Aries, 1962).

Historians have described the separation of work place from home during the industrial revolution in England.* A village study by Edgar Morin documents the radical restructuring of work and leisure in post-World War II Brittany with an increasing penetration of the capitalist mode of production. Changes in the economy accompanied the movement of young people out of small-scale, individual agricultural units and into industrialized farming and service occupations. Women's roles in the public economy declined, and the home, once an undifferentiated area for both sexes, became more exclusively their domain. Many feminine tasks, such as food processing and clothing production, were industrialized, while leisure activities were exclusively defined as what the home (the TV), and the cafe were to provide. Radical restructuring of the peasant economy by modern French capitalism increased the distinction between public and private domains as well as the segregation of the sexes (Morin, 1970).

In this process, power and prestige fall into one sphere while activities surrounding the reproduction and production of people fall into the other. Kinship still organizes this domestic, private economy to a large extent, but its functions and its orientation fall upon women alone. Why upon women? They are the producers and sustainers, the sex that can guarantee the reproduction of the most important resource, people. Men are more likely than women to be drafted into projects for the state, such as massive construction and the military. Those tasks which are essential to the social reproduction of people are increasingly relegated to women as men are mobilized for participation in the public realm. Women's work forms the invisible background against which state societies extract labor power. This is especially true for Western capitalism, with its proclaimed sanctity for the nuclear family; women are separated from an extended family in which work is shared. Women's labor in the care

* See, for example, Hill, 1958, or Moore, 1966, for such a discussion.

and production of people is at once romanticized and trivialized (see the women's magazines in our culture, or in France, for examples).

Work falls unequally upon women of different classes. Upper-class women are often symbols of domesticity while in reality domestic functions are carried out by paid laborers. Domestic functions fall especially heavy on women who are themselves wage-earners (part- or full-time), and who also sustain their families within the private domain. In such a situation, their work in the public domain is usually underpaid in relation to that of men, and discounted by describing the main functions of women to be still domestic ones. Historically, the differing relations to domestic functions by class are illustrated by the relations between urban bourgeois women and peasant women. The former placed their infants with the latter for wet-nursing. In France, this practice is documented into the present century.

Kinship functions in modern state societies do not fall solely upon women; fathers as well as mothers are part of the private, family unit. Kinship also continues to have a certain amount of political potential, although informally. This is seen in the Sicilian Mafia, or in the corporate mergers that accompany ruling-class marriages in the United States. As in pre-state societies, men are usually involved in, or are the controlling forces behind, such kinship as political behavior, yet they are not defined primarily or totally by their participation in this realm.

In modern industrial capitalist states, the privatized kinship realm is increasingly defined as women's work. It is their area of expertise, but also their limitation. The radical separation of home and work place in industrial capitalism transforms and buttresses the distinction between private and public domains that has long had ideological legitimacy through state formation. Women are increasingly defined by their roles within a realm that has been systematically sapped of its resources and authority. Yet the domestic realm produces and sustains the one resource most necessary to all extractive classes: people. Kin groups can be seen as the first colonized structures within emergent states, for their goods and personnel are expropriated by a public authority over which they have little control. It is women's labor that underwrites the capacities of families to produce these resources. Yet this labor is socially unrecognized or accorded a subordinate status while power and prestige are vested in the public domain, which is increasingly controlled by a class of men. The crucial function of kin units in the maintenance of centralized state societies, and especially industrial capitalist ones, is hidden by its ideological submersion into privacy. In the process, the status of women—the holders of kinship functions and powers, a group increasingly defined by its participation in the reproduction and production of families—is reduced.

It must be realized that access to the public sphere alone does not define high status: a menial soldier or an apprentice in a factory does not have high status simply because he or she functions in the public realm. But public mobility, contacts, and certain sorts of jobs within that realm do generate higher status than that held by people who lack any access to public activity. A continuum of differing statuses for women exists, depending on participation in public activities—the trading women of Haiti and West Africa, the nuns of medieval Europe, the female chiefs of East Africa are examples of women holding prestigious positions outside the private realm.

The power associated with the private domain is limited when compared to that available in the public domain. A woman may reign within her family and have the power to control her children, but the state can turn them into soldiers or slaves. While women all over the world, and certainly in Colpied, derive informal prerogatives and status from their roles within the household, codified, legitimate power still rests in a realm from which they are usually excluded. To the extent that the family is a subordinate unit subject to the demands of the state, and to the extent that it is women who are defined by their role within the family, "separate spheres" can never be equal ones.

Susan Harding

Women and Words in a Spanish Village

> What is woven in the loom of fate
> What is woven in the councils of princes
> Is woven also in our veins, our brains
> Is woven like a pattern of living worms
> In the guts of the women of Canterbury.
>
> T. S. Eliot, *Murder in the Cathedral*

Introduction

It was a warm fall afternoon in Oroel. On stone stoops and wooden chairs in the road, a group of women sat in the shade of the houses, sewing and chatting. Three widows and a spinster, they were women with time on their hands. They talked about those in the cemetery, when they had died, how, and what had become of their relatives. They were mending their memories of village families with the thread of their talk, much as they were sewing up hems and cuffs and collars with the thread of their needles.

One hot summer day some men were out in the fields of Oroel overseeing the thresher cut, sort, and sack their wheat. They were sitting in the shade of some bushes, drinking wine and talking.

Many friends helped me in writing this paper and I am very grateful to them. So many contributed so much that the paper is a collective effort. I would especially like to thank Lynn Eden, Roy Rappaport, Rayna Reiter, Gayle Rubin, and Marilyn Young for their encouragement as well as counsel. I am also grateful to the Wenner-Glen Foundation, the Institute for Environmental Quality, and the University of Michigan's Project for the Study of Social Networks in the Mediterranean for their financial support of my fieldwork.

> They exchanged information about the prices, cost, and productivity of several crops, about which was better under what weather and market conditions. They were harvesting each other's knowledge and opinions, much as they were harvesting the wheat of their fields.

The opening images come from Oroel, a small village in northeastern Spain. They suggest that the words of women and men follow the lines of their work. The sexual division of labor in the village is strong and one would think that it would manifest itself in patterns of language use as well. The first section of this paper sketches the division of labor between men and women in Oroel and how this division structures their topics of talk and thought. The division also structures distinct verbal roles in home and village life for the sexes. The second section of the paper describes and discusses in detail the women's side of the verbal division of labor and some of the functions of the skills and genres of speech that comprise the role. In the conclusion, I locate this material in the general debate about the power of women in European peasant societies. As a whole, the paper is about women and words—how women use words and how words use women.

Oroel is an agricultural village. It lies at the base of the first sierra that begins the climb northward to the peaks of the central Pyrenees, and on the fringe of the plain that rolls southward to the Ebro River. The relief of the village land is rugged, alternating among small mesas, valleys, and plains. The primary crops cultivated are cereals, vines, and almond and olive trees; sheep-raising is also an important economic activity for most of the forty-five households that comprise the village.

Changes in the agriculture and demography of the village have accelerated during this century and have affected the sexual division of labor. The population has declined from 400 in 1900 to 180 in 1970, with half the loss occurring since 1950. The decline is both cause and consequence of the mechanization of cereal production, which has occurred in gradual steps through the century and has dramatically cut the hours of labor required in the harvest—what used to take 240 hours now takes one. Vines and olive trees, both labor-intensive crops, have been losing ground rapidly to wheat, the dominant cereal. Before mechanization, women participated in agricultural work, especially in the wheat, olive, and grape harvests. Now, with drastically reduced labor requirements, agricultural work is entirely in the hands of men. So the sexual division of labor that I describe for Oroel is sharper today than it has been at any other time in this century.

Out in the *monte*, as the village land is called, a man walks among cultivated fields and groves of trees. He knows the crops and their varieties, the soil and its possibilities, the *monte* animals and what they do to his crops. He has a name for every wind and knows its character, whether it will bring rain or cold weather, how soon, and how much. He also has a name for every section of the *monte*, and can identify the owner and often the past owners of each parcel of land and knows how it is usually planted. Most of the village men spend most of their days out in the *monte*, usually alone or with a dog, a mule, or a machine. The *monte* is mainly a man's domain.

The way a man feels about his fields is not unlike the way a woman feels about her children. This becomes clear when men talk about why they will have nothing to do with the government concentration program that would assess each man's many scattered fields and redistribute the village land so that each would get an equivalent holding in a single piece. They put forth economic and political arguments about how the program, even though appealing in theory, could not be carried out in practice and would not be carried out justly. But there is something else that holds them firm to their microparcels, something beyond reason, and for many, beyond words. A few will identify this feeling as *cariño*, love, for their land. They and their forebears have poured their thought, sweat, money, their very lives, into those little parcels they own. A man is in his land and his land is in him. To ask him to trade his land for another piece over the hill, just as fertile and productive, is to ask a mother to trade her child for another one just around the corner, just as good-looking and clever.

Some women know the man's *monte*, although they do not know it as well. Nor do they know it from the same perspective, that of its dominator, but as a helper to him who rules. The *monte* that women know best, and one that most men do not know, is much smaller. They know the uncultivated margins and slopes, the places where weeds and herbs and wildflowers grow. They have names for all the wild plants; they know where to find them and how to use them. Though the margins and slopes are privately owned, the women explore and exploit them as if they were public domain.

The village proper is mainly a woman's domain. A woman knows her house and family, as a man knows his fields and trees. She knows where everything is in the house and how to keep it in order. She knows the tastes and moods and needs of her household charges and how to get those in her charge from one day to the next. She knows how to prepare a good cooking fire, how to make bread and sausage, how to cure meat and preserve tomatoes, how to fix dozens of dishes and then use all the leftovers. She knows how to make much of her family's clothing and how to mend and wash it so it will look as well and last as long as possible.

Much as in other Mediterranean villages, the primary work of the men of Oroel is in agriculture and livestock, and a few also work in shops and trades—all places where money is made. Women's primary work is at home, the place where lives are made.

Our work cuts channels in our world of words, creating certain clusters of topics and concerns. We inhabit them and they inhabit us. We say what we do. Thus the division of labor between the sexes in Oroel becomes a division in their use of language as well.

In their talk and thought, village men are primarily occupied with the land and what pertains to it—crops, the weather, prices, wages, inheritance, work animals, and machinery. On the side, they may discuss hunting, play cards, quote facts and figures of all sorts, and argue about sports. In casual dialogue, a man is interested in what a person thinks and in what a person knows and does as a larger social and economic being in the public sphere. His main verbal focus, however, is on his own concerns, not anyone else's.

The talk and thought of women are wrapped around people and their personal lives. The first thing a woman wants to know when she meets someone is about her family. In talking with someone she knows but has not seen in some time, she asks more detailed, precise questions about the person's health and family welfare. In her daily life in the home and village, a woman is likewise more interested in how someone feels than in what someone thinks, in who a person is and what a person does in the private, rather than the public, sphere. From her youth and ongoing conversations and visits, she knows in varying detail about the houses and families in the village, for women are the keepers of kinship ties and tales. In the home, the main focus of her talk and thought is on the needs and concerns of household members. If a man's world of words revolves more around objects and his own concerns, a woman's revolves more around subjects, around persons and their concerns.

The division of men and women in their language use is, however, even deeper. Oroel men and women not only have distinct behavioral roles that influence the content of their speech; they also have distinct verbal roles that structure their use of language and assign to them distinct verbal skills and speech genres. The division of labor, in effect, ascribes to men and women different mental tasks and obligations, in terms of internal and external discourse, as well as different physical tasks and obligations in village life.

The following section of this paper is an examination of the verbal role of Oroel women and of the skills and genres that comprise the role. It is based on material I gathered there during twenty months of fieldwork on several subjects. My information and ideas were gathered informally but consciously; they come out of dozens of conversations with women about their work, and from observations made while participating with them in their work. It was my intention to focus exclusively on women, but it is also true that I could not have participated in and observed the verbal behavior of men in the same way. Comparable material on the verbal role of men in a village will have to be gathered by a man.

The Verbal Role of Women in Oroel

As a wife and mother in Oroel, a woman works all day, every day. She usually spends a third to a half of her hours standing up in the kitchen, cooking, serving, and cleaning up after meals. Between meals she makes the beds, cleans the house, buys and gathers food, and washes, hangs up, irons, and sews clothing. Her daily work is fundamentally reproductive; it reproduces itself every day. Meals are eaten, beds are unmade, rooms are disordered and dirtied, clothes are soiled and torn, daily. Her labor is consumed remorselessly in a ceaseless battle against domestic disorder which she wins only to lose. A woman's work is never done; it is always undone.

Work in the home accounts for most of the physical activity of adult women in Oroel. Likewise, it accounts for most of their verbal activity. The verbal aspect of women's role, or any role, has two manifestations—social speech and inner speech—talk and thought. The two kinds of speech are not the same in structure or content. We do not say just what we think and we do not think just what we say. However, they are related—one follows from the other. It is on the basis of this relationship, and on the basis of what some women told me directly about the content of their thought, that I generalize about women's inner speech in Oroel.

Most of a woman's talk and thought in the home is structured around the requirements of a house and family. Her thought goes into planning, directing, and reviewing the actions that constitute her work, and her talk goes into organizing the activities and events for which she is responsible. As her household work reproduces itself every day, so the words that pertain to it are repeated day after day, year after year.

A woman as a wife and mother must endlessly repeat explanations, answers, and instructions. Sometimes she may yell and nag, for men and children have a tendency not to hear things the more you say them.

Child-rearing is an activity that four-fifths of the adult women in Oroel are or have been engaged in for anywhere from fifteen to thirty-five years of their lives. It is a verbal task as well as a physical and emotional one. An old widow, a mother of six, who is unusually aware of this fact explained to me one reason why a mother must be careful with her words to her children. She illustrated her point by telling me about an exchange she saw between a mother and her two children. One day the children went to the city with their father for the afternoon. When they returned, the mother was all eyes and words for the older son: "Oh, my son, what did you do in the city? I'm so glad you're home. Did you see your uncle? What did he say?" His younger sister stood by, watching out of the corner of her eye, silent. The widow explained that the daughter's jealousy of her brother was the result of this kind of exchange with the mother. A mother must say as much to one child as the other because words are a measure of her affection. A mother who gives her words to one child and withholds them from another is saying that she loves one child more than the other. The widow was quite definite that this was the mother's responsibility and not the father's. When I asked her why, she said, "I suppose it is because a mother is always with the children and the father rarely is. It's she who feeds them and keeps them clothed and clean. She takes care of all their needs. A mother and children are together a lot, especially when the children are very young. A father is hardly ever around, and when he is he doesn't preoccupy himself with the children. His attention is elsewhere."

In child-rearing, the words of women are a means to cultural ends. It is women who are responsible for their children acquiring language and for their primary cultural formation—their preliminary role instruction—through language, in particular for their cultural differentiation as girls and boys who will grow into women and men. A mother may speak equally to her children, but she says different things to them according to their sex. A lot of socialization in Oroel goes on in the kitchen, around the table at mealtime. One standard mother-daughter exchange I have heard in several houses goes like this:

> Mother: "Have another helping."
> Daughter: "No."
> Mother: "Take more."
> Daughter: "No."
> The mother almost puts the helping on her daughter's plate.
> Mother: "Do you want this, yes or no?"
> Daughter: "No."
> The mother withdraws the helping.
> Mother: "No, no, no. You're not going to get a husband if you always say no. You have to say yes."

The last line is tricky, of course. To get married, the girl will have to learn to say yes to a man, but not to say yes to everything until they are married. The fact that the girl's brother heard this exchange is perhaps as important as the girl's hearing it. The line is spoken to the daughter, not the son, so they are learning that they are different. They are learning that boys grow up to ask and give things and girls grow up to answer and take things. This is one instance of child-rearing through words, one of an endless number of such tiny exchanges and events that differentiate and define males and females and cultural men and women.

One capacity that a woman at home in Oroel develops, in conjunction with her household directing and child-rearing skills, is intuition. By "intuition" I do not refer to leaps of the imagination or the faculty of knowing without the use of rational processes. I am referring to what is commonly called "women's intuition," to a combination of empathy and mind-reading that women are known for in our culture as well as Oroel's. In Oroel a woman is called upon to think out certain thoughts and needs of her household charges, to think herself into them and through their activities in search of the needs that it is her responsibility to fulfill. A good woman does not have to be told what her husband and children think or need; she knows, often before they do. It's her job—to know them better than they know themselves, at least in certain ways. One effect of a woman's engaging her thoughts in the lives, minds, and bodies of men and children is to free them from the responsibility of thinking about and meeting certain of their own needs, and thus to give them time, time to work and time to grow up.

What I know about the effects of women's intuition and work on the lives of others in part grew out of my own interaction with a village woman, my structural mother, who thought out my daily needs in distressing detail the first weeks I was in her charge. Gradually I began to discourage her, but beyond a certain point I could not go. On the one hand, she had to help me—I could not help myself *and* do fieldwork. On the other hand, she could not help herself—she had to help me. Interactions with other women provided further evidence of their intuitive capacities, the most striking of which is the ability to predict the course, and often the exact lines, of conversations once given a few situational cues.

A Soviet psychologist named Lev Vygotsky, writing about the structure of inner speech, makes an observation that gives us a clue to the mechanics of intuition. His observation is based on a quotation from a scene in a Tolstoy novel, in which a woman is tending a man on his deathbed: " 'No one heard clearly what he said, but Kitty understood him. She understood because her mind incessantly watched his needs.' We might say that her thoughts, following the thoughts of the dying man, contained the subject to which his word, understood by no one else, referred" (1962:140). Kitty understands the man because she assumes the subject of his thoughts in her own. She assumes his subject as her subject and then deduces the predicate, working with prior knowledge and contextual information, and proceeds to meet the man's needs. The intuitive work of Oroel women seems to operate on the same principle.

A woman is emotionally, as well as physically and verbally, engaged with the concerns of others. She is the emotional center of the household, assuming the anxieties, tensions, sorrows, and joys of her charges as her own. Her role requires that she identify with her charges, especially her children, to such an extent that she may experience insecurities about them as insecurities about herself. Given her position, and as a result of her worldly inexperience and primary cultural formation, a woman becomes unusually vulnerable to fear. If she cannot, for example, account for the whereabouts of one of her children, she may work herself into a virtual state of hysteria, imagining the worst that possibly could have occurred and assuming that it did. It is as if she had lost track of a part of herself. The father's experience is not the same. In one case I observed, when the child finally returned just as the mother, visibly shaking from several hours of anxious worry, was about to call the Guardia Civil, the father's stance was calm, if not unconcerned. He advised his wife to wait until the bad news arrived before she worried. Worry about well-being is distinctly on the women's side of the division of labor.

Women, of course, are more than emotionally dependent on their charges; they are economically dependent on their men, which yields another verbal characteristic, that of finesse. In general, those with resources and power over others learn to protect themselves with a veil of secrecy, which on an individual scale is called a sense of privacy. To penetrate the privacy of their husbands, wives become skilled at asking them questions, tiny and discreet questions, about their actions and activities. A woman seems to assume that she cannot ask a straight question of her husband on some matters and expect a straight answer. So she breaks the question up into piecemeal questions with the aim that together their answers will unobtrusively answer, or give her grounds for inferring the answer, to the question she could not openly ask. Women also may learn to fragment their demands into tiny pieces—first ask for one piece, get it, then another, and so on, until the pieces add up to the whole demand. Another tactic is to make the whole demand at once, but not as such, not by directly or explicitly asking for anything; instead, by talking around what is at issue, focusing on it in fine tuning, going on about details, and so avoid a wholesale, final, negative response. Husbands come to think of their wives as verbally cunning and manipulative, and collectively men imagine that these are natural characteristics of women. But skills of verbal finesse and subterfuge are a function of, and an adaptation to, women's subordinate and dependent position with regard to control over resources.

There is a partially verbal phenomenon typical of and revealing about women in the home which I would like to discuss before going on to women and words in the village, and that is the matter of mothers-in-law. In Oroel, if there is a son and if he marries, he usually inherits the family property intact and takes effective control of it before his parents die. His parents, however, reserve the right to live out their lives in the house and, generally, the right to have final say on many matters. Thus there is the common situation of the wife moving into her husband's mother's house and the consequent conflict. The conflict is exacerbated in Oroel because the impartible inheritance system and the continuing presence and power of the son's parental family converge with a value system that has a mother define her sense of self through her children.

The tension between a mother and her son's wife is thus prescribed by the economic, kinship, and ideological structures of the village. It also exists when a son and his wife make their residence elsewhere, but in an attenuated form since the drama is not acted out every day. The dispute is territorial. It centers on the son, the right and responsibility to think out his daily needs and to meet them, and extends from there to the organization of the lives of other household members and of the house itself. A mother and her daughter-in-law are competing for the same niche. In effect, when a son marries he brings his mother's replacement into the house, another woman who threatens to deprive the mother of part of herself. A mother who does not permit her daughter-in-law any access to her son's welfare, or a wife who tries to usurp all access to her husband's welfare from her mother-in-law, is asking for hell.

In this territorial dispute, a woman's only weapon is her tongue. The mechanism through which it is settled is squabbling, the continual bickering about minute matters and events within the household. With time and pain—sometimes more, sometimes less—lines are drawn and agreements made between a mother and her son's wife. The wife comes into her own when she has children, and, of course, takes full control when her husband's mother dies. Though it is very much he who is at stake, the son experiences the conflict peripherally, and it is probably he who makes up the stories and jokes about it. The women experience the changeover in their guts, in their hearts, not in their heads or humors. They have no rational idiom with which to talk and think out the conflict, and the agreements they come to are largely unspoken and unconscious.

The structurally inevitable conflict between a mother and her son's wife is one of the most serious confrontations that women experience in their lives. But no visible contracts are drawn up, and women have not created elaborate legal systems and institutions that stipulate what is at stake and how it shall pass hands, as men have regarding the transfer of their property. The institutions for the litigation of this dispute are below the cultural surface, embedded in the particular context, beyond the conscious control of the women involved. Not only are there no explicit or formal institutions to deal with the conflict, but there is no tangible recognition of its importance; on the contrary, it is the subject of considerable mockery and derision.

This is a general feature of other conflict situations that involve women in Oroel. The formal institutions for conflict resolution in the village are set up by the church and the state in the persons of the priest and the judge. Women generally do not resort to them with their disputes. If anything, a woman will consult the divinities or the priest for aid and advice. But even these petitions are ultimately not her own, for, in addition to being entirely controlled by men, the church, like the state, is ideologically committed to the principle of male domination. In a legally and ideologically subordinate position and without recourse to effective institutions of their own that they can manipulate, women must defend and advance themselves with whatever everyday verbal skills, such as squabbling, finesse, and gossip, they may develop.

The mother-in-law conflict is a classic scene in village dramas throughout the Mediterranean area. Observing it and other scenes associated with standard relationships mapped from household to household around Oroel, especially those of mother-child and husband-wife, led me to see the village as a theater in a literal sense. The theater-making elements—a stage of reduplicated and common settings and scenes, a cast of predefined roles, a common history and culture, and common activities—ordain a sense of play, of drama, in the village. They join together to render something of a script out of the community's speech. Scenes and lines along with them, such as the mealtime mother-daughter exchange above, are played and replayed, with appropriate improvisations, in households around the village. The play also goes on in the village stage at large. What is said in the passing interactions of persons in the roads and plazas really does seem to be preordained and is most predictable. There are also constraints on the speech behavior of persons from different households in longer, more complex conversations that follow script patterns. This is part of what is behind the uncanny ability that some women have to predict precisely what will be or what was said by others.

When women are not in their houses, they are usually running household errands. The woman in charge of the household goes to one or both of the general stores daily and to the village washbasin at least once a week. In addition, she may make fairly frequent calls on neighbors and kin to arrange, give, or borrow something. This is one of the most flexible components of women's time outside the house. More obligatory are certain formal occasions, official calls a woman makes as her household representative to welcome a new wife to the village, to congratulate a woman for the birth of a child, to aid and encourage in a neighbor's home when someone is sick, and to console in another's home when someone dies. These calls are extensions of a woman's work in the home in the sense that she makes them in the name of her family and that they extend and are the extent of her official interest in the affairs of other households. Collectively, the formal calls women make amount to the social, or public, assimilation of the signal events—marriage, birth, illness, and death—of village households, which are otherwise officially private plays. Another activity that takes women out of their houses and into each other's speaking company is making *mondongo.* Most of the households in Oroel kill one or two pigs in the winter each year; and it is women's work to turn the pigs into meat, that is, to make *mondongo.* Kin and neighbor women aid each other reciprocally on this occasion for the whole day. The forty pigs killed last winter by thirty households in Oroel thus animated dozens of latent networks and friendships among the women.

These are the common occasions women have for speaking with one another. On all of them women are engaging in household work or are engaged as its representative. Insofar as the occasions are public ones, definite limits are placed on a woman's script. Her lines are largely confined to the words of work, to the talk that applies to the task or purpose at hand. Beyond this, there are minor, mundane exchanges about the bric-a-brac of daily living. The women's references are to themselves, perhaps to their children and the physical health of another household charge, or to a relative living elsewhere, and are matter-of-fact reports about their living circumstances. Such chatting defines the actual range of a woman's script on formal calls and, for the most part, on the daily and weekly household chores and errands that engage women outside the home.

There is one more type of talk that is within the public limits of the script on these occasions: stories. The stories women tell each other are about personal, intimate situations, very often about a man, a woman, and a marital problem or anomaly, but the characters are anonymous, unknown, and unnamed, so their affairs may be told in relatively public situations. One story is about a woman who gets separated from her husband on the streets of a strange city on their wedding night. In another honeymoon tale, the newlyweds are offered a large sum of money by a man who wanted to sleep with the bride on the wedding night. They make the deal, and the next day the couple find out the money was counterfeit. In format, the stories are little plays, tiny verbal soap operas in which, once the general playbill is given and the stage is set, the plot unfolds. Each one presents a personal complication or crisis which is the real focus of the story. Its resolution is not very important, and many of the stories end without one: they are simply statements of the problem.

These stories are the myths of women. Like myths in primitive societies, they are repetitious and are repeated often. The characters, situations, and actual events change, but the stories are always the same in the sense that the underlying structures animated and transmitted by them are the same. Like myths, the stories instruct as they entertain. They focus, and they represent a focus of, attention on cultural and social reality, and they structure and interpret that reality. Their tendency not to resolve their complication, just to raise it, suggests that the contradictions which they treat, like the contradictions embedded in the lives of women, are not solved. In any case, these stories belong to women in Oroel; men do not tell them among themselves. The structures they animate and transmit are specific to the role of women.

Gossip between women in Oroel is not unlike the stories they tell each other.* As a genre of speech, it is also personal and intimate, and it develops plots. But if the stories are

*The Spanish equivalent of the English "to gossip" is *charlar*. As in English, the verb has either a negative or a more neutral, harmless connotation, and when used in reference to a woman or women, the negative connotation is usually intended or interpreted. That connotation may be overtly stated by using either *hablar mal* ("to speak badly" of someone), or *criticar* ("to criticize"). Both are usually used in reference to and associated with women more often than men.

myths, then gossip is history, for the characters are real, known, and present—not at the scene of the conversation, but in the local cast. Gossip is about the private affairs of those around the women in their face-to-face society and thus not within the public limits of the script. It is marked by the fact that the speakers would not want the spoken-of to know of the exchange. Gossip also differs from stories in format. It is at once more abbreviated and detailed. Background information is assumed and often only fragments of plots are given at one time. The plots are submerged; they are not explicitly outlined but usually revealed in the course of recounting dialogues. Quotation markers in the form of *dije* and *dijo* ("I said" and "he/she said") are surface cues to the occurrence of gossip. Stories and gossip engage the same cultural structures in women; in addition, gossip engages their personal and social structures. The women are participants, not observers. As characters in the drama, they have a vested interest in how the plot unfolds, in words if not in fact.

A woman may initiate gossip in response to a question or because she has a purpose in mind for communicating some information or an opinion. Sometimes it seems that the women cannot help themselves, that they cannot resist "passing the news." Women have mastered the art of asking questions of each other, as they have of their husbands, of subtly eliciting certain kinds of information from one another to an almost coercive degree. There is a stock of words and responses that are used to lead on someone who has a tale and has begun to tell it. They are along the lines of "Look at that," "I'll be," and a drawn-out "Yes?" A teller often does not know what her listener really wants to know, but can see her take in real news by her expressions, both facial and verbal. Crucial tidbits may appear to slip out inadvertently, either because the teller has disguised them by putting them in a context of mundane observations in order to protect herself, or because the teller did not know how important they were to the listener and they came out accidentally.

Vital words, about death and serious illness, pass around the village as fast as women can open their windows and call down to their neighbors. More confidential information does not move so fast or freely. It encounters resistance and moves in smaller networks. Words flow, stumble, die, are fed back, reborn, and transformed. Each piece of news cuts its own path through the village. Some make things better, some make things worse, some make no difference at all. The overall movement and effect of the messages seem random and beyond any individual control or design. But at each link the movement and effect are not random or accidental. A woman usually has her reasons for saying the things she does. Even when she cannot help herself, she is at least getting something out of her system.

Gossip may be about current events in the village, or it may be about past events which, more strictly speaking, are history. Gossip about past events reviews and provides background information necessary to gossip about current events. When the characters are known but dead and gone, as in the women's talk in the opening image, there are fewer constraints on talk about them. This may or may not be true of talk about past events involving persons known and still present. The exchange that the old widow described to me between the mother and her children who had returned from the city was a past event, but it was understood that I was not to reveal my knowledge of the event or who told me about it. The widow's explicit purpose in telling me about it was to advise me to speak equally to the children I might have. Implicitly, and perhaps unknowingly, she was also informing me of a rivalry between the mother's two children of which I was unaware. Finally, it seemed to me she was simply enjoying the telling for its own sake, enjoying the opportunity to express an interesting observation she had made which perhaps she could have expressed to no one else.

Gossip between women generally occurs around the edges of the occasions I discussed above. It occurs "incidentally" to family business, while one is borrowing something from a neighbor or on the way to the store. It does not occur on the purely formal visits women make and they do not openly visit each other in Oroel just to talk. In fact, visiting by women for which there is no apparent working or formal purpose does occur, but it is clandestine; if the man of the house appeared, some household matter would be contrived to account for the visit.

An appropriate situation for gossip in Oroel is defined by whether or not *confianza* may be invoked. To have *confianza* in someone means you believe you can tell them normally private things in good faith, with the confidence that they will not use what you say against you. In particular, you trust they will not go directly to a person spoken of and tell them everything you said. *Confianza* is not usually invoked when there are more than two women speaking to each other at a time. The criterion of two women talking at a time is not part of my definition of a gossip situation, but it usually applies in Oroel now, perhaps for entirely de facto reasons. The only place where women still gather regularly in groups and talk is the village washbasin. When the village bakery opened twenty years ago it ended their breadbaking circles, and ready-made clothes and more money to buy them has curtailed the sewing circles. The circles had, and the washbasin has, a reputation for gossip, slander, and attack. Perhaps it was true in a time when the village was more crowded and poorer—tensions were higher and tempers shorter. Today, however, the washbasin is a place where much more dirty linen is washed literally than figuratively. Even the washbasin is being challenged as a place for women to gather in groups, since families are beginning to buy washing machines. Women are regularly engaged with one another less, the village is less a village and more "a collection of houses, like a housing estate" (Gluckman, 1963:313).

Oroel is by no means rife with women's gossip, although it is not easy to say precisely how much of it occurs. Its incidence varies for each woman and each week. It is difficult to observe at all because what is socially visible lasts only a few minutes at a time and how often it lasts longer is impossible to say. Moreover, its definition is subjective. Some Oroel men told me that all women do when they talk to one another is gossip. Clearly, its definition depends on one's notion of privacy. I define gossip in terms of the privacy being probed on the one hand—in Oroel, the privacy of the household—and the privacy, or *confianza*, invoked in the exchange on the other hand—speakers do not want the spoken-of to know about the exchange. Given these criteria, I suppose gossip accounts for a rather small portion of a woman's verbal time during an average week.

Although quantitatively perhaps not so important, gossip among women is socially quite significant. On one level, men and women in Oroel are working in contrary social directions. Men are the producers and protectors of household plays, since their role assigns them control over economic and political affairs in and between households. For men's part, in secrecy is power and defense; in privacy is peace and order. Men create and maintain a hierarchy of households in the village that depends on distance and separation; their inclination is toward isolation and self-sufficiency. If it is the role of men to build and keep up the figurative fences, it is the role of women to climb them from time to time.

Often gossip appears to be the simple reporting of conversations and events from scenes participated in, observed, or heard about by the reporter, as if women were quite neutrally keeping each other up on the many village plays. Gossip is a system for circulating real information, but that is never all that is circulated. Although overt criticism is rare, covert evaluation is constant. The evaluation is conveyed by editing if not by editorializing. There is a yes/no evaluation built into the report or failure to report a conversation or event. As the report is given, editing continues by highlighting and omitting portions so that further evaluation is written between the lines when it is not stated in so many words.

Gossip, then, is the collection, circulation, and analysis of certain portions of village script. It is a verbal specialty of women in Oroel, one which many women pursue with vigor but also with considerable care and caution. Women probe privacies; they do not invade them. They are not out telling and gleaning family secrets; they are piecing together plays within and between households according to their definition of relevance. They are responsible for the integration of the village play. Without women talking to each other, there would be little to call village society.

However, gossip among women is not appreciated as a healthy process in Oroel. It is considered unhealthy and disruptive of the peace and order of the village. It is disdained by both men and women, and by the church. The tongues of women—and their thoughts about others as well—are dangerous, wicked, and sinful. The constant cultural campaign against women's gossip and certain changes in their work requirements are on the verge of making gossip among them an entirely underground activity, so swift and secret as to be socially invisible, if not impossible.* In fact, women's gossip is not as destructive as it is made out to be, nor as corrosive and erosive of the village hierarchy and order as all believe. If anything, women's climbing of the figurative fences between households contributes to the maintenance of the village hierarchy. Women in their gossip, no less than in their other talk, are operating with their family interest in mind; it is their vested interest. They are not operating outside the value system but precisely within it; they are not simply speaking the value system, it is determining what they speak. But all this is beside the point. The point is that in gossiping, women

* In another northern Spanish village, a woman, in a conversation about how she spoke with Christ and why women prayed more than men, said, "It's not that I have bad deeds to reveal, it's the bad thoughts. The mind never stops producing them." "Men pray a lot less, that is for sure. We pray more, and we are worse! We are more boorish; we have wicked tongues" (Christian, 1972:141).

According to Pitt-Rivers (1961:144), writing of a southern Spanish village: "Gossiping is shameless behavior, and the accusation of it even couched in euphemistic terms may provoke a violent quarrel."

The same cultural posture is suggested by the comments about women and gossip in *Gifts and Poison*, a 1971 collection of articles about nine European communities edited by Bailey. These comments apply to a village in the French Alps:

> For men to sit around in public and gossip is quite acceptable, it is generally assumed, this exchange is *bavarder:* a friendly, sociable, light-hearted, good-natured, altruistic exchange of news, in-

are behaving politically because they are tampering with power. Their words are the stuff that reputations are made of, and in small communities reputations are powerful because they, in part, determine one's relations and behavior. But power is not the cultural prerogative of women; it is men's. Gossip is potentially a challenge to the male hierarchy, a challenge to men's control of the hierarchy. It is the politics of the officially powerless, and thus is imbued with the connotation of malice, wickedness, sin, and pollution. Gossip is dirty work in Oroel, not because it is so intrinsically, but because women do it.

Women do not have equal voices in the village gossip networks. The potential power of their voices varies with how many village women they are closely related to by kinship and marriage, and with how many women they have forged bonds on the basis of shared work, school, or neighborhood experience. Clearly, a woman who was born in the village, who has lived there all her life, who is related by blood to women in other houses, and who married a village man related to other village women is in the strongest of possible positions: she has the most sources of inputs and outlets for her voice. In practice, the power of her voice also depends on her own finesse at dealing with the information and evaluation she is party to. If, for example, she becomes known for

---

> formation and opinion. But if women are seen talking together, then something quite different is happening: very likely they are indulging in *mauvaise langue*—gossip, malice, "character assassination." (Bailey, in Bailey, ed., 1971:1)

> Friendship amongst women is considered "dangerous" as it threatens family solidarity. (Hudson, in ibid.:42)

> [Women] are expected to keep to themselves and to refrain from gossiping. A woman who has friends and is frequently seen out of the house is suspected of telling family secrets and gossiping maliciously. (Ibid.:46)

I suspect such a posture toward women and gossip is general, as general as male dominance is, but how much of it women actually do and with how much impunity surely varies from society to society and time to time.

negligence regarding her sources, for doubling back to the subject of some gossip and telling her or him what was said by whom, then her channels of information will close up around her. One cannot have *confianza* in her.

Depending on the number and nature of her channels and her reputation for being trustworthy, a woman develops a basis for making her voice heard, for impressing her images and interpretations of village events on others, and so influencing their opinions and behavior. The primary circulation of these images and interpretations is restricted to women themselves. The way they reach and exert any influence over men is on a one-to-one basis; specifically, by wives talking to their husbands. A man who is not married has no direct access to the pool of information, images, and interpretations of village events that women command; likewise, a woman who is not married has no direct access to male-dominated decision-making processes. Actually, the situation is not all or nothing in either case, for sisters and mothers may be links for unmarried men and brothers and fathers may be links for unmarried women. But marriage is the strongest link of all for both a man and a woman to the world of knowledge and power controlled by the opposite sex. If a new *practicante*, a paramedic, is being engaged by the village, the most direct influence a woman can have over his hiring, pay, and living arrangements is through her husband, since all the actual decisions are in the hands of men. Her influence also depends on her ability to garner information about who and what is being considered through other women because her husband is by no means obliged to tell her what he knows, though she may marshal her skills of intuition and finesse in an attempt to find out.

Such are the mechanics of how women may wield power with their words. First, through their ability to influence the information, images, and interpretations of other women, and second, through their ability to influence those of one man at a time. The first involves the use of gossip for political purposes, that is, for power, and the second involves the use of other verbal skills for political purposes. A woman's ability to influence her husband depends specifically on her intuition and finesse, her ability to outguess and manipulate her husband, which are skills she also uses in interactions with other women. For example, a woman can garner information from other women about home improvements in other households and then use it to lobby with her husband for improvements in her own home. And the conflict and the resolution of the conflict between a mother and her daughter-in-law is largely carried out through their verbal skills.

The point is not that women are unique in their use of verbal skills for political ends, but that these skills must be uniquely developed by them in their exercise of power, given the absence of explicit, formal institutions to lobby for their desires and needs, their subordinate economic and political position in both the household and village spheres, and their lack of formal access to the decision-making processes in the society. Whatever recognition the desires and needs of Oroel women get derives from their verbal skills, from their ability to have their voices heard, remembered, and responded to by other women and men on an informal basis. Thus, not only gossip but women's words in general earn a reputation for politicking, and the reputation is a bad one because politics is not women's prerogative.

Conclusion

Women are clearly not powerless persons in Oroel society. If power in a social relationship is the control that is exercised by a person over the environment of another person (Adams, 1967:32; also see Blok, 1974), then the ways women use words confer upon them real power over men. Women direct the organization and daily conduct of households. And they participate with men in making many household decisions that are not in their domain of housekeeping and child care. How much power women have in making these decisions varies with the person and the decision, but the most important decisions made in terms of the future of the household are probably mutual. Examples of such decisions are the sale and purchase of machines, animals, and land; major household and agricultural improvements; and work, marriage, and inheritance arrangements concerning children. Women, furthermore, influence decisions that men make among themselves outside the households, drawing on information and evaluations derived from talking to other women.

So women are hardly downtrodden, inert, voiceless creatures in Oroel. They do have power, but the question remains, how much power? Do we want to say, for example, that women are as, or even more, powerful than men? The argument for women having the upper hand in peasant society runs something like this: The informal power that women have in the household and the village is effectively greater than the formal power that men have in either domain. In the household, women either make the decisions, or, when they are mutual or made by men, women invariably get their own way. In the village, decisions are not worked out so much in formal organizations, which men control, as in informal networks, which women dominate. The "appearance" is that men have more power; the "reality" is that women do. In this context, the ideology of male dominance becomes a myth which appeases men and obscures the real power situation.*

There are several general criticisms I have of this line of argument. First, it seriously underestimates the power in men's hands in the household economy and the village polity. Secondly, it isolates the village from the larger structural context from which men derive much of their economic, political, and ideological power in the village. In this larger context, the role of women in the running of everyday life in the

* Ernestine Friedl presented a moderate version of the argument for female dominance in her 1967 analysis of the position of women in a Greek village. The "appearance versus reality" dichotomy comes from her article. In an unpublished paper, Susan Rogers develops a stronger and more elaborate version of this argument, based on information she gathered in a northeastern French village.

village is dwarfed by the role of men in running the structures that determine the conditions of everyday life. Finally, male dominance is not just a myth in European peasant societies; it is a structural fact. Women may not experience themselves as subordinate, but they are structurally in a subordinate position with respect to men.

More specifically, and in terms of the material presented in this paper, I think the argument seriously overestimates the power in women's hands by not recognizing the nature, limits, and consequences of that power. The informal mechanisms of women's power have been described in this paper as essentially verbal skills that women develop in the household and in the community. Each skill has a double edge, so that as it cuts for a woman, it cuts against her. If gossip provides a forum for a woman to influence the opinions and behavior of others, it also provides the others with a forum to influence her opinions and behavior. Gossip creates among those who participate in it a sense that there is no such thing as privacy, and Oroel women have a saying that goes "All things done that ought not be done are sooner or later known." This sense, if not the fact, of being under constant verbal surveillance restricts the behavior of women and helps keep them in their place. The irony is that it is the collective effect of their own behavior that restricts them as individuals. In a similar fashion, a woman's intuition and inclination to think out the thoughts and needs of others give her knowledge that binds her to comply with their thoughts and needs no less than it frees her from ignorance. The stories she tells and hears remind her of what can happen if she steps out of the moral order, in particular if she violates the marriage code. They not only express but reinforce the structures that govern her thought and behavior. Even her manipulative skills, her skills of finesse and subterfuge, conspire against her. They may be good enough to ferret out a vital piece of information or to bring about a household improvement, but they are by no means powerful enough to challenge basic assumptions about decision-making and the power differential. They keep a woman on a perpetual treadmill of her own immediate, though not ultimate, design. Each gain she makes means that the same game starts over again, reproducing itself, instead of building up toward some kind of solution or progressive strategy.

Verbal skills and speech genres are framed for women by cultural and social structures that exist. A woman develops the skills in acting out the structures and the role dictated by them; the skills are first of all essential to, integrated with, or an extension of the tasks and obligations of a woman as a wife and mother. She may also use them to reach out of the structures and make her voice heard beyond the strict limits of her role. But she cannot use those verbal skills to break out of or break down the structures that framed them.

Both parties in a relationship of interdependence have powers over each other. If the relationship is to endure without—or with only occasional—exercise of physical coercion on the part of the dominant group or persons, those in the subordinate position must be accorded powers that are sufficient in nature and scope to preserve their pride and self-respect. The powers women have in Oroel and other peasant societies are the kind accorded to the subordinate group in an enduring relationship of interdependence. If women have any power to affect the conditions of their lives it is through men and on an individual basis. This is the hallmark of the subordinate position in a hierarchical relationship: the prohibition, whether implicit or explicit, of deliberate collective action to effect a change in living conditions. The nondeliberate, but collective, power that village women exert in the form of gossip operates as much, if not more, to control their own behavior as that of men. The powers of village women are very real, but within the given structures and relationships they do not constitute, nor do they provide women with, the last word.

Sydel F. Silverman

The Life Crisis as a Clue to Social Function: The Case of Italy

Attempts to identify the economic, political, or other functions of women generally concentrate upon the structure and operation of social institutions. However, an alternative approach might also be useful—the point of view of the women themselves, as they go through the experience of learning, assuming, practicing, and discarding roles and functions. I would like to explore the possibility of revealing such functions through a look at the life cycle of women, particularly those transitional points in the life cycle that become recognized, culturally defined crises. Life crises may be taken to mean those periods in the life span at which there is some interruption in continuity—a transition from one culturally defined stage of life to another, and at which there is regularly expected individual stress. Such crises are frequently but not necessarily ritualized; they may coincide with but are not the same as *rites de passage*.

The life crisis is fundamentally a cultural phenomenon, though it may be based upon a biological transition. Cultures may or may not emphasize physiological changes occurring during the life cycle, and thus they may increase or minimize the likelihood of experiential stress at such times. Life crises may readily be analyzed at noncultural levels of explanation —for instance, as physiological events, or as sets of psycho-

---

This article originally appeared in *Anthropological Quarterly* 40:3 (July 1967) and is reprinted with permission.

logical problems. My own interest in this problem derives from some exploratory work on the menopause in American women, a phase at which measurable physiological events (changes in hormonal levels) interact with psychological conflicts and role changes to create a significant degree of regularly expectable stress. I was struck by the fact that the menopause crisis had been very little studied in terms of the status transitions involved. Yet it seems to me that examining crisis periods such as the menopause as social-cultural phenomena might not only clarify the crises themselves but might also suggest some new ideas about the position of women. My assumption is that transitions in statuses—particularly where such transitions become emotionally turbulent—may make the nature of those statuses, and their relation to the social functions of women, stand out more clearly.

I do not hope to arrive at statements of general cross-cultural applicability about the occurrence or severity of crises. Rather, it is my intention to approach the life crisis as a kind of "event analysis"—a way of detecting what functions women have in their society, the relative importance of different functions, and their timing and interweaving through the life cycle. The first step in such an analysis is to uncover the structuring of the life cycle of women in a particular culture—how the life span is divided into periods or stages, the nature of continuity from one stage to the next, and finally those points of transition that involve fundamental status change or for other reasons become stressful. Once these periods of crisis (if any) are identified, a number of different kinds of questions may be asked about them:

1. The timing of the crisis. What specific transitions does it coincide with (physiological changes, psychological reorientation, status transition)? In particular, what social functions are assumed or discarded at this point?

2. Regularized variations in the experience of crisis. What kinds of women—in terms of social positions—have crises of greater or lesser severity?

3. The nature of the identity crisis involved. What do conflicts concerning self-concepts reveal about the experience of assuming or discarding social functions?

4. Changes in social relationships. Does the crisis consist of any breaks in former relationships, formation of new ones, changes in the nature of ongoing ones? What social ties are exploited during the crisis period—who is called on to do what?

5. Economic aspects of the crisis. Does the crisis period involve any economic exchanges or expenditures? Does the woman or any individual or group associated with her undergo changes of economic significance?

6. The ritualization of the crisis. If there is ritual connected, what does it express—what social functions are dramatized and in what way?

These questions represent some of the lines of inquiry that may be relevant to different situations. As an initial illustration of how they might lead to insights into the social position of women, consider how this kind of approach might be applied to the problems of the menopause crisis of American women. In the United States, the continuity of the life span seems to be disrupted at two different periods, which are experienced as crisis—puberty (adolescence) and menopause (climacterium). Concentrating on the second of these, it can be seen that the crisis period coincides with the contracting of the nuclear family and the discarding of the most vital functions of the woman's role in that unit. This fact points up the isolation of the nuclear family unit: the "empty nest" crisis is a reflection of the process by which the loss of members of this small family group, one by one, leaves the remaining members stranded. Similarly, it is useful to consider the nature of the climacteric identity crisis, involving threats of the loss of youth and beauty and conflicts over the renunciation of unachieved youthful ambitions. These aspects of the crisis suggest (among other things) that the curve of achievement and prestige in the life cycle has an early peak, that statuses achieved are not permanently secure but must be actively maintained throughout life, and that for women success is most readily attained through winning and keeping a successful husband.

I turn now to the life cycle of women in Italian culture. My data are drawn entirely from a community in the province of Perugia in central Italy.* Colleverde (a pseudonym) has a population of about 2,000, some 300 of whom reside in the nucleated village that is the focus of community life. These villagers consist of noncultivating landowners and the nonagricultural population (professionals, clerks, merchants, artisans, laborers, etc.). The remainder of the population live, for the most part, on farms scattered across the countryside. The community is located on a tertiary road in the rural hill country of Umbria; although not on a major route of communication, it is easily accessible to the market towns and administrative cities of the region. The economic base of Colleverde is a mixed agriculture, combining a variety of subsistence products with marketed wheat, olives, grapes, and calves. The only real industry in the immediate vicinity is a tobacco-processing factory, the majority of whose employees are women. The agricultural land is organized mainly into self-sufficient family farms. Although some of these farms are in peasant proprietorship, most are cultivated under the *mezzadria* system. Under this system of share-farming, a family of peasants—often a patrilocal extended family and usually landless—enters into a contract with a landowner for the cultivation of the farm, on the basis of a (theoretically) fifty-fifty division of expenses and products.

Evidence on the cultural definition of the phases of the life cycle in Colleverde was derived from three main sources. Most important were observations of the interactional patterns of women of different ages; different periods of life could be distinguished according to gross differences in activities, persons interacted with, customary behaviors, and the like. Second, I noted volunteered statements and elicited ex-

* Fieldwork in Italy was carried out between August 1960 and September 1961, under a research grant from the National Institute of Mental Health, United States Public Health Service (M-3720).

planations of how the women themselves structure the various phases of the life cycle. For example, adult women repeatedly declared, "I was born in Colleverde, I married in Colleverde, and I shall die in Colleverde!" A third source of data was the folk taxonomy of terms referring to the various age groups and periods of life.

According to these data, the life cycle of women in this culture may be subdivided roughly as follows:

—Birth to forty days (life is tentative, the infant protected).

—Forty days to three years (baby accompanies adults, is the center of attention).

—Four to six years (transition to peer-group activity, child is "on her way").

—Seven years to puberty (small groups of girls together, in relatively active play).

—Adolescence, from puberty until readiness to marry (more circumspect activity, with small groups of girls and with female relatives, concerned primarily with preparation for marriageability).

—Courtship (begins with the first steps toward engagement, may involve a series of courtships, continues until marriage).

—Bride (the early months of marriage, or until pregnancy).

—Wife and mother.

—Old woman (begins when the daughter-in-law assumes charge of the household, or when the woman is considered "old").

In my initial attempts in the field to identify the periods of crisis, I considered first those phases that are defined as stressful in American culture, adolescence and climacterium. In Colleverde, however, adolescence is a rather peaceable time, during which girls speculate about courtship rather than actively engage in courtship activities: they communicate with boys only tentatively and sporadically, in groups. Their activity involves the development of marriageable assets—learning housewifely skills, beautifying themselves, and preparing their dowries. As for possible crises surrounding the menopause period, the evidence was negative; not only was there little indication of stress or even concern, but the matter was of little interest to anyone.

At the same time, there were repeated suggestions that the status transition of major importance to women concerned marriage, and that the courtship period leading up to marriage and the months immediately following marriage was a time of expected and experienced anxiety and stress. (Interestingly, a personal communication from Anne Parsons, who was working in a mental institution in Naples, indicated a high incidence of breakdowns in girls during the engagement period.) I then attempted to isolate the crisis period more precisely, by relating it to specific events in the sequence of courtship-engagement-marriage-first child. What eventually emerged from this effort was the view that these several phases do not form a series of separate events, but that there is a single, more or less continuous crisis beginning with the initiation of the first courtship and extending through the early months of marriage. Within this rather long period, the crisis appears to intensify as the time of marriage approaches and to wane after the marriage has taken place.

In the first steps of courtship, the boy indicates his interest (*fa corte*); if the girl accepts his attentions, "they start to walk together," and they are now said to have begun to *fare l'amore*. This phase is typically short. Generally within a few months, the boy comes "into the house" and asks permission of the girl's parents for a formal engagement. This act initiates the *fidanzamento*. This period rarely lasts less than a year; the ideal is two to three years, and engagements of five to ten years are not unusual. During this time, the girl must amass her *corredo* (the dowry), and the boy must attempt to establish his financial position. Characteristically, it is a stormy period, involving quarrels, breakups, reconciliations, often initiations of new courtships. Girls must follow strict rules of conduct: when not with the *fidanzato* they are always accompanied by another female, they do not talk lightly or unnecessarily to a male, and in general they become "serious"—less vivacious in personality, modest, and industrious. Engaged girls are extremely vulnerable to scandal, which often comes in the form of vicious anonymous letters to the *fidanzato.* The occurrence of gossip—even when unfounded—is generally assumed to be evidence of misbehavior, precipitating a crisis between the pair and, frequently, a break-up. Subsequent engagements then become increasingly more delicate for the girl.

Sexual relations between the engaged couple, however, are quite common, as is evidenced by the fact that approximately one-fourth of the brides are pregnant at the time of marriage. In most cases (perhaps 90 percent), marriage to the fiancé follows a premarital pregnancy, generally with the wedding date hastened. There may be some damage to the girl's reputation, but this possibility is lessened by the fact that as long as the boy intends to go through with the marriage, it is in his interest to attempt to conceal or minimize the lapse in his future wife's virtue.

It is worthy of note that the engagement period—precisely the time I have identified as involving the greatest personal stress—is idealized in Italian popular belief and remembered by older women as, in retrospect, "the best time of life." That this is so may not be paradoxical at all. It is a time of intensity of emotional experience, ranging from one extreme to another; exhilaration and despair occur regularly in rapid succession. Undoubtedly, this emotional fluctuation is in itself an important source of the stress. In addition, there is the ever-present uncertainty that the matter will be successfully concluded.

The tension lessens but does not end with the marriage. For a bride entering a patrilocal extended family, there is the problem of fitting into the household presided over by her mother-in-law. It is the bride who is expected to make the major adjustments, and sanctions to detach herself from her own kin are strong. The bride taking charge of a neolocal household faces different problems but only slightly less difficult ones.

The first child usually arrives quite soon after marriage. The first birth is never willingly postponed, although birth control (by means of the withdrawal method) is widely practiced after the first or second birth. The new bride is observed critically by her mother-in-law, and when pregnancy is evident she suddenly assumes an honored and cherished position. She becomes visibly serene and transformed into a "mamma." Clearly, at this point the crisis is over. In general, if pregnancy does not occur, the crisis period continues until the woman and her family make their peace with the misfortune.

The cultural selection of this period as a life crisis suggests the often stated but nonetheless important observation that marriage is the key transition both in the life of the woman and in the life of the society. At the individual level, it is the fundamental status change. It is a stressful change because it is not automatically attained, and to be left "for Sant'Antonio" (a spinster) is an unenviable fate. However, once achieved, the status of the married woman is irrevocable. At the societal level, marriage constitutes a reorganization of economic and social resources. In the marriage is vested the continuity over time of the dominant productive unit: it represents the link from existing nuclear families to new ones, or the perpetuation of extended families. The movement of women at marriage involves, above all, a flow of economic resources from the existing units, with the aid of which the new or enlarged units are supported. While this fact is to some degree true of marriage in most societies, in peasant societies it assumes special significance because of the overriding importance of the family as the landholding or land-working unit.

The life-crisis perspective may permit some refinement of this view of marriage as a reorganization of resources. It is possible here to explore only one line of questioning—the implications of variation in the severity of the crisis between different segments of the population. The description of the courtship and early marriage period given above refers to patterns typical to Colleverde as a whole. However, there is a significant difference between categories within the community. The main line of differentiation in this connection appears to be between the *mezzadria* peasants, on the one hand, and peasant proprietor, nonagricultural, and landowning families, on the other. For simplicity, I will (somewhat inaccurately) refer to the latter group as "villagers."

My impression is that the crisis is considerably less severe for the *messadre* than for the village girls. Among the *mezzadre*, the engagement period tends to be earlier and shorter, for the couple need not have its own economic provisions. They simply join the boy's family on their farm; the only problem may be in arranging their sleeping space. Moreover, there appears to be less tension concerning sexual behavior. Lapses in virtue are not regarded as particularly serious, and a premarital pregnancy may be welcomed almost as much as a postmarital one; in fact, "trial marriage," to assure the boy's family of the fecundity of the future wife, is not unheard of. In general, the stresses surrounding the imminent scandal, the behavioral restrictions, and the turbulent breakups of the village engagements are less evident. I believe this variation to be related to the difference between *mezzadri* and villagers in the kind of resources involved in the marriage transition, which in turn reflects a difference in the economic functions of women in the *mezzadria* and in the village family.

The major resource of the *mezzadria* family is its labor. As a rule it owns no land and little capital, but its access to land is determined by the amount of labor it commands. Improvements in its position come about through quantitative increase in its labor supply and through better organization of that labor: an expanding family can obtain a contract for a larger farm, and a large family group is usually a more productive unit per capita than the same number of persons would be if they were divided into two or more working groups. In this context, the woman's function is measured in terms of labor—her own and that of the children she can potentially produce.

That the work of women is absolutely essential to the *mezzadria* family in its role as a productive unit is reflected in the fact that the minimum family that can enter into a *mezzadria* contract must include a female adult, designated as the *massaia.* She is defined as having charge of the house; she directs the work of the other women and is considered responsible for them and for the small children. Where there are several women, some—particularly the younger ones—work regularly in the fields, and all may help out in those field tasks demanding a large labor pool. For the most part, however, the women's work sphere is around the farmhouse (preparing food, caring for the small animals, tending the kitchen, garden, etc.).

In some cases, the family may use its female labor resources to bring in cash. The farm women derive a small income from the local sale of fowl and eggs; the courtyard animals are their complete responsibility. Traditionally, they often maintained household industries, such as silkworm-raising and weaving. More recently, the tobacco factory has opened new opportunities. In some *mezzadria* families, a few women will be assigned to manage the household, others to work in the fields, while one or more will be sent to wage-earning work in the factory—with the income going into the family till. In such instances, the contribution of all the women is defined as similar in kind, and their roles are largely interchangeable.

In contrast, the economic functions of women in the village families are diverse. A woman's labor is, of course, fundamental, both in the household and, in the case of peasant proprietors, on the family's land. In addition, however, she often owns some of the family's property. In this segment of the population, the dowry may include cash or land, or the woman may come into an inheritance at some time after her marriage. Where this is the case, the woman retains control over this property, although it is managed by her husband. Moreover, village women frequently are income-producers in their own right. Women in Colleverde are professionals (most of the teachers are women, as is the local pharmacist), merchants (two or three of the shops are in the complete charge of a woman, and the wives and daughters of merchants are active in all business places), artisans (the several dressmakers and professional knitters), domestics, and so on. Because of the different family organization (most villagers live in nuclear families), and because of the individual skills involved in most such activities, this wage-earning constitutes a different kind of contribution to the family economy than that of the *mezzadria* women employed in the tobacco factory.

Although the courtship period is defined in terms of the romantic inclinations of the couple, it actually involves a mutual assessment on the part of both families of the relative assets that each has to bring to the marriage. To a large extent, this is done implicitly by the young people themselves before the courtship is initiated. Where this does not occur, and where the relative assets of the pair are markedly out of balance, almost inevitably the courtship is broken off. A slight imbalance, however, is common. This fact, together with the possibility that deficiencies in some areas can be compensated by assets in other areas, is the basis of social mobility.

Among the *mezzadri*, the assessment of a bride involves, above all, the factor of her potential contribution of labor: Is she capable, industrious, and cooperative? Is she likely to be fertile? Her other personal qualities, including her behavior in the sexual sphere, are of secondary value. Similarly, her dowry is a minor concern. It consists of linens, bedroom furniture, and personal items; productive property is not involved. In effect, almost all *mezzadria* girls need have little fear that they will be desired as brides by some family of a rank approximately equivalent to their own.

For the village girl, the matter is more complex. Her value is measured on several bases. The dowry itself may include, in addition to the household and personal trousseau, cash or property. In any case, her eventual share of her family's patrimony will be calculated. Of prime importance, also, are the skills she may have that can be converted into cash income, as well as equipment associated with her trade (for example, a sewing machine). Her housekeeping and mothering skills are also an asset to consider. (However, because numerous children represent an economic liability to a village family, her fertility is not prized.) In this more complicated picture, where a girl's marriageability (at least to someone of non-inferior rank) is not assured but is dependent upon many circumstances, her personal qualities—above all, her virtue—assume a value. The measure of her virtue, her reputation, can significantly add to or detract from her total contribution to the new family unit. "Reputation" is used advisedly here: the fact that a girl who is the innocent victim of gossip is penalized as severely as one who is guilty of misconduct suggests that it is the public estimation of her virtue rather than the virtue itself that is valued. This emphasis on reputation is particularly important where a girl's strictly economic assets are not the equal of her fiancé's. It seems to me that these facts underlie the concern with protecting her honor and the constant threats to it during the courtship period.

It would appear that the difference in the severity of the crisis between *mezzadria* girls and village girls can be directly related to differences in at least three factors: the duration of the courtship period, the value placed on fertility (and thus, the attitude toward premarital sexuality), and the significance of "virtue" in the calculation of a bride's assets. These factors, obviously, are not independent variables. They are consequences of the economic basis of the family unit created or enlarged by the marriage and, most particularly, of the specific functions of the bride in that unit.

These economic functions are fundamental to an understanding of the overall status of women, for they set the limits of their decision-making power. The differences between the *mezzadria* women and the village women are again suggestive. When women's functions are limited to domestic aspects of the family economy and to labor alone, as among the *mezzadri*, the kinds of decisions they have the power to make are similarly limited. The village women, on the other hand, tend to have a role in some of the family's economic activity outside the household. Women who own property maintain an active concern in its management by their husbands, and some income-earning village women have an important area of decision-making almost completely independent of their husbands.

For all women, however, decision-making is restricted to family matters. No formal political role in the community—either in the bureaucracy, in the party in power, or in the various opposition groups—is occupied by a woman. Women are not supposed to be interested in political matters, and few venture to express such an interest openly. Women act within the orbit of the family and its immediate concerns, and in this society the family is structurally separate from the political life of the community and nation. Here there are no lines of extension from the domestic unity up to the state (as is the case in the Arab Mediterranean, for instance).

In looking into the foundations of the variation in severity of the life-crisis experience among different categories of women in Colleverde, we are led to consider a range of feminine economic roles, which can be emphasized or combined in quite different form. Clearly, the question of the "position of women" is not simply a matter of the degree of power or importance that women have in a given society or segment of that society. More to the point, the problem is to determine the basis of their significance, in terms of the particular kinds of functions they fulfill.

Susan E. Brown

Love Unites Them and Hunger Separates Them: Poor Women in the Dominican Republic

For the majority of Dominicans, life is conditioned by the economic deprivation that they suffer. Up to 90 percent of the entire Dominican population belongs to the lowest economic sector (Sanchez-Cordoba, 1966:1; Wiarda, 1969:234). Many urban dwellers belong to this sector, and so do most rural inhabitants, who comprise 65 percent of all Dominicans (Wiarda, 1969:92). While the Dominican Republic has many wealth-producing resources, an elite minority of capitalists—3 to 5 percent of the total population—control the major sources of wealth. In this predominantly agricultural country, less than 1 percent of all landowners control 47.5 percent of all land, while 82 percent of those who work the land possess only 5 percent of it. (*Ahora*, 1971:1-2). Unemployment and underemployment are pervasive, with about 50 percent of the total labor force falling into these categories (Sanchez-Cordoba, 1966:1). Only two-fifths of the rural population is able to obtain even seasonal wage employment (Wiarda, 1969:91). Population growth is rapid, but per capita income dropped from $265 in 1959 to $254 in 1968 (Peña, 1970:2). High inflation in consumer prices has accompanied unemployment and decreasing per capita income. For example, in 1971 a rural day laborer could earn $1.00 plus two meals a day, while meat sold for 50 to 70 cents per pound. Less luxurious staples are even more expensive in the light of the dollar-a-day seasonal income.

* "El amor los une y el hambre los separa" is a common Dominican proverb.

As recently as forty years ago, the majority of Dominicans produced most of their own daily necessities within the household unit; today the majority are unavoidably involved in a market economy, depending on it for most of the foodstuffs they consume. But while market involvement is growing, most Dominicans receive only marginal benefits from it. Meeting daily subsistence needs is a basic struggle for most people.

As an illustration of this struggle, the following is the budget of a household in an agricultural community (in an area considered more prosperous than most). The household depends solely on agriculture: the head sharecrops 15 *tareas* (2.3 acres) and earns annually about $250 to $300. Income from tobacco and corn is augmented by raising a few pigs. The daily maintenance expenses for four persons come to $1.20:

rice (2 pounds)	$ .25
oil	.30
seasonings	.10
tomato sauce	.05
sugar	.15
spaghetti (½ pound)	.08
*viveres**	.20
soap	.04
lamp gas and matches	.03
total	$1.20

Most of the *viveres*, beans, coffee, and an occasional chicken consumed are produced by the household itself, but even at a meager $1.20 per day an annual income of $300 is insufficient.

The majority of Dominicans live under poverty conditions such as these, lacking adequate food, shelter, clothing, health care, and education. But while poverty conditions affect everyone, they affect men and women differently. I will examine the ways in which poor Dominican women manage

* *Viveres* include starchy staples such as manioc, sweet potatoes, plantains, etc.

to cope with poverty and maximize their meager resources.

Recent fieldwork in a rural Dominican village showed me that, contrary to what is suggested by Oscar Lewis (1966) and other, mostly male, social scientists, women of the Spanish Caribbean are dynamic and decisive, continually devising strategies to maximize those means of subsistence available to them. Many authors have viewed domestic organization in the poverty sector as a morass of social disorganization (for example, see Frazier, 1939; Blake, 1961; Henriques, 1954; Moynihan, 1965; Simey, 1946). Because these households are often headed by women, are matrifocal, have variable membership, and are characterized by female multiple-mating patterns and unstable unions (instead of being patrifocal and containing stable nuclear families), they are seen as deviant and in need of reform. Yet my own research confirmed what others have suggested, both for the Caribbean and for American blacks (see E. Clark, 1966; Gonzalez, 1969; Hannerz, 1969; Schneider and Smith, 1973; Stack, 1974; Valentine, 1968; Whitten and Szwed, eds., 1970): that having various male mates in a serial fashion is a major means by which women cope with their difficult socioeconomic circumstances. Here the multiple-mating pattern for women is neither deviant nor an undesirable variation of the middle-class, single-partner pattern. Rather, it is a dynamic female adaptation to life under severe poverty. In fact, it appears to provide these women with a *better* existence than the single-mate pattern could under the same circumstances (S. Brown, 1972).

In the community I studied, there is an acknowledgment of how things "should" be and how individuals "should" behave. These ideal values can be termed "community-held" or middle-class ideals because they reflect the consensus of the dominating society—the elite, trend-setting sectors of the larger Dominican society and of the influential United States society. Village consensus presumes, for example, that both men and women will abstain from sexual relations until after marriage, and that, once married, they will remain faithful to their spouses. In fact, village women generally follow this norm and receive considerable reinforcement for doing so. Men, on the other hand, are expected to have premarital sexual experiences and receive positive reinforcement (at least from their male peer group) for extramarital sexual relationships. The double sexual standard characteristic of Hispanic and many other societies is thus basic to the norms of village mating conduct.

Another community-held, middle-class ideal is that women should be formally married to their mates (preferably within the Catholic Church), and should remain faithful through thick and thin, use and abuse. The husband is responsible for providing his household with sufficient income and goods; the wife is supposed to care for her husband and their children. Ideally, the woman is in charge of intra-household affairs, while the man has responsibility for almost all extra-household affairs. Women are expected to accept this pattern.

As we have noted, in poverty areas this ideal single-partner female mating pattern is seldom obtained. More frequently, one finds a multiple-partner pattern in which a woman has more than one mate, usually more than two, and has them serially. Women who take on one mate after another, thus violating the norm, are labeled "free women" by the other villagers, reflecting social condemnation rather than personal liberation.

Each mating pattern exhibits opposing views and expectations of the man-woman relationship. Those who follow the "ideal" pattern view marriage as a matter of luck and women's duty to suffer whatever comes and make the best of it. The general ideology goes somewhat as follows: "A woman has to marry; she marries, and marriage is like a lottery—you cannot predict what you will get. The man may turn out to be a *gallero* [afficionado of cockfighting], a heavy drinker, or a womanizer. Whatever happens, however, it is the woman's duty to bear [literally, support] it all, and remain faithful and responsible—remain a 'serious woman.' If she behaves properly, then one day her husband will stop his irresponsible behavior and dedicate himself to his wife

Characteristics of the Two Female Lifestyles as Distinguished by Mating Pattern

	Single-partner pattern	*Multiple-partner pattern*
Type of union	Formal marriage (usually within the Catholic Church)	Informal free and visiting unions*
Duration of union	Permanent	Temporary
Post-marital residence	Patrilocal, i.e., on land of or near husband's family	Matrilocal, i.e., on land of or near woman's family
Household composition	Nuclear, i.e., husband, wife, and children	Non-nuclear, i.e., a woman and her children
Household headship	Male	Female
Child-rearing responsibilities	The nuclear household	Children are often "farmed out," especially to maternal kin
Major income provider	Male head of household	Female head of household
Most likely mutual aid interaction	With husband's kin	With woman's kin

[usually, only when he is too old, or perhaps too broke, to do otherwise]."

Women who follow the multiple-partner pattern also view the length of union as a matter of luck, but hold that a

* In a free or consensual union, a couple lives together without the sanction of religious or civil authority. A visiting union also lacks formal sanction, but it differs in that no co-residence is involved; instead, one party (the male), visits the household of the other.

woman's first obligation is to herself and her children, and emphasize the irresponsibility and undependability of men. While they would like to find a stable provider, they know that the chances of this happening are poor. They hold that "a man can be more trouble than he's worth; it is better to check him out before establishing a union as permanent as marriage, for once married, the man has more control over you and your money." If more benefits result from discontinuing a relationship than in maintaining it, they will end it.

These two patterns represent two very different lifestyles, and each is tied to a distinguishable constellation of diametrically opposed characteristics, as can be seen from the accompanying table.

The development of different patterns for married and free-union women can to a large extent be explained by the economic circumstances of each group. The single-mate pattern reflects a response to the life of a small landholding peasant, where the household, which is the unit of both production and consumption, requires the presence of both men and women to function smoothly. In contrast, the second mating pattern is found among people with the most marginal and unstable resources. Landless, unskilled, and with dim economic prospects (increased by discrimination on the basis of color), they need to develop more flexible networks in place of the nuclear family.

Marta, for example, is a poverty-sector woman who unsuccessfully attempted to adhere to the single-mate ideal. Now in her late fifties, Marta lives in her own house with two adult sons, a teen-age grandson (whose father is Marta's eldest son and is divorced from this grandson's mother), and a nonrelated middle-aged woman. One of the sons is preparing for marriage by building a house next to his mother's, on her land. The other works his mother's small landholdings and has recently taken on a mate, who lives in the nearby house of another brother. The nonkin woman, Marta's friend, is reported to have come to visit some fourteen years ago and never left. In exchange for her keep, she assists Marta in the daily chores. Marta, who frequently attends the local Catholic church, feels that a woman should have only one mate during her life and should be officially married to him, but she has never successfully maintained the ideal. Her first mate was a man from a neighboring village. He built her a house there, where they lived for many years and had two children. The relationship was not satisfactory to Marta. As she explains it, "This first man had many other women and he didn't support me and the children adequately." She left him, moving the house he had built back to her own village, onto her parents' plot of land. She supported herself and her children by baking and selling bread in the same oven her mother had used to support Marta and her sisters and brothers. After she had been alone for some years, her first mate rejoined her, moving into her village. Over the next six years, Marta bore four more children; she then decided to leave him again. Although she would have liked to adhere to the single-mate pattern, the union was economically unworkable. It was she who provided for the children, while he had many other women and spent money carelessly. Furthermore, he abused Marta and the children. They separated and Marta lived alone for the next three years. She then took on another man, with whom she lived for only two years, and by whom she had one child. In her words, "I realized that he was as bad as the first, so I left him." This man did little to support Marta or the children; he had the same vices as the first man. Within two years, Marta took on her third mate. They lived together for several years, and Marta decided she must either get married or "repent" her illicit behavior. So she married him and had a child. Although this union was smoother than the other two, it didn't last, and after a few years they agreed to separate. Marta felt she would be economically better off without her husband, supporting herself by raising and selling a few pigs. While Marta recognizes the ideal of a single lifetime mate, she never found it practical to remain with any of her three men. All in all, she says, it was her oven and not her men who brought up the children. Marta, like many other women, feels that men actually detract from the basic tasks of household maintenance by spending needed money for luxuries.

There are many reasons why the single-partner pattern might not represent the most advantageous form of domestic organization for poor Dominican women. In adhering to the single-partner pattern, a woman becomes predominantly dependent upon her spouse, a situation with little advantage in the poverty sector. The division of labor by sex and the responsibility implied in the single-partner pattern is much more viable among more affluent economic sectors, as well as among more prosperous peasants, because the men of the households are more able to adequately support them. A woman under such circumstances can afford to work exclusively within the household, while depending upon her husband for maintenance. Also, within landholding peasant households where subsistence is often meager, the combined daily labor of both men and women is imperative. The man works the fields, cares for the livestock, maintains the necessary tools, and the like; the woman spends her day in food preparation, household maintenance, child care, and so on.

Within the poverty sector, on the other hand, circumstances are different. Poor women who take on multiple mates can provide for themselves and their children more efficiently than poor women who have only a single mate. Women of both groups verbalize the advantages that the more flexible free and visiting unions offer: "Once married, a woman is subject to her husband. Not only can he use his own money as he sees fit but also he has access to the wife's resources." A woman living in a free union vividly explained why she would rather live this way than marry: "I would rather not marry the man with whom I live. If I marry him I will not be free to move about and find the work I choose and, anyway, he would have some control over the money I earn. As it stands now, if he fails to provide for me and my children, or if he abuses me, or if he turns *gallero* and spends all his money on cockfights, women, and alcohol, then I will leave him. I would leave the children with my mother [who already lives with her] and go, as I have gone before, to Santo Domingo to work."

Living near or with one's mother allows greater interchange and mutual aid in food procurement and preparation, child care, and assistance in times of illness or emergency. The strong mother-daughter dyad also allows for greater personal mobility: a woman (as in the case cited) can leave her children with her mother and seek employment elsewhere, returning to the village only intermittently and sending money to her mother for the children's care.

To understand the specifics of the two female mating patterns, we must recognize the importance of having only one mate at a time, and the importance of having children, both highly valued in the culture. Even though a woman may have several mates, she has them one at at time. There are several reasons for this. Given the prevalent *macho* complex, men tend to demand exclusive rights over the women with whom they unite. While male infidelity is common and tolerated, more than one village union has been broken by men who feel their women have been unfaithful. Further, a woman feels she must be able to know who the father of her child is in order to demand some responsibility for its upbringing. And children are considered of paramount importance. Being unmarried and twenty-six, I learned this lesson very well. Almost daily I was asked by one woman or another, "When are you going to get married and begin having children?" As a rule, this question was followed by advice: "You are getting on in years, you are no longer a child and you must marry soon while you are still attractive. A woman must marry and have children, for it is your children who will take care of you in your old age. Imagine what it would be like to grow old having no one to live with and no one to care for you." Then they cite the misfortunes of some elderly village women suffering the plight of childlessness. It is explained that while not all of one's children turn out as they should, and many forget their parents when they leave their natal households, one or two children will turn out to be "good" children and remember their mothers in their old age. In a society where there is little chance for saving and no old-age insurance, it is children one looks to in one's old age. Children are important, particularly to women living in poverty.

Poor women want and need children, but they often have difficulty adequately supporting them. While women of the single-partner pattern generally raise all their children within the nuclear household, women of the multiple-partner pattern often avail themselves of child-shifting procedures in which they temporarily "loan" their children to other households. The child, in exchange for room, board, a small wage, clothing, and medical attention if required, is expected to help with the chores. Girls are more often involved in these child-shifting arrangements than boys, since they assist in the "female" chores of laundry, cleaning, food preparation, and child care. There are obvious benefits to the women involved. For instance, a woman can have more children than she could otherwise. If a child is only lent out temporarily, which is usually the case, he or she remains loyal to the mother and eventually returns to the natal household. In the meantime, the child has been cared for and the mother has obtained an additional, if small, income from the household to which the child was lent. The alliances this child-shifting procedure establishes between families are also important. A child is usually shifted into a household that is better off, or "more powerful," than her or his natal household, and even after the child has left, the family may request and receive goods, such as garden produce, from the household where the child lived.

All in all, the constellation of features associated with the multiple-partner pattern allows for greater flexibility in making the most of one's limited resources. In cases where the male fails to fulfill his role as major household provider, the woman may leave him and take on another, who might provide for her better, even if only for a short period. On the other hand, she might decide to live alone with her children or to return with her children to live with her mother.

Mother-daughter ties are strong. For example, one village woman, Carmen, would not go live in the village of her third mate because she did not want to leave her mother (with whom she and her children lived) alone. Her relationship to her mother was obviously more important than her relationship to her third mate. She anticipated, and so it happened, that this mate was to be but another transitional partner. Carmen ran her own household as she saw most fit. During the harvest she worked in the local tobacco warehouse, and with her earnings she gradually repaired the house they lived in. Although at this time Carmen's fourth mate lived with them and contributed to the household maintenance, Carmen was the household head. She "farmed out" some of her children to neighborhood and kin families, so that she did not have all seven children in the small house at once; at the same time her household received a few dollars a month for each child living in another household. If things were to turn very bad in the village and Carmen needed additional money, she would go to find work elsewhere for a while, leaving the children with her mother.

A woman following the single-mate pattern does not have all these options. She must make the best of what her mate provides for her. Even the possibility of supplementing the household income with her own outside work is subject to her husband's approval. Social customs and considerations as to what is proper behavior deny to these women many of the ways poor Dominican women have come to cope with poverty. It is not considered "proper" for a woman to participate in free or visiting unions; to farm out some of her children; to be the head of her own household; to make decisions about household economics; to represent the household in extra-household affairs; to be the major provider for the household; and so on.

In economic terms, things are getting worse (Brown, 1972) for a majority of village inhabitants. If economic conditions continue to deteriorate, more women will find themselves subject to poverty conditions. More will be searching for ways to stretch their inadequate resources and will be forced to weigh the benefits of the ideal pattern against those of the multiple-mate pattern. And due to its advantages for life under poverty, as time passes more Dominican women are likely to take on the multiple-mate pattern.

Anna Rubbo

The Spread of Capitalism in Rural Colombia: Effects on Poor Women

This essay will focus on peasant and lower-class urban women in the rapidly modernizing Puerto Tejada region of the Cauca Valley, western Colombia. As the process of rural proletarianization gathers momentum in this region, it appears that sex roles are not only altered in rather fundamental ways, but that possibly the new sex roles facilitate the docility of the work force that the new economy requires. One of the main conclusions drawn from this study is that, with the transition from a peasant to a rural proletarian community, the position of women has deteriorated both in the absolute sense and in relation to men, and that this deterioration has counter-progressive or even counter-revolutionary consequences.

By peasant I mean a person who has more or less secure control over the use of an area of land. In this region such areas are usually quite small, but in all cases they provide a significant part of the household income. By and large all people residing outside the town are classified as "peasants" in the above sense, while most people living in the town are landless. The peasants live in dispersed settlements within five miles of the township.

In tracing the recent history of this group of black peas-

The material for this essay was collected over one and a half years in the region during two periods: January 1970 to March 1971, and September to December 1972. The author wishes to thank June Nash and Michael Taussig for their suggestions and comments on earlier versions of this essay, and the people of Puerto Tejada, without whom this essay could not have been written.

ants, the ecological effects of commercialized agriculture will be touched on, as will the social disruption of rural society. The focus of the discussion will be on the position of women in peasant and in plantation modes of production, and the ways in which patterns of social organization are affected by the change from one mode to the other. The role of sorcery in mediating these new relationships between men and women will also be discussed, and some comparisons will be made with middle-class women to differentiate class values in regard to gender.

The Region and Its History

According to nineteenth-century travelers, the Cauca Valley was a paradise of flora and fauna. Simon Bolivar, the famous South American liberator, called it a Garden of Eden. But that once-varied ecology has now been replaced by large-scale mono-cropping, predominantly sugarcane. Rice, soya, corn, and a variety of beans are also grown commercially, and lower quality areas are devoted to cattle raising. This relatively seasonless, equatorial valley is approximately 90 miles long by 10 miles wide and nestles between the central and western *cordilleras* ("chains") of the Colombian Andes. The change in ecology from past to present is dramatic, and the remaining peasant farms are reminders of that past: a "jungle" of bamboo, coffee and cocoa trees, plantains, bananas, fruits, and plants for thatching and making twine, etc. The peasants call the monotonously regular green desert of cane *el monstruo verde* ("the green monster")—the god of the landlords.

The majority of the population are blacks, descendants of slaves brought to work the gold mines for the Spanish in the sixteenth and seventeenth centuries. Following abolition in 1852, they refused to work as day laborers on the haciendas, instead squatting on adjacent land. They cleared the thick jungle and began farming alongside communities of runaway slaves who had been growing contraband tobacco since the late eighteenth century. These "new" peasants grew corn, plantains, fruits, and sugarcane for domestic consumption, and were basically self-sufficient until the early twentieth century. In the 1920s coffee was introduced and quickly became an important cash crop along with cocoa.

Farm work is (and always has been) constant but does not require daily or full-time input. Coffee and cocoa are perennials, and they produce for most of the year. Each has two peak crop seasons annually, but are balanced so that while one is rising the other is falling, and total farm production is fairly constant. Twice a year the undergrowth beneath the coffee, cocoa, and plantains must be cleared, but in a farm with adequate shade trees and a mixture of tree types, the sun barely penetrates to allow much weed growth. Given the nature of the work, the crops, and the overall ecology, it was easy for women to own, manage, and work a farm as well as raise children, thus giving an economic base to female independence. There is no clear-cut sexual division of productive labor as far as the crops are concerned. In this culture women are as adept as men at handling the basic technology, but men rarely partake in domestic chores. Hence, women do both "women's" and "men's" work, while men do only "men's" work.

With the construction of a railway to the Pacific Ocean port of Buenaventura in 1914, the valley was opened up to foreign markets, and foreign investment occurred at an unprecedented rate (Rippy, 1931:152). Subsequently, sugar production (all on large estates) rose dramatically, and this was due in part to the appropriation of peasant plots. Production in the Puerto Tejada region increased from 2,000 metric tons in 1938 to over 90,000 in 1969. But it was not until the Violencia that plantations made significant inroads into the Puerto Tejada area of the valley. The Violencia was a ten-year war (1948-1958), ostensibly between the Liberal and Conservative parties. It was not only a war between political parties, but in some ways, a frustrated social revolution in which an estimated 200,000 people lost their lives (Guzman et al., 1963:1:292). But in addition, rich speculators capitalized on the fear of people and bought land cheaply. The plantations introduced aerial spraying of pesticides, and local people tell the story of how the airplanes sprayed peasant farms, killing shade trees vital for healthy coffee and cocoa. Furthermore, farms were flooded intentionally by the plantations as the latter acquired control of water canals. Some peasants had their crops stolen or destroyed, while others had their access blocked as the plantations acquired the surrounding land. The people describe the Violencia as a many-headed beast, not the least threatening part of it being the land-hungry plantations.

However, there was another factor. Since the expansion of the sugarcane plantations there have always been local peasants and plantation workers willing to collaborate with the plantation owners, some working as brokers persuading their neighbors to sell, others reporting back any signs of unrest or subversion, either within the work force or outside of it. Curiously, it is often said that women do not report on their fellow female workers. Apart from state law enforcement, there is an extensive network to combat "subversion"—from the workers who "sing" to the bosses, to the local parapolice organization, Defense Civil (Civil Defense), and the sugar growers' organization, Asocaña.

The plantation owners, cattle ranchers, and absentee aristocratic families who own the land today view the people with varying degrees of racism and fear (although racism as a national characteristic is always denied), and plantation owners move in convoys with armed guards supplied by the state. The foremen and administrative staff drive powerful jeeps and stay close to their two-way radios. To these people, the work force is an unhappy necessity and they would prefer a mechanized sugar industry if it were politically and economically possible. As long as that is not possible, certain steps are taken to minimize the troublesome factors of a recalcitrant work force, the *sindicatos patronales* (owner-controlled trade unions), and the *contratista* system being the most significant steps.

The latter is a system whereby the plantations contract a set piece of work to a local contractor, who in turn subcontracts to local workers. This type of "casual" worker has no right to form trade unions or to receive social service benefits. It is crucial to realize that women, especially townswomen, are being drawn increasingly into this *contratista* system, as the contractors consider them to be less trouble than men, and can hire them at lower wages.

The changes necessitated by modern capitalist enterprises are difficult ones, and clearly result in both social atomization and individual alienation. Witness the men who work from 6:00 a.m. to 5:00 p.m. in the canefields five and a half days a week, and then spend most of Saturday afternoon waiting for pay; or the women who must leave their young children while they work an eight-hour day far from home. Emerging leaders are frequently co-opted, and self-interest nearly always supersedes collective interest. As one local put it: "The problem with Colombia is that there is too much imperialism, egoism, and poverty."

Most of the plantation workers live in the township. With the coming of the sugarcane plantations, the town itself has changed from being a service and market center into a rural slum, little more than a barracks and dormitory of landless sugarcane workers. In the 1960s the flood of black immigrants from the Pacific coast added to the number of locally dispossessed peasants. The town's population more than doubled in the thirteen years between 1951 and 1964, with the immigrants constituting 26 percent of the population. By 1964 most of the land was in sugarcane, and only one-fifth of the area's population lived in the countryside. In a short space of time, the majority of the people changed from semi-subsistence farmers to landless rural proletarians (DANE [Departamento Administrativo Nacional de Estadistica], 1954, 1964).

Although Puerto Tejada is the richest municipality in the department of Cauca in terms of material output, it is one of the poorest in services. There is neither sewerage nor clean drinking water. Production taxes go to the national government, and no local taxes are exacted from the plantations. Use of the roads, for instance, is vital to the plantations, but the roads are maintained at local expense. The plantations do not feed profits back into the town, and workers have little power to demand better working conditions or a more responsible involvement of plantations in urban improvement. For instance, the major source of drinking water, the Palo River, is dangerously contaminated with fecal bacteria. One of the sugar mills, located upstream from the town, draws water from the river to clean its machinery and pigpens, and then returns the water to the river. Not surprisingly, the incidence of intestinal parasites is widespread. Periodically the impurity of the water is protested, but to date the situation has not changed. People of the upper and middle classes bring their drinking water from nearby Cali or have their own purification plants.

Household Social Structure and Women—General Considerations

Some general remarks can be made about women in the region with reference to their lifestyles and the attitudes of women toward men (and vice versa), although there are variations according to location, age, civil status, and so on.

Domestic work is "women's work." This includes marketing (all buying and much of the selling), cooking, cleaning, washing, mending, fetching water, chopping wood, and caring for the children in general. Women often do "men's work" as well, as agricultural day laborers and peasants. Men, however, rarely do "women's" work.

In their relationships with men, women are frequently subjected to male jealously and possessiveness, which apply in descending degrees to legal wives, free-union wives, daughters, and lovers. Men, although they cause women to be jealous, do not accept any claims on their freedom of movement, nor do they modify their behavior on account of female pressures. For the men it is considered customary and "correct" to come and go as they please, to go drinking and dancing, and to have a concubine or "woman in the *calle* [street]." Women's activities in public places are curtailed, and subject to much malicious gossip. Women cannot go to the cinema, bars, or cafes alone, or even with female friends. Men often demand that women leave the house only for a specific destination and that they must be accompanied by a child or friend. Women can stroll in the plaza at dusk, if accompanied, and are free to go to church alone. Women's most social meeting places are the marketplace and the riverbank where they wash several times a week. However, if a man is ambitious he will forbid his wife to wash in the river, in which case she will be forced to do it in the isolation of her own backyard or, money permitting, hire a washerwoman.

These restrictions apply generally more to townswomen than rural women, more to officially married women than to those living in free unions, more to whites than to blacks, and more to women of higher than lower class.

If we look at the social structure of households—either statically or over time—we see that the restrictions imposed by men must be weakened in many cases, since households headed by women are quite common, as are free unions in comparison with official (i.e., church) marriages.

Fluidity and flux are the keynotes in the social organization of this culture. The outstanding characteristics of household structure are the high degree of those headed by women, and of extended, rather than nuclear, units. The latter, in fact, account for less than half the households, whether they are in the town or the countryside. Serial polygamy is very common, as are "visiting" or extraresidential liaisons between women and men. Inheritance is partible, shared equally between males and females, and offspring from all the deceased's sexual unions are entitled to share. Blood ties are considered to be far more important than marriage or affinal ties, and of those blood ties the mother-child bond is the most important of all. These patterns of residence, mating, and inheritance lead to an extremely diffuse series of social networks in which it is possible for any individual to claim kinship with a vast number of people. On the other

Table 1
Comparison of Household Structures Between Rural and Town Areas in 1973 (as percentages of all households)

Household type	*Rural household* (N = 36)	*Town household* (N = 35)
Simple nuclear	32	45
Extended	32	26
Denuded nuclear:		
headed by women	8	6
headed by men	2	0
Denuded extended:		
headed by women	24	23
headed by men	2	0
	100%	100%

Table 2
Comparison of Affinal Statuses Between Rural and Town Samples in 1971 (as percentages of household chiefs)

	Rural sample (N = 36)	*Town sample* (N = 35)
Church married	18	14
Free union (co-resident)	50	49
Visiting union	9	18
No spouse	23	19
	100%	100%

hand, such claims are bound to be ambiguous and conflicting and are by no means necessarily binding.

We now turn to some of the differences between the town and the countryside seen in Table 1. In the town the nuclear type of household is much more common than in the countryside (45 percent of all households as against 32 percent). There is also a marked increase in the proportion of sexual unions that are visiting or extra-residential (18 percent as compared with 9 percent). Households headed by women form roughly the same proportion in both areas.

It would appear that these two major differences are a result of basic differences in the modes of production that are associated with each locality. Whereas peasant women invariably have an economic base in their land, the townswomen do not have land and are forced to unite with those who have some economic security, fragile as that might be—the male plantation workers. As a general rule townswomen depend on male wage-earners to a far higher degree than do peasant women, and this would seem to account for most of the differences between their mating and residential patterns.

Although the nuclear type of household is more common in town than in the countryside, the rate of marriage (church or consensual) is not more frequent, as seen in Table 2. Rather, there are fewer church marriages in the town than in the countryside. This apparently contradictory phenomenon needs explanation. It appears that in the past (including the slave past) church marriage was considered customary, but statistics show that the rate has continually fallen over the past forty years. Some informants say this is due to landlessness. As one young married peasant male expressed it: "Parents made one marry. But now young people have nothing to look forward to in the future. They have no land." Furthermore, divorce is impossible, and with women becoming more dependent on men, the restrictions and obligations of church marriage are not all that enticing. By contrast, peasant women, with their relative economic independence, have not felt the same "negative" pressures that marriage can exert upon lower-class townswomen.

The latter quite consciously regard marriage as a silly or even bad thing to do, and in this way they are joined by the male folk. Women say, for example, that marriage "spoils a relationship," "gives the spouse too much control," "is not necessary now since a 'natural child' [i.e., a bastard] has the same rights as a 'legitimate' one," and that marriage "is worse than living in a free union if [as is highly likely], the marriage breaks up and one is forced into sin [living with another man out of wedlock, or just the fact of separation itself]." A common saying is that marriage brings seven years of bad luck, and most persons, of either sex, energetically regard marriage as a severe restriction on one's liberty.

These remarks apply far more to lower-class women, whether town or rural, than to middle-class townswomen. Married, middle-class townswomen are materially better off than those of the lower class, but for all that they are in some ways even more dependent on men—i.e., their husbands. The following two examples bring this out in concrete terms, and are offered as illustrations of some of the abstract forces we have discussed such as class and economic dependence.

Doña Marta is twenty-five years old, the mother of four children, and married to a storekeeper. Both are white. She was married at sixteen to her first boyfriend. She talks freely about the lack of love and respect between her husband and herself, but knows she must stay with him because of the children and the business. When they married they moved into the central plaza and began a haberdashery. Now it is flourishing, and they have bought a bar which the husband runs while Marta stays in the haberdashery. She rarely goes out, because the shop cannot be left unattended. It is open seven days a week, fourteen hours a day. She has a maid who cooks and cleans, and the washing is sent out. She is very depressed, is always crying, and wonders if her sterilization operation has anything to do with it. She believes that her husband despises her, and she laments the freedom of men to have intercourse (social and sexual) with women outside the house. But it is, on balance, better to be married because this demands a show of respect. "People wouldn't call you *doña* if you weren't married." If she were to leave him, she suspects he would keep the business, and her nine years of labor with the business and the children would count for nothing. However desolate her personal feelings, she has, in large part, control over the children, as well as status in the eyes of many of the townsfolk. She also has daily contact with people, which many other middle-class women do not have.

Rosa is the "wife" of a doctor and politician, but although they have been living together for fifteen years she does not have the respect of the people (according to Marta). Being middle-class, she has the same restrictions as a married woman, but not the advantage of being the legal wife. Her husband does not like her to walk in the streets, so she is seen there mainly when he is away. He frequents the brothels in the *zona de tolerancia* and has many girl friends, but, "What can I do? If a woman doesn't run things right, then her man will leave her." She consoles herself that she is the *señora* and that the other women do not mean anything to him. "All they want is a few presents while they love another man." Thus, he is respected in the community because of his professional capabilities, and his private behavior is considered normal. She is aware of her dependency, and by and large she conforms to his wishes.

Peasant Women

Peasant women have the possibility of leading a life relatively free from the restraints imposed by men and by the system of wage labor. Because of partible inheritance they can own land, and it is not uncommon, for example, to find instances of a nuclear family with the women as the sole landowner. In such cases the restrictions on women described above apply with much less force, if they apply at all. Men in this situation are sometimes maintained as cheap labor and are occasionally considered to be untrustworthy and unreliable in providing for offspring. A common saying goes: "*Se pican y se van*" ("they sting and they leave," or, they get you pregnant and go). In extended families (often headed by women due to the widowhood of the mother), the mother frequently decides to exclude men from the household, with her daughters' approval. It is not expected that the daughters will remain childless. Rather, each child will be a welcome addition to the family.

In the practice of traditional agriculture (the cultivation of coffee, cocoa, plantains, etc.), the work can be, and often is, done by women. During harvest, extra labor from kin and neighbors can always be found if necessary, but the peasant ecology and crop types are such that not only is there year-round production with harvesting every two weeks, but a few hands can generally cope. Labor input and income vary little over the annual cycle. It appears that traditionally there was reciprocation of labor during harvests, but now every job and exchange is mediated by money. In a situation where men and women have various mates, and have children by each mate, it is usual to find wives working for husbands for cash, sons working for mothers for cash, mothers working for sons for cash, and so on. The mediation of the cash nexus is not necessarily the same, and need not imply the ubiquity of the profit motive. To the contrary, these peasants orient themselves to certain subsistence goals, as defined by the culture, and the prevalence of cash transactions testifies to the fact that even the peasantry depend on store-bought goods for a significant part of their daily consumption.

Let us sketch out a typical day for a woman from an extended, woman-headed household. She rises at 6:30 a.m. and over a wood fire makes breakfast of deep-fried plantains and sweet black coffee, with corn cakes or bread occasionally substituted for plantains. Her very young children stay with her mother; others go to school or work. Work may be helping the mother, or working on neighboring commercial farms or as casual day laborers. By the time children are three or four years old they can do a variety of tasks, such as helping in the house, running messages, and caring for younger brothers and sisters. They are disciplined but not passive, and are brought up to be honest and trustworthy.

At 7:30 the woman will go to work picking coffee, cocoa,

fruits, or plantains, or weeding around the trees. If she is close to home she will come home at 11:00 for lunch, then leave again until her return at 3:30. At 4:00 she will begin making the evening meal of soup, rice, and perhaps meat or beans, although these latter are rare. At 5:30 dinner will be over and the family will sit talking by candlelight, or listen to the *novelas* (serialized dramas) on the transistor radio (if they have one). It is not necessary to farm every day, and two or three days a week will be allocated to washing, marketing, sewing or mending, visiting, etc. Sunday is a festive day, a day for fine clothes, dancing, drinking, visiting, and marketing.

If a woman likes agricultural life and has sufficient land (three to four acres), she will pass her working life in this way. If not, she may turn to higgling—wholesaling and retailing agricultural products from neighboring peasant holdings in various local markets. If she does not have sufficient land to support her family, she or a teen-age daughter may go to the nearby big city to work as maids, but they are not likely to stay long. They will say the work "bores" them, a boredom arising out of a master-slave relationship, low wages, and virtual imprisonment in the employer's house (except for a half-day off every week or two weeks). Generally a maid is an object for abuse from the master, mistress, and their offspring.

The peasant woman can lose her independence if her landholding produces too little, or alternatively when agricultural methods and crops start to change. Such a transformation is now frequently given an impetus by government agencies like the agricultural extension agency, ICA, which tries to persuade peasants to cut down their perennial coffee and cocoa trees and replace them with seasonal "green revolution" crops such as corn, soybeans, tomatoes, etc. The decision to cut down the trees is usually made after a struggle between the older women and the young men in the house. The women are adamantly against such a change, realizing that although the aging and sometimes diseased trees do not produce much, they always produce something. It is a form of agriculture the women understand, and a landscape they love. But when the chaotic-looking jungle of plants and trees is replaced by open fields full of the same plants, tractors driven by men are required to plough the ground, and fertilizers are necessary to enrich the soil. Pesticides become essential to keep the insect population under control, and delicate plants such as tomatoes need constant care and spraying. The new agriculture requires much greater capital and labor inputs than did the traditional agriculture, and the financing organizations usually prefer to do business with men than with women. Likewise, ICA is an all-male organization and conducts all its dealings with the male peasants, even when the women may be substantial landowners.

The struggle tends to be won increasingly by the young men as the old women die, and the hope of making a lot of money quickly becomes irresistible. Although credit to the small farmer is limited and interest rates are high, many peasants with small landholdings are turning to these seasonal crops. What the young men do not realize is that the risks are high and that a bad season can ruin the small farmer. An example (and not an isolated one) is the case of Elberto. He borrowed the equivalent of $800 to plant tomatoes. One month before harvesting. Some exceptionally heavy rains washed the plants away. Now Elberto cannot pay the penalty interests imposed on the loan, let alone the loan itself. It is probable that ultimately his land will be confiscated and made available to one of the plantations.

It would seem that the old women are right, and that to cut down the coffee and cocoa trees is to court disaster. A critical time is coming, due to the fact that there has not been any systematic tree replanting over the years. Now that the trees are old, production is dropping, and people have no savings to fall back on.

Lower-Class Townswomen

The life of the townswomen is very different from that of the peasants. Many peasant women will say town life is much better because you do not have to fetch water and chop wood, there is more company, and there are more things happening *(ambiente)*. But living in town is expensive, and "free" farm products such as water, fuel, a house, etc., have to be paid for, thus accentuating the need for a paying job. However, there are few jobs for women, especially in the town, and they tend to go to the lower middle class rather than to the lower class: i.e., jobs as shop assistants or waitresses. Some women make a living selling baked goods, drinks, and food on the two weekly market days. Others station themselves daily outside the prison, the bus station, dance halls, or in the *zona de tolerancia*. Women with capital often buy a sewing machine, and dressmaking can be a relatively lucrative profession. Lower-class women without capital tend to become prostitutes, and little stigma is attached to this by persons of the same class. As one woman explained, "*Vendo mis carnes para mis hijos*" ("I sell my flesh for my children"). Alternatively, some of these women work in agriculture, sometimes combining both prostitution and agricultural work according to what is offered. The majority of jobs for townswomen are found in the fields, as casual day laborers rather than permanent, affiliated workers with health and retirement benefits. It is extremely important to point out that contractors prefer to employ women because they are thought to be *más mansa* (more docile) than the men, and will work for lower wages. They are *más mansa* because they frequently have numerous children to feed, often with minimal help (or none at all) from the father of the children. These are the women from the extended or female-headed families experiencing the difficulties of the proletarian role.

The work these women do is tiring and often extremely harmful to their health, as in the common case where they must apply powerful organo-phosphorous pesticides by hand, plant by plant, from a small container. They work in the cane and soybean fields sowing and weeding, and in the cornfields sowing, weeding, fumigating, and harvesting. The bean crops are harvested mechanically, but the harvesters fail to pick up the whole crop. What remains (the *requisa*) is harvested by gleaners who give half to the owner and keep the other half for themselves. Many poor families rely heavily on the *requisa* to augment their incomes. From this activity has grown the derogatory use of the word *iguaza* (a small duck that digs in the earth) to describe the female lumpenproletariat. Their earnings barely suffice for basic necessities. Emergencies such as a death, sickness, accidents, or something special for school nearly always require that the family pawn a possession, such as a watch, a pair of pants, a dress, or a bed. The four pawnshops are all owned by whites who live outside the town, and they charge 10 percent interest a month!

Misia* Juana, age thirty-four, is the mother of four children. She has had seven pregnancies. The oldest child is thirteen, the youngest five. A year ago she was abandoned by her "husband," who went to live with another woman who had only one child and a small *finca,* or garden plot. He is a cane cutter and supplies the family each week with basic but insufficient foods, such as rice, flour, potatoes, noodles, and cooking fat, all purchased in the company store. Juana has to supplement the food, pay the rent, and provide clothes, school books, and medicine. She works as a day laborer and after a harvest will glean with one or two of the children. She works intermittently because of her ill health and because often something needs to be done for the children. When she works, the five-year-old stays home alone because his sisters go to school. He is either locked in or out of the one-room house because of the fear of thieves.

Juana describes her childhood on the Pacific Coast where food was plentiful and nobody worked for cash. Their economy was subsistence farming and fishing. She came with her husband, José, to the *valle* to make money to buy some luxury items. Now, fifteen years later, there is no possibility of her returning to the Coast (where she has land) because she could never raise the capital necessary for the return

* The prefix *misia* is the lower-class equivalent of *doña* and carries the same connotation of respect.

journey and to support the family for the first few months. (Although she says that the latter objection is not so important, because on the Coast people help one another.) In the pueblo, nothing is given away. Of the separation of herself and her husband she said, "It is terribly serious to lose your man, because then you live very badly. It is a sin against the children and it is very bad for me. I am left in the street when he goes to another woman. If we lived on the Coast, however, it would not be so bad."

With the strain of her responsibilities and the lack of food in the house (it is usual to hear one of the children crying after a meal, "*Mama, tengo hambre*" ["Mama, I'm hungry"]), she periodically goes "mad." She takes off her clothes and dances in the streets until someone catches her and takes her inside. If she does not recover she goes to the mental hospital in the nearby city, but she never stays more than a few days because she worries about the children.

She does not know what to do. She wants to buy a house so that at least the family will have a permanent roof over their heads, but working as a day laborer (and an irregular one at that) she does not make enough money. She talks of going to the city to work as a maid, but what would happen to the children? It would be difficult for her to find work, since she neither reads nor writes, and most employers want a literate person. Her chances of bettering her life seem dismal. Her ill health and disposition make it impossible to make the "best" out of day laboring. She has no capital to try anything else. Her life is a holding operation—against hunger, sickness, and sadness; yet she has a tenderness and gentleness for her children and other people that survives under extraordinary privation.

Misia Graciela, age twenty-eight, was born in the town and is the mother of three children. She has given birth to five, but two died at about nine months of age. She was brought up in a convent by nuns, who taught anticommunism as well as religion. Her parents are both dead, and what little land they owned has been dissipated among the inheritors, who over time have sold it to meet debts. Graciela owns the one room she lives in and the land on which it stands. Her children have all been fathered by the same man. He comes from the Pacific Coast, where he had a "wife" and children. He has another woman in the pueblo who also has a child by him. Graciela did not believe that Pablo had another woman until she saw her with him one day in the street, pregnant. She was very angry and jealous, not so much out of spurned love as out of pride and annoyance that his meager wages would be further divided. For they must now be divided among the woman on the Coast, Pablo's aging father, herself, her children, and the new woman and child. Their relationship had not been good for some time, and he had been seeing other women. He stayed out late at night drinking and dancing, and gave her little help with the children. One night she was sick and the baby was crying. After trying to console the baby she asked him to help, but he rolled over and went to sleep, saying, "It's your job, you're the mother, aren't you?" Subsequently she tried to keep him out of the room, and when he came home at 4:00 a.m. she barred the door. But this was ineffective, because he told her that if there was no intercourse, she would receive no money. Consequently, she became pregnant again. Piedad was born, and a month later the baby Cecilia died of pneumonia. The hut was damp, and there was no money for medicine. Then Pablo began working on a sugarcane plantation three hours away, coming back only on Sundays.

Since Graciela was dependent on him for money, she had to comply with his wishes. The money she received for herself and the children came irregularly and was barely enough. He would give her about $2.00 (U.S.) a week, but this only provided her with the most meager necessities (rice, the staple, costs 15¢/pound; meat, 40¢; a tin of powdered milk, $1.00). She has had several jobs but always finds it difficult to hold a job and care for the three young children, who are nine months, five, and six years old. She has worked frying small things to eat in the streets, but that was not profitable. She had a job cooking at one of the plantations, but there were so many mosquitos and insects in the plantation-provided room that the children could not sleep. She then had a job living in, cooking and cleaning for an elderly grain merchant. However, he became sick and was frightened that he was going to die without kin in the house. On two days' notice he fired her. Her only solution was to return to her room and wait for her husband to come with money. The corner storekeeper gives credit, but on many items his prices are 10 to 20 percent higher than in the government-operated store.

There is little accord between members of her extended family, so child care cannot be taken care of collectively; nor does she have any security in case of an emergency, such as when she went to have a sterilization operation. The care of the children during her eight-day absence became a problem. She did not want to leave them with the sister she lives with; nor could she leave them with her childless sister. Finally she left them with her husband's lover, reasoning that she was the person who had the most obligation to look after them. The woman recognized her obligation, and the children were well treated.

Graciela can see few ways out of her situation. Her hope is to go to the nearby big city and work as a maid for a middle-class family for $20 to $30 a month. She would be unable to take the children with her and might leave them with the husband's lover or with a relation of his some two hours away. The separation from her children would be very painful, but she is matter-of-fact about the realities of her situation and her lack of choice. She tries to invoke magic in a half-hearted way to win back Pablo's affections so that he will give her enough money for her and the children's survival.

His life is not easy either, although he does not have the constant responsibilities of young children. He cuts cane and lives in a plantation camp three hours from the pueblo. He works under the hot sun, nine hours a day, five days a week. Saturday is a five-hour workday, after which the workers wait for two or three hours while the pay is given out. He suffers from back and eye trouble, and at thirty-three appears almost a physical wreck. On Sunday he puts on his silk shirt and dark glasses and tries to forget the canefields.

Unlike Graciela, Felipa is coping a little better with her life and has even been involved in some industrial strikes. She comes from the Pacific Coast and has no kin ties in the town. The wage she earns is not enough to support a family if they are to eat anything much other than rice. Hence, women like Felipa are under great pressure to work regularly, and to get their children into the work force as soon as possible. In contrast to country children, town children are frequently undisciplined, untrained in traditional customs, and likely to get involved in petty crime at an early age.

Felipa is twenty-seven and has three primary-school-age children. She lives alone with the children in one room, which she rents. She works as a day laborer and manages to do so fairly consistently, as she is strong and in reasonably good health. She makes one dollar a day and sometimes more. She has been involved in two strikes, although strikes among the women workers are rare. Other poor townswomen described the situation this way:

> We went to work at five in the morning. Don Juan, the *contratista*, offered us 15¢ per sack of corn that we picked. But we had heard that he was being paid 35¢ a sack. So we left and walked home, which was a good three-hour walk. There were no leaders; we were unanimous. The *mayordomo* of the hacienda spoke to him, and the next day he offered us 25¢. We weren't satisfied, but we need the money. If I don't work, we don't eat.

> One day we went to weed corn. The rows of corn were very long, as far as you could see. They were offering 20¢ a row, and each was about 400 meters long. We told the *contratista* that rows were worth 30¢, because besides weeding we had to drop pesticide on each plant from a bottle. We have heard that these pesticides are very dangerous to one's health. He refused to raise the pay, so we left. We walked for one and one-half hours when the *contratista* caught up with us and offered us 25¢. We decided, reluctantly, to take the money. We all have children at home.

These examples are typical of the desperate situation. Whereas a peasant woman could combine farming and child-rearing with a degree of emotional and economic stability for all, the poor townswoman struggles to earn a living and to raise children as she would like to, that is, as *formal* ("polite") and worthy members of society. For peasants, especially the women, householding includes domestic work, child-rearing, and farming, and in a very real sense these are organically interconnected. For the townswomen, however, these basic aspects of life are structurally differentiated, and what is more, seem incapable of synthesis.

Sorcery

The new dependence on men induces competition between women that is dramatically illustrated in the use of sorcery and love magic. Sorcery *(brujeria)* is used to capture a man's affections, or to keep a straying man in line. It need hardly be said that it is more widely used in the town than in the country.

There are various methods women can use to capture a man's affections. Most involve some ritual use of potions, the ingredients for which are bought from the Amazon Indian traders in the local marketplace. The simplest *liga* is achieved by placing some of the special potion on the man's clothing. Others are more complex and ritualized. The commonly known recipes, or methods, follow.

Light and smoke a cigar about halfway. Take a candle (preferably bought with the money of the man you are trying to attract) and break it in half. Light one piece of it. Sprinkle sugar or pepper onto the burning cigar and puff very hard. Concentrate on the man. When the ash is ready to drop, let it fall and then stamp on it while saying three times, "So and so, *hijo de puta*" (son of a prostitute). It should be noted that this expression is a very common form of abuse, but normally it is used more often by men than women. It is believed that the smoke can penetrate the brain of the man.

Homemade *ligas* are also effective; two commonly used ones are as follows. Take some hair from the head, armpits, and pubic areas and mix them with the sperm of the lover. (The sperm is obtained after intercourse during which the woman does not have an orgasm, so as to maintain the purity of the sperm.) Place the ingredients in a bottle and mix them with alcohol. Then bury the bottle inside the house. For the second *liga*, take some armpit and pubic hair, toast it, grind it, and mix it with the man's coffee. If the sorcery is strong enough, the man can be turned into a fool *(tonto)* and will forever "walk behind" *(anda atrás)* the woman.

In the case of love rivalries and the tensions arising from a triangular relationship, it is not the male who is reproached for the affair, but the woman. It is commonly said that one of the women will try to use sorcery to harm or kill the other woman, or to at least terminate the relationship. It is supposed that she will frequently employ the services of a female sorcerer. Such was the case with Dolores and Julia.

Dolores had a husband who was having an affair with another woman. At that time she was working as a day laborer, and it was usual for the workers to eat a cooked lunch. One day she ate a lunch prepared by a friend, and from that day her stomach began to swell. At first she thought she was pregnant, but the swelling became very extreme and remained. Shortly after the swelling had begun her husband left her to live with the other woman. Two years later, Dolores was very sick, and the rest of her body was emaciated. She was sure that it was sorcery administered through the food. (Food is commonly considered to be a medium for magic; for this reason salt, for example, can never be borrowed.) Her old, blind mother became very angry upon hearing this and said that if the other woman should hear of her suspicions she would use more sorcery to finish her off.

Julia and Carlos have been married for ten years and have seven children. He has a photography business in which she helps occasionally. Their newly purchased television set seems to indicate that the business is going well. He comes from an agricultural family with little land, and she comes from the Pacific Coast. Carlos has a lover and a child by her. When he brought the "new sister" to the house one day, the children would have nothing to do with her. In spite of having a lover, he is extremely possessive of his wife and will not allow her to walk alone in the street. Recently he became very vicious toward her, and he beats her frequently. She is afraid, as are his brothers and his mother, that he will kill her but they feel powerless because they believe him to be bewitched. It is presumed that Carlos' lover is behind it.

Some time ago a strange woman came to the door and gave one of the children three beautiful oranges. Julia said they must be thrown away, which they were. Shortly thereafter the woman came again with more oranges, and this time they were put aside and stayed in the house until they began to go bad. From approximately this time Julia and Carlos' relationship began to deteriorate. They went to a curer, but Carlos refused to take the herbal remedies he prescribed. The situation worsened and Julia sent to the mayor's office to file a complaint and to take out a *caucion* against Carlos in case he should become more violent. The judge ordered them to see a psychiatrist (!) but neither of them wants to do that. Neither has any understanding of the workings of psychiatry, and they cannot imagine that a white, middle-class psychiatrist can help them.

Although women employ sorcery in questions of love, they do not employ sorcery as a means of directly improving their material situation. In contrast, some men working in the sugar plantations make a pact with the devil to increase production. The pact allows the worker to increase the amount of cane cut or loaded, but there are conditions attached to it—usually a time limit on one's life, and an unpleasant death. It is said that the money thus earned cannot be turned into productive capital and must be spent on consumer luxuries. A pig bought with the money would die, a business started with it would founder. It is indeed devil's money, fit only for drinking and gambling. Like the townswomen, peasants (men and women) do not make pacts with the devil. The making of such a pact seems to be an expression of alienation from both land and work. The peasants do not suffer that alienation, and the townswomen cannot "afford" to, in the sense that to make such a pact would jeopardize their ability to provide food for their children.

In summary, it is important to note the role of sorcery. In a rapidly "modernizing" world, sorcery is not losing out. On the contrary, it appears to be patching up some of the gaping cultural, economic, and social holes produced by rural capitalism in its plantation form. Although it crosses racial lines (the most respected curers and sorcerers are Indians from the Upper Amazon), it does not often cross class lines; it therefore serves to unite lower-class people in some ways. Sorcery also unites women as a group, but in a complex way, because it both divides women, and serves as an acceptable rationalization of men's mistreatment of them. It contributes to their oppression, but is also one of their few sources of power.

Conclusion

In conclusion, it should be said that women in this modernizing situation have a difficult role and that they live it with great courage. Change in the mode of production works in this case to the disadvantage of women. Women have lost their economic independence while often retaining sole responsibility for raising their children. As peasants, women often chose to be singly responsible for their children, but it becomes very difficult to do so as proletarians or lumpenproletarians. This has resulted in women having to seek work wherever they can and under adverse conditions, as we saw in the case of the *iguazas*, the female agricultural laborers. We see also that tensions in interpersonal relations are exacerbated by an ambivalent acceptance of dependence on men, and an ambivalent reluctance of men to be depended on.

It is not so much the "sexist" culture that is the fundamental problem (although there is much sexism), but the new relations of production and lack of land that are disrupting the lives of both men and women, thus altering the function of traditional mating patterns that previously allowed great flexibility for both sexes.

The ability of women to change their lives for the better is seriously inhibited as they become increasingly dependent on men who now exercise a new power over them by virtue of the availability and nature of work. This new power arises from a fundamental and total change in the social relations of production: from a peasant mode of production to a capitalist mode. In turn, it is important to emphasize the growing dependence of the men themselves on these macroeconomic structures, and the declining control they have over their own lives. For women, the effect of this growing dependence on males might be more accurately described as a sub-dependence—a dependency merely mediated by the male wage laborer, which serves to bind women emotionally, economically, and often unwillingly, to men, and through them to the wider system.

Dorothy Remy

Underdevelopment and the Experience of Women: A Nigerian Case Study

My concern in this paper is with developing a theoretical framework for the analysis of the economic and ideological constraints on the autonomy of women in urban Africa. My approach entails an examination of the evolution of the urban environment, the nature of the social structure that has emerged, and, finally, the adaptive responses used by individuals or groups occupying different structural positions in the political economy. An analytic framework which incorporates recognition of the processes of underdevelopment and class formation is particularly relevant here, for it focuses attention on the structural and situational variables that generate and maintain women's relative poverty and powerlessness.

The pattern of economic development in Nigeria under colonial and indigenous rule has generated and perpetuated structural inequalities between sectors of the economy, between tribes, and between sexes. The government promotes externally financed extractive, processing, and manufacturing industries through a variety of financial inducements, as well as through an infrastructure oriented explicitly toward its needs (Remy and Weeks, 1973). The small externally oriented sector of the economy, with its largely expatriate managerial staff and imported technology, is supported at the expense of the capital and infrastructural requirements of the indigenous economy. Consumer goods produced in Nigerian factories for the elite market both undersell indigenously produced goods and serve as symbols of wealth and status. Differential distribution of wage employment opportunities between regions and between ethnic groups emerged early in the colonial period as schools and industries were concentrated in southern Nigeria. They are perpetuated as those with jobs seek to consolidate their position through the selective advancement of people from their communities of origin. Income inequalities widen as those who obtain employment in state-supported industries and in the administrative bureaucracy earn substantially higher incomes than the average earned in the impoverished indigenous economy.

Within both the state-supported and indigenous economies, women are at a structural disadvantage. Fewer women than men attend school. Those who do are channeled into a narrow range of occupations, none of which includes the government or private sector jobs through which high incomes and social status are obtained. Further, women's indigenous economic activities are undermined by competition both from manufactured products and from men able to accumulate capital from wage employment and invest it in trade or craft production in the indigenous economy. At an ideological level, religion provides a rationale for the existing social order while at the same time providing an institutional framework through which women are able to fulfill the economic and social roles assigned them.

In this paper I shall discuss, in the context of the city of Zaria in northern Nigeria, the implications for women of this pattern of economic development. I shall examine a woman's economic independence from two perspectives: the degree to which she is economically independent of her husband or family, and the extent to which she is able to participate directly in the economic or social life of the community. She is economically independent if she pays for her own food, room, and clothing, or would be able to do so should her husband die or leave her. She participates directly in the economy when she buys and/or sells goods and services without the intervention of a third person.

Zaria, established in its present location in 1536, was founded as the southernmost capital of a loose federation of Habe city-states. In the early nineteenth century, Fulani pastoralists used the mechanism of a religious *jihad*, or holy war, against the pagan population to incorporate the Habe cities into a centralized theocratic state. The Fulani, who intermarried with the Moslem Hausa ruling class, created an administrative system which the British employed a century later to govern the Protectorate of Northern Nigeria. As a means of maintaining the existing politico-religious hierarchy, the British excluded Christian missions from Moslem areas. Since virtually all education was provided by mission schools, the majority Hausa population lacked the training necessary for the growing number of administrative and commercial jobs and Christians from the south, where mission schools were permitted, migrated to Zaria to work for the Europeans. In addition, traders, both Christian and Moslem, migrated north because of the concentration of wage workers and the improved transportation system.

A loose tripartite division of the town emerged, which was reflected in its settlement pattern. The Hausa Moslem population lived in the precolonial walled town of Birnin Zaria. They were primarily farmers, but were also craftsmen and merchants. Outside the city walls, northern, largely Moslem, migrants lived in a planned settlement called Tudun Wada. Across a belt of rich farmland bordering the Kubbani River, a new town, Sabon Gari, developed. It drew Christians from the north and south—Tiv, Idoma, Igala, people from the south of Zaria province, and Ibo and Yoruba. These are the groups that had had access to the Western schooling necessary to gain entry into the commercial and bureaucratic economy.

The dominant commercial, bureaucratic, and manufacturing establishments are alien to Zaria in two ways. First, virtually all the capital, managerial staff, technology, and work practices are European and differ fundamentally from those of the indigenous economy. The enterprises themselves, and those who manage them, are also physically isolated from the rest of the population. Second, the nonmanagerial labor force in the state-supported enterprises comes from outside of Zaria. In 1970, 80 percent of the nonmanagerial workers at the largest factory, the Nigerian Tobacco Company (NTC), were not native to Zaria.

It is the workers in the NTC factory and their families who are the focus of the following analysis. In 1970-1971 I spent several hours a day observing work-place interaction in the factory. As I established friendships, I would ask the men to introduce me to their wives. In this manner, I acquired access to a group of people largely invisible in the anthropological literature, the married working-class women (Remy and Weeks, 1973).

Three-quarters of the male NTC employees are married and live with their wives. These workers are linked through their wives to the indigenous economy; in complementary fashion, through marriage to factory employees, women from diverse backgrounds are part of the small Zaria working class. The households of the permanent workers at NTC are economically secure in comparison with those of small-scale businessmen and traders, and the main source of income is the husband's wage packet. Only one of the twenty-four women interviewed was wage-employed herself; the remainder either hoped to be, or were, active in Zaria's indigenous economy.

The indigenous economy is characterized by face-to-face interactions among buyers and sellers of goods and services, and by a high degree of product specialization, transfers in very small units, and the widespread use of short-term credit. The social relations of economic transfer are thus responsive to the poverty of the urban population and to the sharp seasonal and yearly fluctuations in income. In a situation in which there are large numbers of buyers and sellers, economic success comes through the careful maintenance of "customer" relations. In Nigerian usage, a "customer" may be either the buyer or the seller of a product or a service. A "customer relationship" implies, at the minimum, a regular relationship. It also frequently means that a friendship has been built between buyer and seller through the extension of credit or the practice of giving a "dash"—a small increase in the quantity of the goods over the amount sold at the agreed-upon price. The buyer maintains her side of the relationship by regularly buying from the same seller. The system gains its continuity in Nigerian markets as children learn from their parents the economic and social behavior associated with being a good "customer" (Remy, 1968).

Access to customers, then, is critical to a woman's capacity to earn a regular cash income through her economic activities, whether they involve the home-based production of goods or participation in the market as a trader. Fixed operation from a shop or stall in a neighborhood or marketplace further facilitates maintenance of customer relationships. Women who live in sparsely settled areas of the city and cannot establish a stall in the market must develop compensatory mechanisms if they are to insure regular and frequent interaction with a large number of customers.

Women who come to Zaria from rural areas are poorly equipped for participation in the urban indigenous economy, where there is a more complex division of labor and a greater reliance on specialized skills. Trading agricultural products or processing food, both common activities of Nigerian rural women, become more complex in the city, where the raw agricultural products must be purchased in the market or acquired from "customers." The former requires an initial capital investment and the latter a well-developed network of customers. Urban home-based crafts, such as knitting, crocheting, and embroidery, require access to a teacher and a small amount of initial capital to pay for equipment and materials. Potentially more profitable urban skills, such as sewing, require a period of apprenticeship, which the learner must pay for, as well as a substantial investment in a sewing machine (Boserup, 1970).

The ability of women in Zaria to obtain a regular cash income over which they have control is thus constrained by structural limitations on their capacity to acquire the capital and skills that are relevant in an urban context. Access to economic opportunity is further constrained by the prevailing belief that a woman's economic activities should be confined to the domestic sphere.

The interaction between the ideological and structural limitations on full participation in the urban economy entails somewhat different considerations for women who are restricted to their houses and those who have greater physical mobility. The wives of the Hausa ruling class experience the most restrictive form of marriage, *auren kulle.* This is marriage of complete seclusion in which a woman may never go outside the confines of her husband's compound. Many of the household duties are carried out by servants, and social contact and common interests between husband and wife are minimal. During the colonial period, a new elite developed among those Hausa men who had been to school and assumed positions of responsibility in the government bureaucracy. Wages from employment at NTC have enabled other Moslem workers, whether Hausa or not, to express similar values. In describing this category of Nigerian men, Rachel Yeld observed:

> This new elite group has firmly adopted the status symbols of the Moslem Hausa aristocracy of the cities and towns of the Northern Region, particularly their emphasis on Moslem rather than Western culture, including a strict conformity to Islamic custom on the seclusion of wives and general attitudes towards the position of women. (Yeld, 1964:66)

The close relationship between economic resources and the degree of wife seclusion can be seen in the marital histories of the men in my sample from Birnin Zaria. They began work at NTC as unskilled laborers and the women they married are in *auren tsare,* or partial seclusion (where the wife is allowed to visit her relatives and attend the health clinic if necessary). However, in the households of the two men who had been promoted to skilled jobs, total seclusion was imposed on the youngest wife, who is not allowed to leave her husband's compound under any circumstances.

The degree of seclusion practiced among the Hausa and other ethnic groups which have come under Moslem influence is justified in religious terms. Women are expected to observe Moslem practices, such as praying, in the privacy of their rooms, but they may not attend the gatherings for prayer at the mosques or the religious celebrations of the great annual festivals. Nor do young girls in some provinces of the North attend Koranic schools. "With the Moslem emphasis on public prayer and ceremonial, it means that women are excluded from the formal religious life of the community" (ibid.:65).

Secluded Moslem women are cut off from direct access to the economic life of the community. With the exception of a limited range of goods and services provided by Moslem women traders who enter the compounds, all food, clothing, and raw materials used in productive activities are purchased by a child or a male member of the household. Similarly, a child or a man will sell the goods a woman has produced. The household and the degree of cooperation within it thus become a major determinant of a woman's economic activities. From kin and friends a woman learns the skills by which she can earn a cash income. Although secluded, women make articles of clothing or process and cook food ("snacks") for sale; they also sell soap, perfume, oil, and similar small items. In Hausa households the women cook an evening meal and sometimes a morning one as well. All other food is referred to as "snacks" and is bought in the market or from women who prepare it in their compounds. While much of the cooked food is sold to men, women also buy mid-day snacks from each other through the intermediary of children. Processing food and making these "snacks" are the most widespread economic activities of Hausa women, both rural and urban.

Secluded women also earn money by embroidering men's caps, an occupation which is less arduous and has a higher status. The caps, which are worn by most Moslem men in Zaria, consist of a narrow circular band of cloth sewed to a round crown. Patterns are sold in the market and the women embroider in the design with colored thread. The variation in the complexity of the design, the quality of work, and the thread determines the price of the completed cap. All of the women I interviewed had learned how to embroider from another adult member of the household. The capital investment is small, and it is possible for a woman to become established in business by working with her teacher on only one cap and dividing the proceeds.

As the following case illustrates, rural Moslem women who move to the city after marriage lack this household base for participation in the urban economy. Asabe's father and his three wives grew cotton and food crops on a farm in a village near Zaria. Asabe's mother was not in strict seclusion: she occasionally worked on the farm and regularly sold homespun cotton thread and a porridge-like drink in the village market. Asabe attended Koranic school until her marriage to a man from the village; he had attended technical college and now worked at the Nigerian Tobacco Company as a mechanic. They moved to the Tudun Wada section of Zaria, where they lived in two rooms facing an enclosed courtyard shared by five other families. The other women in the compound were not Hausa, but they spoke Hausa as a second language. The women helped each other with cooking and child care, but Asabe did not consider them her friends. In fact, she had no friends in Zaria largely because there was no older female relative in the area who could take her to ceremonial gatherings where she could meet other women (Yeld, 1960). Asabe wanted to sell prepared food as her mother had done, or set up a loom so she could weave, but her landlord forbid her to dig loom posts and her husband objected to her doing either. Further, even if she had been allowed to weave, it would have been unlikely that she could earn very much because the demand for factory-produced printed cotton cloth has drastically reduced the market for the cloth woven by Hausa women. Selling prepared food might have been more profitable, but Asabe's social isolation ruled this out because she would have had to either sell it in her compound or through children in the market. So Asabe's days were spent sitting quietly listening to the radio, cooking one meal for herself and her husband, and cleaning the two rooms. She wanted to have a child so that she would have more to do.

The degree of social isolation and inability to participate fully in the economy make secluded women economically vulnerable should their marriages end in divorce; equally, the high incidence of divorce mitigates against these women developing enduring relationships with their co-wives. An effective adaptive strategy for the urban Hausa woman requires that she maintain a long-term relationship with her extended family and with her women friends, one that will continue through changes in marital status. Regular gift exchanges, requiring an independent income, facilitate the maintenance of such relationships. Asabe's two best friends from childhood live in her home village, which she has not revisited since her marriage. Since she has no income of her own, she is unable to maintain her relationships with them by sending gifts. She is dependent on her husband's generosity for these gifts, and if she cannot fully maintain her end of the relationship, it will be difficult for her to draw on it for support should any marital difficulties make it necessary.

The restrictions on the public activities of women, especially Northern Moslem women, does not imply that they do not want a greater degree of economic participation or that they do not in fact seek independent sources of income whenever possible. As one woman expressed it: "It is not right for a woman to be idle. It does not take long to cook and care for the children and I like to work for the rest of the time. I do not like to ask my husband for money each time I want to buy something."

A Christian woman, regardless of tribe, may also be financially dependent on her husband but she is able to participate more directly in the economy as a consumer, and often as a trader or producer as well. Further, through the women's association of her tribe or through her church she can participate directly in the social life of her community. However, it is very difficult for illiterate women from agricultural communities to earn an income in Zaria. Unskilled NTC workers often cannot afford to pay for their wives' instruction or provide them with capital. The wife of one such man has lived in Zaria for six years but has been unable to translate her ability to trade in agricultural produce into a successful urban trade. Her husband, who worked as a seasonal laborer prior to his employment as an unskilled worker at NTC, had been unable to provide her with sufficient capital to operate a successful business. Furthermore, the family has moved several times during the course of their residence in Zaria, which has increased the wife's difficulty in establishing a neighborhood base for her trade.

A few of the other women interviewed, who were also married to unskilled workers, appeared to be in a position to acquire specialist skills. The husbands of three young Christian women had paid their tuition at sewing classes and planned eventually to buy them sewing machines. When this happens, these women will be able to earn independent incomes, but they will be in a highly competitive business—itself an indication of the popularity of this strategy. There is an oversupply of tailors and seamstresses in Zaria. Price competition is keen and women who cannot establish shops in the market are at a competitive disadvantage because they are dependent upon the custom of women in their neighborhoods.

Without exception, the women in my sample who were able to acquire sufficient skills and capital to earn an income through trade or as seamstresses had attended primary school and were married to skilled workers who themselves had at least secondary educations. All of the women had learned to read, write, and speak some English. Because of their husbands' higher incomes, they had been able to devote several years to acquiring specialist skills. Their husbands had also provided the initial capital for them to become established in business. Once well established, these women had been able to reinvest their profits into expanding their enterprises.

A Yoruba woman, Mary, attended class at a sewing institute in Zaria for one year and spent a second year in advanced training in Ibadan while her husband was in training for his position as foreman. At the time of the interview she owned two sewing machines, which her husband had bought for her, and had six apprentices. She had rented a stall in the market, where her apprentices sell cloth, cosmetics, and the clothing they have made. Women also come to her house to buy clothing. While both her training and her initial capital were provided by her husband as part of their marriage agreement, Mary is now economically independent of him. Sissi, another Yoruba woman, whose husband worked at NTC as a mechanic, probably earned less than Mary by selling provisions from a stall in the Sabon Gari market. Most of her daily turnover was reinvested in her business. She would have liked to rent a shop in the market, but had been unable to accumulate the necessary capital.

In addition to their skills and capital, Sissi and Mary benefited from being able to establish stalls in the market. The long-standing tradition of urban trade among Yoruba women, both Christian and Moslem, insured them ethnic community support for their economic activities. All of Mary's apprentices and many of her customers were Yoruba, as were the women with whom Sissi worked in the market.

Most women from areas of Northern Nigeria, however, where the Hausa influence is strong and educational influence weak, conduct their businesses from their homes. Work as a seamstress is a favored occupation for these women, although isolation from the marketplace can be a disadvantage. The market seamstress or tailor enjoys an irregular but substantial trade from passers-by, while the home-based seamstress must depend entirely on regular customers. It is therefore important for the home seamstress to maintain relationships with a large number of potential customers over a long period of time in order to benefit from their custom when they have money available for the purchase of clothing. An obvious advantage of trading from the home is that a woman can sell while performing her domestic chores.

Urban migration and the need for specialized skills creates a discontinuity in the transmission of female roles. Women are unable to teach their daughters the skills that are most relevant in the urban environment, and these must be acquired through public or private schools. The public school system is the major gate-keeping mechanism determining access to wage employment. Schooling for girls in Northern Nigeria is restricted both by the number of openings and by parental attitudes. Even for schooled women, however, public attitudes about the appropriate occupations for women, as well as the intense competition among men for jobs, has generally resulted in the concentration of women with schooling in a limited number of "female" occupations. As a consequence, there is a two-tiered division in women's economic activities. A few women with professional training work as teachers, nurses, or secretaries, while the majority of women—those who have only primary schooling or none—work as unskilled workers or in the trade-based indigenous economy.

Most nonsecluded women participate in religious and ethnic associations. These provide networks of relationships that can be called upon, particularly in times of personal crisis—they are for the urban "strangers" what kinship is for the urban Hausa. The effectiveness of these associations appears, however, to be a function of a woman's economic resources: her participation depends in part on her ability to make financial contributions to the associations, and, as we have seen, her ability to do this is in turn largely dependent on her husband's ability to finance her training or start in trade.

At the same time that the ethnic associations and churches provide an institutional form through which women can obtain emotional and other support, they reinforce an ideology of subordinate status for women and of their dependence on marriage. No woman sits on a church's governing body, although their husbands, who do not participate in the activities of their church with the frequency of their wives, serve on the committees which make decisions affecting the entire congregation. In the ethnic associations men and women meet separately. The women meet to discuss common problems, to assist women who are sick, and to care for the families of members when there has been a death. The men, on the other hand, are much more active in advancing the common interests of the group in the home community: they collect money to establish a member in business, to pay for the schooling of a member's son, or to send back to the home community to finance a school or clinic. To draw this distinction in function is not to imply that the men do not provide financial and personal support to members when necessary, but to point out that it is the women who are *restricted* to this more personal function, which is only part of the more far-reaching concern of the men for the group as a whole.

There is also, in the ethnic and church associations, a strong emphasis on "correct" behavior in terms of attitudes toward elders and husbands. One of the women traders told me that the members of her ethnic association met to "give advice to each other about how to stay happy with our husbands." The associations are explicitly for married women, which means that a divorced woman is often simultaneously isolated from both male and female support, beyond that provided by her brothers and sisters. The ideology of subordinate status for women and of a restricted, dependent role as wife, and the associated limitations on an ability to become economically self-sufficient, are mutually reinforcing. Without an independent income women cannot finance activities that would advance their collective status or promote the further training of their daughters. They are dependent upon husbands and kin, and on the collective security provided by the church and/or ethnic association. Supporting these by maintaining "correct behavior" insures the continuation of this security while at the same time making it necessary. The system is not, however, sufficiently pervasive to still the desire of women from all backgrounds and conditions to participate in the commercial economy.

To summarize, capitalist economic development has either introduced or reinforced structural inequalities within the Nigerian economy. But while economic options for men have widened, and they have assumed new roles which permit varying degrees of personal autonomy, the same is not true for women. Within the urban economy intense competition for wage jobs and a restrictive range of "appropriate" jobs for women has channeled those few women with schooling into a narrow range of occupations. The increasing demand for manufactured goods and their relative cheapness has reduced demand for the craft products of women, thus undermining an important avenue to economic autonomy. Men, because they can accumulate more capital through wage employment, are able to buy and sell agricultural and manufactured goods in volume at lower prices, and in the process they reduce the profit margins of women traders. Many men have the option of transferring economic resources from the wage sector of the economy to the indigenous economy. Women, with only few exceptions, must confine their economic activities to this relatively impoverished sector.

European and Nigerian men share the belief that the primary role of a woman is that of wife and mother. School curricula, course offerings in technical schools, and hiring practices fail to include economic options beyond a narrow range of service occupations. The capitalist economy undermines the customary economic activities of women while at the same time failing to train or provide a supporting infrastructure that would enable women to provide for their own economic security.

Religion reinforces and perpetuates these structural inequalities. While *kulle* is restrictive, at least in large kin-based households the domestic productive role of women is maintained. Wage employment, however, enables men to maintain their wives in *kulle*, but in small, isolated families, which leaves the women without the female support that made seclusion psychologically bearable. At the same time, the husband's income makes the women's productive activities less economically important. While the Christian churches have in a sense liberated some Nigerian women by providing, through their schools, the opportunity for women to become economically active, this has also occurred in the context of households in which women are isolated from a female support system with its own viable economic base.

Norma Diamond

Collectivization, Kinship, and the Status of Women in Rural China

The marked improvements in the status of women in China since Liberation have attracted the attention not only of scholars but also of those of us involved in the women's liberation movement. Some observers feel that the question of women's equality has been solved in China through the destruction of feudalism and capitalism, by the introduction of new legislation (particularly the 1950 Marriage Law), and by the entry of large numbers of women into the agricultural and industrial work force. Others, more skeptical, point to the undeniably lesser participation of women in positions of leadership and in political life, to the problem of lower pay rates for women, and the continuation of a sexual division of labor despite the presence of women in a wide variety of jobs. They take these as evidence that a socialist system still fails to come to grips with the basic question of male oppression and the special conditions of women.

Janet Salaff and Judith Merkle (1973), for example, argue that while the revolution freed women to the extent that it removed the legal restrictions that bound them to the family and prevented them from participating in production, it

---

Earlier versions of this paper were presented at the meetings of the American Anthropological Association, New Orleans, November 29-December 1, 1973, and at a Committee of Concerned Asian Scholars panel in Boston in early April 1974. For their criticisms and suggestions during the development of this paper I would like to extend thanks to Delia Davin, Irene Eber, Gayle Rubin, Brooke Grundfest Shoepf, and Marilyn Young.

failed to take the final step of liberating women from their special form of oppression within "the most intimate private areas of life," or from the male-supremacist thinking imbedded in the traditions and historical experience of the society. The Chinese do not deny that there is a struggle against continuing male chauvinism in the home and the local community. Salaff and Merkle's position is that these male-chauvinist attitudes are perpetuated and buttressed by (1) the continuation of the nuclear family, (2) the cost considerations of socializing housework, and (3) the relative non-participation of women in the military either now or during earlier stages of the revolution; and they are pessimistic that China can or will end the oppression of women as a social group.

In her rebuttal, Nancy Milton (1973) points out that the demands of revolutionary Chinese women never included the total abolition of the family, but only of the feudal-patriarchal family and the restriction on free choice in marriage. The goal was a happier family life, not universal divorce. Speaking to the point of women gaining the means of coercion (armed force), she points to the inclusion of women in the PLA since 1958 and the military role of women in the mass media. And on the third point, she argues that it is a question of time and economic means in a society like China's, which is not yet an advanced industrial society. The question of housework is gradually being resolved as living standards rise and more funds become available for child-care facilities, services, and simplification of household tasks. In brief, she counsels patience, as opposed to the school of thought which says "once again we have been betrayed by promises."

Both analyses are wrong in part, in what they fail to include in their discussions. The problem is more than one of "bourgeois" versus "revolutionary" feminist demands, or of traditional versus modern industrializing societies.

In 1972 Soong Ch'ing-ling, head of the All-China Federation of Women and a vice-chairman of the People's Republic, wrote a key article discussing these issues (1973:201-209).

She is less sanguine than Milton. Although she asserts that women's liberation, which begins with a democratic revolution, will be completed only within the socialist revolution, she states firmly that it is not yet time for the women's movement in China to close up shop or for the women's associations to disband. Among the peasantry, still 85 percent of the population, the "feudal-patriarchal ideology" continues despite the presence of women in many kinds of work, in the schools, and in the military. There are still real problems to be grappled with: unequal pay, unequal access to education, the pressure to produce sons, and the burden of household chores hindering women from full participation in public life.

More recent statements also stress the problem of the persistence of older thinking. Fu Wen (1974:16-18) and Hsu Kwang (1974:12-15) point to the existence of backward elements representing the landlord and capitalist classes, those who look down on women, bar their way to full participation in society, and try to turn back the clock. These and other recent commentators on the woman question see the campaign to criticize Lin Piao and Confucius as a mass movement that will sweep away the old ideas about women and propel China's women to win complete liberation.

To some extent the problem may be ideology, as the Chinese say it is. But it is my feeling that this analysis also fails to ask certain questions, specifically what is there in the current organization of society, particularly rural society, that allows for the continuation of the feudal-patriarchal ideology, or that creates it in new guise? Must we assume that male oppression of women is so deeply rooted in the human species that even revolution and major restructurings of society are insufficient to abolish it?

What I shall do in this paper is try to deal with how the rural sector has been reorganized since 1949, how this has affected women, and to what extent traditional structures *were* abolished (since everyone seems to assume blithely that they have been). Everywhere in China the process of socialist transformation of the countryside followed the same sequence: equalization of landholdings during land reform, the formation of mutual-aid teams which gradually became the basis for cooperatives, the organization of these into collectives, and the coordination of these under the commune system after 1958. However, units smaller than the commune have considerable autonomy. The production brigade, usually based on the natural village, is the unit for collective ownership of land, livestock, machinery, and small workshops. The smaller production team, which often coincides with hamlet or neighborhood, is the basic accounting unit in many communes. These residential units hold land-use rights and own some machines, tools, and livestock. Below that, there is also some property ownership at the household level, including the private plots that represent 5 percent of the total agricultural land.

Before Liberation landholding took two basic forms: household ownership and lineage ownership (with perhaps a third variant of corporate business ownership in the late Ch'ing and Republican periods). Both local and absentee landlordism could result either from small household ownership of surplus lands or from lineage ownership. In either case, the title to land and control over it passed along male lines of descent. Since surname exogamy was mandatory, women usually were married to men outside of their natal community. Villages and hamlets were often composed of large clusters of male kinsmen whose wives came from outside and whose sisters left the community at marriage. A different pattern was found in those areas where recurrent political upheavals, natural disasters, and/or the pressures of landlordism led to frequent population movement. There villages tended to be more heterogeneous in terms of surname, and women stood a better chance of remaining in their home communities after marriage. This was particularly true in the north and northwest.

Within the traditional system, women were essentially propertyless, save for the dowry goods they received at marriage. They did not inherit land or receive it as part of their dowry, and in poor families they often did not even receive a dowry. At all social levels women were the means through which to produce sons and continue the family (male) line. At all but the top social level, they also represented an input of labor to the household economy. Sometimes this was crucial, particularly in the southern rice area, and where tea, silk, cotton, or production of cloth constituted a major part of household income. In addition, women were responsible for domestic chores and child care. Their labor was under the direct control of male household heads or an older woman (mother-in-law, eldest sister-in-law) acting as a surrogate for male authority. Where women earned agricultural wages, these were paid directly to the household head. Women's powerlessness in the economic sphere was reflected in the customary inheritance rulings that gave widows only temporary control over household-owned land. They held it in trust for their minor sons, and as sometimes happened, the land reverted in use and ownership to the deceased husband's brothers or lineage cousins.

Along with lack of economic power went lack of social power. Women had little or no role to play in lineage organizations. They were lost to their lineage of birth when they married and were never fully incorporated into their husband's lineage until death, when they were commemorated as ancestors.

The land-reform program destroyed the landlords as a class, cut the power of the rich peasants, and undercut the base of lineage power and wealth by breaking up and redistributing lineage estates. These corporate forms of land ownership disappeared as land reverted to household ownership, although technically it was distributed to individuals. In many places, even though women received title to land, their status was not markedly changed. Their lands continued to be worked and administered by fathers, husbands, or sons. Isabel and David Crook, for example, comment that in the area of Hopei where they were, the individual land deeds were in the keeping of the male family head, who also controlled household finances. Women's consent was needed for selling the land, but it was difficult for women to exercise the right of withholding their consent (1966:242). Secondly, women often lacked the agricultural expertise needed to take over control of their newly received land. In some regions, women were not involved in agricultural labor at all, or they worked only at certain tasks during peak seasons (weeding, transplanting, harvesting). In a speech in 1947, Teng Ying-chao foresaw the problems that women would have during land reform (1949:40-46). She urged that there be training of women in all facets of production, including side occupations and handicrafts, but most importantly in all aspects of agricultural production as determined by the particular conditions of the area. This organized training for women does not seem to have been universal policy. Had it been, it would have made more realistic the exhortations to women to engage in production in order to win economic equality. As it was, many women remained untrained and unable to participate in agriculture. Their threat to withdraw their landholdings in the course of a divorce was a somewhat empty one: they might have been left economically helpless. The holdings of unmarried daughters were also treated as household property. The writings of the period are unclear about what would be done with a daughter's share when she married. Since marriages continued to be village-exogamous, the best she might do would be to "lease" her share to her father or brothers. However, we are talking about a short period of time. By 1952, with the formation of mutual-aid teams and lower-level cooperatives, a new situation emerged. What were essentially male groups pooled their household lands and labor resources into a larger work unit than the household.

Thirdly, during the land-reform period women were encouraged to participate and to throw off all remaining oppression. "Speaking bitterness" through the forum of the women's associations was at first difficult, but as it gained momentum and the criticisms targeted in on male oppression within the family, the women were persuaded to desist. Poor peasant men were in the forefront of the struggle for land reform. Attacks directed at them were thought by some to be a way of aiding the class enemy. Most of the early activists in the women's associations were women from poor peasant households: the husbands, fathers, or fathers-in-law of whom they complained were at the same time the activists in the revolutionary struggle, and as such, "erring comrades to be reasoned with" rather than the main oppressors (Crook, 1966:241). There may have been some truth in this, but it took the edge off criticisms of male-chauvinist thinking at that time.

With the development of collectives in the mid-1950s, a new situation emerged. Little property was retained by the household, and economic powers were vested in a larger group based for the most part on neighborhood and/or former social ties. This development created the conditions for a reconstitution of the localized lineage in ways neither planned nor anticipated. The lineage, minus its gentry/landlord/rich peasant leadership and stripped of religious functions, too often formed the basis of the new cooperative units. Together, a group of male kinsmen held usage rights over land, ponds, forests, orchards, livestock, and equipment. A woman usually became a member of her husband's team when she joined his residence at marriage. Many of the current small-production teams are still referred to by family name, except in multi-surname hamlets or in the case of specialized production teams that recruit across neighborhood boundaries.

With the work unit based on neighborhood, there is often no way to avoid the overlap with kinship ties. Nor is it necessarily undesirable. Ties of kinship, like ties of friendship, feed into cooperative efficiency and help meet the goal of greater productivity, assuming that kin loyalties do not override class awareness. That teams and brigades often have a kinship base is not a new observation. John Lewis, in his study of leadership, makes reference to this (1963:236-38). He presents a chart analysis of a production team in Hupei in which the team leader, the assistant leader in charge of field management, and the section leader guiding subsidiary occupations are all members of the Yang family of the same generation level, while two other men of the Yang family of another generation are in charge of livelihood and techniques. He further comments:

> In still another production team in Kiangsu which received national recognition in 1960, moreover, the team leader is Liu So-chin. His first elder brother is a secretary of the party branch, his second elder brother is a group work leader, his fourth younger brother is an "advanced worker" and his two sisters are Young Communist League members. For a team of 105 households, it is highly revealing that this single family has attained such a pervasive leadership position. The "proletarian" relationships among family members must be assumed to be of an order different from the strictly neutral relationships dictated by Communist ethics. Although a great deal of research is still required to demonstrate the prevalence of family-dominated leadership at the production levels, it is probable that at this level Confucian concepts of "relational leadership" have found considerable tacit support. (Ibid.:238)

The same frequency of "relational leadership" is evident also in Jan Myrdal's study (1965) where the sons, daughters, nephews, and other kin of Li Yueh-hua, the old Party secretary, hold positions of responsibility from the team level up to the commune. At the time of Myrdal's writing, a son and a daughter served with him on the management committee of the brigade. Another son was a team bookkeeper. Two nephews served as leader and member of the management committee of a second team within the brigade. Two others were in cadre posts at the commune level. The daughter and two of the nephews were Party members. The Li households came to the village as migrants in the 1930s, but most of the current residents are also migrants who came fleeing the famines of the late 1920s, the war, and the KMT White terror. In this situation, the Lis formed a significantly large solidarity block. They comprised seven or eight of the village's fifty households, including its most complex extended ones, easily outnumbering any other surname group in the brigade. But they by no means held a clear majority: cadre positions were filled by a range of surnames, while some Li family members held no positions of responsibility at all. However, in communities with more time-depth and stable population, a single surname group can dominate decision-making simply because they clearly outnumber any other contenders.

Nanwang village, cited as a model in the early days of cooperativization, is a case in point (Li Kai and Ching Shen, 1957:115-27). It is clearly a lineage village, and the three founders of the first cooperatives were Wang Yu-kun, Wang Hsiao-chi, and Wang Hsiao-pang—all poor peasants. They were joined by three upper-middle-peasant Wang households, which led to struggle between those who were from poor peasant households and those who were better off. On one occasion "some of the members wanted to elect Li Wu, a Party member [as chairman], but he [Wang Wen-shuang, an upper-middle peasant] made them elect Wang Tan-tan, who was politically backward and no good as a leader" (ibid.:120). The situation was eventually resolved successfully, with 85 percent of the village households being drawn into the cooperative under poor peasant leadership, but the struggle to put national and collective interests in first place and to be aware of class struggle still goes on in what is now Nanwang Village Production Brigade, according to recent reports (*Hung-chi*, March 1974).

The dangers resulting from the lack of attention to class struggle are not only the move backward to the individualistic "capitalist road," but a return to an even older order. The Kwangtang press in the early 1960s printed critiques of several production brigades in the region which were apportioning collective funds to repair the ancestral halls, paint new ancestral tablets, and rebuild local temples (Ting Chung, 1962).

Western scholars and Chinese commentators alike have made little connection between the patrilineal structure and lineage control of collective work units, and the difficulties of realizing the goal of full equality for women in the rural areas. The household in many rural teams and brigades remains embedded in a network of male kinsmen that has been strengthened by collectivization. To avoid this development, it would have been necessary to force massive transfers of the population, with all the attendant economic chaos and psychological suffering—clearly unfeasible and undesirable. The equalization of women's status has thus been held back by the necessities of the situation.

One of the results of the current structure is that team and brigade affiliations are seen as passing from father to sons. Women still are either in-marrying strangers who have to prove themselves or temporary residents who will soon be departing to get married. There is little incentive for the work unit to recommend girls over boys for higher education or specialized training, or to prepare them for increasing degrees of responsibility and leadership. Of course, there *are* some women in positions of leadership and responsibility. In the rural areas women are cited as making up anywhere from 10 percent to 37 percent of the cadres. But this figure includes those assigned to "women's work"—creche and nursery attendants, and the leaders of all-female small work groups within the team or brigade. When it comes to holding wider powers, including leadership over men, the number of women is small.

Moreover, the women who become leading cadres in the rural areas seem often to have led atypical lives. This assertion can be documented somewhat by the existent literature and by the small amounts of interviewing I was able to do over a two-month period in 1973 during a visit to China. In Myrdal's study, referred to earlier, the leading woman cadre was not only the daughter of the Party secretary and kinswoman to several other male cadres, but in addition she resided after marriage in her father's house while her husband worked in nearby Yenan city. In short, an atypical marriage allowed her to stay in the village of her birth and to advance politically. The Crooks' earlier study (1959:43) similarly points out that the first woman activist in the community had "the advantage over most married women of Ten-Mile Inn of being a native of the village." Contrary to local custom, she married a man from a nearby hamlet. Her daughter followed the same pattern, thus giving her a wide range of ties.

Matrilocal marriage obviously works in women's favor. But there are other atpyical patterns as well that produced cadres and activists. The first labor heroine in Ten-Mile Inn was an adopted daughter-in-law, brought in as a small child to be a future wife and treated as a household slave. When the Peasant Women's Association formed, she was the first to take her domestic grievances to them, and when they resolved her case successfully, she became one of the most active members. After years of humiliation, she set out to earn respect for herself by becoming a pacesetter in spinning and weaving (ibid.:73). The first head of the Peasant Women's Association was herself an adopted daughter-in-law in a family that had sunk into poverty. She worked in the fields at heavy labor, though this was not usual for women. Her husband died when she was thirty-six, and she had her first taste of independence. She became an active supporter of the anti-Japanese village government, an opera fan, and the only female member of the village music club. She even took up smoking in public. When the Peasant Women's Association formed, she "found herself pushed to the fore by the rather shy and timid members of the new organization because she was one of the few poor women who never feared to speak her mind" (ibid.:106).

The outstanding woman cadre of a village two miles from where the Crooks did their original study was separated even earlier in life from male authority. Her father died before she was born. She and her mother were thrown on their own resources, living as fuel gatherers and doing coolie labor. She was married at fifteen, but soon abandoned. At seventeen, she was completely on her own. Contacted as a representative of the poorest peasants by a Communist cadre, she sheltered her for two years, aided the anti-Japanese guerrilla forces, and at twenty-four became a Party member herself. The following year (1944) she became a labor heroine and was elected as head of her village's women's association. When her husband finally returned to the community, well after Liberation, she was already firmly established as a cadre, heading the first mutual-aid group in the village and later the first lower-level Agricultural Producers' Cooperative (Crook, 1966:16-19).

Moreover, as the Crooks indicate, the initial members of the Peasant Women's Association were recruited from among the poorest in the village. They were those who had suffered the most from both class oppression and male oppression. Some had been forced into prostitution. Others had been abandoned without any means of livelihood and either forced to find their own way or to take temporary husbands. Some were runaways from cruel husbands or unbearable household circumstances. Generally, they were seen as "disreputable" women by the middle peasants, including middle-peasant women who had led more conventional lives.

And there were still others whose lives took them beyond "Confucian morality" and male authority. C. K. Yang cites the case of the woman representative who in the old society was a "female sorcerer." She was a poor peasant woman who made a living through shamanistic séances in the old days. After Liberation she developed into an articulate and politically sophisticated cadre. Her earlier skills in human relations and her verbal abilities, Yang suggests, were invaluable assets. So was her class background, and even more so, her marginal position—since, "unlike economically more fortunate women, she had apparently not had a man to speak for her and thus had overcome *before* the revolution one of the traditional patterns of 'proper' behavior that restrained women from direct action" (1959:132). In short, she was not tied into the kinship system through marriage ties, but in order to survive had been forced to create a position of influence for herself—in this case, one where backing by supernatural authority would override male authority.

My own limited interviewing elicited a high percentage of similar life experiences. In Shashihyu Brigade, Tsunghwa County, the leading woman cadre and head of the women's association was a former adopted daughter-in-law who remained in the community after marriage. The leader of the crack women's work group of "Iron Wives" was village-born, and had married within the village to another cadre. In

Hsuhang Commune, near Shanghai, the leading woman cadre at the commune level was locally born and had moved back to her native village with her husband after many years of working in city industry. A second of the women's leaders was a former adopted daughter-in-law who at the time of Liberation demanded the right to free choice in marriage, in this case a young man living in the hamlet where she had been raised. Adopted daughters-in-law as cadres and activists in the over-forty age group also turned up at Ch'i-li-ying in Honan and elsewhere, as did women who had essentially made matrilocal marriages.

It is still unusual for women to stay in their home communities after marriage unless they are married to someone in the People's Liberation Army or a worker in the nearby city or county town. However, in the current birth-control campaigns, families are being urged to have no more than three children and to think about bringing in a son-in-law if all three should turn out to be girls. Joining your wife's residence no longer carries the stigma it did in the past, when it was an unfilial act that only the poorest men would agree to. Resettlement of educated youths in the countryside also widens the marriage pool and makes it possible for young women to remain in their home communities.

The adoption of child brides stopped at Liberation, as well it should, but in some areas it has had negative effects on the recruitment of women cadres in the younger generation of women. In some teams in Hsuhang, almost 70 percent of the women over forty had been adopted as small children, and in overall terms women's participation in political life was high (25 percent of the commune Party Committee and 30 percent of the commune Revolutionary Committee were women; and women led not only all of the all-women work teams, but some mixed work teams and one brigade). Yet there was concern about the absence of upcoming new cadres among the younger women. The teams, many of which were dominated by one surname group, were less willing to educate and train their own daughters. Brides were selected from outside the team, and often from outside the commune. Like departing daughters, the new brides lacked training and experience. They were also under pressure to produce sons during the early years of marriage. They were not in the work force full time for several years (although in this commune women were 55 percent of the agricultural work force and 40 percent of the industrial work force). Even when their children all reached school age, these women were ineligible for responsible posts because of their broken work records, their lesser participation in political work, their lack of experience, and their lack of special skills. When I visited, the women cadres were grappling with the problem of how to recruit new leadership from out of this younger group.

There remains the need to look at the problem in terms of ideology and the retention of traditional ways of thinking about women. The long legacy of second-class status is not that easily obliterated. In many areas, women are excused or even barred from doing agricultural work during menses: the reason given is that it would be detrimental to their health, but the underlying reason is that in traditional thinking, menstruating women were polluting and would affect the crops. This kind of thinking is still being struggled against.

The evaluation of the work that women do also reflects older thinking. Housework, for example, continues to go unrewarded and is defined as "nonwork." There is no payment for food preparation, cooking, child care, laundry, or clothing production unless it is done outside of the home in a team or brigade workshop. Moreover, these tasks are seen as women's responsibilities, particularly in the countryside. A recent article in the *Kuang-ming Daily* reflects the ambivalence toward sharing of household tasks:

> . . . due to the influence of feudalism and capitalism, there are still persons who tend to look down upon and discriminate against women. This has been reflected in many of their activities. Some of them merely pay lip service to the role of women who must shoulder half of the worldly responsibilities, while refusing to take any action to bring that role into full play. Others assign women cadres as much housework as possible, as if women are

> cut out only for household chores which they consider to be outside their own responsibility. (Lu Yuan, 1973)

That last line can only refer to husbands or male household heads, since housework is hardly "assigned" by the team, brigade, factory, or office unit. The article continues, in a somewhat compromising vein:

> It is true that after marriage, a woman must spend much of her time and energy on household chores. Yet a revolutionary woman certainly does not allow such chores to cut into her social responsibilities. Men comrades should *offer to share a portion* [italics mine] of the household chores from the standpoint of equality, to enable the women comrades to participate properly in socialist revolution and socialist construction. (Ibid.)

In short, household chores remain the responsibility of the woman: a man can choose to "help her with her work," but if he does not, the woman must still manage to find time to engage in political activity and productive labor. This may be a big step forward from saying women's place is in the home or that men have no responsibility for the management of the household, but it's still a long way from egalitarianism. In many households, the young wife's source of help is an older woman whose age and state of health precludes her participation in productive labor outside the home. This transfer has changed the daughter-in-law/mother-in-law relationship considerably, but it has not changed the relationship between men and women or improved the status of women.

Just as household tasks continue to be sex-typed, productive labor may continue to be assigned by sex. Throughout the work force there are now women doing jobs that were once thought of as "men's work." Some are exceptional cases such as aviators and high-tension powerline operators who stand as symbols for the promise that "anything male comrades can do, female comrades can do." In the countryside, women continue to be excluded from some jobs. To some degree this is necessary for the protection of pregnant women, for the convenience of those who are breast-feeding, or for older women whose feet were bound. But women are pregnant or breast-feeding for a relatively short span of years, and sometimes the division of labor by sex seems to reflect earlier role definitions and attitudes toward women.

A case in point is the report of an investigating team of the county Revolutionary Committee in Ch'i-tung county, Kiangsu (*Hung-ch'i*, March 1973). The team investigated a fishing village where 85 percent of the agricultural work force was women. As in pre-Liberation times, few or none were engaged in fishing. Tasks like soil loosening, weeding, fruit picking, and cotton trimming were assigned to women. Other tasks were regarded as only suitable for men:

> Some women have high enthusiasm and demand farm jobs which are beyond their capacity, and they are urged to think of the long-range interests and work realistically within their capacity. (Ibid.)

The article goes on to approve the example of a hard-working woman who was permanently removed from agricultural work and assigned to be an attendant in the creche after having an operation, and to explain that pregnant, lactating, and menstruating women were all excluded from transplanting work. Men were excluded from other things: "domestic work should be shared by men and women, but some household chores, such as looking after children, sewing, etc., should generally be done by women."

In some places, women have been insistent that they have the same capacities as men, or at least some of them do. There are teams of "Iron Girls" or "Iron Wives" that do heavy and difficult work or all phases of agricultural work and often take on more than the normal quota to prove their point. It seems to be easier to prove that point in the northern areas where women did little agricultural work prior to Liberation. Their relatively recent entry into the work force, doing "men's work" has raised their consciousness and that of the men as well. But in areas where some agricultural jobs were traditionally done by women, agricultural labor is more sex-typed and not always given equal payment.

Productive agricultural labor is rewarded by work points, converted into cash paid to the individual. There is a guiding principle of equal pay for equal work, and certainly some women earn as much as some men. But often, women are less productive and efficient in the same job. They work a shorter labor day in order to meet domestic responsibilities, and lose several work days a month during menses, which further reduces their income. Women's work groups often do tasks which receive a lower work-point evaluation in terms of effort or skills required. These tend to be jobs done by women before Liberation.

At Holo Brigade, near Wuxi, yearly income for women falls between 280 *yuan* and 360 *yuan*. Men's income ranges between 480 and 520. The women's income range reflects shorter work days, fewer work days per month, and sex-assigned tasks. The highest earners in the brigade are those in male work groups raising pond fish and cultivating pearls. Both men and women work in grain-production teams, but women work only twenty-five days of the month and receive lower work points for what they do. In the brigade-run embroidery shop, the women workers' points and earnings are determined not by the market value of what the shop produces, but what their husbands' or fathers' team accords them—these women earn between 6½ and 9 points a day, but never a full 10.

Impressionistically, it would seem, then, that where women continue to do the same productive jobs they did before Liberation, the demand for equal pay is less easily won. The value of women's work was adjudged long ago. Another, and admittedly extreme, example of this occurs in the tea brigades near Hangchow. The major income of the community stems from women's labor. Tea accounts for 90 percent of brigade income, with women engaged in tea picking eight months of the year and also doing most of the processing. Men work in forestry and rice production, which accounts for most of the remaining 10 percent. Yet a man's work day is given 10 points, while a woman's is worth 8. Accounting is done at the brigade level, rather than at the level of the production team, as is still the rule elsewhere. Since work points are unequal, almost every man in the brigade receives a higher cash income than any woman. If accounting were done at the team level, the all-women tea teams would be earning anywhere from eight to nine times more than the men. With the accounting at the brigade level, income could still be equal if women received the same number of work points. Instead, males, as a group, receive the difference between the wages of the actual producers and the market value of the item produced. I was told that this system followed the Tachai model: in form, yes, by accounting at the brigade level and thus equalizing team incomes; but in spirit, no. And one wonders whether the system would be so enthusiastically followed if the men's work produced a markedly more valuable product. Certainly that was not the case in our earlier example of Holo Brigade.

Of course, this is not an economic rip-off, as in the days when the landlord pocketed the difference between the market price of tea and the meager wages of his women day workers. It all becomes household income now, shared with spouse, children, and aged parents. But it's a political rip-off: despite their importance in production and being 51 percent of the work force, women are only 27 percent of the cadres in the brigade and commune committees, and 40 percent of the leaders and specialists at the small team levels.

However, the various failures to achieve total equality do not cancel out the tremendous progress that has been made. Chinese women, prior to Liberation, were victims of the most terrible kinds of oppression. They had no economic independence or access to education or political leadership. Today they come close to being half the work force. Even though they participate politically in lesser numbers than the ideal, it is a tremendous leap forward from their total powerlessness in traditional society. They have come a long way since 1949, and we should look at the recent developments that may serve to realize the goal of sex equality more completely.

One such development is the encouragement to move up to the brigade level of accounting, coupled with equalization of work points for all tasks (as in Tachai). This assures women of a potentially equal income. In addition, the move to the brigade as the major social unit beyond the household could lead to more rationalized decision-making about education and training of women for leadership. In multi-surname villages, a young woman may have to leave her parental team at marriage, but she will not always be leaving the brigade. The growth of commune industry, and commune- or brigade-sponsored work groups similarly take decisions about women out of the hands of the localized lineage.

A second development is the relocation of educated youths in the countryside. Some of these are permanent assignments, bringing in potential marriage partners. The educated young women are unlikely to accept a traditional role, and will serve also to spur people into reconsidering their expectations for their own daughters. And if the educated young men marry into the community, their wives will have more status and leverage than if they were coming as strangers into a new place.

Thirdly, there are the stirrings in the newly revived women's associations which were disbanded during the Cultural Revolution. Starting in 1972, they were reorganized and quickly became involved in educational projects, family planning, encouragement of women into production, and concern for the special needs of women. Starting in the summer of 1973, women's congresses were held at the county, regional, and municipal levels, and by late summer were beginning to convene at the provincial level.* The provincial congresses,

* It is improbable that the Chinese press and radio did not give more detail about the resolutions and speeches at these congresses. Our various government-sponsored monitoring services did not find the subject very important. *Daily Report,* for example, confined its efforts to translating only the speeches given by the high-ranking invited male guest at each opening session. One such appeared under the incredible lead line composed by someone at *Daily Report:* "XXX Lauds Distaff Role." Fortunately, he had done no such thing! And although the *Jen-Min-Jih-Pao* literally devoted pages to articles by, for, and about women during the first two weeks of March, the *Survey of the China Mainland Press*

each of which met for five or six days, dealt with such issues as implementation of the principle of equal pay for equal work, labor protection for women, sharing of housework, planned parenthood, encouragement of late marriage, greater participation of women in production, increasing the number of women cadres and bringing women into more political activity and study, recruitment of more women into the Party and the Young Communist League, attention to the special problems of educated young women resettling in the countryside, and criticism and struggle against the forces of old ideas and habits reflecting male-chauvinist thinking. Press reports available here unfortunately did not detail the resolutions that came out of these meetings, but one from the Hainan Administrative Region is perhaps indicative:

"There must be women Party members in each brigade by the end of this year and in each production team by the end of June next year" (*Daily Report*, October 18, 1973).

Also encouraging is the fusion of the woman question with the campaign to criticize Lin Piao and Confucius. Direct linkages still seem to be limited to the writings of women cadres and women's collectives, but they have been very much in evidence in the press since the onset of the mass movement. Since at least early January 1974, Lin Piao has been targeted as a spokesman and symbol for male-chauvinist thinking. He has been charged with slandering women as being "backward in thought and ideas" (*Kuang-ming-jih-pao*, January 14,

---

seems to have regarded them as just so many blank pages. Anyway, according to the radio monitoring done by *Daily Report*, from mid-July to the beginning of the Tenth Party Congress in late August, women's congresses were held in Kwangtung, Fukien, Kansu, Heilungkiang, Tibet, the Kwangsi-Chuang Autonomous Region, Chekiang, Szechuan, Yunnan, Shensi, Liaoning, Kiangsu, Kiangsi and various regions of Sinkiang. All of these made some linkage between Liu Shao-chi and the persistence of old ideas about women. After the Tenth Party Congress, there were meetings in Shanghai and Peking, Honan, Hunan, Kweichow, Hainan, and Inner Mongolia. I was not able to find reports for the remaining provinces. These later meetings added criticism of Lin Piao and study of the Tenth Party Congress documents to the discussion agendas.

1974), and with having said such things as "a woman cannot be expected to have a bright future" (Fu Wen, 1974), "a woman's future is determined by that of her husband," and "a woman must devote herself to her husband." He is accused of having urged a return to "loyalty, filial piety, chastity, and righteousness" (New China News Agency, March 8, 1974), in order to once again bind women with "reactionary, feudal ethics." He is also said to have stated that women "think only about how to get oil, salt, soy sauce, vinegar, and firewood" (NCNA, March 12, 1974). All of these attacks on mistaken ideas about women are, of course, part of a larger criticism of worship of the past and the desire to restore capitalism or even aspects of feudalism. The women's movement is strengthened by being a part of that wider criticism.

Also encouraging, but more muted in the anti-Confucian campaign, are the attacks on clan loyalties over class unity. Several articles have appeared discussing the experiences in the brigades in Chufu County, Shantung, which is the home of the K'ung lineage, the descendants of Confucius (NCNA, January 31, 1974; see also *Jen-Min-Jih-Pao*, March 1, 1974). Pointing to the problems of landlordism and exploitation in the old society that involved those of the same surname, and to the class struggle that continued after Liberation, the message of the articles is that "those of the same class are dear, not those of the same clan," and that historical experience proves the hypocrisy of the Confucian principles of "jen" and "I."

Class awareness versus clan loyalties appears in another context, one that praises women's political astuteness. In one such article the director of the commune women's association was singled out for commendation because when an unreformed landlord in her production brigade

> . . . used clan relations to corrode a cadre, she aroused *the masses of women* to struggle against him. She mobilized an elderly woman who had worked as a servant for the landlord in the old society to pour out her grievances and expose his crimes. This helped raise the women's consciousness of class struggle. (NCNA, March 7, 1974; italics added)

And who is better suited to do this than the women, who are outsiders to the male solidarity group and have no special interest in protecting clan privilege?

Merged also into the anti-Confucius campaign is discussion of the underlay of traditional religious beliefs that defined women as polluting agents either in agriculture or in the fishing industry (NCNA, February 27, March 10, March 11, 1974). The old taboos are criticized as a part of the doctrine of "male superiority," linked to Confucian thought even if not discussed in the Confucian classics.

At the same time, there is still reluctance within the anti-Confucian campaign to separate the issue of oppression of women as women, from the question of class struggle. In many, though by no means all, of the articles, Confucian ideas are said to have oppressed the "working women" (*lao-dung-fu-nu*), rather than women in general.

> For over two thousand years until Liberation, the working women were subjected to oppression by the reactionary political authority, clan authority, religious authority, and the authority of the husband and downtrodden at the lowest stratum of society. . . . The establishment of the socialist system in China has eliminated the class cause of oppression and exploitation of working women and liberated the masses of women politically, economically, and culturally. (*Jen-Min-Jih-Pao*, March 8, 1974; see also NCNA, February 22, 1974)

Undeniably, working women suffered the most: their oppression as women was an added element to their oppression as peasants and workers, to their oppression as youth in a gerontocracy. But one could argue that all women shared some of the same oppression because of the value assigned to gender. The oppression stemming from clan authority, religious authority, and the authority of the husband touched the lives of all but an exceptional handful. There were few Empress Dowagers through the two thousand years of history.

There are still other developments which are of positive value in raising the status of women. Birth-control methods are being actively promoted and increasingly adopted, thus giving women control over their own bodies and providing alternatives to motherhood as women's only or major role. Child-care facilities are expanding. And finally, there is the sincere concern with the problem of training and promoting more women cadres. The December 1973 issue of *Hung-ch'i* contained an article specifically on the need to train and recruit more women cadres and bring them into the Party. The same month an article in the *Jen-Min-Jih-Pao* on training of new cadres in Linhsi County, Hopei, pointed out that since the Ninth Party Congress half of the cadres promoted to commune and county posts have been women, and that at the production-brigade and team levels, 37 percent of the cadres are women (*Jen-Min-Jih-Pao,* December 12, 1973). Similarly, we might assume that the campaign in Hsinfang County, Kwangtung, is not an isolated case: there, over the past two years, some 209 women went through special training classes preparing them for positions at the commune and county levels, while another 3,720 attended commune-sponsored classes to enable them to move into lower-level posts (*Jen-Min-Jih-Pao,* October 9, 1973). Some of the educated youth resettled in the area were drawn into the educational work with women, particularly literacy classes to bring them up to the level where they could become involved in ideological study.

There is also sharp protest in the press when local situations are markedly out of line with government policy. Recently there was a letter in the *Kuang-Ming Daily* strongly criticizing the school system in the Kwangsi-Chuang Autonomous Region (*Kuang-Ming Daily,* September 21, 1973). The writer complained that in his/her commune only 12 percent of the teachers were women, none of whom were allowed to hold any positions of responsibility. Within the country, where women were between 20 percent and 30 percent of the teachers, only one had been given a responsible post as deputy director of the Revolutionary Leadership Group in a brigade primary school. The letter concluded by strongly urging more female representation, and investigation of the situation by responsible persons.

Looking at the overall situation some twenty-five years since Liberation, there is still cause for optimism. Although the changes have not been as far-reaching as some might have hoped, they are considerable, and recent developments are encouraging. The anti-Confucius movement is very complex and deals with a number of issues. The scholarly polemics on the Spring and Autumn Period, on the nature of slave society and the rise of feudalism, and on the meaning of Confucian terms and phrases are but one part of it. To the anthropologist's eye, there is more importance to the meetings and discussions going on in the countryside and in urban neighborhoods and work places. The past is not being discussed for its own sake, but because of its relevance to contemporary life, in this case its negative effects on the current scene. In relating this discussion to their own lives and experiences, it is conceivable that people's consciousness will be raised and further changes will occur. Some of those changes will have to be structural ones. Consciousness alone does not resolve the problem of realizing full equality for women, just as years of exposure to the concept of class struggle have not always led to success in breaking down the insularity of kinship groups and expanding the size of the cooperating group. There are still backward communes, like the one I visited near Canton, where almost every team represented a single surname group, each clearly separated from the others in residence clusters and guarding its own resources, and hesitant to pool some of its wealth into brigade projects and enterprises. The revolution is not yet completed, but one can hope that it will continue to move along the right path, breaking down the last vestiges of privilege and inherited power and doing away with outmoded social structures and and ideas whose origins go back to tribal society.

Bibliography

Aberle, David F. 1961. "Matrilineal Descent in Cross-cultural Perspective." In *Matrilineal Kinship*, edited by David M. Schneider and Kathleen Gough. Berkeley: University of California Press.

Adams, Richard N. 1967. *The Second Sowing: Power and Secondary Development in Latin America.* San Francisco: Chandler.

Ahora. 1971. "Agraria reforma," pp. 1-2.

Althusser, Louis. 1969. "Freud and Lacan." *New Left Review* 55: 48-65.

———, and Balibar, Etienne. 1970. *Reading Capital.* London: New Left Books.

Anderson, Tom; Gorelick, Arlene; and Rubin, Gayle. 1970. "Workers Paid Off in Thing Called Love." Unpublished manuscript.

Aries, P. 1962. *Centuries of Childhood.* London: Jonathan Cape.

Bachofen, Jacob J. 1967. *Myth, Religion, and Mother Right.* Translated by Ralph Manheim. Princeton: Princeton University Press.

Bailey, F. G., ed. 1971. *Gifts and Poison: The Politics of Reputation.* Oxford: Blackwell.

Bamberger, Joan. 1974. "The Myth of Matriarchy: Why Men Rule in Primitive Society." In *Women, Culture, and Society*, edited by Michelle Zimbalist Rosaldo and Louise Lamphere. Stanford, Calif.: Stanford University Press.

Bandura, A., Ross, D., and Ross, S. A. 1961. "The Transmission of Aggression Through Imitation of Aggressive Models." *Journal of Abnormal and Social Psychology* 63: 575-82.

Barry, H. H., Bacon, M. K., and Child, I. L. 1957. "A Cross-Cultural Survey of Some Sex Differences in Socialization." *Journal of Abnormal and Social Psychology* 55: 327-32.

Bartram, John. 1895. *Observations on the Inhabitants, Climate, Soil, Rivers, Productions, Animals, and Other Matters Worthy of Notice.* Reprint ed.: Geneva, N.Y.: W. F. Humphrey.

Bates, Daisy. 1938. *The Passing of the Aborigines.* London: John Murray.

Beauchamp, William M. 1900. "Iroquois Women." *Journal of American Folk-Lore* 13 (April-June): 81-91.

Benston, Margaret. 1969. "The Political Economy of Women's Liberation." *Monthly Review* 21, no. 4: 13-27.

Berger, Peter, and Luckmann, T. 1967. *The Social Construction of Reality.* Garden City, N.Y.: Doubleday Anchor.

Berndt, Ronald. 1962. *Excess and Restraint.* Chicago: University of Chicago Press.

Biesele, Megan. 1972. "A !Kung Bushman Folk Tale." *Botswana Notes and Records,* vol. 4. Gaborone: Botswana Society.

———. In press. "Religion and Folklore." In *The Bushmen,* edited by P. V. Tobias. Cape Town: Human and Rousseau.

———. In press. "Some Aspects of !Kung Folklore." In *Kalahari Hunter-Gatherers,* edited by R. B. Lee and Irven DeVore. Cambridge, Mass.: Harvard University Press.

Blake, Judith. 1961. *Family Structure in Jamaica.* New York: Free Press.

Bloch, M. 1961. *Feudal Society.* Chicago: University of Chicago Press.

Blok, Anton. 1974. "A Comment on Physical Strength and Social Power." Unpublished manuscript.

Borun, M. *et al.* (The Philadelphia Collective). 1971. *Women's Liberation: An Anthropological View.* Pittsburgh: Know, Inc.

Boserup, Ester. 1970. *Woman's Role in Economic Development.* New York: St. Martin's.

Briffault, Robert. 1927. *The Mothers: The Matriarchal Theory of Social Origins.* New York: MacMillan.

Brown, Judith K. 1970*a.* "Economic Organization and the Position of Women among the Iroquois." *Ethnohistory* 17, nos. 3-4: 131-67.

———. 1970*b.* "A Note on the Division of Labor by Sex." *American Anthropologist* 72: 1073-78.

Brown, Susan E. 1972. "Coping with Poverty in the Dominican Republic." Ph.D. dissertation, University of Michigan.

Buettner-Janusch, J. 1966. *Folia Primatologica 4;* cited in Thelma Rowell, *Social Behavior of Monkeys.* Baltimore: Penguin Books, 1972.

Bulmer, Ralph. 1969. "Political Aspects of the Moka Ceremonial Exchange System Among the Kyaka People of the Western Highlands of New Guinea." *Oceania* 31, no. 1: 1-13.

Carpenter, C. R. 1948. "Life in the Trees: The Behavior and Social Relations of Man's Closest Kin." In *A Reader in General Anthropology*, edited by C. Coon. New York: Henry Holt.

Carr, Lucien. 1887. "On the Social and Political Position of Woman Among the Huron-Iroquois Tribes." *Annual Report of the Trustees of the Peabody Museum of American Archaeology and Ethnology* 3: 207-32.

Chasseguet-Smirgel, J. 1970. *Female Sexuality*. Ann Arbor: University of Michigan Press.

Christian, William. 1972. *Person and God in a Spanish Valley*. New York: Seminar Press.

Clark, Alice. 1968. *Working Life of Women in the Seventeenth Century*. London: Frank Cass & Co.

Clark, Edith. 1966. *Land Tenure and the Family in Four Selected Communities in Jamaica*. London: George Allen and Unwin.

Cohen, Yehudi. 1969. "Ends and Means in Political Control: State Organization and the Punishment of Adultery, Incest, and the Violation of Celibacy." *American Anthropologist* 71: 4.

Coult, Allan D. 1965. *Cross Tabulations of Murdock's World Ethnographic Sample*. University of Missouri.

Crook, Isabel and David. 1959. *Revolution in a Chinese Village: Ten-Mile Inn*. New York: Humanities.

———. 1966. *The First Years of Yangyi Commune*. New York: Humanities.

Current Anthropology. 1968. Social Responsibilities Symposium. Reprint from December 1968 issue.

Dalla Costa, Mariarosa, and James, Selma. 1972. *The Power of Women and the Subversion of the Community*. Bristol: Falling Wall Press.

D'Andrade, Roy G. 1966. "Sex Differences and Cultural Institutions." In *The Development of Sex Differences*, edited by Eleanor Maccoby. Stanford, Calif.: Stanford University Press.

DANE (Departamento Administrativo Nacional de Estadistica). 1954. *Censo de Poblacion de 1951*. Bogota.

———. 1964. *Censo Agropecuario de 1960*. Bogota.

Davis, Elizabeth Gould. 1971. *The First Sex*. New York: G. P. Putnam.

Davis, J. 1969. "Town and Country." *Anthropological Quarterly* 42, no. 3.

de Beauvoir, Simone. 1953. *The Second Sex*. New York: Alfred Knopf.

Deloria, Vine Jr. 1969. *Custer Died for Your Sins: An Indian Manifesto*. New York: Macmillan.

Denich, Bette S. 1974. "Sex and Power in the Balkans." In *Women, Culture, and Society*, edited by Michelle Zimbalist Rosaldo and Louise Lamphere. Stanford, Calif.: Stanford University Press.

Derrida, Jacques. 1972. "Structure, Sign, and Play in the Discourse of the Human Sciences." In *The Structuralist Controversy*, edited by R. Macksey and E. Donato. Baltimore: Johns Hopkins Press.

Deutsch, Helene. 1948*a*. "The Significance of Masochism in the Mental Life of Women." In *The Psychoanalytic Reader*, edited by R. Fleiss. New York: International Universities Press.

———. 1948*b*. "On Female Homosexuality." In *The Psychoanalytic Reader*, edited by R. Fleiss. New York: International Universities Press.

Devereaux, George. 1937. "Institutionalized Homosexuality Among Mohave Indians." *Human Biology* 9:498-529.

DeVore, I., and Washburn, S. L. 1961. "Social Behavior of Baboons and Early Man." In *Social Life of Early Man*, edited by S. L. Washburn. Chicago: Aldine.

Diamond, Stanley. 1971. "The Rule of Law Versus the Order of Custom." In *The Rule of Law*, edited by Robert Wolff. New York: Simon & Schuster.

———. 1974. *In Search of the Primitive*. New Brunswick, N.J.: Transaction Books.

Diner, Helen. 1965. *Mothers and Amazons*. New York: Julian Press.

Dolhinow, Phyllis Jay, ed. 1971. *Primate Patterns: Studies in Adaptation and Variability*. New York: Holt, Rinehart, and Winston.

Douglas, Mary. 1963. *The Lele of Kasai*. London: Oxford University Press.

———. 1966. *Purity and Danger: An Analysis of Concepts of Pollution and Taboo*. New York: Praeger.

Draper, Patricia. 1972. "!Kung Bushmen Childhood." Ph.D. dissertation, Harvard University.

———. 1973. "Crowding Among Hunter-Gatherers: The !Kung." *Science* 182: 301-303.

———. In press. "Social and Economic Constraints on Child Life Among the !Kung." In *Kalahari Hunter-Gatherers*, edited by R. B. Lee and Irven DeVore. Cambridge, Mass.: Harvard University Press.

———. In preparation. "!Kung Subsistence Work at /Du/da: Variation in Adult Work Effort Among the !Kung."

Elkin, A. P. 1939. Introduction to Phyllis M. Kaberry, *Aboriginal Woman: Sacred and Profane*. London: Routledge and Kegan Paul.

Ember, Carol. 1972. "Residential Variation Among Hunter-Gatherers." Paper presented at the 71st Annual Meeting of the American Anthropological Association, Toronto, December 1972.

Engels, Frederick. 1891. *The Origin of the Family, Private Property, and the State.* 4th ed. Moscow: Foreign Languages Publishing House.

———. 1972. *The Origin of the Family, Private Property, and the State,* edited by Eleanor Leacock. New York: International Publishers.

Evans-Pritchard, E. E. 1951. *Kinship and Marriage Among the Nuer.* London: Oxford University Press.

———. 1970. "Sexual Inversion Among the Azande." *American Anthropologist* 72: 1428-34.

Faithorn, Elizabeth. In press. "Women as Persons: Aspects of Female Life and Male-Female Relations Among the Káfe." In *Sex Roles in the New Guinea Highlands,* edited by Paula Brown Glick and Philip Newman. Special issue of *Anthroplogical Studies.*

Fee, Elizabeth. 1973. "The Sexual Politics of Victorian Social Anthropology." *Feminist Studies* (Winter/Spring): 23-29.

Fenton, William N. 1957*a*. "Long-term Trends of Change Among the Iroquois." Proceedings of the 1957 Annual Spring Meetings of the American Ethnological Society. Seattle.

———. 1957*b*. "Seneca Indians by Asher Wright (1859)." *Ethnohistory* 4 (Summer): 302-21.

———. 1969. "J.-F. Lafitau (1681-1746), Precursor of Scientific Anthropology." *Southwestern Journal of Anthropology* 25 (Summer): 173-87.

Firestone, Shulamith. 1970. *The Dialectic of Sex: The Case for Feminist Revolution.* New York: Bantam.

Ford, Clellan, and Beach, Frank. 1972. *Patterns of Sexual Behavior.* New York: Harper.

Foucault, Michel. 1970. *The Order of Things.* New York: Pantheon.

Fox, Robin. 1967. *Kinship and Marriage.* London: Pelican Books.

Frazier, E. Franklin. 1939. *The Negro Family in the United States.* Chicago: University of Chicago Press.

Freud, Sigmund. 1932. "Concerning the Sexuality of Women." *Psychoanalytic Quarterly* 1: 191-209.

———. 1943. *A General Introduction to Psychoanalysis.* Garden City, N.Y.: Garden City Publishing Company.

———. 1961*a*. "Some Psychical Consequences of the Anatomical Distinction Between the Sexes." In *The Complete Works of Sigmund*

Freud, vol. 19, edited by J. Strachey. London: Hogarth.

———. 1961*b*. "Female Sexuality." In *The Complete Works of Sigmund Freud*, vol. 21, edited by J. Strachey. London: Hogarth.

———. 1965. "Femininity." In *New Introductory Lectures in Psychoanalysis*, edited by J. Strachey. New York: W. W. Norton.

Friedan, Betty. 1963. *The Feminine Mystique*. New York: W. W. Norton.

Friedl, Ernestine. 1967. "The Position of Women: Appearance and Reality." *Anthropological Quarterly* 40, no. 3: 97-108.

Fu Wen. 1974. "Doctrine of Confucius and Mencius—The Shackle That Keeps Women in Bondage." *Peking Review* 17, no. 10 (March 18): 16-18.

Gale, Fay, ed. 1970. *Woman's Role in Aboriginal Society*. Australian Aboriginal Studies No. 36. Canberra: Australian National Institute of Aboriginal Studies.

Gardiner, Jean. 1974. "Political Economy of Female Labor in Capitalist Society." Unpublished manuscript.

Garfinkel, Harold. 1960. "The Rational Properties of Scientific and Common Sense Activities." *Behavioral Science* 5, no. 1: 72-83.

Gason, S. 1879. "The Dieri." In *The Folklore, Manners, Customs and Languages of the South Australian Aborigines*, edited by G. Taplin. Adelaide: E. Spiller.

Gerstein, Ira. 1973. "Domestic Work and Capitalism." *Radical America* 7, nos. 4 and 5: 101-28.

Glasse, R. M. 1971. "The Mask of Venery." Paper read at the 70th Annual Meeting of the American Anthropological Association, New York City, December 1971.

Gluckman, Max. 1963. "Gossip and Scandal." *Current Anthropology* 4, no. 3: 307-16.

Goldenweiser, Alexander A. 1912. "On Iroquois Work, 1912." *Summary Report of the Geological Survey of Canada*, Anthropology Division, sessional paper 26, pp. 464-75. Ottawa: Government Printing Bureau.

———. 1914. "On Iroquois Work, 1913-1914." *Summary Report of the Geological Survey of Canada*, Anthropology Division, pp. 365-73. Ottawa: Government Printing Bureau.

Gonzalez, Nancie L. 1969. *Black Carib Household Structure*. Seattle: University of Washington Press.

Goodale, Jane C. 1971. *Tiwi Wives*. Seattle: University of Washington Press.

———, and Chowning, Ann. 1971. "The Contaminating Woman."

Paper read at the 70th Annual Meeting of the American Anthropological Association.

Goodall, Jane Van Lawick. 1965. "Chimpanzees of the Gombe Stream Reserve." In *Primate Behavior*, edited by I. DeVore. New York: Holt, Rinehart, and Winston.

Goody, Jack, and Tambiah, S. J. 1973. *Bridewealth and Dowry*. Cambridge, England: Cambridge University Press.

Gough, Ian. 1972. "Marx and Productive Labour." *New Left Review* 76: 47-72.

Gough, Kathleen. 1959. "The Nayars and the Definition of Marriage." *Journal of the Royal Anthropological Institute* 89: 23-24.

———. 1961. "The Modern Disintegration of Matrilineal Descent Groups." In *Matrilineal Kinship*, edited by David M. Schneider and Kathleen Gough. Berkeley: University of California Press.

———. 1971. "The Origin of the Family." *Journal of Marriage and the Family* 33 (November): 760-71.

———. 1972. "An Anthropologist Looks at Engels." In *Woman in a Man-Made World*, edited by Nona Glazer-Malbin and Helen Youngelson Waehrer. Chicago: Rand McNally.

Gribble, E. R. 1940. *Forty Years with the Aborigines*. Sydney: Angus & Robertson.

Guzman, G., *et al.* 1963. *La Violencia en Colombia*. Ediciones Tercer Mundo.

Hackett, Amy, and Pomeroy, Sarah. 1973. "Making History: The First Sex." *Feminist Studies* 1, no. 2: 97-108.

Hamburg, David A., and Lunde, Donald T. 1966. "Sex Hormones in the Development of Sex Differences in Behavior." In *The Development of Sex Differences*, edited by Eleanor E. Maccoby. Stanford, Calif.: Stanford University Press.

Hamilton, Annette. 1970. "The Role of Women in Aboriginal Marriage Arrangements." In *Woman's Role in Aboriginal Society*. Australian Aboriginal Studies No. 36. Canberra: Australian Institute of Aboriginal Studies.

Hamilton, John P. 1827. *Travels Through the Interior Provinces of Colombia*. 2 vols. London.

Hannerz, Ulf. 1969. *Soulside: Inquiries into Ghetto Culture and Community*. New York: Columbia University Press.

Harpending, Henry. 1972. "!Kung Hunter-Gatherer Population Structure." Ph.D. dissertation, Harvard University.

———. In press. "Genetic and Demographic Variation in !Kung Populations." In *Kalahari Hunter-Gatherers*, edited by R. B. Lee and Irven DeVore. Cambridge, Mass.: Harvard University Press.

Harrison, Jane Ellen. 1962. *Epilegomena to the Study of Greek Religion and Themes.* New York: University Books.

Hart, C. W. M., and Pilling, Arnold R. 1960. *The Tiwi of North Australia.* New York: Holt, Rinehart, and Winston.

Hefner, Robert. 1974. "The *Tel Quel* Ideology: Material Practice Upon Material Practice." *Substance* 8: 127-38.

Henriques, Fernando. 1954. *Family and Colour in Jamaica.* London: Eyre and Spottiswoode.

Herskovitz, Melville. 1937. "A Note on 'Woman Marriage' in Dahomey." *Africa* 10, no. 3: 335-41.

Hertz, Robert. 1960. *Death and the Right Hand.* Glencoe: Free Press.

Hewitt, John N. B. 1933. "Status of Woman in Iroquois Policy Before 1784." *Annual Report of the Board of Regents of the Smithsonian Institution for 1932*, pp. 475-88. Washington: U.S. Government Printing Office.

Hiatt, Betty. 1970. "Woman the Gatherer." In *Woman's Role in Aboriginal Society.* Australian Aboriginal Studies No. 36. Canberra: Australian Institute of Aboriginal Studies.

Hill, C. 1958. *Puritanism and Revolution.* London: Secker & Warberg.

Hockett, Charles F., and Ascher, Robert. 1968. "The Human Revolution." In *Man in Adaptation: The Biosocial Background*, edited by Yehudi A. Cohen. Chicago: Aldine Press.

Horney, Karen. 1973. "The Denial of the Vagina." In Karen Horney, *Feminine Psychology.* Edited by Harold Kelman. New York: W. W. Norton.

Howell, Nancy. In press. "The Population of the Dobe Area !Kung." In *Kalahari Hunter-Gatherers*, edited by R. B. Lee and Irven DeVore. Cambridge, Mass.: Harvard University Press.

———. In press. "The Feasibility of Demographic Studies of Anthropological Populations." In *Method and Theory in Anthropological Genetics*, edited by Michael Crawford and Peter Workman. Albuquerque: University of New Mexico Press.

Hsu Kwang. 1974. "Women's Liberation Is a Component Part of the Proletarian Revolution." *Peking Review* 7, no. 10 (March 18): 12-15.

Hudson, Susan. 1971. "Social Ranking in a French Alpine Village." In *Gifts and Poison*, edited by F. G. Bailey. Oxford: Basil Blackwell.

Hultkrantz, Ake. 1961. "Bachofen and the Mother Goddess: An Appraisal After One Hundred Years." *Ethnos* 26: 75-85.

Hung-ch'i. March 1973. Investigating Team of the County Revolutionary Committee, Ch'i-tung County, Kiangsu, "Bring into Fuller Play the Role of Women as a Labor Force"; translated in *Survey of China Mainland Magazines 1973-1974*, pp. 51-54.

———. March 1974. Party Branch, Nan Wang Village Production Brigade, Anping County, Hopei, "Lienxi Luxian Doujeng: Shiji Pi Lin Pi Kung," pp. 45-57.

Hymes, Dell, ed. 1972. *Reinventing Anthropology*. New York: Random House.

Ingliss, Gordon. 1970. "Northwest American Matriliny: The Problem of Origins." *Ethnology* 9 (April): 149-59.

Jakobson, Roman, and Halle, Morris. 1971. *Fundamentals of Language*. The Hague: Mouton.

Jen-Min-Jih-Pao. October 9, 1973. "CCP Committee of Hsinfeng County, Kwangtung, Actively Help Women Cadres Improve Their Leadership." Translated in *Daily Report* 1, no. 214 (November 6, 1973).

———. December 12, 1973. Reporting Unit, Linhsi Hsien Revolutionary Committee, "Training of New Cadres." Translated in *SCMP*, January 9, 1974.

———. March 8, 1974. Editorial for International Women's Day. NCNA English release, Peking.

Jenness, Diamond. 1932. *The Indians of Canada*. Bulletin no. 65 of the National Museum of Canada, Ottawa.

Jones, Ernest. 1933. "The Phallic Phase." *International Journal of Psychoanalysis* 14: 1-33.

Kaberry, Phyllis M. 1939. *Aboriginal Woman: Sacred and Profane*. London: Routledge and Kegan Paul.

Kagen, Jerome, and Moss, H. A. 1962. *From Birth to Maturity*. New York: John Wiley and Sons.

Kaplan, David, and Manners, Robert A. 1972. *Culture Theory*. Englewood Cliffs, N.J.: Prentice-Hall.

Katz, Richard. In press. "Education and Transcendence: Trance-Curing with the Zhun/wasi." In *Kalahari Hunter-Gatherers*, edited by R. B. Lee and Irven DeVore. Cambridge, Mass.: Harvard University Press.

Kelly, Raymond. 1974. "Witchcraft and Sexual Relations: An Exploration of the Social and Semantic Implications of the Structure of Belief." Paper read at the 73rd Annual Meeting of the American Anthropological Association, Mexico City.

Kephart, Jane. 1970. "Primitive Woman as Nigger, or, The Origin of the Human Family as Viewed Through the Role of Women." M.A. dissertation, University of Maryland.

Konner, M.J. 1972. "Aspects of Developmental Ethnology of a Foraging People." In *Ethnological Studies of Child Behavior*, edited by N. Burton Jones. Cambridge, England: Cambridge University Press.

———. In press. "Maternal Care, Infant Behavior and Development Among the !Kung Bushmen." In *Kalahari Hunter-Gatherers*, edited by R. B. Lee and Irven DeVore. Cambridge, Mass: Harvard University Press.

Kuang-Ming Daily. September 21, 1973. Translated in *Daily Report* 1, no. 203 (October 19, 1973).

Kuang-ming-jih-pao. January 14, 1974. "Women Can Prop Up Half of Heaven." Translated in *SCMP*, February 4-8, 1974.

Kummer, Hans. 1968. *Social Organization of Hamadryas Baboons*. Chicago: University of Chicago Press.

Lacan, Jacques. 1968. "The Function of Language in Psychoanalysis." In Anthony Wilden, *The Language of Self*.

———. 1970. "The Insistence of the Letter in the Unconscious." In *Structuralism*, edited by J. Ehrmann. Garden City, N.Y.: Doubleday Anchor.

———. n.d. "The Signification of the Phallus." Translated by Larry Shields and Rayna Reiter. Unpublished manuscript.

Lafitau, Joseph F. 1724. *Moeurs des sauvages ameriquains, comparées aux moeurs des premiers temps*. 4 vols. Paris: Saugrain l'aîné.

Lampl de Groot, Jeanne. 1933. "Problems of Femininity." *Psychoanalytic Quarterly* 2: 489-518.

———. 1948. "The Evolution of the Oedipus Complex in Women." In *The Psychoanalytic Reader*, edited by R. Fleiss. New York: International Universities Press.

Landes, Ruth. 1938. *The Ojibwa Woman: Male and Female Life Cycles Among the Ojibwa Indians of Western Ontario*. Reprint ed.: New York: W. W. Norton, 1971.

Landy, David. 1959. *Tropical Childhood*. Chapel Hill, N.C.: University of North Carolina Press.

Langness, L. L. 1967. "Sexual Antagonism in the New Guinea Highlands: A Bena Bena Example." *Oceania* 37, no. 3: 161-77.

Larguia, Isabel, and Dumoulin, John. 1972. "Towards a Science of Women's Liberation." *NACLA Newsletter* 6, no. 10: 3-20.

Lasch, Christopher. 1974. "Freud and Women." *New York Review of Books* 21, no. 15: 12-17.

Lattimore, Owen. 1957. *Inner Asian Frontiers of China*. New York: Capitol Publishers.

Leach, Edmund. 1971. *Rethinking Anthropology*. New York: Humanities Press.

Leacock, Eleanor. 1972. Introduction to Frederick Engels, *The Origins of the Family, Private Property, and the State*, edited by Eleanor Leacock. New York: International Publishers.

Leavitt, Ruby R. 1972. "Women in Other Cultures." In *Woman in Sexist Society: Studies in Power and Powerlessness*, edited by Vivian Gornick and Barbara Moran. New York: New American Library.

Lee, R. B. 1965. "Subsistence Ecology of !Kung Bushmen." Ph.D. dissertation, University of California, Berkeley.

———. 1968*a*. "The Sociology of !Kung Bushman Trance Performances." In *Trance and Possession States*, edited by Raymond H. Prince. Montreal: R. M. Bucke Memorial Society.

———. 1968*b*. "What Do Hunters Do for a Living, or, How to Make Out on Scarce Resources." In *Man the Hunter*, edited by R. B. Lee and Irven DeVore. Chicago: Aldine.

———. 1969. "Eating Christmas in the Kalahari." *Natural History* 78.

———. 1972. "Population Growth and the Beginnings of Sedentary Life among the !Kung Bushmen." In *Population Growth: Anthropological Implications*, edited by Brian Spooner. Cambridge, Mass.: MIT Press.

———. In press. "Male-Female Residence Arrangements and Political Power in Human Hunter-Gatherers." Paper presented at the workshop in "Male-Female Behavior Patterns in Primate Societies" at the IV International Congress of Primatology. To appear as a special issue of *Archives of Sexual Behavior*, edited by Jane B. Lancaster.

Lee, Richard, and DeVore, Irven. 1968. "Problems in the Study of Hunters and Gatherers." In *Man the Hunter*, edited by R. B. Lee and Irven DeVore. Chicago: Aldine.

Lee, R. B. and DeVore, Irven, eds. 1968. *Man the Hunter*. Chicago: Aldine.

LeVine, Robert A., and LeVine, Barbara. 1963. "Nyansongo: A Gusii Community." In *Six Cultures*, edited by Beatrice Whiting. New York: John Wiley.

Lévi-Strauss, Claude. 1965. "The Future of Kinship Studies." *Proceedings of the Royal Anthropological Institute*, pp. 13-22.

———. 1969. *The Elementary Structures of Kinship*. Boston: Beacon Press.

———. 1970. *The Savage Mind*. Chicago: University of Chicago Press.

———. 1971. "The Family." In *Man, Culture, and Society*, edited by H. Shapiro. London: Oxford University Press.

Lewin, Ellen, *et al.* 1971. "Power Strategies and Sex Roles." Paper presented at the 70th Annual Meeting of the American Anthropological Association.

Lewis, A. 1965. *The Development of Southern French and Catalan Society*. Austin: University of Texas Press.

Lewis, Diane. 1973. "Anthropology and Colonialism." *Current Anthropology* 14: 581-602.

Lewis, John. 1963. *Leadership in Communist China*. Ithaca: Cornell University Press.

Lewis, Oscar. 1966. *La Vida: A Puerto Rican Family in the Culture of Poverty: San Juan and New York*. New York: Random House.

Li Kai and Ching Shen. 1957. "The Road for Five Hundred Million Peasants." In *Socialist Upsurge in China's Countryside*, edited by Mao Tse-tung. Peking: Foreign Languages Press.

Lindenbaum, Shirley. 1972. "Sorcerers, Ghosts, and Polluting Women: An Analysis of Religious Belief and Population Control." *Ethnology* 11, no. 3: 241-53.

———. 1973. "A Wife Is the Hand of Man." Paper read at the 72nd Annual Meeting of the American Anthropological Association.

Livingstone, Frank. 1969. "Genetics, Ecology, and the Origins of Incest and Exogamy." *Current Anthropology* 10, no. 1: 45-49.

Loskiel, George H. 1794. *History of the Mission of the United Brethren Among the Indians in North America*. Translated by Christian LaTrobe. London: The Brethren's Society for the Furtherance of the Gospel.

Lowie, Robert H. 1961. *Primitive Society*. New York: Harper.

Lu Yuan. 1973. "Hail to Them for Shouldering Half of the Worldly Responsibilities." *Kuang-ming Daily*, July 8, 1973. Translated in *Daily Report* 1, no. 180 (August 3, 1973).

Maccoby, Eleanor E. and Jacklin, Carol N. 1974. *The Psychology of Sex Differences*. Stanford, Calif.: Stanford University Press.

Mafeje, Archie. 1971. "The Ideology of Tribalism." *Journal of Modern African Studies* 9: 253-61.

Malinowski, Bronislaw. 1913. *The Family Among the Australian Aborigines*. London: University of London Press.

———. 1929. *The Sexual Life of Savages*. London: Routledge and Kegan Paul.

———. 1970. "The Primitive Economics of the Trobriand Islanders." In *Cultures of the Pacific*, edited by T. Harding and B. Wallace. New York: Free Press.

Maples, William R. 1971. "Farming Baboons." Paper presented at the 1971 Meeting of the American Association of Physical Anthropologists, Boston, Mass.

Marmor, Judd. 1965. *Sexual Inversion*. London: Basic Books.

Marshall, John. 1958. "Hunting Among the Kalahari Bushmen." *Natural History* 67: 291-309; 376-95.

———. n.d. "The Hunters," "An Argument About Marriage," "Nlum Tchi," "N!owa T'ama: The Melon Tossing." Film Study Center, Peabody Museum, Harvard University.

Marshall, Lorna. 1957. "The Kin Terminology System of the !Kung Bushman." *Africa* 27: 1-25.

———. 1957. "N!ow." *Africa* 27: 232-40.

———. 1959. "Marriage Among !Kung Bushmen." *Africa* 29: 335-65.

———. 1960. "!Kung Bushman Bands." *Africa* 30: 323-55.

———. 1961. "Sharing, Talking and Giving." *Africa* 31: 231-52.

———. 1962. "!Kung Bushman Religious Beliefs." *Africa* 32: 221-52.

———. 1965. "The !Kung Bushmen of the Kalahari Desert." In *Peoples of Africa*, edited by James L. Gibbs. New York: Holt, Rinehart, and Winston.

Marx, Karl. 1969. *Theories of Surplus Value*, Part I. Moscow: Progress Publishers.

———. 1971*a*. *Pre-Capitalist Economic Formations.* New York: International Publishers.

———. 1971*b*. *Wage-Labor and Capital.* New York: International Publishers.

———. 1972. *Capital*, vol. 1. New York: International Publishers.

Mauss, Marcel. 1967. *The Gift.* New York: W. W. Norton.

McMurtrie, Douglas. 1914. "A Legend of Lesbian Love Among North American Indians." *Urologic and Cutaneous Review* (April): 192-93.

Mead, Margaret. 1935. *Sex and Temperament in Three Primitive Societies.* New York: William Morrow.

———. 1950. *Male and Female: A Study of the Sexes in a Changing World.* New York: Morrow.

Meggitt, M. J. 1964. "Male-Female Relationships in the Highlands of Australian New Guinea." *American Anthropologist* 66, no. 4, part 2: 204-24.

Mehlman, Jeffrey. 1972. *French Freud: Structural Studies in Psychoanalysis.* New Haven: Yale French Studies # 48.

Milliken, Charles. 1924. "A Biographical Sketch of Mary Jemison, the White Woman of the Genesee." *Researches and Transactions of the New York State Archaeological Association* (Lewis H. Morgan Chapter, Rochester, New York) IV, no. 3: 81-101.

Milton, Nancy. 1973. "A Response to 'Women and Revolution.' " In *Women in China*, edited by Marilyn Young. Michigan Papers in Chinese Studies No. 15. Ann Arbor: University of Michigan Center for Chinese Studies.

Minturn, L., and Hitchcock, John T. 1963. "The Rajputs of Khalapur, India." In *Six Cultures*, edited by Beatrice Whiting. New York: John Wiley.

Mitchell, Juliet. 1971. *Women's Estate*. New York: Vintage.

———. 1974. *Psychoanalysis and Feminism*. New York: Pantheon.

Money, John and Ehrhardt, Anke A. 1972. *Man and Woman, Boy and Girl*. Baltimore: Johns Hopkins University Press.

Montagu, M. F. Ashley. 1937. *Coming into Being Among the Australian Aborigines*. London: Routledge.

Moore, B. 1966. *Social Origins of Dictatorship and Democracy*. Boston: Beacon Press.

Morgan, Lewis H. 1954. *The League of the Ho-De'No-Sau-Nee, Iroquois*. Human Relations Area Files.

———. 1962. *League of the Iroquois*. New York: Corinth Books.

———. 1963. *Ancient Society*. Edited by Eleanor Leacock. Cleveland: World Publishing Co.

———. 1965. *Houses and House-Life of the American Aborigines*. Chicago: University of Chicago Press.

Morin, E. 1970. *The Red and the White*. New York: Pantheon.

Morris, Desmond. 1967. *The Naked Ape*. New York: McGraw Hill.

Moynihan, Daniel P. 1965. *The Negro Family: The Case for National Action*. U.S. Department of Labor, Office of Policy Planning and Research. Washington, D.C.: U.S. Government Printing Office.

Murdock, George P. 1934. *Our Primitive Contemporaries*. New York: The Macmillan Co.

———. 1949. *Social Structure*. New York: The Macmillan Co.

———. 1957. "World Ethnographic Sample." *American Anthropologist*.

———. 1967. *Ethnographic Atlas: A Summary. Ethnology* 6, no. 2: 109-236.

Murphy, Robert. 1959. "Social Structure and Sex Antagonism." *Southwestern Journal of Anthropology* 15, no. 1: 81-96.

Myrdal, Jan. 1965. *Report from a Chinese Village*. New York: Pantheon.

NCNA (New China News Agency). January 31, 1974. "Former Tenants of Confucius' Descendants Denounce Lin Piao." English release, Peking.

———. February 22, 1974. "Women Alternate Members of Party Central Committee Criticize Lin Piao, Confucius." English release, Peking.

———. February 27, 1974. "East China Peasant Women Criticize Lin Piao, Confucius." English release, Nanking.

———. March 7, 1974. "Central China Region Actively Trains Women Cadres." English release, Changsha.

———. March 8, 1974. "Tachai Women Criticize Lin Piao and Confucius." English release, Peking.

———. March 10, 1974. Interview with all-woman fishing team in Shantung. English release, Tsinan.

———. March 11, 1974. "Chinese Fisherwomen Criticize Lin Piao's Contempt for Women's Notions as Reactionary." English release, Shenyang.

———. March 12, 1974. "Woman Oil Tender Goes to College." English release, Peking.

Noon, John A. 1949. *Law and Government of the Grand River Iroquois.* Viking Fund Publications in Anthropology 12. New York: Viking Fund.

Oakley, Ann. 1973. *Sex, Gender, and Society*. New York: Harper & Row.

Oliver, Pamela Elaine. 1972. "Women and Men in Social Exchange: A Cross-Cultural Study." Master's thesis, University of North Carolina, Chapel Hill.

Ortner, Sherry B. 1974. "Is Female to Male as Nature Is to Culture?" In *Woman, Culture, and Society*, edited by Michelle Zimbalist Rosaldo and Louise Lamphere. Stanford, Calif.: Stanford University Press.

Parker, Arthur C. 1910. *Iroquois Uses of Maize and Other Food Plants.* New York State Museum Bulletin 144. Albany: University of the State of New York.

———. 1913. *The Code of Handsome Lake, the Seneca Prophet.* New York State Museum Bulletin 163. Albany: University of the State of New York.

———. 1916. *The Constitution of the Five Nations.* New York State Museum Bulletin 184. Albany: University of the State of New York.

———. 1926. "An Analytical History of the Seneca Indians." *Researches and Transactions of the New York State Archaeological Association* (Lewis H. Morgan Chapter, Rochester, N.Y.) VI, nos. 1-4: 1-162.

Patai, Daphne. 1974. "Utopias." *Aphra* 5, no. 3: 2-16.

Peña, Silvio H. 1970. "Dudan ricos retormen al pais." *El Nacional*, June 11.

Peterson, Nicolas. 1970. "The Importance of Women in Determining the Composition of Residential Groups in Aboriginal Australia." In *Woman's Role in Aboriginal Society*. Australian Aboriginal Studies No. 36. Canberra: Australian Institute of Aboriginal Studies.

Pitt-Rivers, J. A. 1961. *The People of the Sierra*. Chicago: University of Chicago Press.

Plath, Sylvia. 1965. *Ariel*. New York: Harper and Row.

Quain, B. H. 1961. "The Iroquois." In *Cooperation and Competition among Primitive Peoples*, edited by Margaret Mead. Boston: Beacon Press.

Randle, Martha C. 1951. *Iroquois Women, Then and Now*. Bulletin of the Bureau of American Ethnology 149: 167-80. Washington.

Rappaport, Roy, and Buchbinder, Georgeda. In press. "Fertility and Death Among the Maring." In *Sex Roles in the New Guinea Highlands*, edited by Paula Brown and G. Buchbinder. Cambridge, Mass.: Harvard University Press.

Read, Kenneth. 1952. "The Nama Cult of the Central Highlands, New Guinea." *Oceania* 23, no. 1: 1-25.

———. 1965. *The High Valley*. New York: Charles Scribner's Sons.

Reay, Marie. 1959. *The Kuma*. London: Cambridge University Press.

Reed, Evelyn. 1972. *Is Biology Women's Destiny?* New York: Pathfinder Press.

———. 1972. "Engels and Women's Liberation." *International Socialist Review* 33, no. 4.

Reisman, Paul. 1972. *New York Times Book Review*, October 22, p. 7.

Remy, Dorothy. 1968. "Social Networks and Patron-Client Relations: Ibadan Market Women." Unpublished manuscript.

———, and Weeks, John. 1973. "Employment and Inequality in a Nonindustrial City." In *Employment in Emerging Societies*, edited by Karl Wohlmuth. New York: Praeger.

Remy Weeks, Dorothy. 1973. "Adaptive Strategies of Men and Women in Zaria, Nigeria: Industrial Workers and Their Wives." Ph.D. dissertation, University of Michigan.

Richards, Audrey I. 1950. "Some Types of Family Structure Amongst the Central Bantu." In *African Systems of Kinship and Marriage*, edited by A. R. Radcliffe-Brown and Daryll Forde. New York: Oxford University Press.

Richards, Cara B. 1957. "Matriarchy or Mistake: The Role of Iroquois Women Through Time." *Proceedings of the 1957 Annual Spring Meeting of the American Ethnological Society*, pp. 36-45. Seattle.

Rippy, J. Fred. 1931. *The Capitalists and Colombia*. New York.

Rogers, Susan. 1973. "Female Forms of Power and the Myth of Male Dominance: A Model of Female/Male Interaction." Unpublished manuscript.

Róheim, Géza. 1933. "Women and Their Life in Central Australia." *Journal of the Royal Anthropological Institute* 63.

Rosaldo, Michelle Zimbalist, and Lamphere, Louise, eds. 1974. *Woman, Culture, and Society*. Stanford, Calif.: Stanford University Press.

Rowell, Thelma. 1972. *Social Behavior of Monkeys*. Baltimore: Penguin.

Rowntree, M. and J. 1970. "More on the Political Economy of Women's Liberation." *Monthly Review* 21, no. 8: 26-32.

Sacks, Karen. 1971. "Economic Bases of Sexual Equality: A Comparative Study of Four African Societies." Ph.D. dissertation, University of Michigan.

———. 1971. "Comparative Notes on the Position of Women." Paper given at the 70th Annual Meeting of the American Anthropological Association.

———. 1974. "Engels Revisited: Women, the Organization of Production, and Private Property." In *Woman, Culture, and Society*, edited by Michelle Zimbalist Rosaldo and Louise Lamphere. Stanford, Calif.: Stanford University Press.

Sahlins, Marshall. 1960*a*. "The Origin of Society." *Scientific American* 203, no. 3: 76-86.

———. 1960*b*. "Political Power and the Economy in Primitive Society." In *Essays in the Science of Culture*, edited by Robert Dole and Robert Carneiro. New York: Crowell.

———. 1963. "Poor Man, Rich Man, Big Man, Chief: Political Types in Melanesia and Polynesia." *Comparative Studies in Society and History* 5: 285-303.

———. 1968. *Tribesmen*. Englewood Cliffs, N.J.: Prentice-Hall.

———. 1972. *Stone Age Economics*. Chicago: Aldine-Atherton.

Salaff, Janet, and Merkle, Judith. 1973. "Women and Revolution: The Lessons of the Soviet Union and China." In *Women in China*, edited by Marilyn Young. Michigan Papers in Chinese Studies No. 15. Ann Arbor: University of Michigan, Center for Chinese Studies.

Salter, Elizabeth. 1972. *Daisy Bates*. New York: Coward, McCann & Geoghegan.

Sanchez-Cordoba, L. R. 1966. *Diagnostico Rural de la Republica Dominicana*. Santo Domingo: Oficina Nacional de Planificacion.

Sanday, Peggy R. 1973. "Toward a Theory of the Status of Women." *American Anthropologist* 75: 1682-1700.

Schaller, George B. 1964. *The Year of the Gorilla*. Chicago: University of Chicago Press.

Schein, M., and Lopate, C. 1972. "On Engels and the Liberation of Women." *Liberation* 16 (February).

Schneider, David, and Gough, Kathleen, eds. 1961. *Matrilineal Kinship.* Berkeley: University of California Press.

———, and Smith, R. T. 1973. *Class Differences and Sex Roles in American Kinship and Family Structure.* Englewood Cliffs, N.J.: Prentice-Hall.

Schoolcraft, Henry R. 1847. *Notes on the Iroquois, or, Contributions to American History, Antiquities, and General Ethnology.* Albany: Erastus H. Pease & Co.

———. 1860. *Archives of Aboriginal Knowledge.* 6 vols. Philadelphia: J. B. Lippincott & Co.

Scott, John Finley. 1965. "The Role of Collegiate Sororities in Maintaining Class and Ethnic Endogamy." *American Sociological Review* 30, no. 4: 415-26.

Sears, Robert; Maccoby, Eleanor E.; and Levin, Harry. 1957. *Patterns of Childbearing.* New York: Harper and Row.

———; Rau, L.; and Alpert, A. 1965. *Identification and Child Rearing.* Stanford, Calif: Stanford University Press.

Seaver, James E. 1880. *Life of Mary Jemison: Deh-he-wä-mis.* Buffalo: Matthews Brothers & Bryant.

Secombe, Wally. 1973. "Housework Under Capitalism." *New Left Review* 83: 3-24.

Semyonov, Y. I. 1967. "Group Marriage, Its Nature and Role in the Evolution of Marriage and Family Relations." In *Seventh International Congress of Anthropological and Ethnological Sciences,* vol. 4. Moscow.

Service, E. R. 1966. *The Hunters.* Englewood Cliffs, N.J.: Prentice-Hall.

Shapiro, Judith. 1972. "Male Bonds and Female Bonds: An Illustrative Comparison." Paper presented to the 70th Annual Meeting of the American Anthropological Association, New Orleans, December 1971.

Shostak, Marjorie. In press. "A Zhun/twa Woman's Memories of Childhood." In *Kalahari Hunter-Gatherers,* edited by R. B. Lee and Irven DeVore. Cambridge, Mass.: Harvard University Press.

Simey, T. S. 1946. *Welfare and Planning in the West Indies.* Oxford: Clarendon Press.

Singer, Alice. 1971. "Bridewealth and the Exchange of People." Paper presented at the Northeast Regional Meetings of the American Anthropological Association.

Snyderman, George S. 1951. "Concepts of Land Ownership Among the Iroquois and Their Neighbors." *Bulletin of the Bureau of American Ethnology* 149: 13-34.

Solanis, Valerie. 1967. *S.C.U.M. Manifesto (Society for Cutting Up Men).* New York: Olympia Press.

Sonenschein, David. 1966. "Homosexuality as a Subject of Anthropological Investigation." *Anthropological Quarterly* 2: 73-82.

Soong Ching-ling. 1973. "Women's Liberation." In *Women in China,* edited by Marilyn Young. Michigan Papers in Chinese Studies No. 15. Ann Arbor: University of Michigan, Center for Chinese Studies.

Speck, Frank G. 1945. "The Iroquois, a Study in Cultural Evolution." *Bulletin of the Cranbook Institute of Science* 23 (Bloomfield Hills, Michigan).

Spencer, Baldwin, and Gillen, F. J. 1927. *The Arunta,* vol. 2. London: Macmillan.

Spindler, George D. 1970. *Being an Anthropologist.* New York: Holt, Rinehart, and Winston.

Stack, Carol. 1974. *All Our Kin.* New York: Harper and Row.

Stern, Bernhard J., ed. 1933. "The Letters of Ashur Wright to Lewis Henry Morgan." *American Anthropologist* 35: 138-45.

Steward, Julian H. 1970. "Cultural Evolution in South America." In *The Social Anthropology of Latin America,* edited by Walter Goldschmidt and Harry Hoijer. Los Angeles: University of California Latin American Center.

Stites, Sara H. 1905. *Economics of the Iroquois.* Bryn Mawr College Monographs 1, no. 3.

Stocking, George. 1968. *Race, Culture, and Evolution.* Glencoe, Ill.: Free Press.

Strathern, Marilyn. 1972. *Women in Between.* New York: Seminar.

Sweet, L., ed. 1967. "Appearance and Reality: Status and Roles of Women in Mediterranean Society." *Anthropological Quarterly* 40, no. 3.

Teleki, Geza. 1973. "The Omnivorous Chimpanzee." *Scientific American* 228: 1.

Teng Ying-chao. 1949. "Tudi Gaige yu Funu Gongzuoti Xin Renwu." In *Funu Yundong Wenxian.* Hong Kong: Xinminju Publishers.

Thomas, Elizabeth Marshall. 1958. *The Harmless People.* New York: Random House.

———. 1963. "Bushmen in the Kalahari." *National Geographic* 123: 866-88.

Thompson, E. P. 1963. *The Making of the English Working Class.* New York: Vintage.

Thurnwald, Richard. 1916. "Banaro Society." *Memoirs of the American Anthropological Association* 3, no. 4: 251-391.

Tiger, Lionel and Fox, Robin. 1971. *The Imperial Animal.* New York: Holt, Rinehart, and Winston.

Ting Chung. May 3, 1962. "Repair of Temples and Preservation of Cultural Objects." In *Southern Daily* (Canton); reprinted in Ralph Crozier, *China's Cultural Legacy and Communism.* New York: Praeger, 1970.

Valentine, Charles. 1968. *Culture and Poverty.* Chicago: University of Chicago Press.

———. 1972. *The Relevance of Anthropology to Black Studies.* McCaleb Module No. 15. Reading, Mass.: Addison-Wesley.

Van Baal, J. 1966. *Dema.* The Hague: Nijhoff.

Vance, Carol. 1975. "Sexual Stratification in Anthropology: 1974-75." *Anthropology Newsletter* 16, no. 4 (April).

Vogel, Lise. 1973. "The Earthly Family." *Radical America* 7, nos. 4 and 5: 9-50.

Vygotsky, Lev. 1962. *Thought and Language.* Cambridge, Mass.: MIT Press.

Warner, W. Lloyd. 1937. *A Black Civilization.* New York: Harper and Brothers.

Washburn, Sherwood, and Lancaster, C. 1968. "The Evolution of Hunting." In *Man the Hunter,* edited by R. B. Lee and Irven DeVore. Chicago: Aldine.

Waugh, F. W. 1916. "Iroquois Foods and Food Preparation." *Memoir of the Canada Department of Mines, Geological Survey* 86 (Anthropological Series 12). Ottawa: Government Printing Bureau.

White, Isobel M. 1970. "Aboriginal Woman's Status: A Paradox Resolved." In *Woman's Role in Aboriginal Society.* Australian Aboriginal Studies No. 36. Canberra: Australian Institute of Aboriginal Studies.

Whiting, J. W. M., and Whiting, Beatrice B. 1973. "Altruistic and Egoistic Behavior in Six Cultures." In *Cultural Illness and Health,* edited by Laura Nader and Thomas W. Maretzki. Washington, D.C.: American Anthropological Association.

Whitten, Norman E., Jr., and Szwed, John, eds. 1970. *Afro-American Anthropology.* New York: Free Press.

Wiarda, Howard J. 1969. *The Dominican Republic: Nation in Transition.* New York: Praeger.

Wilden, Anthony. 1968. *The Language of the Self.* Baltimore: Johns Hopkins Press.

———. 1972. "Libido as Language." *Psychology Today* 5, no. 12.

Williams, F. E. 1936. *Papuans of the Trans-Fly.* Oxford: Clarendon.

Wittig, Monique. 1973. *Les Guérillères.* New York: Avon.

Wolf, E. 1969. "Society and Symbols in Latin Europe and in the Islamic Near East." *Anthropological Quarterly* 42, no. 3.

Wolff, Charlotte. 1971. *Love Between Women.* London: Duckworth.

Woodburn, James. 1968. "An Introduction to Hadza Ecology." In *Man the Hunter*, edited by R. B. Lee and Irven DeVore. Chicago: Aldine.

———. 1968. "Stability and Flexibility in Hadza Residential Groupings." In *Man the Hunter*, edited by R. B. Lee and Irven DeVore. Chicago: Aldine.

Yalman, Nur. 1963. "On the Purity of Women in the Castes of Ceylon and Malabar." *Journal of the Royal Anthropological Institute* 93, no. 1: 25-58.

Yang, C. K. 1959. *The Chinese Family in the Communist Revolution.* Cambridge: The Technology Press.

Yeld, Rachel. 1960. "Islam and Social Stratification in Northern Nigeria." *British Journal of Sociology* 51: 112-28.

———. 1964. "Education Amongst Women and Girls in the Kebbi Emirate of Northern Nigeria." In *Education and Politics in Nigeria*, edited by H. N. Weilder. Freiburg: Verla Romach.

Yellen, John E. In press. "Settlement Pattern of the !Kung: An Archaeological Perspective." In *Kalahari Hunter-Gatherers*, edited by R. B. Lee and Irven DeVore. Cambridge, Mass.: Harvard University Press.

Yellen, John E., and Harpending, Henry. 1972. "Hunter-Gatherer Populations and Archaeological Inference." *World Archaeology* 4: 244-53.